Clinical Neuropsychological Foundations of Schizophrenia

This volume is the first practitioner-oriented source of information on the neuropsychology of schizophrenia that conveys the growth in the field in terms of what is known about cognition in schizophrenia, its assessment, and how this informs clinical practice.

It provides the practicing clinical neuropsychologist, and other professionals working with persons with schizophrenia, with the knowledge and tools they need to provide competent professional neuropsychological services. It includes an overview of developmental models of schizophrenia and its associated neuropathologies, so that the clinician can fully understand how vulnerability and progression of the disorder influence brain development and functioning, and how cognition and functioning are associated with these changes. In addition, the volume covers contemporary evidence-based assessment and interventions, including cognitive remediation and other cognitive oriented interventions. Throughout, the research findings are synthesized to make them clinically relevant to clinical neuropsychologists working in outpatient or inpatient psychiatric settings.

The book is an invaluable resource for practicing professional neuropsychologists, clinical psychologists, psychiatrists, and neuropsychiatrists, as well as graduate students of these disciplines, interns, and postdoctoral residents and fellows who work with schizophrenic patients.

American Academy of Clinical Neuropsychology/Psychology Press Continuing Education Book Series

Series Editors: Joel E. Morgan and Jerry J. Sweet

AACN/Psychology Press Continuing Education Series publishes authored and edited volumes containing a blend of cutting-edge primary research and practical/professional material for clinicians, researchers, and students of clinical neuropsychology and clinical psychology.

Each volume is written or edited by leading scholars in the field and is specifically designed to assist readers in advancing their relevant research or professional activities in clinical neuropsychology. Volumes in this series have been selected by the series editors because they provide one or more of the following: overview of a core or emerging area of concern to clinical neuropsychologists; in-depth examination of a specific area of research or practice in clinical neuropsychology; update of a neglected or controversial clinical application; information pertaining to relevance of a new interdisciplinary discovery/technique to neuropsychological function; or current ethical matters and other professional considerations in the application of new knowledge or methods to the understanding of neuropsychological functions.

AACN Online System

Any licensed psychologist who reads one of the books in the AACN/Psychology Press series will be able to earn CE credits by reading designated books and completing an online quiz.

To Receive Online Credit:

- Read one of the CE-designated books in its entirety
- Access the CE quiz online at the AACN website (www.theaacn.org)
- Register for the specific book for which you wish to receive CE credit, and
- Complete all questions on the quiz.

The estimated time to read the book and complete the related quiz is determined by the length of each book, which also determines the number of possible credits.

The cost of CE credits is noted on the AACN website, and is reduced for AACN members and affiliates. Credit will be awarded to individuals scoring 80% or higher on the quiz. Participants will receive an immediate confirmation of credits earned by email.

CE Accreditation Statement

AACN is approved by the American Psychological Association to sponsor continuing education for psychologists. AACN maintains responsibility for this program and its content.

For more information on new and forthcoming titles in the Series and for instructions on how to take the accompanying online CE tests, please visit **www.theaacn.org** or **www.psypress.com/AACN**

Clinical Neuropsychological Foundations of Schizophrenia

Edited by

Bernice A. Marcopulos
and
Matthew M. Kurtz

American Academy of Clinical Neuropsychology

Routledge
Taylor & Francis Group
NEW YORK AND LONDON

First published 2012
by Routledge
711 Third Avenue, New York, NY 10017

Simultaneously published in the UK
by Routledge
2 Park Square, Milton Park, Abingdon, Oxon OX14 4RN

First issued in paperback 2017

Routledge is an imprint of the Taylor & Francis Group, an informa business

Library of Congress Cataloging in Publication Data
Clinical neuropsychological foundations of schizophrenia / edited by Bernice A. Marcopulos and Matthew M. Kurtz.
p. cm. — (American academy of clinical neuropsychology/psychology press continuing education series)
ISBN 978-1-84872-877-6
1. Schizophrenia. 2. Neuropsychology. I. Marcopulos, Bernice A. II. Kurtz, Matthew M., 1967–
RC514.C565 2012
616.89'8—dc23
2011047684

ISBN 13: 978-1-138-10993-3 (pbk)
ISBN 13: 978-1-84872-877-6 (hbk)

Typeset in New Caledonia and Korinna
by EvS Communication Networx, Inc.

Dedicated to my parents Donald and Gizela Marcopulos,
and my husband and daughters,
Thomas, Alexandra, and Halina Guterbock

To my parents Seymour and Ruth Kurtz,
for teaching me the value
of intellectual curiosity.

Contents

List of Figures

Preface

This book has two goals. First, we have endeavored to present the information that a clinical neuropsychologist would need to provide competent, scientifically-informed services to persons with schizophrenia-spectrum illness. Second, we wanted to provide a state-of-the art summary of contemporary empirical work in many of the most exciting research areas in the neuropsychology of schizophrenia, directly linking these findings with practice. We hope this volume will highlight the fascinating complexity of this richly deserving and fascinating patient population and aid the clinician in fully considering the myriad factors that influence cognition.

Over the years we have taught and trained many practicum students, predoctoral interns, and post-doctoral fellows at our respective psychiatric and academic institutions, focusing on the clinical science of assessment and rehabilitation of persons with schizophrenia-spectrum illness. Even as the scientific neuropsychology literature on schizophrenia has grown exponentially, we became frustrated that there were no comprehensive neuropsychology-oriented resources for clinicians working with persons with schizophrenia that integrated this new clinical science with practice. Our hope is that this volume will help to fill this void.

We also hope that this volume might spur more clinical and academic interest in this population among our neuropsychologist colleagues. The recent TCN/AACN survey shows that very few neuropsychologists are working in primary psychiatric settings and this has changed little since the previous surveys (Sweet, Meyer, Nelson, & Moberg, 2011). Only 20% of referrals come from psychiatry, and we surmise that few of these are for patients with schizophrenia-spectrum illness. In our opinion this is regrettable, as neuropsychology has much to offer in the clinical care of these patients, in the development of new treatment and assessment strategies, as well as understanding the neurodevelopmental mechanisms underlying the clinical correlates of the illness. While the TCN/AACN survey does not show an increase in neuropsychologists working with schizophrenia, a review of the key terms "neuropsychology" and "schizophrenia" in PsycINFO shows a steady increase in the number of published scholarly articles that include both terms. During the decade from 1980 to 1990, 182 articles were published in peer reviewed journals; from 1990 to 2000 the number jumped to 745; and by 2000 to 2010 there were 2,197 such articles! While stigma about the disorder among the public remains high, and living with the symptoms of the disorder will always present significant challenges for those affected, with these new research findings (many described in the pages of this book) there is the potential for true innovations in the care of people with schizophrenia in the near future. Thus, we hope this book will also inspire a new generation of scientist-practitioners to focus their energies on implementing these many new scientific findings into clinical practice for the enhancement of care of people with schizophrenia.

We envisioned this volume to be a compendium of critical clinical issues a neuropsychologist must consider to provide competent and scientifically-informed evaluations and interventions for persons with schizophrenia-spectrum disorders. Our volume begins with an overview of cognition in schizophrenia (Kurtz & Marcopulos), then moves to a contemporary perspective on the neuro-scientific origins of schizophrenia in Chapter 2 (Keshavan & Diwadkar). Chapter 3 provides an approach to the neuropsychological evaluation, highlighting salient issues in each section of the report (Marcopulos & Fujii). Kurtz reminds us of the importance of functional outcome as the ultimate target of treatment in Chapter 4 and provides a critical review of appropriate methods for assessment. As with all clinical assessments, cultural variables must be considered and there are several unique issues regarding schizophrenia that Fujii covers in Chapter 5. Chapters 6 and 7 consider schizophrenia from a developmental lifespan perspective. DeMarco and Marcopulos reflect upon developmental histories of learning disabilities, ADHD, and intellectual abilities vis-à-vis schizophrenia-spectrum disorders. Depp, Loughran, and Palmer review the growing literature on aging and schizophrenia and cognition. Individuals with schizophrenia-spectrum illnesses are at high risk for a number of medical comorbidities that can cause cognitive impairment and can profoundly impact performance during cognitive evaluation (Stone & Keshavan, Chapter 8). Given the highly elevated rates of head injury in schizophrenia and the putative role in its etiology in some cases, we include this topic as well (Chapter 9, Flashman, McAllister, & Ferrell). At least 50% of persons with schizophrenia have comorbid substance abuse; thus a thorough understanding of the effects of substance abuse on the presentation, course and treatment of schizophrenia is crucial for the practicing neuropsychologist working with this patient population (Chapter 10, Mueser & McGurk). Sestito and Goldberg (Chapter 11) review the possible cognitive enhancing and cognitive impairing effects of the most commonly prescribed psychotropic medications in schizophrenia. In recent years the implementation of behavioral treatment approaches for improving cognitive function in schizophrenia has burgeoned with many empirically validated in randomized controlled trials. Reviewing and contributing to this new literature, Medalia and Bellucci (Chapter 12) show us that rather than just delineating the nature of cognitive deficits via assessment, neuropsychology is having an impact on the remediation of these deficits as well. Finally, because of the dramatic changes in the mental health system with failures in community-based treatment, many persons with schizophrenia end up with legal charges and require forensic assessment. In the last Chapter (13), Tussey and Marcopulos contend that neuropsychology plays a vital role in forensic assessments.

We would like to thank Jerry Sweet and Joel Morgan, the AACN CE series book editors, for giving us the opportunity to pursue this project. We would like to thank Paul Dukes, Stephanie Drew, and Lee Transue at the Psychology Press for their guidance and help. We would like to thank Anthony Giuliano for his very insightful editorial comments on several the chapters, which resulted in great improvements in the manuscript. He was also instrumental in the early conceptualization of the volume contents and in suggesting appropriate authors. We both would like to thank our "teachers" (our patients at Western State Hospital and at The Institute of Living) for what we learned about neurocognitive implications of schizophrenia, not only in the lab but in day-to-day functioning. We would also like to thank the mentors and colleagues who introduced us to the field of clinical neuropsychology in schizophrenia, Paul Moberg, Ruben and Raquel Gur, Alice Medalia, and Michael Green. Finally, we would like to thank all the chapter authors for donating their time and energy towards this project. We learned a tremendous amount from their scholarly contributions.

REFERENCE

Sweet, J. J., Meyer, D. G., Nelson, N. W., & Moberg, P. J. (2011). The *TCN/AACN* 2010 "salary survey": Professional practices, beliefs, and incomes of U.S. neuropsychologists. *The Clinical Neuropsychologist*, 25, 12–61.

Contributors

Dona Bellucci
Department of Psychology
Essex County Hospital Center

Anthony P. De Marco
Department of Psychiatry and Neurobehavioral Sciences
University of Virginia Health System

Colin A. Depp
Department of Psychiatry
University of California, San Diego

Vaibhav A. Diwadkar
Department of Psychiatry
Wayne State University School of Medicine

Richard Ferrell
Section of Neuropsychiatry,
Department of Psychiatry,
Dartmouth Medical School,
Dartmouth-Hitchcock Medical Center Dartmouth Medical School

Laura A. Flashman
Section of Neuropsychiatry,
Department of Psychiatry,
Dartmouth Medical School,
Dartmouth-Hitchcock Medical Center

Daryl Fujii
Veterans Affairs Pacific Island Health Care System

Terry E. Goldberg
Zucker Hillside Hospital/ Feinstein Institute/AECOM

Matcheri S. Keshavan
Beth Israel Deaconess Medical Center and
Massachusetts Mental Health Center
Harvard Medical School

Matthew M. Kurtz
Department of Psychology
Wesleyan University

Casey Loughran
Department of Psychiatry
University of California, San Diego
Veterans Administration Medical Center, San Diego

Bernice A. Marcopulos
Department of Graduate Psychology
James Madison University

Thomas McAllister
Section of Neuropsychiatry,
Department of Psychiatry,
Dartmouth Medical School,
Dartmouth-Hitchcock Medical Center

Susan R. McGurk
Associate Professor of Occupational Therapy
Boston University.

Alice Medalia
Department of Psychiatry
Columbia University College of Physicians & Surgeons

Kim T. Mueser
Executive Director of the Center for Psychiatric Rehabilitation, and Professor of Occupational Therapy
Boston University

Barton W. Palmer
Department of Psychiatry; University of California, San Diego.
Veterans Administration Medical Center, San Diego

Nicole Sestito
Zucker Hillside Hospital/ Feinstein Institute/AECOM

William S. Stone
Massachusetts Mental Health Center Division of Public Sector Psychiatry
Beth Israel Deaconess Medical Center Department of Psychiatry
Harvard Medical School

Chriscelyn M. Tussey
Bellevue Hospital Center
New York University School of Medicine

1

Cognition in Schizophrenia

MATTHEW M. KURTZ, Ph.D.
Department of Psychology, Wesleyan University, Middletown, CT

BERNICE A. MARCOPULOS, Ph.D.
Department of Graduate Psychology, James Madison University, Harrisonburg, VA

The purpose of this first chapter is to provide an introduction and overview of the relevant historical basis and clinical research identifying cognitive impairment as a core feature in schizophrenia spectrum disorders. This chapter will briefly review epidemiology and etiology, and what is known and presumed about the natural history of neurocognitive impairment in schizophrenia as related to the clinical course of the illness (from the premorbid period to multi-episode or established illness). We will review what is known about deficits in youth at risk for schizophrenia from family risk and follow-back studies, as well as cognition in the prodromal period from clinical high risk studies. We will cover cognitive predictors of illness onset, the profile and magnitude of deficits in first episode schizophrenia, cognitive changes in people recovering from acute exacerbation, and longitudinal studies of neurocognitive impairment in established schizophrenia. We will also provide a brief description of the cognitive profiles of people with schizophrenia and related or spectra disorders. This chapter will conclude with an overview of pertinent clinical issues, many of which will be elaborated in much greater detail in subsequent chapters in this volume.

EPIDEMIOLOGY/ETIOLOGY

Schizophrenia is a relatively uncommon mental disorder, with lifetime prevalence rates worldwide ranging from one half to 1%, but pockets of higher prevalence have also been reported. As schizophrenia is typically a chronic disorder, incidence rates are lower: approximately 15.2 in 100,000 (McGrath et al., 2004). Incidence rates vary by gender (males greater than females) as well as geographic location (greater at higher latitudes), and also vary within countries (Menezes, 2004). Despite its low prevalence, it is one of the most disabling with fewer than 20% of individuals with this disorder able to hold full or even part-time competitive employment (Marwaha & Johnson, 2004). By far the majority of long-term psychiatric hospital beds are used for patients diagnosed with schizophrenia (Lay, Nordt, Rössler, 2007; Pillay & Montcrieff, 2011). Hallucinations, delusions, and disorganized behavior may be the most noticeable symptoms to observers, but it is the cognitive symptoms that most interfere with independent living and quality of life. Consequently, in recent years, treatment has begun to focus on ameliorating cognitive symptoms.

Although the etiology of schizophrenia remains an enigma, there does appear to be a clear genetic influence on emergence of the disorder. First-degree, biological relatives of individuals with schizophrenia have a risk for developing the disorder that is 10 times that of the general population. Concordance rates are higher in monozygotic than dizygotic twins. Lastly, biological relatives of adoptees who develop schizophrenia have increased risk for schizophrenia whereas adoptive relatives do not have increased risk (Tsuang, Stone, & Faraone, 1999). Environmental stress early in development also plays a role in the emergence of the disorder. For example, data from the 1957 influenza pandemic suggest that mothers who were in their second trimester of pregnancy during the outbreak were more likely to give birth to children who subsequently developed schizophrenia (Mednick, Machon, Huttunen, & Bonett, 1988). Maternal starvation during pregnancy has also been linked to increased rates of incidence (Susser & Lin, 1992). Birth complications have also been linked to increased rates of schizophrenia (Clarke, Harley, & Cannon, 2006). While at this point in time there is little evidence that psychological stresses produce schizophrenia *de novo*, a variety of well-controlled studies have revealed that family levels of expressed hostility and over-involvement have a marked deleterious influence on the course of the disorder (Butzlaff & Hooley, 1998).

HISTORICAL PERSPECTIVES ON ETIOLOGY, TREATMENT AND THE IMPORTANCE OF COGNITION IN SCHIZOPHRENIA

Early in the 20th century, psychologists and psychiatrists recognized that there were cognitive deficits in patients with schizophrenia and these deficits looked similar to patients with documented brain damage. Kraepelin (1920) observed cognitive impairment in schizophrenia, which he called dementia praecox:

> the fact is decisive that the morbid anatomy has disclosed not simple inadequacy of the nervous constitution but destructive processes in the background of the clinical picture.

The discovery of neuroleptic drugs which block the brain neurotransmitter dopamine in the 1950s and the growth of biological psychiatry during the same period promoted the idea that schizophrenia is a brain disease and should be viewed from a neuropathological perspective (Kleist, 1960).

While the current scientific literature recognizes the probable neurobiological underpinnings of schizophrenia, there was a time during the middle of the 20th century that psychosocial or psychoanalytic etiologies were favored. One such theory surmised that the "schizophrenogenic mother" who is both overprotective and rejecting, causes their child's psychopathology (Fromm-Reichmann, 1948; Hartwell, 1996). Bateson's "double-bind" hypothesis pointed to disordered patterns of family communication (Bateson, Jackson, Haley, & Weakland, 1956) as a causative factor. Others countered that childhood schizophrenia is not due to rejection by the mother, but rather due to an organic brain deficit affecting interpersonal relationships (Anderson, 1952). Anderson theorized that the deficit involved the associational areas of the cortex.

While schizophrenia is currently seen as a brain disease, environmental and social factors play an important role in disease expression. Current theories do not favor poor parenting as a primary etiology, however, family communication patterns (i.e., "expressed emotion") have been found to correlate with relapse among persons with schizophrenia (Butzlaff & Hooley, 1999). Psychoanalysis, the most popular approach to psychotherapy for much of the 20th century, has not been found to be an effective treatment, and may even be harmful (Mueser & Berenbaum, 1990). As the neuroscience of mental illness has been more studied and neuropsychological characteristics better understood, biological and cognitive treatments have become more prominent. Pharmacotherapy is a standard method for reducing the positive symptoms of schizophrenia. Psychotherapeutic techniques, such as CBT for hallucinations and delusions have shown benefit for symptoms targeted by the therapy in controlled trials, although effects have been more modest in more carefully controlled trials (e.g., Wykes, Steel, Everitt, & Tarrier, 2008; Dixon et al., 2010). These interventions are typically predicated on the notion that the way in which psychotic phenomena are experienced have implications for feelings and behavior, and that distress and behavioral disability associated with the disease can be changed by modifying persistent biases in the interpretations of psychotic experiences through a psychotherapeutic process (Morrison & Barratt, 2008). Cognitive remediation, a group of behavioral interventions designed to improve elementary cognition, either directly via drill-and-practice or through the acquisition and implementation of compensatory strategies has shown much promise and several approaches have been developed and researched (see Medalia & Bellucci, this volume).

PATTERN AND MAGNITUDE OF IQ AND NEUROCOGNITIVE IMPAIRMENT IN SCHIZOPHRENIA

A wealth of studies of neuropsychological function in schizophrenia has been conducted over the past 20 years (Harvey & Reichenberg, 2007). In this section of the chapter we review findings for specific neuropsychological domains in schizophrenia. To facilitate comparisons of findings across very different neuropsychological measures, for each domain we provide a standardized estimate of effect-size impairment in schizophrenia (Cohen's d). We use the metric of small, d = .2 – .5, medium d = .5 – .8 and large effect-size (d > .8) impairment.

Full-Scale IQ

Since Charles Spearman's work at the beginning of the 20th century, psychologists have made distinctions between general cognitive capacity or "g" that represent crystallized skill such as oral vocabulary that are resistant to the effects of neural insult, and tests of specific neurocognitive skills, these include attention, verbal and non-verbal memory, working memory, problem-solving, processing speed, and sensory-motor functioning that are assessed with standardized neuropsychological instruments and that are more sensitive to neural damage.

Most studies of full-scale IQ in schizophrenia have shown effect-size impairment in the large range for full-scale IQ (e.g., Dickinson, Ramsey, & Gold, 2007; d = .98) with impairments in Performance IQ that are typically 50% greater than that observed for verbal IQ (e.g., Heinrichs & Zakzanis, 1997). These findings suggest that deficits in specific neuropsychological function in schizophrenia are frequently evident in concert with high levels of global IQ impairment.

Attention Attention has been most commonly assessed through the use of measures of sustained visual vigilance: most frequently the Continuous Performance Test (CPT). Some of these CPT measures place greater demands on visual identification, by having clients respond to a single target (the "X" version of the CPT) while other versions place greater demands on working memory, by asking the client to respond as rapidly as possible when they see one stimulus but only when it is preceded by a second stimulus (the "A–X" version of the CPT). Other versions place greater visual demands by degrading the target (making the target blurred; the "degraded stimulus" version of the CPT). Regardless of task type, patients show deficits in the moderate-large (.66 – 1.16) range on these tasks (Dickinson et al., 2007; Heinrichs & Zakzanis, 1998) relative to matched healthy controls.

Verbal and Non-Verbal Episodic Memory Verbal episodic memory has typically been studied with the use of tests of list learning (e.g., California Verbal Learning Test, Hopkins Verbal Learning Test, Rey Auditory Verbal Learning Test) or verbal prose recall (e.g., Logical Memory from the Wechsler Memory Scale). In each of these measures the client is asked to recall a list of words, or a passage of text. Delayed recall and recognition measures are administered as well. Results have revealed that patients show severe levels of impairment on verbal memory measures (d = 1.20 – 1.22; Aleman, Hijman, deHaan, & Kahn, 1999). Comprehensive literature reviews have suggested that as a group, studies of episodic memory impairment reveal that memory deficits in schizophrenia lie largely at the level of encoding and retrieval. Studies have suggested that these encoding deficits may be linked to the fact that people with schizophrenia are less likely to "deeply" encode to-be-remembered information. They are more likely to use phonemic, rather than semantic cues for encoding, based on the types of errors they make on forced choice recognition (choosing words that sound alike rather than those that are semantically related).

When information is encoded successfully on an initial presentation, retention for that material remains strong across a retention interval for most patients (Cirillo & Seidman, 2003). We note that some studies have suggested that this pattern of impairment (poor learning but intact retention) is often a characteristic of frontal lobe impairment. Studies of retrieval have been used to assess disruptions in the storage vs. retrieval process for episodic memory—if recognition performance is stronger than recall this would suggest evidence of disruption in the retrieval of memories rather than disruptions in storage. One meta-analysis has revealed that recall is considerably more diminished than recognition memory in schizophrenia even when task difficulty is carefully titrated between the response formats (Aleman et al., 1999), suggesting disruptions in memory retrieval in the illness. However other studies have suggested similar levels of recall and recognition impairment regardless of recognition cues (Paulsen et al., 1995).

Studies of non-verbal memory typically use difficult-to-verbalize figures which are in some cases complex (Rey Complex Figure Test), in some cases simple (Visual Reproduction subtest of the WMS-III). In some cases non-verbal learning is assessed over trials (Benton Visual Retention Test; BVRT). Effect sizes impairment in these studies is nearly identical to those for verbal memory measures, in the moderate-large range (d = .74 – 1.03; e.g., Heinrichs & Zakzanis, 1996; Aleman et al., 1999).

Verbal and Nonverbal Working Memory In these studies a series of items are presented and the participant has to both store the items for later recall as well as perform mental operations on the memoranda. Digits backward is a protoypical example of this type of task requiring the individual to both remember a set of items and then perform a manipulation (placing them in a reverse order). Findings are similar to those of episodic memory and are in the large (d = .8 1.1) range of impairment (Park & Lee, 2005; Aleman et al., 1999).

Language Impairment in language has been recognized in earliest descriptions of the disorder as part of the four As of schizophrenia (association; Bleuler, 1951). Interestingly, single word reading, spelling and vocabulary skills acquired early in life in schizophrenia appear largely spared (Townsend, Malla,

& Norman, 2001) and for this reason they have frequently been selected as indices of premorbid intellectual function. In contrast, studies of other aspects of language ability, including word fluency and verbal comprehension have shown large effect size impairment (d = .83 – 1.41; Heinrichs & Zakzanis, 1997; Dickinson et al., 2007; Bokat & Goldberg, 2003).

Processing Speed This is an index of the general speed of cognitive operations (e.g., the ability to complete a simple visual-motor task quickly) that has been hypothesized to serve as a rate-limiting step across a variety of elementary cognitive operations such as encoding, recall, mental manipulation and decision-making in schizophrenia (Dickinson et al., 2007). David Wechsler (1955), in his original description of the WAIS, noted that patients with schizophrenia are most severely disrupted on measures of processing speed on the WAIS. Consistent with this idea, an important meta-analysis suggests that processing speed may be more impaired (d = 1.57) than other commonly studied neurocognitive functions such as verbal memory, executive function or working memory in schizophrenia—however more recent work has suggested that impairment on processing speed measures is more closely linked to dosage of antipsychotic medications than other neurocognitive functions, and thus may reflect, at least partially, a treatment rather than illness variable (Knowles, David, & Reichenberg, 2010).

Executive Function Executive functions include the ability to mentally represent a goal, to develop steps to complete that goal and then to evaluate whether the goal was successfully attained. Many of the features of schizophrenia are suggestive of dysfunction in executive function—reduced spontaneity, avolition, mental rigidity, and lack of social judgment. Probably the most commonly used measure of executive function is the Wisconsin Card Sorting Test (WCST), to assess rule learning and cognitive flexibility, the Stroop Color Word Test with its emphasis on verbal inhibition, Trail Making Test B which is focused on set-shifting, and the Controlled Oral Word Association Test (COWA) a measure of word generation. Mean effect-sizes on these tasks have been typically in the large range (e.g., WCST total = .88; Heinrichs & Zakzanis, 1998).

Sensory Motor Function Most studies have indicated only moderate level deficits on measures of sensory processing, while most studies have suggested moderate-to-severe severe deficits in simple motor speed (e.g., Dickinson et al., 2007).

HETEROGENEITY OF NEUROPSYCHOLOGICAL TEST FINDINGS

There is considerable discrepancy in the literature regarding whether the typical cognitive pattern of schizophrenia is best characterized by generalized deficits that vary from patient to patient by severity, or multiple, heterogeneous specific deficits that differ across patients and can be grouped into subtypes. In the previous section we delineated impairment in a variety of commonly assessed neuropsychological domains. In all cases, however, findings represented mean values from groups of patients, rather than the patterns of neuropsychological impairment evident in individually assessed patients. Studies of inter-individual differences in patterns of neuropsychological test scores can help show whether patterns or subtypes of neurocognitive deficit are evident in different groups of patients. Heinrichs and Zakzanis (1998) concluded that schizophrenia is characterized by a generalized cognitive impairment. More recently Dickinson, Iannone, Wilk, and Gold (2004) attempted to answer the "heterogeneity question" using structural equation modeling on a sample of 97 patients who were administered the WAIS III and WMS III. They found that for over two-thirds of the patients a common factor accounted for the relationship between diagnosis and cognitive test performance. Other studies have suggested that patients can be parsed into distinct groups according to patterns of neuropsychological deficits.

Cognitive Subtypes

Factor-Analytic Studies Neuropsychologists have investigated possible distinctive cognitive subtypes within schizophrenia (Goldstein, Shemansky, & Allen 2005; Heinrichs & Awad, 1993; Heinrichs, Ruttan, Zakzanis, & Case, 1997). Studies using cluster analytic studies have delineated three cognitive subtypes, including a high cognitive functioning, "neuropsychologically normal" group (Palmer, Heaton, Paulson, Kuck, & Braff, 1997; Silverstein & Zerwic, 1985), a very low cognitive functioning group (similar to dementia), and a group with motor impairment but relatively preserved verbal abilities (Seaton, Goldstein, & Allen, 2001). The "neuropsychologically normal" individuals tend to be younger at the time of testing and tend to have a relatively benign course characterized by a low number and short length of hospitalizations, stable in the community and more likely to be seen in outpatient clinics. They tend to have fewer negative symptoms and more positive symptoms. In contrast, the very low cognitive functioning group tends to be older, less well-educated, and may have a more severe prodrome with an earlier onset of the disorder. While the high functioning group tends to be normatively average, it is not clear whether their cognitive functioning would have been above average had they not become mentally ill. Kremen, Seidman, Faraone, Toomey, and Tsuang (2004) argue that these presumably neuropsychologically normal patients are impaired relative to their expected premorbid level.

Memory-Based Subtypes

Patients with schizophrenia have also been grouped based on memory performance. Turetsky et al. (2002) found three subtypes based on the profile of memory deficits exhibited on the California Verbal Learning Test (CVLT): subcortical, cortical and relatively unimpaired. The "subcortical" group showed moderate to severely impaired free recall, normal retention across a delay interval, and disproportionate improvement on recognition testing. These patients tended to have a longer duration of illness and more severe psychiatric symptomatology and evidenced ventricular enlargement and isolated frontal lobe gray matter reductions. The "cortical" group exhibited impaired learning, rapid forgetting of learned material, elevated cued-recall intrusions, and limited ability to benefit from recognition testing. "Cortical" patients tended to be younger and had earlier illness onset, and they evidenced reduced temporal lobe gray matter and hypometabolism in temporal lobe structures linked to language and memory processes. More recent studies have supported the temporal stability of these subtypes (Bell, Johannesen, Greig, & Wexler, 2010).

Evidence for Neuropsychological Normality in a Subgroup of Schizophrenia?

Findings regarding heterogeneity of neuropsychological test findings in schizophrenia might suggest that there is a subgroup of patients with schizophrenia who are neuropsychologically normal. For example, in a study of 171 outpatients with schizophrenia and 63 inpatients, ratings of scored neuropsychological test protocols were conducted by blind, highly experienced neuropsychologists. Of this sample, 27% of the people with schizophrenia were classified as neuropsychologically normal. The authors concluded that the pathophysiology of the cognitive deficits are most likely distinct from the pathophysiology producing symptoms. Neuropsychologically normal clients were similar in terms of most demographic, psychiatric and functional characteristics, except that normal patients had fewer negative and extrapyramidal symptoms, were on less anticholinergic medication, socialized more frequently and were less likely to have had a recent psychiatric hospitalization (Palmer, Heaton, Kuck, & Braff, 1997).

Others studies however have concluded that most patients with schizophrenia are impaired neuropsychologically when baseline IQ levels are considered for. For example, Kremen, Seidman, Faraone, and Tsuang (2001) grouped a sample of thirty-six patients into IQ bands of low average (81–94) and average (95–119) IQ scores. Clients in the two groups had different overall levels of neurocognitive impairment but both groups' performance was impaired relative to matched healthy controls, and the patterns of performance in the groups were similar. Wilk Gold, McMahon, Humber, Iannone, & Buchanan (2005) found that patients matched for full-scale IQ with healthy controls showed similar levels of memory impairment whether mean patient IQ scores were in the "high" (> 110) or low (< 90) range. Taken together, these findings suggest similar patterns of elementary neurocognitive impairment across different levels of IQ that may represent a stable neurocognitive signature for the disorder. Neurocognitive impairment is evident in virtually all patients when baseline IQ is accounted for.

Clinical Sources of Heterogeneity

One potential source of heterogeneity of cognitive deficits in schizophrenia is age of onset of psychosis. Rajji, Ismail, and Mulsant (2009) conducted a meta-analysis on cognition in early onset (by the age 19), late onset (age 40) and first episode schizophrenia. They found that early onset was associated with greater cognitive deficits, while later onset had relatively preserved cognitive function. More severe neuropsychological deficits are associated with more relapses, but it is unclear whether the relapses are a cause or result of cognitive impairment (Rund et al., 2007). In summary, the neuropsychologist evaluating an individual who has been diagnosed with schizophrenia should not necessarily expect to find a "typical" profile of cognitive strengths and weaknesses, but will find enduring neurocognitive impairments in any number of IQ or neurocognitive domains.

SOCIAL COGNITIVE IMPAIRMENTS IN SCHIZOPHRENIA

While a seminal paper on social cognitive deficits was published in 1997 (Penn, Corrigan, Bentall, Racenstein, & Newman, 1997), it is only over the past 5 to 10 years that increased attention is being paid to social cognitive deficits in schizophrenia. Social cognition refers to how people think about themselves and others in the social world. In the schizophrenia literature, deficits have typically been grouped into four general domains: the interrelated abilities of processing facial emotion and interpreting and responding to social cues, such as body language or voice intonation perception; theory-of-mind (ToM), or the ability to understand that other people have different mental states from their own; and attributional style or the ability to make appropriate causal inferences regarding the causes of events. Like deficits on traditional neuropsychological test instruments, these impairments are resistant to the effects of typical and atypical antipsychotic medication and are present at illness onset (Penn, Sanna, & Roberts, 2008). There is some evidence that deficits exist before diagnosis and in samples with genetic high risk (Gibson, Penn, Prinstein, Perkins, & Belger, 2010). Furthermore, deficits in facial affect recognition and social perception have been linked to greater supervision in living status and poorer occupational status (Hooker & Park, 2002), as well as poor performance on social role plays and inappropriate personal appearance (Meyer & Kurtz, 2009; Pinkham & Penn, 2006). ToM has been found to be correlated with community function in outpatients and behavioral problems in both in and outpatient samples (Roncone et al., 2002; Brune, 2005). While there has been less attention paid to attributional style, one study has showed that a tendency to make stable attributions of the causes of life events is linked to a greater number and higher quality of social interactions (Lysaker, Lancaster, Nees, & Davis, 2004).

While measures of facial affect recognition, social cue perception, ToM, and attributional style are not standard tests in a neuropsychologist's armamentarium of assessment tools, recent results suggest that these measures explain variance beyond that measured by standard neuropsychological assessment tools. Pinkham and Penn (2006) argue that assessment of social cognition can provide incremental value for assessing clients' ability to live independently and negotiate their social world. It should be noted that these measures are indices of capacity, not function in a client's naturalistic environment, and thus may overestimate the ability to read facial affect, social cues and take other perspectives as these operations most likely take greater effort in individuals with diminished cognitive capacity and where motivation may be lower to engage in effortful cognitive operations.

PATTERNS OF NEUROPSYCHOLOGICAL IMPAIRMENT IN DIFFERENT PHASES OF THE DISORDER

Schizophrenia is best conceptualized as a neurodevelopmental disorder. Recent research has sought to characterize the course of the disorder, particularly in reference to the nature of cognitive deficits in the prodrome, during the first episode and throughout the course of the illness.

Neuropsychological Impairment in Children with Schizophrenia and those at Elevated Genetic Risk for the Disease

Children and adolescents with schizophrenia also show cognitive deficits in attention, memory, and executive functioning (Asarnow et al., 1994; Bedwell, Smith, Hamberger, Kumra, & Rapoport, 1999; Goldberg, Karson, Leleszi, & Weinberger, 1988; Kenny et al., 1997; Kumra et al., 2000; Øie & Rund, 1999). Cognitive deficits, primarily in attention, predate onset of the illness and are present in at risk children before the onset of symptoms (Cornblatt & Erlenmeyer-Kimling, 1985; Cornblatt & Keilp, 1994; Erlenmeyer-Kimling et al., 2000).

Intellectual Deficits in Children and Young-Adults Who Go On to Develop Schizophrenia

"Follow-back" as well as longitudinal studies of clinical and genetically high-risk individuals have informed us that cognitive deficits are present well before the presence of psychotic symptoms indicating the onset of the schizophrenia. For instance, Woodberry, Giuliano, and Seidman (2008) found in their meta-analysis that many years prior to the onset of psychotic symptoms, individuals later diagnosed with schizophrenia score one-half a standard deviation below normal controls on IQ tests. It is well-known that low pre-morbid IQ is a risk factor for the development of schizophrenia (e.g., Aylward, Walker, & Bettes, 1984). Furthermore, epidemiological cohort studies have revealed that intellectual impairment is evident even during childhood in those destined to develop psychosis (e.g., Cannon et al., 2000) and a growing number of studies now also suggest that there are declines in estimated IQ in a substantial population of people with the illness between childhood and late adolescence (e.g., Reichenberg et al., 2005). Even for those individuals within the normal range of IQ, for those who go on to develop schizophrenia there is a greater probability of significant intra-individual variability between subtests on measures of IQ (Reichenberg et al., 2006).

Neuropsychology of Individuals at Clinical High Risk for Schizophrenia

Studies of individuals at clinical high risk (CHR) for schizophrenia, which is defined as evidence of attenuated positive symptoms upon interview and history in at least one of five categories: unusual thought content, suspicion/paranoia, grandiosity, perceptual anomalies, and/or disorganized communication, have revealed deficits on a variety of neuropsychological measures that are typically somewhere between healthy control performance and performance in full-blown illness. The most extensive study to date, the North American Prodrome Longitudinal Study (NAPLS), which consists of coordinated data collection at 8 sites, has revealed that neuropsychological functioning is poorer in high-risk participants who went on to develop psychosis versus those who do not. Tests of processing speed and verbal learning and memory discriminated controls from high-risk participants most effectively, but the magnitude of impairment in these participants was still less than in those with full-blown psychosis. There was evidence that poorer performance on verbal learning and memory tests predicted more rapid transition to psychosis, but performance on neuropsychological tests did not provide incremental validity for likelihood of conversion beyond clinical factors (Seidman et al., 2010).

First-Episode

The profile and magnitude of deficits in first episode schizophrenia are similar to deficits seen later during the course of the illness. Sponheim et al. (2010) compared recent onset (mean length of illness 2.6 years) and chronic (mean length of illness 14 years) patients with schizophrenia with matched controls. They found that recent onset schizophrenic patients had similar deficits compared with chronic patients, except that timed motor tests and problem-solving were worse in chronic patients. Motor deficits seemed to be associated with first generation antipsychotic use in the chronic patients. Lower intellectual functioning, achievement scores and planning were also seen in these patients. Episodic memory was more impaired in individuals with longer duration of illness, but this accounted for only 6.7% of the variance. Their findings fit the model of fairly stable cognitive functioning across the life span of schizophrenia.

Mesholam-Gately, Giuliano, Goff, Faraone, and Seidman (2009) completed a landmark study, conducting a comprehensive meta-analysis of 47 studies of first episode psychosis to characterize the cognitive profile of individuals with schizophrenia very early during the disease course. They examined 10 cognitive domains including memory, attention (divided into three subdomains of processing speed, working memory, and vigilance), nonverbal memory, general cognitive ability, language functions, visuospatial abilities, delayed verbal memory and learning strategies, executive functioning, social cognition, and motor skills. They compared their findings with those of Heinrichs and Zakzanis (1998), a meta-analysis that included patients throughout the course of the illness. Mesholam-Gately et al. found medium to large effect sizes showing impairments in all neurocognitive functions compared with controls. Their findings also support previous studies suggesting that there is a decline in IQ between the premorbid phase and the first episode. Deficits evidenced in the first episode were comparable to older, more chronic samples, such as those included in the Heinrichs and Zakzanis study. The largest cognitive domain effect sizes were in verbal learning and memory (ES = –1.20) and attention/processing speed (ES = –0.96), and the smallest effect size was in motor functioning (ES = –0.64). Nonverbal learning and memory was also substantially impaired (ES = –0.91). General cognitive ability, language, and visuospatial skills showed large effect size impairments (ES = –0.91, –0.88, and –0.88, respectively). The executive function domain, which include only Wisconsin Card Sorting Test variables, was ES = –0.83. The largest test effect size was for Digit Symbol coding (ES = –1.59). Their analysis also included measures of social cognition, showing an ES of 0.77. Mesholam-Gately and colleagues found that there was considerable heterogeneity within the cognitive domains and measures, also consistent with Heinrichs and Zakzanis. Based on consistency of findings between first-episode and more chronic samples, they concluded that illness severity or long-term exposure to neuroleptics cannot account for the deficits seen in first-episode individuals and this reflect core features of the disorder. Their study also showed that these cognitive deficits are widespread and generalized, but also heterogeneous even against this generalized cognitive impairment with more salient deficits in memory relative to other neurocognitive domains.

Older Patients

Data from 29 cross-sectional studies showed large effect-size impairment across all measures of global cognition and specific neuropsychological functions for older (mean age approximately 65 years) patients with schizophrenia. Demographic (e.g., age, race, gender) and clinical factors (inpatient vs. outpatient status, positive and negative symptoms, etc.) played a role in the size of the effects (Irani, Kalkstein, Moberg, & Moberg, 2010). Figure 1.1 compares levels of impairment on measures of IQ and specific neurocognitive domains across different age-groups and stage of illness derived from the meta-analyses described in this section of the chapter. As can be seen, effect sizes are in the moderate-large range (.75–1.00) for all areas of neurocognition, regardless of illness stage, with some evidence of somewhat larger levels of impairment in immediate verbal memory for FE and chronic samples.

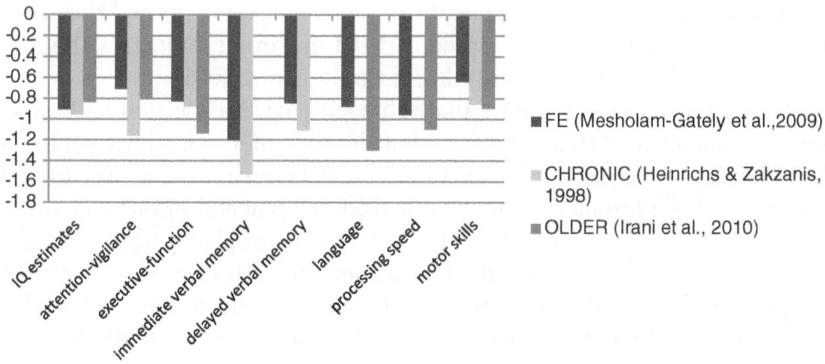

Figure 1.1 Mean effect-size impairment in a variety of np domains in FE, chronic and older samples of patients with schizophrenia.

STUDIES OF LONGITUDINAL COURSE OF NEUROCOGNITIVE DEFICITS IN SCHIZOPHRENIA

While cross-sectional studies reviewed in this chapter so far suggest similar levels of cognitive impairment in different illness stages (see Figure 1.1), only longitudinal studies avoid "cohort" effects and increase power for detecting change in performance by studying the same patients over time. Early follow-up studies evaluated very brief 6-month to 1-year test-retest intervals (e.g., Nopoulos, Flashman, Flaum, & Arndt, 1994; Sweeney, Haas, Keilp, & Long, 1991) during which it would be highly unlikely to detect gradually progressive cognitive decline. In more recent years a growing number of studies have begun to evaluate longer test-retest interval of 5 and even 10 years.

Controversy concerning the longitudinal course of cognitive deficits in schizophrenia can be traced back to earliest descriptions of the disorder. Whereas Kraepelin had adopted the label "dementia praecox" for the disease (a term first used by the French psychiatrist Morel in 1860), as Kraepelin believed the disease had a chronic, deteriorating course (1919), Bleuler (1950) disagreed, noting in a review of 515 cases at Burgholzli Hospital in Zurich, Switzerland, that after the first episode of disease the majority of patients had only mild deterioration, as evidenced by a continuing ability to work and live outside a structured hospital setting. While not mutually exclusive, to this day these two views of the course of the disease have persisted and they have influenced the presumed trajectory of cognitive deficits across the life span: in the first view schizophrenia represents a degenerative neuropsychiatric disorder characterized by onset of the disease in young adulthood followed by a lengthy period of gradual symptomatic, neurocognitive and psychosocial decline. Consistent with this view, some studies have documented a decline on some neurocognitive measures, particularly on overall mental status measures and abstraction (Fucetola et al., 2000; Harvey et al., 1999). These findings are also supported by reports of a reduction in frontal and temporal gray matter regional brain volumes and ventricular enlargement over a 4-year period beyond that associated with healthy aging, as measured by MRI in chronic patients with schizophrenia (e.g., Mathalon, Sullivan, Lim, & Pfefferbaum, 2001).

An alternative view suggests that schizophrenia is associated with neurocognitive impairment that is expressed at the time of, or possibly even before, clinical onset of the disease but that these deficits remain stable over time. By this view, schizophrenia represents a neurodevelopmental disorder characterized by early neural insult that produces a "static encephalopathy" evident for the remainder of the patient's life. Consonant with this view, several research groups have documented a relative consistency of performance on both brief screens of overall mental status (e.g., Waddington & Youssef, 1996; Zorrilla et al., 2000) as well as more comprehensive neuropsychological test batteries (e.g., Censits, Ragland, Gur, & Gur, 1997; Hyde et al., 1994). This view is also consonant with reports on phenomenology and psychosocial outcome in the disorder (see Harrow & Jobe, 2010).

The implications of these alternative views for many of the common tasks that clinical neuropsychologists will engage with in the care of people with schizophrenia, such as the accurate assessment of the effects of pharmacologic and behavioral strategies targeted at neurocognitive deficits, cannot be overemphasized. If schizophrenia is characterized by a gradually worsening cognitive course, interventions that stabilize cognitive deficits over time would be judged efficacious. Alternatively, if cognitive status is static over time, measurable improvements in cognitive test performance associated with administration of a therapeutic intervention would be a minimally necessary benchmark to conclude a potentially positive effect of the intervention.

For stable outpatients with schizophrenia, with the exception of motor slowing, there is little evidence for a reduction in cognitive test performance over a 1.5- to 5-year test-retest interval. This observation is true whether patients are tested initially at first-episode (Censits et al., 1997; Hoff et al., 1999) or after many years of illness (Censits et al., 1997; Heaton et al., 2001), and whether raw scores are examined (Gold, Arndt, Nopoulos, O'Leary, & Andreasen, 1999) or test results are corrected for the effects of aging by comparing obtained scores to those of healthy matched-controls (Heaton et al., 2001; Hoff et al., 1999). This stability was evident even when patients were neuroleptically-naïve at initial testing but were retested on neuroleptic medication with decreased symptoms. Consistent with the findings of this section, a recent meta-analysis of cognitive functioning over the life span in schizophrenia showed a stable course, and even some evidence for a slight improvement in functioning (Szöke et al., 2008).

Results from long-term hospitalized, highly impaired samples of patients, however, reveal a very different pattern of results. These studies suggest that for this sample of patients, high levels of cognitive impairment are evident at a relatively young age, e.g., at least by the second or third decade of life, but that these patients are at-risk for even more profound levels of cognitive impairment as they age past 60 years. Studies have indicated that these patients show significant decreases in overall mental status in the sixth and seventh decade of life and the probability of higher levels of impairment increase tremendously as the patient ages (Friedman et al., 2001). Additional information on changes in cognitive function in the aged patient with schizophrenia can be found in Depp, Loughran, and Palmer, this volume.

THE RELATIONSHIP BETWEEN SYMPTOMS AND NEUROCOGNITION

What is the relationship between symptoms of schizophrenia and neurocognitive deficits? Some authors have argued that there is little or no relationship between cognitive performance and clinical symptom profiles (e.g., Heinrichs & Awad, 1993; Hughes et al., 2003; Rund et al., 2004; Seaton, Allen, Goldstein, Kelley, & van Kammen, 1999). Green (1998) noted that while the correlations between symptoms and cognitive performance were significant, they only explained about 10% of the variance in cognition. When relationships are found, negative symptoms are more likely than positive symptoms to correlate with cognitive deficits (Liddle & Morris, 1991). Liddle and Morris found that a negative symptom factor correlated with deficits in verbal fluency and general slowing in information processing. A disorganized symptom factor correlated with deficits in verbal fluency and inhibition of inappropriate responses.

More recently, several meta-analytic studies have been conducted to examine the relationship between positive and negative symptoms of schizophrenia and neuropsychological functions. Kerns & Berenbaum (2002) found that executive function and semantic memory were associated with a positive symptom (thought disorder). Nieuwenstein, Aleman, and de Haan, (2001) found that negative symptoms were associated with poor WCST performance, but not CPT performance. Dominguez, Viechtbauer, Simons, van Os, and Krabbendam (2009) conducted a comprehensive meta-analytic review of 58 studies of patients with schizophrenia-spectrum illness performance on neuropsychological tests to further clarify the relationship between symptoms and neuropsychological test performance. They examined positive/affective and negative/disorganized symptoms and six neurocognitive constructs based on the constructs included in the NIMH-initiated MATRICS test battery. The number of cognitive variables analyzed was quite extensive and included IQ, reasoning and problem solving, processing speed, attention/vigilance, verbal fluency, executive functions, verbal working memory, verbal learning and memory, and visual learning, and memory. Positive symptoms included delusions, ideas of reference, unusual thought content, hallucinations, grandiosity, and suspiciousness/persecution. Affective symptoms include depression, hopelessness, self-depreciation, guilt, early awakening, suicidal ideation, anxiety, and social avoidance. The negative symptoms included alogia, affective flattening, avolition, apathy, anhedonia, asociality, social withdrawal, stereotyped thinking, and motor retardation. Disorganized symptoms included positive formal thought disorder, difficulty in abstract thinking, derailment, tangentiality, incoherence, illogicality, circumstantiality, associative loosening, inattention/distractibility, disorientation, inappropriate affect, bizarre behavior, mannerisms, and posturing. Consistent with previous studies, negative symptoms correlated with cognitive test performance, particularly verbal fluency, verbal learning and memory, and IQ. Disorganized symptoms correlated with attention/vigilance, visual learning and memory, and IQ. The only correlation between positive symptoms and neuropsychological tests was processing speed.

NEUROCOGNITIVE DEFICITS AND ACUTE SYMPTOM STATES

In general, while "state" effects can occur, the core cognitive deficits of schizophrenia are quite robust and relatively impervious to positive symptoms such as hallucinations and delusions and depression (Gladsjo et al., 2004).

CONCLUSIONS

With respect to the aims of this chapter, we can conclude the neuropsychological deficits in schizophrenia are evident across a broad array of neurocognitive and social cognitive domains in the moderate to large effect-size range. While some studies have indicated that impairment on neuropsychological measures in schizophrenia is reflective of a common deficit across tests, many studies have effectively subtyped patients according to patterns of memory impairment or other factors. Current research suggests that while a group of patients may score within the normal range on neuropsychological tests, these scores typically represent a reduction from expected test scores based when IQ levels are accounted for. Studies of genetic and clinical high-risk individuals indicate that deficits are evident across a variety of neuropsychological measures at a level intermediate between patients with full-blown illness and controls, while "follow back" studies of patients who have schizophrenia suggest that patients have a half-standard deviation impairment on IQ measures, on average, before formal disease onset. There is no evidence that neuropsychological impairment serves as a predictor of who develops schizophrenia, but deficits in verbal learning have been linked to more rapid onset of the disease. Once patients are diagnosed, cross-sectional and longitudinal studies have shown that deficits on neuropsychological tests are similar in first-episode, middle-aged, and older patients with schizophrenia. These findings argue against the idea that either the effects of the disease process or long-term medication exposure produce degenerative changes in neurocognitive function in outpatients. There is evidence of cognitive decline in the smaller subpopulation of patients with schizophrenia who are long-term hospitalized secondary to severe functional impairment. There are modest relationships between negative and disorganization symptoms and neuropsychological impairment with less evidence for relationships between positive symptoms and neuropsychological test performance.

REFERENCES

Aleman, A., Hijman, R., deHaan, E. H., & Kahn, R .S. (1999). Memory impairment in schizophrenia: a meta-analysis, *American Journal of Psychiatry, 156*(9),1358–1366.

Anderson, C. M. (1952). Organic factors pre-disposing to schizophrenia. *Nervous Child, 10,* 35–42.

Asarnow, R. F., Asamen, J., Granholm, E., Sherman, T., Watkins, J. M., & Williams, M. E. (1994). Cognitive/neuropsychological studies of children with a schizophrenic disorder. *Schizophrenia Bulletin, 20,* 647–669.

Aylward, E., Walker, E., & Bettes, B. (1984). Intelligence in schizophrenia: Meta-analysis of the research. *Schizophenia Bulletin, 10,* 430–459.

Bateson, G., Jackson, D. D., Haley, J., & Weakland, J. (1956). Toward a theory of schizophrenia. *Behavioral Sciences, 1,* 251–264.

Bedwell, J. S., Keller, B., Smith, A. K., Hamberger, S., Kumra, S., & Rapoport, J. L. (1999). Why does postpsychotic IQ decline in childhood-onset schizophrenia? *American Journal of Psychiatry, 156,* 1996–1997.

Bell, M. D., Johannesen, J. K., Greig, T. C., & Wexler, B. E. (2010). Memory profiles in schizophrenia: Categorization validity and stability. *Schizophrenia Research 118,* 26–33

Bleuler, E. (1950). *Dementia praecox or the group of schizophrenias* J. Zinkin (trans.). New York: International Universities Press.

Bleuler, E. (1951). The basic symptoms of schizophrenia. In D. Rapaport (Ed.), *Organization and pathology of thought: Selected sources* (pp. 581–649). New York: Columbia University Press.

Bokat, C. E., & Goldberg, T. E. (2003). Letter and category fluency in schizophrenia patients: a meta-analysis. *Schizophrenia Research, 64*(1), 73–78.

Brune, M. (2005). Emotional recognition, 'theory of mind,' and social behavior in schizophrenia. *Psychiatry Research, 133,* 135–147.

Butzlaff, R. L., & Hooley, J.M. (1998). Expressed emotion and psychiatric relapse: A meta-analysis. *Archives of General Psychiatry, 55*(6), 547–552.

Cannon, T. D., Bearden, C. E., Hollister, J. M., Rosso, I. M., Sanchez, L. E., & Hadley, T. (2000). Childhood cognitive functioning in schizophrenia patients and their unaffected siblings: a prospective cohort study. *Schizophrenia Bulletin, 26,* 379–193.

Censits, D. M., Ragland, J. D., Gur, R. C., & Gur, R. E. (1997). Neuropsychological evidence supporting a neurodevelopmental model of schizophrenia: a longitudinal study. *Schizophrenia Research, 24,* 289–298.

Cirillo, M. A., & Seidman, L J., (2003). Verbal declarative memory dysfunction in schizophrenia: from clinical assessment to genetics and brain mechanisms. *Neuropsychology Review, 13*(2), 43–77.

Clarke, M. C., Harley, M., & Cannon, M. (2006). The role of obstetric events in schizophrenia. *Schizophrenia Bulletin, 32,* 3–8.

Cornblatt, B. A., & Erlenmeyer-Kimling, L. (1985). Global attentional deviance as a marker of risk for schizophrenia: Specificity and predictive validity. *Journal of Abnormal Psychology, 94,* 470–486.

Cornblatt, B. A., & Keilp, J. G. (1994). Impaired attention, genetics, and the pathophysiology of schizophrenia. *Schizophrenia Bulletin, 20,* 31–46.

Deifendorf, A., & Kraepelin, E. (1907). *Clinical psychiatry: A text-book for students and physicians.* New York: Macmillan.

Dickinson, D., Iannone, V. N., Wilk, C. M. & Gold, J. (2004). General and specific deficits in schizophrenia. *Biological Psychiatry, 55,* 826–833.
Dickinson, D., Ramsey, M. E., & Gold, J. (2007). Overlooking the obvious: A meta-analytic comparison of digit symbol coding tasks and other cognitive measures in schizophrenia. *Archives of General Psychiatry, 64*(5), 532–542.
Dixon, L. B., Dickerson, F., Bellack, A. S., Bennett, M. Dickinson, D., Goldberg, R. W., et al. (2009). The 2009 schizophrenia PORT psychosocial treatment recommendations and summary statements. *Schizophrenia Bulletin, 36,* 48–70.
Dominguez, M., Viechtbauer, W., Simons, C., van Os, J., & Krabbendam, L. (2009). Are psychotic psychopathology and neurocognition orthogonal? A systematic review oftheir associations. *Psychological Bulletin, 135,* 157–171.
Erlenmeyer-Kimling, L., Rock, D., Roberts, S. A., Janal, M., Kestenbaum, C., Cornblatt, B., et al. (2000). Attention, memory, and motor skills as childhood predictors of schizophrenia-related psychoses: The New York High Risk Project. *American Journal of Psychiatry, 157,* 1416–1422.
Friedman, J. I., Harvey, P. D., Coleman, T., Moriarty, P. J., Bowie, C., Parrella, M., et al. (2001). Six-year follow-up study of cognitive and functional status across the lifespan in schizophrenia: A comparison with Alzheimer's disease and normal aging. *American Journal of Psychiatry, 158*(9), 1441–1448.
Fromm-Reichmann, F. (1948). Notes on the development of treatment of schizophrenics by psychoanalytic therapy. *Psychiatry: Journal for the Study of Interpersonal Processes, 11,* 263–273.
Fucetola, R., Seidman, L. J., Kremen, W. S., Faraone, S. V., Goldstein, J. M., & Tsuang, M. T. (2000). Age and neuropsychologic function in schizophrenia: A decline in executive abilities beyond that observed in healthy volunteers. *Biological Psychiatry, 48,* 137–146.
Gibson, C. M., Penn, D. L., Prinstein, M. J., Perkins, D. O., & Belger, A. (2010). Social skill and social cognition in adolescents at genetic risk for psychosis. *Schizophrenia Research, 122,* 179–184.
Gladsjo, J. A, McAdams, L. A., Palmer, B. W., Moore, D. J., Jeste, D. V., & Heaton, R. K. (2004). A six-factor model of cognition in schizophrenia and related psychotic disorders: Relationships with clinical symptoms and functional capacity. *Schizophrenia Bulletin, 30,* 739–754.
Gold, S., Arndt, S., Nopoulos, P., O'Leary, D. S., & Andreasen, N. C. (1999). Longitudinal study of cognitive function in first-episode and recent-onset schizophrenia. *American Journal of Psychiatry, 156,* 1342–1348.
Goldberg, T. E., Karson, C. N., Leleszi, J P., & Weinberger, D. R. (1988). Intellectual impairment in adolescent psychosis: A controlled psychometric study. *Schizophrenia Research, 1,* 261–266.
Goldstein, G., Shemansky, W. J., & Allen, D. N. (2005). Cognitive function in schizoaffective disorder and clinical subtypes of schizophrenia. *Archives of Clinical Neuropsychology, 20,* 153–159.
Green, M. F. (1998). *Schizophrenia revealed: From neurons to social interaction.* New York: W.W. Norton.
Harrow, M., & Jobe, T. H. (2010). How frequent is chronic multiyear delusional activity and recovery in schizophrenia: A 20-year multi–follow-up. *Schizophrenia Bulletin, 36,* 192–204.
Hartwell, C. E. (1996). The schizophrenogenic mother concept in American psychiatry. *Psychiatry: Interpersonal and Biological Process, 59,* 274–297.

Harvey, P. D., Parrella, M., White, L., Mohs, R. C., Davidson, M., & Davis, K. L. (1999). Convergence of cognitive and adaptive decline in late-life schizophrenia. *Schizophrenia Research, 35,* 77–84.

Harvey, P. D., & Reichenberg, A. (2007). Neuropsychological impairments in schizophrenia: Integration of performance-based and brain imaging findings. *Psychological Bulletin, 133*(5), 833–858.

Heaton, R. K., Gladsjo, J. A., Palmer, B. W., Kuck, J., Marcotte, T. D., & Jeste, D. V. (2001). Stability and course of neuropsychological deficits in schizophrenia. *Archives of General Psychiatry, 58,* 24–32.

Heinrichs, R. W., & Awad, A. G. (1993). Neurocognitive subtypes of chronic schizophrenia. *Schizophrenia Research, 9,* 49–58.

Heinrichs, R. W., Ruttan, L., Zakzanis, K. K., & Case, D. (1997). Parsing schizophrenia with neurocognitive tests: evidence of stability and validity. *Brain & Cognition, 35*(2), 207–224.

Heinrichs, R. W., & Zakzanis, K. K. (1998). Neurocognitive deficit in schizophrenia: A quantitative review of the evidence. *Neuropsychology, 12*(3), 426–445.

Hoff, A. L., Sakuma, M., Wieneke, M., Horon, R., Kushner, M., & DeLisi, L. E. (1999). Longitudinal neuropsychological follow-up study of patients with first-episode schizophrenia. *American Journal of Psychiatry, 156*(9), 1336–1341.

Hooker, C., & Park, S. (2002). Emotion processing and its relationship to social functioning in schizophrenia patients. *Psychiatry Research, 112,* 41–50.

Hughes, C., Kumari, V., Soni, W., Das, M., Binneman, B., Drozd, S., et al. (2002) . Longitudinal study of symptoms and cognitive function in chronic schizophrenia. *Schizophrenia Research, 59,* 137– 146.

Hyde, T. M., Nawroz, S., Goldberg, T. E., Bigelow, L. B., Strong, D., Ostrem, J. L., et al. (1994). Is there cognitive decline in schizophrenia? A cross sectional study. *British Journal of Psychiatry, 164,* 494–500.

Irani, F., Kalkstein, S., Moberg, E. A., & Moberg, P. J. (in press). Neuropsychological performance in older patients with schizophrenia: a meta-analysis of cross-sectional and longitudinal studies. *Schizophrenia Bulletin.*

Kenny, J. T., Friedman, L., Findling, R. L., Swales, T. P., Strauss, M. E., Jesberger, J. A., et al. (1997). Cognitive impairment in adolescents with schizophrenia. American *Journal of Psychiatry, 154,* 1613–1615.

Kerns, J. G., & Berenbaum, H. (2002). Cognitive impairments associated with formal thought disorder in people with schizophrenia. *Journal of Abnormal Psychology. 111,* 211–224

Kleist, K. (1960). Schizophrenic symptoms and cerebral pathology. *Journal of Mental Science, 106,* 246–255.

Knowles, E. E., David, A. S., & Reichenberg, A. (2010). Processing speed deficits in schizophrenia: re-examining the evidence. *American Journal Psychiatry, 167*(7), 828–835.

Kraepelin E. (1920). *Dementia Praecox and Paraphrenia* (R. M. Barclay,Trans.; G. M. Roberston, Ed.). E 7 S Livingstone, Edinborough.

Kremen, W. S., Seidman, L. J., Faraone, S. V., & Tsuang, M. T. (2001). Intelligence quotient and neuropsychological profiles in patients with schizophrenia and in normal volunteers. *Biological Psychiatry, 50,* 453–462.

Kumra, S., Wiggs, E., Bedwell, J., Smith, A. K., Arling, E., Albus, K., et al. (2000). Neuropsychological deficits in pediatric patients with childhood-onset schizophrenia and psychotic disorder not otherwise specified. *Schizophrenia Research, 42,* 135–144.

Lay, B., Nordt, C., & Rössler, W. (2007). Trends in psychiatric hospitalization of people with schizophrenia: A register-based investigation over the last three decades. *Schizophrenia Research, 97,* 68–78.

Lee, J,. & Park, S. (2005). Working memory impairments in schizophrenia: A meta-analysis. *Journal of Abnormal Psychology, 114*(4), 599–611.

Liddle, P. F., & Morris, D. L. (1991). Schizophrenic syndromes and frontal lobe performance. *British Journal of Psychiatry, 158,* 340–345.

Lysaker, P. H., Lancaster, R. S., Nees, M. A., & Davis, L. W. (2004). Attributional style and symptoms as predictors of social function in schizophrenia. *Journal of Rehabilitation Research and Development, 41*(2), 225–232.

Marwaha, S., & Johnson, S. (2004). Schizophrenia and employment: A review. *Social Psychiatry and Psychiatric Epidemiology, 39,* 337–349.

Mathalon, D. H., Sullivan, E. V., Lim, K. O., & Pfefferbaum, A. (2001). Progressive brain volume changes and the clinical course of schizophrenia: A longitudinal magnetic resonance imaging study. *Archives of General Psychiatry, 58,* 148–157.

McGlashan, T. H. (1988). A selective review of recent North American long-term follow-up studies of schizophrenia. *Schizophrenia Bulletin, 14*(4), 515–542.

McGrath J., Saha, S., Welham, J., El Saadi, O. E., MacCauley, C., & Chant, D. (2004). A systematic review of the incidence of schizophrenia: the distribution of rates and the influence of sex, urbanicity, migrant status and methodology. *BMC Medicine, 2.*

Mednick, S. A., Machon, R. A., Huttunen, M. O., & Bonett, D. (1988). Adult schizophrenia following prenatal exposure to an influenza epidemic. *Archives of General Psychiatry, 45,* 189–192.

Menezes, P. (2004). Incidence and outcome of schizophrenia across the globe. In W. F. Gattaz & Busatto, G. (Eds.), *Advances in Schizophrenia Research 2009.* doi: 10.1007/878-1-4419-0913-8_1, Springer Science+Business Media, LLC,2010

Mesholam-Gately, R. I. Giuliano, A. J., Goff, K. P., Faraone, S. V., & Seidman, L. J. (2009). Neurocognition in first-episode schizophrenia: A meta-analytic review. *Neuropsychology, 23,* 315–336.

Meyer, M., & Kurtz, M. (2009). Elementary neurocogntive function, focial affect recognition, and social skills in schizophrenia. *Schizophrenia Research, 110,* 173–179.

Morrison, A. P., & Barratt, S. What are the components of CBT for psychosis? A Delphi study. *Schizophrenia Bulletin, 36,* 136–142.

Mueser, K. T., & Berenbaum, H. (1990). Psychodynamic treatment of schizophrenia: Is there a future? *Psychological Medicine, 20,* 253–262.

Nieuwenstein, M. R., Aleman, A., & de Haan, E. H. F. (2001). Relationship between symptom dimensions and neurocognitive functioning in schizophrenia: A meta-analysis of WCST and CPT studies. *Journal of Psychiatric Research 35,* 119–125.

Nopoulos, P., Flashman, L. Flaum, M., & Arndt, S. (1994). Stability of cognitive functioning early in the course of schizophrenia. *Schizophrenia Research, 14*(1), 29–37.

Øie, M., & Rund, B. R. (1999). Neuropsychological deficits in adolescent onset schizophrenia compared with attention deficit hyperactivity disorder. *American Journal of Psychiatry, 156,* 1216–1222.

Palmer, B., Heaton, R. K., Kuck, J., & Braff, D. (1997). Is it possible to be schizophrenic yet neuropsychologically normal? *Neuropsychology, 11,* 437–446.

Penn, D. L., Corrigan, P. W., Bentall, R. P., Racenstein, J. M., & Newman, L. (1997). Social cognition in schizophrenia. *Psychological Bulletin, 121,* 114–132.

Penn, D. L., Sanna, L. J., & Roberts, D. L. (2008). Social cognition in schizophrenia; An overview. *Schizophrenia Bulletin, 34,* 408–411.

Pillay, P., & Montcrieff, J. (2011). Contributions of psychiatric disorders to occupation of NHS beds: Analysis of hospital episode statistics. *The Psychiatrist, 35*, 56–59.

Pinkham, A. E., & Penn, D. L. (2006). Neurocognitive and social cognitive predictors of interpersonal skill in schizophrenia. *Psychiatry Research, 143*, 167–178.

Rajji, T.K., Ismail, J., & Mulsant, B. H. (2009). Age at onset and cognition in schizophrenia: Meta-analysis. *British Journal of Psychiatry, 195*, 286–293.

Reichenberg, A., Weiser, M., Rapp, M.A., Rabinowitz, J. Caspi, A., Schmeidler, J., et al. (2005). Elaboration on premorbid intellectual performance in schizophrenia. *Archives of General Psychiatry, 62*, 1297–1304.

Reichenberg, A., Weiser, M., Rapp, M. A., Rabinowitz, J., Caspi, A., Schmeidler, J., et al. (2006). Premorbid intra-individual variability in intellectual performance and risk for schizophrenia: A population-based study. *Schizophrenia Research 85*, 49–57.

Roncone, R., Falloon, I. R. H., Mazza, M., De Risio, A., Pollice, R., Necozione, S., et al. (2002). Is theory of mind in schizophrenia more strongly associated with clinical and social functioning than with neurocognitive deficits? *Psychopathology, 35*, 280–288.

Rund, B. R., Melle, I., Friis, S., Johannessen, J. O., Larsen, T. K., Midbøe, L. J., et al. (2007). The course of neurocognitive functioning in first-episode psychosis and its relation to premorbid adjustment, duration of untreated psychosis, and relapse. *Schizophrenia Research 91*, 132–140

Rund, B. R., Melle, I., Friis, S., Larsen, T. K., Midboe, L. J., Opjordsmoen, S., et al. (2004). Neurocognitive dysfunction in first-episode psychosis correlates with symptoms, premorbid adjustment, and duration of untreated psychosis. *American Journal of Psychiatry, 161*, 466–472.

Seaton, B. E., Allen, D. N., Goldstein, G., Kelley, M. E., & van Kammen, D. P. (1999). Relationship between cognitive and sympton profile in hetrogeneity in schizophrenia. *Journal of Nervous and Mental Disease, 187*, 414–419.

Seaton, B. E, Goldstein, G., & Allen, D. N. (2001). Sources of heterogeneity in schizophrenia: The role of neuropsychological functioning. *Neuropsychology Review, 11*, 45–67.

Seidman, L. J., Giuliano, A. J., Meyer, E. C., Addington, J., Cadenhead, K. S., Cannon, T. D., et al. (2010). Neuropsychology of the Prodrome to psychosis in the NAPLS Consortium: Relationship to family history and conversion to psychosis. *Archives of General Psychiatry, 67*, 578–588.

Silverstein, M. L., & Zerwic, M. J. (1985). Clinical psychopathologic symptoms in neuropsychologically impaired and intact schizophrenics. *Journal of Consulting and Clinical Psychology, 53*, 267–268.

Sponheim, S., Jung, R. E., Seidman, L. J., Mesholam-Gately, R. I., Manoach, D. S., O'Leary, D. S. et al. (2010). Cognitive deficits in recent-onset and chronic schizophrenia. *Journal of Psychaitric Research, 44*, 421–428.

Susser, E. S., & Lin, S. P. (1992). Schizophrenia after prenatal exposure to the Dutch hunger winter of 1944–1945. *Archives of General Psychiatry, 49*, 983–988.

Sweeney, J. A., Haas, G. L., Keilp, J. G., & Long, M. (1991). Evaluation of the stability of neuropsychological functioning after acute episodes of schizophrenia: One year follow-up study. *Psychiatry Research, 38*, 63–76.

Szöke, A.,Trandafir, A., Dupont,, M.-E., Méary, A., Schürhoff, F., & LeBoyer, M. (2008). Longitudinal studies of cognition in schizophrenia: Meta-analysis. *British Journal of Psychiatry*, 192, 248–257.

Townsend, L. A., Malla, A. K., & Norman, R. M. (2001). Cognitive functioning in stabilized first-episode psychosis patients. *Psychiatry Research, 104*, 119–131.

Tsuang, M. T., Stone, W. S., & Faraone, S. V. (1999). Schizophrenia: A review of genetic studies. *Harvard Review of Psychiatry, 7*, 185–207.

Turetsky, B. I., Moberg, P. J., Mozley, L. H., Moelter, S. T., Agrin, R. N., Gur, R. C., et al. (2002). Memory-delineated subtypes of schizophrenia: Relationship to clinical, neuroanatomical and neurophysiological measures. *Neuropsychology, 16*, 481–490.

Waddington, J. L., & Youssef, H. A. (1996). Cognitive dysfunction in chronic schizophrenia followed prospectively over 10 years and its longitudinal relationship to the emergence of tardive dyskinesia. *Psychological Medicine, 26*, 681–688.

Wechsler, D. (1955). *The range of human capacities.* Baltimore: Williams & Wilkins.

Wilk, C. M., Gold, J. M., McMahon, R. P., Humber, K., Iaonnone, V. N., & Buchanan, R. W. (2000). No, it is not possible to be schizophrenic yet neuropsychologically normal. *Neuropsychology, 19*, 778–786.

Woodberry, K., Giuliano, A. J., & Seidman, L. J. (2008). Premorbid IQ in schizophrenia: A meta-analytic review. *American Journal of Psychiatry, 165*(5), 579–587.

Wykes, T., Steel, C., Everitt, B., & Tarrier, N. (2008). Cognitive behavior therapy for schizophrenia: effect sizes, clinical models, and methodological rigor. *Schizophrenia Bulletin, 34*, 523–537.

Zorrilla, L. T. E., Heaton, R. K., McAdams, L. A., Zisook, S., Harris, M. J., & Jeste, D. V., (2000). Cross-sectional study of older outpatients with schizophrenia and healthy comparison subjects: No difference in age-related cognitive decline. *American Journal of Psychiatry, 157*, 1324–1326.

BOX 1.1 PREVALENCE AND ETIOLOGY

1. Prevalance rates are one half to 1% worldwide with pockets of higher prevalence reported.
2. While etiology of the disorder remains unclear, genetic factors clearly influence emergence of the disorder. First degree relatives of probands have an approximately 10% chance of developing the disease.
3. Monozygotic twins have a substantially higher concordance rates (approximately 50% in some studies) than dizygotic twins.
4. Maternal stress during pregnancy, such as influenza during the second trimester of gestation and maternal starvation along with birth complications, are risk factors for subsequent diagnosis in offspring.

BOX 1.2 PATTERN AND MAGNITUDE OF IQ AND NEUROCOGNITIVE DEFICITS IN SCHIZOPHRENIA

1. There is large effect-size impairment in full-scale IQ relative to healthy controls with some evidence that performance IQ is, on average, 50% more impaired than verbal IQ scores.
2. Moderate-large effect size impairment is evident on neuropsychological measures of attention, verbal and non-verbal episodic memory, verbal and non-verbal working memory, language, processing speed, and executive-function.
3. There is some evidence that processing speed is more impaired than other neuropsychological functions.
4. These neuropsychological deficits are evident at illness onset, during middle-age and into senescence. For the majority of patients, these deficits do not worsen with time. Both cross-sectional and longitudinal studies support the stability of these deficits over time.
5. While still a relatively new area of research, studies of social cognition, that is the ability of patients to think about themselves and the social world, have shown that patients also have marked deficits in this sphere of cognition that are not reducible to other aspects of cognition.

BOX 1.3 SUBTYPES OF NEUROCOGNITIVE DEFICIT IN SCHIZOPHRENIA

1. Deficits on neuropsychological measures in schizophrenia can best be understood as reflecting a common factor evident across different domains of neuropsychological function. These findings suggest that differences in performance between patients can best be understood as differences in magnitude rather than pattern.
2. Using statistical procedures for grouping patients according to patterns of neuropsychological performance, some studies have supported distinguishing patients into three neurocognitive subtypes: a neuropsychologically normal group, a low cognitive functioning group and a group with spared verbal skills but impaired motor functioning.

3. Dividing patients according to patterns of deficits on verbal memory measures has revealed groups of patients labeled "subcortical" with marked retrieval impairments and frontal pathology, "cortical" patients with deficits in encoding and storage and temporal lobe abnormalities and relatively unimpaired patients.
4. While some studies have shown that as many as approximately 30% of patients with schizophrenia are neuropsychologically normal when neuropsychological test protocols are judged by experts, more recent work suggests that when IQ measures are carefully matched to healthy controls, almost all patients with schizophrenia show some level of neuropsychological impairment.

BOX 1.4 NEUROPSYCHOLOGICAL IMPAIRMENT IN PEOPLE AT GENETIC HIGH RISK FOR SCHIZOPHRENIA, CLINICAL HIGH RISK AND "FOLLOW-BACK" STUDIES OF PATIENTS DIAGNOSED WITH THE DISEASE

1. Impaired attention is evident in individuals at elevated genetic risk for schizophrenia.
2. People at clinical high-risk for the disorder have deficits across a range of neuropsychological measures that are intermediate in magnitude between healthy control and patient's performance.
3. Individuals later diagnosed with schizophrenia score one-half a standard deviation below healthy controls on IQ tests.
4. There is no evidence that neuropsychological deficits predict the onset of schizophrenia: current research suggests that deficits in verbal memory predict a more rapid transition to formal diagnosis.

CONTINUING EDUCATION QUESTIONS

1. A first degree relative of someone with schizophrenia has a _____ chance of developing the disease.
   A. 1%
   B. 10%
   C. 50%
   D. 80%

2. There is some evidence that deficits in _________ are greater in magnitude than in other areas of neuropsychological functioning.
   A. Processing speed
   B. Attention
   C. Verbal memory
   D. Executive-function
   E. None of the above
3. Neurocognitive deficits in schizophrenia, generally speaking___________ across the lifespan.
   A. Worsen
   B. Improve
   C. Stay stable
   D. None of the above
4. Memory-delineated subtypes in schizophrenia suggest abnormalities in the ______ lobe in patients with a "cortical" pattern of memory impairment.
   A. Frontal
   B. Temporal
   C. Occipital
   D. Parietal
5. Research has shown that patients with schizophrenia who scored in the average range on IQ tests premorbidly still showed unusual IQ scores in that
   A. Verbal IQ was abnormally high
   B. Digit Span was highly impaired
   C. There were unusually large discrepancies between IQ subtests.
   D. None of the above.

2

Schizophrenia as a Developmental Brain Disorder

MATCHERI S. KESHAVAN, M.D.
Department of Psychiatry, Beth Israel Deaconess Medical Center and Massachusetts Mental Health Center, Harvard Medical School

VAIBHAV A. DIWADKAR, Ph.D.
Ph.D., Department of Psychiatry, Wayne State University School of Medicine

INTRODUCTION

Cognitive impairments are a core feature of schizophrenia, and are a royal road to follow in investigating neurobiological impairments as well as models of pathogenesis in this illness. The dominant model of schizophrenia during the past century has been the Kraepelinian concept of a degenerative disease, based on observations of cognitive decline, and captured in the term *dementia praecox*. However, the view that abnormal neurodevelopment may underlie schizophrenia has been gaining acceptance in recent decades. This idea is not new; the observation of deficits in social interaction as well as premorbid signs in childhood was noted by Bleuler and Kraepelin (see Malmberg, Lewis, David, & Allebeck, 1998; Marenco & Weinberger, 2001) and Clouston (1891) who observed developmental dysmorphic abnormalities, such as high arched palate, in patients he considered as having "adolescent insanity." Southard at the Boston Psychopathic Hospital (now the Massachusetts Mental Health Center) observed brain changes in schizophrenia that were attributed to developmental deviations (Casanova, 1995). Bender (1953) and subsequently Fish and Hagin (1972) argued that schizophrenia might reflect a developmental "encephalopathy."

At least three developmental formulations have been suggested, those positing altered pre- or perinatal brain development, those that implicate periadolescent developmental abnormalities, and those proposing neuroregressive processes after illness onset. In this chapter, we will review and attempt to integrate these models of schizophrenia and associated neuropathologies to enable the practicing neuropsychologist to fully understand how these brain dysfunctions emerge, and how impaired cognition and functioning can result from such changes. We first examine clinical evidence of schizophrenia reflecting a neurodevelopmental diathesis. We then examine the anatomy, function, neurochemistry, and neuropathology of brain structures or networks that may explain the developmental manifestations of the illness. We will also examine pathogenesis, that is, when during development the disease related processes might begin, and etiology of brain developmental alterations, with reference to the genetic and environmental determinants of the illness and their interaction. Finally, we will outline a potential integrative model of this illness and discuss future directions of research.

CLINICAL AND NEUROCOGNITIVE EVIDENCE OF DISORDERED BRAIN DEVELOPMENT IN SCHIZOPHENIA

The strongest, though indirect, evidence of disordered neurodevelopment in schizophrenia derives from observations of premorbid behavioral, neurocognitive, and minor physical anomalies. Subtle deficits in general intellectual function are seen as well as selective deficits in a variety of cognitive functions (i.e., attention and executive functions, psychomotor abilities, language and memory); minor physical anomalies, indicating disordered early development. Prospective general population cohort studies, studies of relatives with increased risk for schizophrenia ("high-risk" studies; Keshavan, 2004), and retrospective studies of individuals with already manifest illness (archival–observational studies; Walker, Savoie, & Davis, 1994) are in support of these observations.

Attention and Executive Functions

Schizophrenia is marked by impaired spatial and verbal working memory beginning early in the illness as well as in those at risk for the illness (Elvevag & Goldberg, 2000). Impairments in attentional processing and executive function have also been observed in high risk offspring of schizophrenia patients (Cornblatt, Obuchowski, Roberts, Pollack, & Erlenmeyer-Kimling, 1999; Keshavan et al., 2010). Decreased speed of performance is seen in first degree relatives on the Stroop color-naming task that indexes selective attention and executive function (Zalla et al., 2004). Deficits have also been consistently observed on the Wisconsin Cart Sort task which indexes executive function; the performance of relatives is intermediate between healthy control subjects and schizophrenia patients (Egan et al., 2001;Keri, Kelemen, Benedek, & Janka, 2001; Wolf,

Cornblatt, Roberts, Shapiro, & Erlenmeyer-Kimling, 2002). Patients and at-risk relatives also show deficits in tasks where decisions must be based on contextual information (MacDonald, Pogue-Geile, Johnson, & Carter, 2003). In such continuous performance tasks (e.g., the AX-CPT), subjects must respond to targets in a sequence only if they are preceded by particular items (e.g. A followed by an X), but not others. Attentional impairment is trait related, stable over time, and related to genetic vulnerability (Michie et al., 2000). In one of the early High Risk studies, the New York High Risk Project (NYHRP), attentional impairment in childhood predicted 58% of the offspring of schizophrenia subjects who developed schizophrenia spectrum disorders in adulthood (Erlenmeyer-Kimling, 2000).

Neuromotor, Memory and Language Abilities

An association between motor coordination problems or delayed motor milestones and later schizophrenia appears to be substantiated by retrospective studies of home movies of individuals who subsequently developed schizophrenia (Walker et al., 1994), as well as population cohort studies (Rosso, Bearden, et al., 2000). In a pioneering prospective study of infants and children, Fish (1984) originally observed neuromotor deviations (which she termed pandysmaturation) in about a half of the offspring at risk. Similar neuromotor dysfunctions have been observed in other studies, including the Pittsburgh High Risk study (Prasad, Sanders, et al., 2009), and may predict affective flattening in adolescence (Dworkin et al., 1993).

A deficit in short term verbal memory was seen in 83% of offspring who later developed schizophrenia in the NYHRP study (Erlenmeyer-Kimling, 2000) though high false positive rates (28%) were seen as well. Attentional impairments had lower sensitivity (58%) and lower false positive rates (18%) for prediction of later schizophrenia. Population cohort studies suggest premorbid language impairments including decreased speech intelligibility (Bearden et al., 2000). Receptive language difficulties appear to predict a significant increase in risk for later schizophrenia (Cannon et al., 2002).

Minor Physical Anomalies

Minor physical anomalies (MPAs), including malformations of the ear, palate, and facial dysmorphic features, may offer clues to the neurodevelopmental deviations underlying schizophrenia. MPAs may reflect altered development of the ectoderm and may shed light on the timing of the neurodevelopmental deviations. MPAs predict later emergence of schizophrenia spectrum disorders in offspring at risk in some (Dworkin et al., 1993) but not all studies (Lawrie, Byrne, et al., 2001).

Clearly, premorbid clinical and neurobehavioral evidence points to neurodevelopmental pathology in schizophrenia. However, such data do not shed light on the neuroanatomy of such pathology; careful in vivo imaging, electrophysiological, and neuropathological studies, as will be discussed below, will elucidate this issue.

DEVELOPMENTAL ABNORMALITIES UNDERLYING SCHIZOPHRENIA: NEUROANATOMICAL ALTERATIONS

Neurocognitive deficits outlined above strongly suggest involvement of several cortical and subcortical circuits, as well as disordered connectivity in the association cortices. However, critical regions of the brain, such as the prefrontal cortex, may be particularly vulnerable to abnormal neurodevelopment in schizophrenia (Lewis, 1997; Weinberger et al., 2001).

Brain structural studies in young relatives at risk for schizophrenia are of considerable value, given that MRI measurements of brain volume are sensitive to normative brain maturational processes (Giedd et al., 1999). Significant reductions in gray matter volume in the heteromodal association cortex and basal ganglia (McCarley et al., 1999; Shenton, Dickey, Frumin, & McCarley, 2001) have been observed in first-episode schizophrenia patients. Studies of unaffected relatives at risk for schizophrenia have uncovered gray matter reductions in structures such as the prefrontal cortex (Gogtay et al., 2003), temporal cortex (Lawrie, Whalley, et al., 2002), hippocampus (Keshavan, Diwadkar, et al., 2002; Schulze et al., 2003; Seidman et al., 2002; Tepest, Wag, Miller, Falkai, & Csernansky, 2003), amygdala (Keshavan, Diwadkar, et al., 2002; Keshavan, Montrose, et al., 1997; Seidman et al., 1999), and thalamus (Lawrie, Whalley, Abukmeil, et al., 2001; Lawrie, Whalley, Kestelman, et al., 1999). Other findings in schizophrenia include ventricular enlargement (Staal et al., 2000), lack of cerebral asymmetry (Bhojraj et al., 2010; Sharma et al., 1999) and reductions in whole-brain white matter volume (Hulshoff et al., 2004). These anatomic alterations involve brain areas serving cognitive domains such as language, spatial and verbal working memory, and executive function (Mesulam, 1998); as discussed earlier, relatives appear to show cognitive impairment in these domains; relatives with cognitive impairments appear to have the most prominent structural brain alterations (Bhojraj et al., 2010).

BRAIN DEVELOPMENT, ALTERATIONS IN BRAIN FUNCTION IN SCHIZOPHRENIA

The application of in vivo imaging techniques to the study of schizophrenia is too extensive to permit an adequate summary. Methodologically, the application of in vivo functional MRI studies to the study of schizophrenia and to an understanding of developmental and genetic contributions to schizophrenia is fraught with several conceptual challenges. For example, the electrophysiological bases of the endogenous Blood Oxygen Level Dependent (BOLD) based contrast agent is complex, more closely related to the lower frequency local field potentials than higher frequency spike discharges (Heeger, Huk, Geisler, & Albrecht, 2000; Logothetis, 2002). As a result, the term *activation* in fMRI is somewhat simplistic and difficult to interpret in the face of general deficits in performance that characterize schizophrenia (Carter, 2005). Hypoactivation, in the sense of PET-related "hypofrontality" that has been previously documented (Andreasen, Endicott, Spitzer, & Winokur, 1977) may reflect a basic failure to engage task-relevant circuitry (Barch et al., 2001) or a failure to engage regions commensurate with changes in task difficulty (Manoach, 2003). When task difficulty is carefully matched between patients and controls, it appears that the schizophrenia brain is *inefficient* in its dependence on cortical resources (Cairo, Woodward, & Ngan, 2006; Callicott et al., 2000; Jansma, Ramsey, van der Wee, & Kahn, 2004; Potkin et al., 2009) requiring greater "activation" to sustain behavioral performance approaching that of controls.

Understanding the role of development in fMRI-measured activation and risk and vulnerability for schizophrenia is also challenging as functional brain development is highly nonlinear (Huttenlocher & Dabholkar, 1997), variable and interactive (Edin, Macoveanu, Olesen, Tegner, & Klingberg, 2007). Similarly, the link between genes and genetic polymorphisms, brain activation and schizophrenia (Tan, Callicott, & Weinberger, 2007), is intriguing but it is presumably also complex. Nevertheless fMRI has been successful in documenting widespread differences not only between first-episode schizophrenia patients and controls, but also between young and old nonpsychotic relatives on tasks of working memory, attention, and emotion processing (Barbour et al., 2010; Callicott et al., 2003; Keshavan, Dick et al., 2002). Also, aberrant (failure to suppress) activity of the default state networks has been demonstrated in relatives of schizophrenia patients and found to be correlated with psychopathology (Whitfield-Gabrieli et al., 2009).

Clearly, available evidence indicates that premorbid abnormalities in brain development might lead to anatomical and physiological alterations in widely distributed cortical and subcortical networks. An understanding of the micro-structural and neurochemical underpinnings of such deficits is critical for our efforts to determine the causative factors that determine their emergence.

NEUROPATHOLOGY OF THE DEVELOPMENTAL BRAIN ALTERATIONS

Brain changes in schizophrenia as discussed above may include neuronal and glial cell abnormalities, synaptic dysfunction, and cellular disarray (Cho, Gilbert, & Lewis, 2003), and may behind neurochemical alterations underlying the emergence of psychopathology. Postmortem evidence in schizophrenia suggests a 5 to 10% reduction in cortical thickness in the dorsal prefrontal cortex (Harrison & Lewis, 2001). Cell packing density has been reported to be increased without any change in the number of neurons (Selemon et al., 1995); this may reflect reductions in axon terminals, and dendritic spines that comprise the cortical synaptic neuropil. Such reductions in neuronal size may also underlie reduced cortical thickness (Pierri, Volk, Auh, Sampson, & Lewis, 2001; Rajkowska et al., 1998). Reductions in pyramidal neuron size in the cortex may result from aberrant thalamocortical projections arising during development. Reduced somal size and dendritic spine density (Pierri et al., 2001; Rajkowska et al., 1998) may result from a loss of afferent inputs to the cortex. Glial abnormalities have also been implicated in schizophrenia; historically, the absence of gliosis was considered supportive of an early neurodevelopmental origin of schizophrenia and was taken as evidence against a neurodegenerative pathology. There may be regionally specific reductions of glial cells in the orbitofrontal, anterior cingulate, and motor cortices (Benes, Davidson, & Bird, 1986; Benes, McSparren, et al., 1991; Cotter, Pariente, & Everall, 2001; Rajkowska et al., 1999). Further studies of glial cell function and their role during development are likely to shed light on neurodevelopmental models of schizophrenia.

Neuronal disarray has been suggested as underlying the development of schizophrenia as evidenced by studies reporting disordered arrangements of neurons in postmortem brains. Several neurodevelopmental processes may be involved including neuronal arrangement and cortical maturation, subplate formation, neuronal migration toward cortical layers, and neuronal orientation. A subset of schizophrenic patients appears to show disordered distribution of subplate neurons in cortical and temporal lobes (Akbarian, Bunney et al., 1993; Akbarian, Sucher, et al., 1996). These data suggest that an aberrant neuronal migration during early development may occur in schizophrenia (Falkai, Schneider-Axmann, & Honer, 2000).

NEUROCHEMICAL MECHANISMS OF DISORDERED BRAIN DEVELOPMENT

Neurotransmitters, such as dopamine, glutamate, serotonin, and gamma-amino butyric acid (GABA) are good candidates to be considered in neurodevelopmental theories of schizophrenia. While dopaminergic abnormalities have been central to neurochemical theories of schizophrenia, considerable evidence of dysfunctional glutamatergic and GABA systems in this illness has also emerged over the past two decades. The neurochemical and molecular mechanisms responsible for neurotransmission play vital roles in early brain development, postnatal plasticity, and brain degeneration. Attempts to develop effective treatments for schizophrenia frequently target these specific systems.

In recent years, a greater understanding of the complex interactions of the dopaminergic system with other neurotransmitter systems, variable DA regulation in different brain regions, and multiple DA receptor types has led to a more complex and broader view of DA's role in schizophrenia. In an elegant formulation, Weinberger (1987) posited that schizophrenia may be related to deficits in the mesocortical DA system leading to mesolimbic DA overactivity. Another influential model by Grace (1991) suggests that schizophrenia may be associated with a deficit in tonic DA drive and an exaggeration of the phasic stress-induced DA release. Aberrant presynaptic storage, release, reuptake, and metabolic mechanisms in DA mesolimbic systems have been observed in positron emission tomography (PET) studies of schizophrenia patients (Laruelle,

2000). Reduced density of cortical DA axons and specific DA regulatory proteins, as well as cortical DA D1 receptor upregulation may contribute to working memory deficits, a common feature of schizophrenia (Abi-Dargham et al., 2002; Akil et al., 1999; Albert et al., 2002; Goldman-Rakic, 1994). It is to be kept in mind, however, that direct evidence of DA abnormality in schizophrenia is still lacking; the DA model best explains positive symptoms, while the cognitive deficits remain in search of clear-cut neurochemical explanations.

Another neurotransmitter system prominently implicated in schizophrenia is glutamate, the most abundant excitatory neurotransmitter in the mammalian brain. It is critically involved in the early developmental processes of neuronal migration and neuronal survival, for brain plasticity during adolescence; glutamate is also important for neuronal excitability and viability throughout life. Given the key role in schizophrenia played by processes of development, neuronal regulation, and neurotoxicity, it is easy to see why glutamatergic alterations might be highly plausible. Early observations of reductions in cerebrospinal fluid glutamate levels (Kim, Kornhuber, Schmid-Burgk, & Holzmuller, 1980) and similarities between the clinical manifestations of schizophrenia and psychosis caused by phencyclidine (PCP), a NMDA receptor antagonist (Coyle, 1996; Javitt & Zukin, 1991; Tamminga, 1998) led to the glutamate hypothesis. Evidence of altered glutamate metabolism in postmortem brains of schizophrenia patients (Tsai & Coyle, 1995), and altered gene expression for NMDA receptor subunits (Akbarian, Sucher, et al., 1996) are in support of this theory. However, these findings have not been consistently replicated. Further, while glutamate is ubiquitously distributed in the brain, alterations in this system do not easily explain the relatively more localized alterations in schizophrenia.

The major inhibitory neurotransmitter in the central nervous system, GABA, has also been importantly implicated in the pathogenesis of schizophrenia. This view is supported by postmortem data suggesting decreased expression of glutamic acid decarboxylase (an enzyme involved in GABA synthesis) in cortical brain regions (Volk, Austin, Pierri, Sampson, & Lewis, 2000). GABAergic interneurons regulate pyramidal cell activity and may be critical for cognitive functions. Abnormalities in cortical GABA and pyramidal neurons have been described in schizophrenic brains. GABA reductions are also seen in a well-known animal model of schizophrenia; that is, rodents deficient in reelin, an extracellular matrix protein (Costa et al., 2001; Liu et al., 2001).

Psychotic symptoms can result from drugs affecting serotonergic systems, such as lysergic acid diethylamide (LSD) and psilocybin. This suggests involvement of this neurotransmitter in schizophrenia. Though there is little direct evidence of this, the therapeutic role of serotonergic-dopaminergic antagonists in the past decade has rekindled a possible role for serotonin in pathophysiology.

Optimum functioning of neurotransmitter receptors, ion channels, and signal transduction is dependent on the integrity of neuronal cell membranes, largely comprising phospholipids. An in vivo imaging technique, magnetic resonance spectroscopy (MRS), allows investigation of abnormal membrane metabolites in psychiatric illness and in at-risk populations. Neurodevelopmental processes, such as neuritic sprouting and myelination, are expressed by changes in concentration of MRS-measurable metabolites, such as phosphomonoesters (PMEs) and phosphodiesters (PDE), among others (Pettegrew, Keshavan, & Minshew, 1993; Stanley, 2002). Higher PME levels are observed at the time and site of neuritic sprouting, and higher PDE levels are observed at the site and time of neuronal membrane breakdown. Reported reductions in PME levels in the PFC of young relatives of schizophrenia patients (Keshavan et al., 2003), reflect a possible reduction in neuritic sprouting or accelerated pruning. A reduction in the ratio of PME to PDE in this population could indicate an alteration in the membrane phospholipid turnover (Keshavan, Stanley, et al., 2003; Klemm et al., 2001; Rzanny et al., 2003).

Another MRS technique (Proton MRS) can quantify levels of N-acetyl aspartate (NAA), considered to be a general marker of neuronal integrity. Emerging studies have documented reductions in this metabolite in young relatives of schizophrenia patients consistent with similar to NAA reductions observed in schizophrenia. Reductions in NAA (expressed as NAA/choline ratios) in the anterior cingulate have been observed in offspring of schizophrenia patients (Keshavan, Montrose, et al., 1997). NAA/Creatine ratio reductions in the hippocampus have also been observed in adult relatives (Callicott, Egan, et al., 1998). Glutamate reductions have been observed in male relatives at risk (Keshavan, Dick, et al. 2009), though increases in glutamatergic metabolites have also been seen (Abbott & Bustillo 2006).

In summary, the above studies suggest that microstructural and neurochemical alterations may predate illness onset and may reflect aberrant brain development. Alterations in glutamate, GABA, and dopaminergic systems may be developmentally mediated and precede illness onset. Given the typical onset of illness during adolescence or early adulthood, the question of when such abnormalities begin, and how they evolve over time assume importance.

PATHOGENESIS AND TIMING OF THE ABNORMAL BRAIN DEVELOPMENT

Potential "windows" into the timing of developmental pathophysiology are suggested by the key "facts" of schizophrenia (Tandon, Keshevan, & Nasrallah, 2008; Wyatt, Alexander, Egn, & Kirch, 1988): (a) premorbid deficits, that date back to early development in many cases (Done, Crow, Johnstone, & Sacker, 1994; Jones & Cannon, 1998); (b) the characteristic onset in adolescence (Hafner, Maurer, Koffler, & Riecher-Rossler, 1993); (c) functional decline that occurs during the early course of schizophrenia (McGlashan & Fenton, 1993). These observations have led to the three neurodevelopmental models discussed below that have been proposed in relation to the timing of pathophysiological processes in schizophrenia.

The "Early" Developmental Processes

Premorbid neurodevelopmental alterations in schizophrenia primarily point to one or other causal factors early in development, that is, intra- or perinatally, perhaps during the second half of gestation. In these models (Murray & Lewis, 1987; Weinberger, 1987), a fixed lesion from early life interacts with normal brain maturation occurring later. This view is supported by neuropathological observations of (a) altered cytoarchitecture that suggest possible errors in neural genesis or migration in schizophrenia; and (b) epidemiological observations suggesting associations between early neurobehavioral deficits and later emergence of schizophrenia, as discussed earlier. The developmental derailment is unlikely to involve the earliest steps of neurogenesis, since neural tube defects (i.e., midline cysts, spina bifida) are not associated with higher incidence of schizophrenia. It is more likely that the processes of programmed cell death, neural migration, or synaptic proliferation, which begin during the second trimester of pregnancy, are involved. These abnormalities can possibly explain premorbid behavioral precursors of schizophrenia (Fish, 1987; Watt, 1978). However, the "early" theory does not easily explain the characteristic onset of schizophrenia in adolescence or early adulthood.

The "Late" Developmental Processes

The onset of schizophrenia in adolescence suggests an alternative view that the pathophysiology of this disorder may begin in or shortly before this critical period of development. Based on data that indicate substantial changes in brain biology during adolescence, Feinberg (1982–1983) initially proposed that schizophrenia may result from an abnormality in periadolescent synaptic pruning. This view is supported by observations that substantive changes in several in vivo neurobiological measures occur in adolescence that may indirectly reflect changes in synapse density. Periadolescent reductions are seen in slow wave sleep, which represents the summed postsynaptic potentials in large assemblies of cortical and subcortical axons and dendrites. Decreases are also seen in synthesis of membrane phospholipids, as measured by phosphorus magnetic resonance spectroscopy studies (Pettegrew et al., 1991), cortical gray matter volumes, as measured by structural MRI (Jernigan & Tallal, 1990) as well as regional prefrontal metabolism (Chugani, Phelps, & Mazziotta, 1987). Similar, but more pronounced decrements are seen in schizophrenia, compared to healthy controls, in slow wave sleep (Keshavan, Lawrie, et al., 1998), membrane synthesis (Pettegrew et al., 1991), gray matter volume (Zipursky, 1992), and prefrontal metabolism (Andreasen et al., 1992). These observations have been taken to indirectly suggest an exaggeration of the normative synaptic pruning process, perhaps more prominently in critical brain regions such as prefrontal cortex in schizophrenia (Keshavan, Anderson, & Pettegrew, 1994; Pettegrew et al., 1997). This hypothesis has been supported by neural network modeling studies (Hoffman & McGlashan, 1997; McGlashan & Hoffman, 2000) and neuropathological studies showing reductions in the synapse rich neuropil and a consequent increase in cortical neuron density (Selemon, Rajkowska, & Goldman-Rakic, 1995). Reductions have also been reported in the expression of synaptophysin, a synaptic marker (Eastwood & Harrison, 1995; Glantz & Lewis, 1997) and in dendritic density (Garey, Patel, & Ong, 1994). In this model, the overall reduction of cortical synapse rich neuropil in schizophrenia may lead to reduced neuronal plasticity, and consequently impaired capacity to handle the normative academic, familial, and interpersonal demands of adolescence. Symptoms and signs of schizophrenia may appear when a critical threshold of such neuropil loss is exceeded.

The Postillness Progressive Changes

The "early" and "late" developmental models discussed above do not satisfactorily account for the functional declines that occur during the first few years after illness onset in schizophrenia (Lieberman et al., 1996; Loebel et al., 1992; McGlashan & Fenton, 1993). There is evidence that prolonged untreated illness predicts a poorer outcome, suggesting a possible "neurotoxic" effect of psychosis (Lieberman, 1993). Additionally, progressive brain structural alterations may be seen in schizophrenia (DeLisi, 1995; Keshavan et al., 1998; Thompson et al., 2001) though not all studies show this (Jaskiw et al., 1994). Some studies suggest alterations in neurophysiological indices such as amplitudes of evoked response potentials (P300) in schizophrenia (Mathalon, Ford, Rosenbloom, & Pfefferbaum, 2000).

Continuing neurochemical changes may underlie such neuroprogressive events. One model suggests that neurochemical "sensitization" may result from repeated exposure to neurochemical stressors (Lieberman, Sheitman, & Kinon, 1997). While stimulants, such as amphetamine and cocaine rarely produce psychosis in healthy humans during acute administration, their intermittent use appears to cause paranoid forms of psychosis. Stimulants also show cross-sensitization; that is, repeated administration leading to increased sensitivity to other drugs or environmental stressors. Such sensitization may lead to increased stimulant induced dopamine release, perhaps with the involvement of NMDA and non-NMDA glutamate receptors (Kalivas & Duffy, 1995). This model is supported by neuroimaging studies which increased striatal amphetamine induced dopamine release in schizophrenia patients (Laruelle et al., 1996) as well in those at clinical high risk for this illness (Howes et al., 2009). Neurochemical systems are tightly regulated with GABA providing the inhibitory regulation and glutamate the excitatory inputs; dopamine has an important modulatory effect on both of these systems (Krystal et al., 1999). An emerging view is that progressive brain changes in schizophrenia might result from an accumulation of oxidative stress related damage, and the failure of the antioxidant system (Reddy, Keshavan, & Yao, 2003).

Not everyone, however, agrees that progressive neurobiological changes occur in schizophrenia. For example, it has been postulated that the observed neurobiological changes during the course of schizophrenia may simply be plastic adaptations of the nervous system to the experience of being psychotic or cognitively impoverished (Weinberger & McClure, 2002).

The three views of the timing of schizophrenia pathogenesis are by no means mutually exclusive. It is possible that an early brain maturational deviation predisposes the individual to a later developmental derailment, and perhaps to postillness neurotoxic processes. A "three hit" model may accommodate all these processes (Keshavan, 1999). The causal mechanisms that might underlie such a cascade of pathogenetic events will need further elucidation, and will be discussed in the next section.

ETIOLOGY OF DEVELOPMENTAL BRAIN ALTERATIONS: GENES, ENVIRONMENT, AND INTERACTIONS

Schizophrenia is currently viewed as a complex disorder with multiple, interactive etiological factors, similar to other common disorders in medicine such as coronary artery disease and diabetes. Given the highly heterogenous nature of the schizophrenia syndrome, it is likely that several genetic and environmental factors may interact to produce the symptoms and signs of schizophrenia.

Genetic Factors

Schizophrenia Highly Heritable. Risk for schizophrenia increases with the percentage of shared genes (Gottesman, 1991). The risk for schizophrenia is about 2% in third-degree relatives, 2 to 6% in the second-degree relatives, and 6 to 17% in first-degree relatives of an affected individual. Twin studies show high concordance for monozygotic twins who share 100% of the genes; if one twin is affected, the risk of schizophrenia in the unaffected twin is approximately 17% for dizygotic twins and about 50% for monozygotic twins (Cardno & Gottesman, 2000). On the other hand, the absence of 100% concordance suggests that environmental factors must be involved. Interestingly, adoption studies have demonstrated that shared environmental factors do not account for the familial features of schizophrenia (Lewis & Levitt, 2002). Thus, neither genetic nor environmental factors by themselves are sufficient causal explanation for the disorder.

Candidate genes have been proposed that stem from several functional areas of neurodevelopment thought to be impaired in schizophrenia. These functions include transcriptional regulatory proteins and cell adhesion molecules (CAMs), which play an important role in neurogenesis, differentiation, and migration as well as the regulation of axonal growth in the developing brain. Neurotrophins, important molecular regulators of neuronal survival and differentiation (Thoenen, 1995) have also been of great interest. Alterations in brain derived neurotrophic factor (BDNF) have been reported in first episode schizophrenic patients (Jindal et al., 2010); these findings, as well as recent evidence of a relationship between a BDNF polymorphism and episodic memory deficits, support BDNF as a putative schizophrenia susceptibility factor (Egan et al., 2003; Muglia et al., 2003). Candidate genes implicated in schizophrenia may also be involved in one or other aspect of glutamatergic function. These include RGS4, a member of the family of regulators of G-protein signaling proteins (Lewis & Levitt, 2002), the DTNBP1 gene (the dystrobrevin-binding protein1, or dysbindin gene; Straub et al., 2002) which regulates nitric oxide synthase that in turn impacts on NMDA receptor function (Moghaddam, 2002) and neuregulin (Stefansson et al., 2002). Genetically mediated impairments in cortical glutamate neurotransmission can predispose to pathologically enhanced stress-activated monoaminergic neurotransmission leading to psychosis (Billingslea, Mastropaolo, Rosse, Bellack, & Deutsch, 2003; Moghaddam, 2002). Altered patterns of gene expression may also be influenced by environmental events occurring during sensitive periods of neurodevelopment, such as the prenatal, perinatal, and adolescence time frames (Lewis & Levitt, 2002).

Environmental Risk Factors

Prospective studies of general population cohorts have provided important information on environmental risk factors for early brain adversity in schizophrenia. Epidemiological and case-control studies suggest an increased frequency of obstetric and perinatal complications (Cannon et al., 2000; Dalman et al., 1999; Rosso et al., 2000). Other potential etiological variables are also implicated; the North Finland Birth Cohort (Rantakallio, Jones, Moring, & Von Wendt, 1997) and the UK National Child Development Study (Leask, Done, & Crow, 2002) showed that childhood infections may be associated with risk for later schizophrenia. Birth cohort studies suggest increased risk for schizophrenia in relation to urban place of birth (Harrison & Owen, 2003), migration (Cantor-Graae, Pedersen, McNeil, & Mortensen, 2003); paternal age (Brown, Schaefer, et al., 2002); birth order (Kemppainen et al., 2001); exposure to prenatal rubella (Brown, Freeman, et al., 2001); and low maternal and birth weights (Wahlbeck, Forsen, Osmond, Barker, & Eriksson, 2001). Prenatal exposure to herpes simplex virus in schizophrenia is associated with cognitive impairment and brain structural alterations (Prasad , Shirts, Yolken, Keshavan, & Nimgaonkar, 2007). Risk factors occurring during the second or third trimester of pregnancy may in particular be associated with the susceptibility. Environmental factors in later development such as substance abuse (in particular cannabis) also contribute to schizophrenia risk. Psychosocial stress including traumatic experiences in childhood may be important as well.

Though recent linkage and genome-wide association studies have identified a large number of candidate genes and specific risk alleles for schizophrenia, replicated findings explain only a small fraction of the heritability. The view that schizophrenia may be caused by multiple common genes each conferring a small effect has not been supported by genome-wide association studies

(GWAS); this view has been replaced in recent years by observations of rare and unique mutations and copy number variations (CNV) conferring possibly severe risks seen in a significant proportion of patients, though no single locus explains more than approximately 1% of cases. Genes involved in cell signaling, brain development, and glutamate appear to be differentially affected, and seem to cut across diagnostic boundaries, being seen in other developmental disorders such as autism (International Schizophrenia Consortium, 2008; McClellan & King, 2010; Stefansson et al., 2008; Walsh et al., 2008). Finally, the relationships between genes (e.g., DISC1, neuregulin) and their neuropathological consequences (such as dendritic morphology) are not straightforward, and are likely to be influenced by profound gene-gene and gene-protein interactions, leading to incredibly complex "interactomes" (Camargo et al., 2007; Hayashi-Takagi et al., 2010; Jaaro-Peled, Ayhan, Pletnikov, & Sawa, 2010).

Any etiological model of schizophrenia needs to integrate genetic risk with environmental factors associated with the disorder (Tandon et al., 2008; van Winkel et al., 2010). An important limitation to bear in mind, however, is that several well-known environmental factors such as prenatal infection, obstetric trauma, trauma, urbanicity, and cannabis exposure, either individually or collectively, can account for only a small proportion of the etiology of schizophrenia. Gene-environmental models suggest that interactive effects of genes and environment on biological pathways may have larger effects than either genes or environment (Meyer & Feldon, 2010). An integrative approach is the "two-hit hypothesis" (Bayer, Falkai, & Maier, 1999; Huttunen, Machon, & Mednick, 1994; Maynard, Sikich, Lieberman, & LaMantia, 2001) which proposes that genetic risk (first hit) and early developmental alterations may prime the person to react to a second hit in the form of an environmental factor later during development leading to the illness. The use of environmental perturbations to treat genetically altered mice with putative mutations can help model such integrative models for this complex mental illness (Robertson, Hori, & Powell, 2006).

An epigenetic model, which is increasingly gaining recognition, posits that environmental impact on gene expression via changes in DNA methylation and chromatin structure may play a role in the etiology of schizophrenia (Petronis, Paterson, & Kennedy, 1999). This research is in its infancy and few definitive findings have yet emerged to support this model in schizophrenia. However, since it is possible by pharmacological approaches to modify epigenetic processes (Gavin & Sharma, 2010), this model has a prominent potential to pave a path to therapeutic advances.

TOWARD AN INTEGRATIVE GENETIC–DEVELOPMENTAL MODEL

Schizophrenia clearly results from genetically mediated alterations in early and late maturational processes of brain development, interacting with environmental epigenetic effects. Further studies investigating gene-environment and gene-gene interactions should significantly improve our understanding of the complex genetic factors that contribute to schizophrenia development. Unitary models that integrate genetic, environmental, and developmental factors and exploring common themes, such as glutamatergic dysfunction, might prove useful in elucidating the etiopathogenesis of this disorder.

Models are needed to simplify and analyze problems that are otherwise complex. While the pathophysiological models reviewed in this chapter offer considerable heuristic power, the strength of any explanatory model lies in its ability to generate testable hypotheses, which can then be examined using appropriate animal models. Three types of heuristic animal models have been used to examine the neurodevelopmental origins of schizophrenia (Lipska, Lerman, Khaing, & Weinberger, 2003). One such model is the neonatal ventral hippocampal lesion model, derived from the theory of disrupted neurogenesis in early development. The second approach is to use pharmacological models such as NMDA receptor blockade (Moghaddam, 2003). Early lesions in the glutamatergic system may inform investigation of the disordered brain development. Third, conditional transgenic models seek to selectively reduce or increase expression of genes involved in critical periods of development. As an example, the heterozygous reeler mouse, which expresses 50% of the brain reeler content of the wild type mouse, expresses many neurobiological characteristics of the schizophrenia phenotype (Liu et al., 2001). Other molecular targets for manipulation studies in animal models include genes involved in glutamatergic and dopaminergic neurotransmission. The complex multifactorial (multiple genes and environmental factors) etiology of schizophrenia makes such efforts extremely challenging.

Young relatives at risk for schizophrenia (familial high risk strategy) as well as those at clinical high risk (individuals with prodromal symptoms) offer a valuable opportunity to study the etiopathogenesis of the illness. The nature, timing, and causal risk factors underlying altered neurodevelopmental trajectories that predispose to schizophrenia may be investigated in prospective studies of these at-risk populations. Noninvasive in vivo neuroimaging techniques, such as functional MRI, diffusion tensor imaging proton magnetic resonance spectroscopy (MRS; Stanley, Pettegrew, & Keshevan, 2000), may be able to address these questions. Using high field magnets (i.e., 3 Tesla or higher) and advanced spectral editing techniques, one can now reliably delineate the GABA, glutamate, and glutamine signals with proton MRS, thus paving the way to definitively test the neurochemical models reviewed in this chapter. These approaches, in combination with clinical data will also potentially allow multivariate prediction of the emergence of psychopathology during adolescence and early adulthood (Eack et al., 2008), as well as elucidate the neurobiology of the transition from the prepsychotic to the psychotic phases of the schizophrenic illness.

In summary, the pathophysiological models reviewed in this chapter suggest that while psychosis begins in late adolescence or early adulthood, the pathogenesis of this illness really begins much earlier from a long-drawn neurodevelopmental deviation. The goal of any pathophysiological model is really to generate hypotheses about novel preventive and therapeutic interventions. It is evident that multiple and sequential etiological factors, many of which might be amenable to be reversed, may interact and contribute to the causation of the illness. Preventive treatments may be tailored to the causal factors in the disease process in individuals predisposed to the disorder. To effectively move forward, an improved understanding and definition of this target population is critical. Accurate identification of risk factors is important for selecting at-risk subjects who are most likely to benefit; development of safe and effective early intervention in such individuals is an active area of research currently.

ACKNOWLEDGMENTS

This work was supported in part by NIMH Grants MH45156, 45203, and a NARSAD established Investigator Award (MSK) and MH 68680 (VAD).

REFERENCES

Abbott, C., & Bustillo, J., (2006). What have we learned from proton magnetic resonance spectroscopy about schizophrenia? A critical update. *Current Opinion in Psychiatry 19*, 135–139.

Abi-Dargham, A., Mawlawi, O., Lombardo, I., Gil, R., Martinez, D., Huang, Y., et al. (2002). Prefrontal dopamine D1 receptors and working memory in schizophrenia. *Journal of Neuroscience, 22*(9), 3708–3719.

Akbarian, S., Bunney, W. E., Potkin, S. G., Wigal, S. B., Hagman, J. O., & Sandman, C. A. (1993). Altered distribution of nicotamine-adenine dinucleotide phosphate-diaphorase cells in frontal lobe of schizophrenics implies disturbances of cortical development. *Archives of General Psychiatry, 50*, 169–177.

Akbarian, S., Sucher, N. J., Bradley, D., Tafazzoli, A., Trinh, D., Hetrick, W. P., et al. (1996). Selective alterations in gene expression for NMDA receptor subunits in prefrontal cortex of schizophrenics. *Journal of Neuroscience, 16*(1), 19–30.

Akil, M., Pierri, J. N., Whitehead, R. E., Edgar, C. L., Mohila, C., Sampson, A. R., et al. (1999). Lamina-specific alterations in the dopamine innervation of the prefrontal cortex in schizophrenic subjects. *American Journal of Psychiatry, 156*(10), 1580–1589.

Albert, K. A., Hemmings, H. C., Jr., Adamo, A. I., Potkin, S. G., Akbarian, S., Sandman, C. A., et al. (2002). Evidence for decreased DARPP-32 in the prefrontal cortex of patients with schizophrenia. *Archives of General Psychiatry, 59*(8), 705–712.

Andreasen, N. C., Endicott, J., Spitzer, R. L., & Winokur, G. (1977). The family history method using diagnostic criteria. Reliability and validity. *Archives of General Psychiatry, 34*(10), 1229–1235.

Andreasen, N. C., Rezzi, K., Alliger, R., Swayze, I. I., Falum, M., Kirchner, P., et al. (1992). Hypofrontality in neuroleptic-naive patients and in patients with chronic schizophrenia. *Archives of General Psychiatry, 49*, 943–958.

Barbour, T., Murphy, E., Pruitt, P., Eickhoff, S. B., Keshavan, M. S., Rajan, U., et al.

(2010). Reduced intra-amygdala activity to positively valenced faces in adolescent schizophrenia offspring. *Schizophrenia Research, 123*, 126–136.

Barch, D. M., Carter, C. S., Braver, T. S., Sabb, F. W., MacDonald, A., 3rd, Noll, D. C., et al. (2001). Selective deficits in prefrontal cortex function in medication-naive patients with schizophrenia. *Archives of General Psychiatry, 58*(3), 280–288.

Bayer, T. A., Falkai, P., & Maier, W. (1999). Genetic and non-genetic vulnerability factors in schizophrenia: The basis of the "two hit hypothesis." *Journal of Psychiatric Research, 33*(6), 543–548.

Bearden, C. E., Rosso, I. M., Hollister, J. M., Sanchez, L. E., Hadley, T., & Cannon, T. D. (2000). A prospective cohort study of childhood behavioral deviance and language abnormalities as predictors of adult schizophrenia. *Schizophrenia Bulletin, 26*(2), 395–410.

Bender, L. (1953). Childhood schizophrenia. *Psychiatric Quarterly, 27*(4), 663–681.

Benes, F. M., Davidson, J., & Bird, E. D. (1986). Quantitative cytoarchitectural studies of the cerebral cortex of schizophrenics. *Archives of General Psychiatry, 43*(1), 31–35.

Benes, F. M., McSparren, J., Bird, E. D., SanGiovanni, J. P., & Vincent, S. L. (1991). Deficits in small interneurons in prefrontal and cingulate cortices of schizophrenic and schizoaffective patients. *Archives of General Psychiatry, 48*(11), 996–1001.

Bhojraj, T. S., Sweeney, J. A., Prasad, K. M., Eack, S., Rajarethinam, R., Francis, A. N., et al. (2010a). Progressive alterations of the auditory association areas in young non-psychotic offspring of schizophrenia patients. *Journal of Psychiatiric Research, 45*, 205–212.

Bhojraj, T. S., Prasad, K. M., Eack, S. M., Francis, A. N., Miewald, J. M., Montrose, D. M., et al. (2010b). Gray matter loss in young relatives at risk for schizophrenia: Relation with prodromal psychopathology. *Neuroimage, 54*, S272–279.

Billingslea, E. N., Mastropaolo, J., Rosse, R. B., Bellack, A. S., & Deutsch, S. I. (2003). Interaction of stress and strain on glutamatergic neurotransmission: Relevance to schizophrenia. *Pharmacology Biochemistry and Behavior, 74*(2), 351–356.

Brown, A. S., Schaefer, C. A., Wyatt, R. J., Begg, M. D., Goetz, R., Bresnahan, M. A., et al. (2002). Paternal age and risk of schizophrenia in adult offspring. *American Journal of Psychiatry, 159*(9), 1528–1533.

Brown, R. T., Freeman, W. S., Perrin, J. M., Stein, M. T., Amler, R. W., Feldman, H. M., et al. (2001). Prevalence and assessment of attention-deficit/hyperactivity disorder in primary care settings. *Pediatrics, 107*(3), E43.

Cairo, T. A., Woodward, T. S., & Ngan, E. T. (2006). Decreased encoding efficiency in schizophrenia. *Bioogicall Psychiatry, 59*(8), 740–746.

Callicott, J. H., Bertolino, A., Mattay, V. S., Langheim, F. J., Duyn, J., Coppola, R., et al. (2000). Physiological dysfunction of the dorsolateral prefrontal cortex in schizophrenia revisited. *Cerebral Cortex, 10*(11), 1078–1092.

Callicott, J. H., Egan, M. F., Bertolino, A., Mattay, V. S., Langheim, F. J. P., Frank, J. A., et al. (1998). Hippocampal N-acetyl aspartate in unaffected siblings of patients with schizophrenia: A possible intermediate neurobiological phenotype. *Biological Psychiatry, 44*, 941–950.

Callicott, J. H., Egan, M. F., Mattay, V. S., Bertolino, A., Bone, A. D., Verchinksi, B., et al. (2003). Abnormal fMRI response of the dorsolateral prefrontal cortex in cognitively intact siblings of patients with schizophrenia. *American Journal of Psychiatry, 160*(4), 709–719.

Camargo, L. M., Collura, V., Rain, J. C., Mizuguchi, K., Hermjakob, H., Kerrien, S., et al. (2007). Disrupted in Schizophrenia 1 Interactome: Evidence for the close connectivity of risk genes and a potential synaptic basis for schizophrenia. *Molecular Psychiatry, 12*(1), 74–86.

Cannon, M., Caspi, A., Moffitt, T. E., Harrington, H., Taylor, A., Murray, R. M., et al. (2002). Evidence for early-childhood, pan-developmental impairment specific to schizophreniform disorder: Results from a longitudinal birth cohort. *Archives of General Psychiatry, 59*(5), 449–456.

Cannon, T. D., Rosso, I. M., Hollister, J. M., Bearden, C. E., Sanchez, L. E., & Hadley, T. (2000). A prospective cohort study of genetic and perinatal influences in the etiology of schizophrenia. *Schizophrenia Bulletin, 26*(2), 351–366.

Cantor-Graae, E., Pedersen, C. B., McNeil, T. F., & Mortensen, P. B. (2003). Migration as a risk factor for schizophrenia: A Danish population-based cohort study. *British Journal of Psychiatry, 182*, 117–122.

Cardno, A. G., & Gottesman, II. (2000). Twin studies of schizophrenia: From bow-and-arrow concordances to star wars Mx and functional genomics. *American Journal of Medical Genetics, 97*(1), 12–17.

Carter, C. S. (2005). Applying new approaches from cognitive neuroscience to enhance drug development for the treatment of impaired cognition in schizophrenia. *Schizophrenia Bulletin, 31*(4), 810–815.

Casanova, M. F. (1995). Elmer Ernest Southard 1876–1920. *Bioogicall Psychiatry, 38*(2), 71–73.

Cho, R., Gilbert, A., & Lewis, D. A. (2003). The neruobiology of schizophrenia. In D. S. Charney (Ed.), *The neurobiology of mental disorders* (pp. 113–128), New York: Oxford University Press.

Chugani, H. T., Phelps, M. E., & Mazziotta, J. C. (1987). Positron-emission tomography study of human brain functional development. *Annals of Neurology, 22*, 487–497.

Clouston, T. S. (1891). *Neuroses of development: The Morrison lectures for 1890.* Edinburgh: Oliver and Boyd.

Cornblatt, B., Obuchowski, M., Roberts, S., Pollack, S., & Erlenmeyer-Kimling, L. (1999). Cognitive and behavioral precursors of schizophrenia. *Developmental Psychopathology, 11*(3), 487–508.

Costa, E., Davis, J., Grayson, D. R., Guidotti, A., Pappas, G. D., & Pesold, C. (2001). Dendritic spine hypoplasticity and downregulation of reelin and GABAergic tone in schizophrenia vulnerability. *Neurobiology of Disease, 8*(5), 723–742.

Cotter, D. R., Pariante, C. M., & Everall, I. P. (2001). Glial cell abnormalities in major psychiatric disorders: The evidence and implications. *Brain Research Bulletin, 55*(5), 585–595.

Coyle, J. T. (1996). The glutamatergic dysfunction hypothesis for schizophrenia. *Harvard Review of Psychiatry, 3*, 241–253.

Dalman, C., Allebeck, P., Cullberg, J., Grunewald, C., & Koster, M. (1999). Obstetric complications and the risk of schizophrenia: A longitudinal study of a national birth cohort. *Archives of General Psychiatry, 56*(3), 234–240.

DeLisi, L. E. (1995). A prospective follow-up study of brain morphology and cognition in first-episode schizophrenic patients: Preliminary findings. *Biological Psychiatry, 38*, 349–360.

Done, D. J., Crow, T. J., Johnstone, E. C., & Sacker, A. (1994). Childhood antecedents of schizophrenia and affective illness: Social adjustments at ages 7 and 11. *British Medical Journal, 309*, 699–703.

Dworkin, R. H., Cornblatt, B. A., Friedmann, R., Kaplansky, L. M., Lewis, J. A., Rinaldi, A., et al. (1993). Childhood precursors of affective vs. social deficits in adolescents at risk for schizophrenia. *Schizophrenia Bulletin, 19*(3), 563–577.

Eack, S. M., Prasad, K. M. R., Montrose, D. M., Goradia, D. D., Dworakowski, D., Miewald, J., et al. (2008). An integrated psychobiological predictive model of emergent psychopathology among young relatives at risk for schizophrenia. *Progress in Neuropsychopharmacology and Biological Psychiatry, 32*(8), 1873–1878.

Eastwood, S. L., & Harrison, P. J. (1995). Decreased synaptophysin in the medical temporal lobe in schizophrenia demonstrated using immunoautoradiography. *Neuroscience, 69*, 339–343.

Edin, F., Macoveanu, J., Olesen, P., Tegner, J., & Klingberg, T. (2007). Stronger synaptic connectivity as a mechanism behind development of working memory-related brain activity during childhood. *Journal of Cognitive Neuroscience, 19*(5), 750–760.

Egan, M. F., Goldberg, T. E., Gscheidle, T., Weirich, M., Rawlings, R., Hyde, T. M., et al. (2001). Relative risk for cognitive impairments in siblings of patients with schizophrenia. *Biological Psychiatry, 50*(2), 98–107.

Egan, M. F., Kojima, M., Callicott, J. H., Goldberg, T. E., Kolachana, B. S., Bertolino, A., et al. (2003). The BDNF val66met polymorphism affects activity-dependent secretion of BDNF and human memory and hippocampal function. *Cell, 112*(2), 257–269.

Elvevag, B., & Elvevag, T .E. (2000). Cognitive Impairment in schizophrenia is the core of the disorder. *Critical Review In Neurobiology, 14*, 1021.

Erlenmeyer-Kimling, L. (2000). Neurobehavioral deficits in offspring of schizophrenic parents: Liability indicators and predictors of illness. *American Journal of Medical Genetics, 97*(1), 65–71.

Falkai, P., Schneider-Axmann, T., & Honer, W. G. (2000). Entorhinal cortex pre-alpha cell clusters in schizophrenia: Quantitative evidence of a developmental abnormality. *Biological Psychiatry, 47*(11), 937–943.

Feinberg, I. (1982–83). Schizophrenia: Caused by a fault in programmed synaptic elimination during adolescence? *Journal of Psychiatiric Research, 17*, 319–334.

Fish, B. (1984). Characteristics and sequelae of the neurointegrative disorder in infants at risk for schizophrenia: 1952–1982. In N. F. Watt, E. J. Anthony, L. C. Wynne, & J. E. Rolf (Eds.), *Children at risk for schizophrenia: A longitudinal perspective* (pp. 423–439). New York: Cambridge University Press.

Fish, B. (1987). Infant predictors of the longitudinal course of schizophrenic development. *Schizophrenia Bulletin, 13*, 395–409.

Fish, B., & Hagin, R. (1972). Visual-motor disorders in infants at risk for schizophrenia. *Archives of General Psychiatry, 27*(5), 594–598.

Garey, L. J., Patel, T., & Ong, W. Y. (1994). Loss on dendritic spines from cortical pyramidal cells in schizophrenia. *Schizophrenia Research, 11*, 137.

Gavin, D. P., & Sharma, R. P. (2010). Histone modifications, DNA methylation, and schizophrenia. *Neuroscience and Biobehavioral Reviews, 34*(6), 882–888.

Giedd, J. N., Blumenthal, J., Jeffries, N. O., Castellanos, F. X., Liu, H., Zijdenbos, A., et al. (1999). Brain development during childhood and adolescence: A longitudinal MRI study. *Nature Neuroscience, 2*(10), 861–863.

Glantz, L. A., & Lewis, D. A. (1997). Reduction of synaptophysin immunoreactivity in the prefrontal cortex of subjects with schizophrenia: Regional and diagnostic specificity. *Archives of General Psychiatry, 54*, 943–952.

Gogtay, N., Sporn, A., Clasen, L. S., Greenstein, D., Giedd, J. N., Lenane, M., et al.

(2003). Structural brain MRI abnormalities in healthy siblings of patients with childhood-onset schizophrenia. *American Journal of Psychiatry, 160*, 569–571.

Goldman-Rakic, P. S. (1994). Working memory dysfunction in schizophrenia. *Journal of Neuropsychiatry and Clinical Neuroscience, 6*, 348–357.

Gottesman, I. I. (1991). *Schizophrenia genesis: The origins of madness.* New York: W. H. Freeman.

Grace, A. A. (1991). Phasic versus tonic dopamine release and the modulation of dopamine system responsivity: A hypothesis for the etiology of schizophrenia. *Neuroscience, 41*(1), 1–24.

Hafner, H., Maurer, K., Loffler, W., & Reicher-Rossler, A. (1993). The influence of age and sex on the onset and early course of schizophrenia. *British Journal of Psychiatry, 162*, 80–86.

Harrison, P., & Lewis, D. (2001). Neuropathology in schizophrenia. In S. Hirsch & D. R. Weinberger (Eds.), *Schizophrenia.* Oxford, UK: Blackwell.

Harrison, P. J., & Owen, M. J. (2003). Genes for schizophrenia? Recent findings and their pathophysiological implications. *Lancet, 361*(9355), 417–419.

Hayashi-Takagi, A., Takaki, M., Graziane, N., Seshadri, S., Murdoch, H., Dunlop, A. J., et al. (2010). Disrupted-in-Schizophrenia 1 (DISC1) regulates spines of the glutamate synapse via Rac1. *Nature Neuroscience, 13*(3), 327–332.

Heeger, D. J., Huk, A. C., Geisler, W. S., & Albrecht, D. G. (2000). Spikes versus BOLD: What does neuroimaging tell us about neuronal activity? *Nature Neuroscience, 3*(7), 631–633.

Hoffman, R. E., & McGlashan, T. H. (1997). Synaptic elimination, neurodevelopment, and the mechanism of hallucinated "voices" in schizophrenia. *American Journal of Psychiatry, 154*(12), 1683–1689.

Howes, O., Montgomery, A., Asselin, M., Valli, I., Tabraham, P., Johns, L. et al. (2009). Elevated striatal dopamine function linked to prodromal signs of schizophrenia. *Archives of General Psychiatry, 66*(1),13–20.

Hulshoff Pol, H. E., Brans, R. G., van Haren, N. E., Schnack, H. G., Langen, M., Baare, W. F., et al. (2004). Gray and white matter volume abnormalities in monozygotic and same-gender dizygotic twins discordant for schizophrenia. *Biological Psychiatry, 55*(2), 126–130.

Huttenlocher, P. R., & Dabholkar, A. S. (1997). Regional differences in synaptogenesis in human cerebral cortex. *Journal of Comparative Neurology, 387*(2), 167–178.

Huttunen, M. O., Machon, R. A., & Mednick, S. A. (1994). Prenatal factors in the pathogenesis of schizophrenia. *British Journal of Psychiatry, 23*(Suppl.), 15–19.

International Schizophrenia Consortium. (2008). Rare chromosomal deletions and duplications increase risk of schizophrenia. *Nature, 455*(7210), 237–241.

Jaaro-Peled, H., Ayhan, Y., Pletnikov, M. V., & Sawa, A. (2010). Review of pathological hallmarks of schizophrenia: Comparison of genetic models with patients and nongenetic models. *Schizophrania Bulletin, 36*(2), 301–313.

Jansma, J. M., Ramsey, N. F., van der Wee, N. J., & Kahn, R. S. (2004). Working memory capacity in schizophrenia: A parametric fMRI study. *Schizophrenia Research, 68*(2–3), 159–171.

Jaskiw, G. E., Juliano, D. M., Goldberg, T. E., Hertzman, M., Urow-Hamell, E., & Weinberger, D. R. (1994). Cerebral ventricular enlargement in schizophreniform disorder does not progress. A seven year follow-up study. *Schizophrenia Research, 14*(1), 23–28.

Javitt, D. C., & Zukin, S. R. (1991). Recent advances in the phencyclidine model of schizophrenia. *American Journal of Psychiatry, 148*(10), 1301–1308.

Jernigan, T. L., & Tallal, P. (1990). Late childhood changes in brain morphology observable with MRI. *Developmental Medicine Child Neurology, 32*, 379–385.

Jindal, R. D., Pillai, A. K., Mahadik, S. P., Eklund, K., Montrose, D. M., & Keshavan, M. S. (2010). Decreased BDNF in patients with antipsychotic naive first episode schizophrenia. *Schizophrenia Research, 119*(1–3), 47–51.

Jones, P., & Cannon, M. (1998). The new epidemiology of schizophrenia. *The Psychiatric Clinics of North America, 21*(1), 1–25.

Kalivas, P. W., & Duffy, P. (1995). D1 receptors modulate glutamate transmission in the ventral tegmental area. *Journal of Neuroscience, 15*(7 Pt 2), 5379–5388.

Kemppainen, L., Veijola, J., Jokelainen, J., Hartikainen, A. L., Jarvelin, M. R., Jones, P., et al. (2001). Birth order and risk for schizophrenia: A 31-year follow-up of the Northern Finland 1966 Birth Cohort. *Acta Psychiatrica Scandinavia, 104*(2), 148–152.

Keri, S., Kelemen, O., Benedeck, G., & Janka, Z. (2001). Different trait markers for schizophrenia and bipolar disorder:A neurocognitive approach. *Psychological Medicine, 31*(5), 915–922.

Keshavan, M. S. (1999). Development, disease and degeneration in schizophrenia: A unitary pathophysiological model. *Journal of Psychiatric Research, 33*(6), 513–521.

Keshavan, M. S. (2004). High risk studies, brain development and schizophrenia. In M. S. Keshavan, J. L. Kennedy & R. M. Murray (Eds.), *Neurodevelopment and schizophrenia*. London: Cambridge University Press.

Keshavan, M. S., Anderson, S., & Pettegrew, J. W. (1994). Is schizophrenia due to excessive synaptic pruning in the prefrontal cortex? *Journal of Psychiatric Research, 28*, 239–265.

Keshavan, M. S., Dick, R. M., Diwadkar, V. A., Montrose, D. M., Prasad, K. M., & Stanley, J. A. (2009). Striatal metabolic alterations in non-psychotic adolescent offspring at risk for schizophrenia: A (1)H spectroscopy study. *Schizophrenia Research, 115*, 88–93.

Keshavan, M. S., Dick, E., Mankowski, I., Harenski, K., Montrose, D. M., Diwadkar, V., et al. (2002). Decreased left amygdala and hippocampal volumes in young offspring at risk for schizophrenia. *Schizophrenia Research, 58*(2–3), 173–183.

Keshavan, M. S., Diwadkar, V. A., Spencer, S. M., Harenski, K. A., Luna, B., & Sweeney, J. A. (2002). A preliminary functional magnetic resonance imaging study in offspring of schizophrenic parents. *Progress in Neuropsychopharmacology and Biological Psychiatry, 26*(6), 1143–1149.

Keshavan, M. S., Haas, G. L., Kahn, C. E., Aguilar, E., Dick, E. L., Schooler, N. R., et al. (1998). Superior temporal gyrus and the course of early schizophrenia: Progressive, static, or reversible? *Journal of Psychiatric Research, 32*, 161–167.

Keshavan, M. S., Kulkarni, S., Bhojraj ,T., Francis, A., Diwadkar, V., Montrose, D. M., et al. (2010). Premorbid cognitive deficits in young relatives of schizophrenia patients. *Frontiers of Human Neuroscience, 9*(3), 62.

Keshavan, M. S., Montrose, D. M., Pierri, J. N., Dick, E. L., Rosenberg, D., Talagala, L., et al. (1997). Magnetic resonance imaging and spectroscopy in offspring at risk for schizophrenia: Preliminary studies. *Progress in Neuropsychopharmacology and Biological Psychiatry, 21*, 1285–1295.

Keshavan, M. S., Reynolds, C. F., Miewald, J. M., Montrose, D. M., Sweeney, J. A.,

Vasko, R. C., et al. (1998). Delta sleep deficits in schizophrenia: Evidence from automated analyses of sleep data. *Archives of General Psychiatry, 55*, 443–448.

Keshavan, M. S., Stanley, J. A., Montrose, D. M., Minshew, N. J., & Pettegrew, J. W. (2003). Prefrontal membrane phospholipid metabolism of child and adolescent offspring at risk for schizophrenia or schizoaffective disorder: An in vivo (31)P MRS study. *Molecular Psychiatry, 8*(3), 316–323.

Kim, J. S., Kornhuber, H. H., Schmid-Burgk, W., & Holzmuller, B. (1980). Low cerebrospinal fluid glutamate in schizophrenic patients and a new hypothesis on schizophrenia. *Neuroscience Letters, 20*(3), 379–382.

Klemm, S., Rzanny, R., Riehemann, S., Volz, H. P., Schmidt, B., Gerhard, U. J., et al. (2001). Cerebral phosphate metabolism in first-degree relatives of patients with schizophrenia. *American Journal of Psychiatry, 158*(6), 958–960.

Krystal, J. H., D'Souza, D. C., Petrakis, I. L., Belger, A., Berman, R. M., Charney, D. S., et al. (1999). NMDA agonists and antagonists as probes of glutamatergic dysfunction and pharmacotherapies in neuropsychiatric disorders. *Harvard Review of Psychiatry, 7*(3), 125–143.

Laruelle, M. (2000). The role of endogenous sensitization in the pathophysiology of schizophrenia: Implications from recent brain imaging studies. *Brain Research Review, 31*(2–3), 371–384.

Laruelle, M., Abi-Dargham, A., van Dyck, C. H., Gil, R., D'Souza, C. D., Erdos, J., et al. (1996). Single photon emission computerized tomography imaging of amphetamine-induced dopamine release in drug-free schizophrenic subjects. *Proceedings of the National Academy of Sciences USA, 93*(17), 9235–9240.

Lawrie, S. M., Byrne, M., Miller, P., Hodges, A., Clafferty, R. A., Cunningham Owens, D. G., et al. (2001). Neurodevelopmental indices and the development of psychotic symptoms in subjects at high risk of schizophrenia. *British Journal of Psychiatry, 178*, 524–530.

Lawrie, S. M., Whalley, H. C., Abukmeil, S. S., Kestelman, J. N., Donnelly, L., Miller, P., et al. (2001). Brain structure, genetic liability, and psychotic symptoms in subjects at high risk of developing schizophrenia. *Biological Psychiatry, 49*(10), 811–823.

Lawrie, S. M., Whalley, H. C., Abukmeil, S. S., Kestelman, J. N., Miller, P., Best, J. J., et al. (2002). Temporal lobe volume changes in people at high risk of schizophrenia with psychotic symptoms. *British Journal of Psychiatry, 181*, 138–143.

Lawrie, S. M., Whalley, H., Kestelman, J. N., Abukmeil, S. S., Byrne, M., Hodges, A., et al. (1999). Magnetic resonance imaging of brain in people at high risk of developing schizophrenia [see comments]. *Lancet, 353*(9146), 30–33.

Leask, S. J., Done, D. J., & Crow, T. J. (2002). Adult psychosis, common childhood infections and neurological soft signs in a national birth cohort. *British Journal of Psychiatry, 181*, 387–392.

Lewis, D. A. (1997). Development of the prefrontal cortex during adolescence: Insights into vulnerable neural circuits in schizophrenia. *Neuropsychopharmacology, 16*, 385–398.

Lewis, D. A., & Levitt, P. (2002). Schizophrenia as a disorder of neurodevelopment. *Annual Review of Neuroscience, 25*, 409–432.

Lieberman, J., Koreen, A., Chakos, M., Sheitman, B., Woerner, M., Alvir, J., et al. (1996). Factors influencing treatment response and outcome of first-episode schizophrenia: Implications for understanding the pathophysiology of schizophrenia. *Journal of Clinical Psychiatry, 9*, 5–9.

Lieberman, J. A. (1993). Prediction of outcome in first-episode schizophrenia. *Journal of Clinical Psychiatry, 54 Suppl*, 13–17.
Lieberman, J. A., Sheitman, B. B., & Kinon, B. J. (1997). Neurochemical sensitization in the pathophysiology of schizophrenia: Deficits and dysfunction in neuronal regulation and plasticity. *Neuropsychopharmacology, 17*, 205–229.
Lipska, B. K., Lerman, D. N., Khaing, Z. Z., & Weinberger, D. R. (2003). The neonatal ventral hippocampal lesion model of schizophrenia: Effects on dopamine and GABA mRNA markers in the rat midbrain. *European Journal of Neuroscience, 18*(11), 3097–3104.
Liu, W. S., Pesold, C., Rodriguez, M. A., Carboni, G., Auta, J., Lacor, P., et al. (2001). Down-regulation of dendritic spine and glutamic acid decarboxylase 67 expressions in the reelin haploinsufficient heterozygous reeler mouse. *Proceedings of the Nationall Acadamy of Sciences U S A, 98*(6), 3477–3482.
Loebel, A. D., Lieberman, J. A., Alvir, J. M., Mayerhoff, D. I., Geisler, S. H., & Szymanski, S. R. (1992). Duration of psychosis and outcome in first-episode schizophrenia. *American Journal of Psychiatry, 149*(9), 1183–1188.
Logothetis, N. K. (2002). The neural basis of the blood-oxygen-level-dependent functional magnetic resonance imaging signal. *Philosophical Transactions of the Royal Society of London B Biological Science, 357*(1424), 1003–1037.
MacDonald, A. W., Pogue-Geile, M. F., Johnson, M. K., & Carter, C. S. (2003). A specific deficit in context processing in the unaffected siblings of patients with schizophrenia. *Archives of General Psychiatry, 60*, 57–65.
Malmberg, A., Lewis, G., David, A., & Allebeck, P. (1998). Premorbid adjustment and personality in people with schizophrenia. *British Journal of Psychiatry, 172*, 308–313.
Manoach, D. S. (2003). Prefrontal cortex dysfunction during working memory performance in schizophrenia:Reconciling discrepant findings. *Schizophrenia Research, 60*(2-3), 285–298.
Marenco, S., & Weinberger, D. R. (2001). The neurodevelopmental hypothesis of schizophrenia: Following a trail of evidence from cradle to grave. *Developmental Psychopathology, 12*, 501–527.
Mathalon, D. H., Ford, J. M., Rosenbloom, M., & Pfefferbaum, A. (2000). P300 reduction and prolongation with illness duration in schizophrenia. *Biological Psychiatry, 47*(5), 413–427.
Maynard, T. M., Sikich, L., Lieberman, J. A., & LaMantia, A. S. (2001). Neural development, cell-cell signaling, and the "two-hit" hypothesis of schizophrenia. *Schizophrenia Bulletin, 27*(3), 457–476.
McCarley, R. W., Wible, C. G., Frumin, M., Hirayasu, Y., Levitt, J. J., Fischer, I. A., et al. (1999). MRI anatomy of schizophrenia. *Biological Psychiatry, 45*(9), 1099–1119.
McClellan, J., & King, M. C. (2010). Genetic heterogeneity in human disease. *Cell, 141*(2), 210–217.
McGlashan, T. H., & Fenton, W. S. (1993). Subtype progression and pathophysiologic deterioration in early schizophrenia. *Schizophrenia Bulletin, 19*, 71–84.
McGlashan, T. H., & Hoffman, R. E. (2000). Schizophrenia as a disorder of developmentally reduced synaptic connectivity. *Archives of General Psychiatry, 57*(7), 637–648.
Mesulam, M. M. (1998). From sensation to cognition. *Brain, 121*, 1013–1052.
Meyer, U., & Feldon, J. (2010). Epidemiology-driven neurodevelopmental animal models of schizophrenia. *Progress in Neurobiology, 90*(3), 285–326.

Michie, P. T., Kent, A., Stienstra, R., Castine, R., Johnston, J., Dedman, K., et al. (2000). Phenotypic markers as risk factors in schizophrenia: Neurocognitive functions. *Australia New Zealnd Journal of Psychiatry, 34*(Suppl. 2), S74–85.

Moghaddam, B. (2002). Stress activation of glutamate neurotransmission in the prefrontal cortex: Implications for dopamine-associated psychiatric disorders. *Biological Psychiatry, 51*(10), 775–787.

Moghaddam, B. (2003). Bringing order to the glutamate chaos in schizophrenia. *Neuron, 40*(5), 881–884.

Muglia, P., Vicente, A. M., Verga, M., King, N., Macciardi, F., & Kennedy, J. L. (2003). Association between the BDNF gene and schizophrenia. *Molecular Psychiatry, 8*(2), 146–147.

Murray, R. M., & Lewis, S. W. (1987). Is schizophrenia a neurodevelopmental disorder? [editorial]. *British Medical Journal (Clinical Research Edition), 295*(6600), 681–682.

Petronis, A., Patterson, A. D., & Kennedy, J. L. (1999). Schizophrenia: An epigenetic puzzle? *Schizophrenia Bulletin, 25*(4), 639–655.

Pettegrew, J. W., Keshavan, M. S., & Minshew, N. J. (1993). 31P nuclear magnetic resonance spectroscopy: Neurodevelopment and schizophrenia. *Schizophrenia Bulletin, 19*(1), 35–53.

Pettegrew, J. W., Keshavan, M. S., Panchalingam, K., Strychor, S., Kaplan, D. B., Tretta, M. G., et al. (1991). Alterations in brain high-energy phosphate and membrane phospholipid metabolism in first-episode, drug-naive schizophrenics. A pilot study of the dorsal prefrontal cortex by in vivo phosphorus 31 nuclear magnetic resonance spectroscopy. *Archives of General Psychiatry, 48*(6), 563–568.

Pettegrew, J. W., McClure, R. J., Keshavan, M. S., Minshew, N. J., Panchalingam, K., & Klunk, W. E. (1997). 31P magnetic resonance spectroscopy studies of developing brain. In M. S. Keshavan & R. M. Murray (Eds.), *Neurodevelopement & Adult Psychopathology* (pp. 71–92). Cambridge, UK: Cambridge University Press.

Pierri, J. N., Volk, C. L., Auh, S., Sampson, A., & Lewis, D. A. (2001). Decreased somal size of deep layer 3 pyramidal neurons in the prefrontal cortex of subjects with schizophrenia. *Archives of General Psychiatry, 58*(5), 466–473.

Potkin, S. G., Turner, J. A., Brown, G. G., McCarthy, G., Greve, D. N., Glover, G. H., et al. (2009). Working memory and DLPFC inefficiency in schizophrenia: The FBIRN study. *Schizophrenia Bulletin, 35*(1), 19–31.

Prasad, K. M., Sanders, R., Sweeney, J., Montrose, D., Diwadkar, V., Dworakowski, D., et al. (2009). Neurological abnormalities among offspring of persons with schizophrenia: Relation to premorbid psychopathology. *Schizophrenia Research, 108*(1–3), 163–169.

Prasad, K. M., Shirts, B. H., Yolken, R. H., Keshavan, M. S., & Nimgaonkar, V. L. (2007). Brain morphological changes associated with exposure to HSV1 in first-episode schizophrenia. *Molecular Psychiatry, 12*(1), 101, 105–113.

Rajkowska, G., Miguel-Hidalgo, J. J., Wei, J., Dilley, G., Pittman, S. D., Meltzer, H. Y., et al. (1999). Morphometric evidence for neuronal and glial prefrontal cell pathology in major depression. *Biological Psychiatry, 45*, 1085–1098.

Rajkowska, G., Selemon, L. D., & Goldman-Rakic, P. S. (1998). Neuronal and glial somal size in the prefrontal cortex: A postmortem morphometric study of schizophrenia and Huntington disease. *Archives of General Psychiatry, 55*(3), 215–224.

Rantakallio, P., Jones, P. B., Moring, J., & Von Wendt, L. (1997). Association between central nervous system infections during childhood and adult onset schizophrenia and other psychoses: A 28-year follow-up. *Inernational Journal of Epidemiology, 26*, 837–843.

Reddy, R., Keshavan, M., & Yao, J. K. (2003). Reduced plasma antioxidants in first-episode patients with schizophrenia. *Schizophrenia Research, 62*(3), 205–212.

Robertson, G. S., Hori, S. E., & Powell, K. J. (2006). Schizophrenia: An integrative approach to modelling a complex disorder. *Journal of Psychiatry and Neuroscience, 31*(3), 157–167.

Rosso, I. M., Bearden, C. E., Hollister, J. M., Gasperoni, T. L., Sanchez, L. E., Hadley, T., et al. (2000). Childhood neuromotor dysfunction in schizophrenia patients and their unaffected siblings: A prospective cohort study. *Schizophrenia Bulletin, 26*(2), 367–378.

Rosso, I. M., Cannon, T. D., Huttunen, T., Huttunen, M. O., Lonnqvist, J., & Gasperoni, T. L. (2000). Obstetric risk factors for early-onset schizophrenia in a Finnish birth cohort. *American Journal of Psychiatry, 157*(5), 801–807.

Rzanny, R., Klemm, S., Reichenbach, J. R., Pfleiderer, S. O., Schmidt, B., Volz, H. P., et al. (2003). 31P-MR spectroscopy in children and adolescents with a familial risk of schizophrenia. *European Radiologyu, 13*(4), 763–770. .

Schulze, K., McDonald, C., Frangou, S., Sham, P., Grech, A., Toulopoulou, T., et al. (2003). Hippocampal volume in familial and nonfamilial schizophrenic probands and their unaffected relatives. *Biological Psychiatry, 53*(7), 562–570.

Seidman, L. J., Faraone, S. V., Goldstein, J. M., Goodman, J. M., Kremen, W. S., Toomey, R., et al. (1999). Thalamic and amygdala-hippocampal volume reductions in first-degree relatives of patients with schizophrenia: An MRI-based morphometric analysis. *Biological Psychiatry, 46*(7), 941–954.

Seidman, L. J., Faraone, S. V., Goldstein, J. M., Kremen, W. S., Horton, N. J., Makris, N., et al. (2002). Left hippocampal volume as a vulnerability indicator for schizophrenia: A magnetic resonance imaging morphometric study of nonpsychotic first-degree relatives. *Archives of General Psychiatry, 59*(9), 839–849.

Selemon, L. D., Rajkowska, G., & Goldman-Rakic, P. S. (1995). Abnormally high neuronal density in the schizophrenic cortex. A morphometric analysis of prefrontal area 9 and occipital area 17. *Archives of General Psychiatry, 52*, 805–818.

Sharma, T., Lancaster, E., Sigmundsson, T., Lewis, S., Takei, N., Gurling, H., et al. (1999). Lack of normal pattern of cerebral asymmetry in familial schizophrenic patients and their relatives—The Maudsley Family Study. *Schizophrenia Research*, 111–120.

Shenton, M. E., Dickey, C. C., Frumin, M., & McCarley, R. W. (2001). A review of MRI findings in schizophrenia. *Schizophrenia Research, 49*(1–2), 1–52.

Staal, W. G., Hulshoff Pol, H. E., Schnack, H. G., Hoogendoorn, M. L., Jellema, K., & Kahn, R. S. (2000). Structural brain abnormalities in patients with schizophrenia and their healthy siblings. *American Journal of Psychiatry, 157*, 416–421.

Stanley, J. A. (2002). In vivo magnetic resonance spectroscopy and its application to neuropsychiatric disorders. *Canadian Journal of Psychiatry, 47*(4), 315–326.

Stanley, J. A., Pettegrew, J. W., & Keshavan, M. S. (2000). Magnetic resonance spectroscopy in schizophrenia: Methodological issues and findings-part I. *Biological Psychiatry, 48*(5), 357–368.

Stefansson, H., Rujescu, D., Cichon, S., Pietilainen, O. P., Ingason, A., Steinberg, S., et al. (2008). Large recurrent microdeletions associated with schizophrenia. *Nature, 455*(7210), 232–236.

Stefansson, H., Sigurdsson, E., Steinthorsdottir, V., Bjornsdottir, S., Sigmundsson, T.,

Ghosh, S., et al. (2002). Neuregulin 1 and susceptibility to schizophrenia. *American Journal of Human Genetics, 71*(4), 877–892.

Straub, R. E., Jiang, Y., MacLean, C. J., Ma, Y., Webb, B. T., Myakishev, M. V., et al. (2002). Genetic variation in the 6p22.3 gene DTNBP1, the human ortholog of the mouse dysbindin gene, is associated with schizophrenia. *American Journal of Human Genetics, 71*(2), 337–348.

Tamminga, C. A. (1998). Schizophrenia and glutamatergic transmission. *Critical Review of Neurobiology, 12*(1–2), 21–36.

Tan, H. Y., Callicott, J. H., & Weinberger, D. R. (2007). Dysfunctional and compensatory prefrontal cortical systems, genes and the pathogenesis of schizophrenia. *Cerebral Cortex, 17*(Suppl. 1), 171–181.

Tandon, R., Keshavan, M. S., & Nasrallah, H. A. (2008). Schizophrenia, "just the facts" what we know in 2008. 2. Epidemiology and etiology. *Schizophrenia Research, 102*(1–3), 1–18.

Tepest, R., Wang, L., Miller, M. I., Falkai, P., & Csernansky, J. G. (2003). Hippocampal deformities in the unaffected siblings of schizophrenia subjects. *Biological Psychiatry, 54*(11), 1234–1240.

Thoenen, H. (1995). Neurotrophins and neuronal plasticity. *Science, 270*(5236), 593–598.

Thompson, P. M., Vidal, C., Giedd, J. N., Gochman, P., Blumenthal, J., Nicolson, R., et al. (2001). Mapping adolescent brain change reveals dynamic wave of accelerated gray matter loss in very early-onset schizophrenia. *Proceedings of the Nationall Academy of Sciences U SA, 98*(20), 11650–11655.

Tsai, G., & Coyle, J. T. (1995). N-acetylaspartate in neuropsychiatric disorders. *Progress in Neurobiology, 46*, 531–540.

van Winkel, R., Esquivel, G., Kenis, G., Wichers, M., Collip, D., Peerbooms, O., et al. (2010). Genome-Wide Findings in Schizophrenia and the Role of Gene-Environment Interplay. *CNS Neuroscience and Therapeutics, 16*, e185–192.

Volk, D. W., Austin, M. C., Pierri, J. N., Sampson, A. R., & Lewis, D. A. (2000). Decreased glutamic acid decarboxylase67 messenger RNA expression in a subset of prefrontal cortical gamma-aminobutyric acid neurons in subjects with schizophrenia. *Archives of General Psychiatry, 57*(3), 237–245.

Wahlbeck, K., Forsen, T., Osmond, C., Barker, D. J., & Eriksson, J. G. (2001). Association of schizophrenia with low maternal body mass index, small size at birth, and thinness during childhood. *Archives of General Psychiatry, 58*(1), 48–52.

Walker, E. F., Savoie, T., & Davis, D. (1994). Neuromotor precursors of schizophrenia. *Schizophrenia Bulletin, 20*(3), 441–451.

Walsh, T., McClellan, J. M., McCarthy, S. E., Addington, A. M., Pierce, S. B., Cooper, G. M., et al. (2008). Rare structural variants disrupt multiple genes in neurodevelopmental pathways in schizophrenia. *Science, 320*(5875), 539–543.

Watt, N. F. (1978). Patterns of childhood social development in adult schizophrenics. *Archives of General Psychiatry, 35*(2), 160–165.

Weinberger, D. R. (1987). Implications of normal brain development for the pathogenesis of schizophrenia. *Archives of General Psychiatry, 44*, 660–669.

Weinberger, D. R., Egan, M. F., Bertolino, A., Callicott, J. H., Mattay, V. S., Lipska, B. K., et al. (2001). Prefrontal neurons and the genetics of schizophrenia. *Biological Psychiatry, 50*, 825–844.

Weinberger, D. R., & McClure, R. K. (2002). Neurotoxicity, neuroplasticity, and magnetic resonance imaging morphometry: What is happening in the schizophrenic brain? *Archives of General Psychiatry, 59*(6), 553–558.

Whitfield-Gabrieli, S., Thermenos, H. W., Milanovic, S., Tsuang, M. T., Faraone, S. V., McCarley, R. W., et al. (2009). Hyperactivity and hyperconnectivity of the default network in schizophrenia and in first-degree relatives of persons with schizophrenia. *Proceedings of the National Acadamy of Sciences U SA, 106*(4), 1279–1284.

Wolf, L. E., Cornblatt, B. A., Roberts, S. A., Shapiro, B. M., & Erlenmeyer-Kimling, L. (2002). Wisconsin Card Sorting deficits in the offspring of schizophrenics in the New York High-Risk Project. *Schizophrenia Research, 57*(2–3), 173.

Wyatt, R. J., Alexander, R. C., Egan, M. F., & Kirch, D. G. (1988). Schizophrenia, just the facts. What do we know, how well do we know it? *Schizophrenia Research, 1*(1), 3–18.

Zalla, T., Joyce, C., Szoke, A., Schurhoff, F., Pillon, B., Komano, O., et al. (2004). Executive dysfunctions as potential markers of familial vulnerability to bipolar disorder and schizophrenia. *Psychiatry Research, 121*, 207–217.

Zipursky, R. O. (1992). Widespread cerebral gray matter volume deficits in schizophrenia. *Archives of General Psychiatry, 49*, 195–205.

BOX 1

1. Schizophrenia is marked by subtle to profound impairments across a wide range of sensorimotor domains, including attention, memory, executive function and language. These impairments are suggestive of deficits in brain function in a wide range of heteromodal cortical regions.
2. In vivo functional imaging studies suggest a pervasive pattern of heteromodal deficits, particular in prefrontal cortical function. These deficits are observed during early stages of the illness and point to the developmental origins of schizophrenia.

BOX, 2

1. Imaging and post-mortem studies suggest stuctural and neurochemical alterations that may predate schizophrenia onset and may reflect aberrant brain maturational processes.
2. Alterations in glutamate, gamma-aminobutyric acid (GABA) and dopaminergic systems may be developmentally mediated and precede illness onset.

BOX 3

3. Schizophrenia begins in late adolescence or early adulthood, but premorbid and prodromal alterations predate clinical onset of psychosis by many years.

4. Genetic factors are among the best established etiological factors. Multiple and sequential environmental factors may interact with genetic liability and additively contribute to the emergence of the illness.

CONTINUING EDUCATION QUESTIONS

1. Disruptions in neurogenesis and neural migration are consistent with:
   a. Disruption of neural maturation during pre-natal stages
   b. Disruption of neural maturation during peri-adolescent stages
   c. Neural degeneration after disease onset
   d. None of the above
2. ______ is a neurotransmitter thought to be in neurogenesis and neural migration.
   a. **Glutamate**
   b. Dopamine
   c. GABA
   d. Serotonin
3. Structural brain imaging findings have most commonly implicated ______ in schizophrenia.
   a. Heteromodal cortical association areas
   b. Primary cortical sensory areas
   c. Primary cortical motor areas
   d. All of the above
4. Which of the following is NOT true regarding the etiology of schizophrenia:
   a. Genes and environment interact to produce the syndrome of schizophrenia
   b. Susceptibility genes for schizophrenia have not yet been identified.
   c. Obstetric complications frequently produce schizophrenia
   d. Paternal age is a risk factor for schizophrenia

3

Neuropsychological Assessment of Persons with Schizophrenia

BERNICE A. MARCOPULOS, Ph.D.

Department of Graduate Psychology, James Madison University, Harrisonburg, VA

DARYL FUJII, Ph.D.

Veterans Affairs Pacific Island Health Care System

INTRODUCTION

The value of neurocognitive assessment in the clinical management and scientific study of schizophrenia has increased considerably over the past 20 years, as evidenced by the dramatic increase in journal articles and conference presentations on this topic. However, cognitive testing in schizophrenia has a much earlier history. Kraeplin (1920) was the first to observe that patients with "dementia praecox" (i.e., schizophrenia) had cognitive impairments that appeared to progress over time. In 1919, a student of Cattell's named Shepard Ivory Franz administered the first neuropsychological test battery in a psychiatric hospital (Barr, 2008) By the 1950s, psychologists were regularly using cognitive tests with psychiatric patients to differentiate "functional" from "organic" conditions and to detect brain damage. In fact, Brackbill opined that

> … psychologists could make a worth-while contribution to the studies of possible central nervous system pathology among schizophrenics. (1956, p. 210)

Clinicians working in psychiatric hospitals in the middle of the 20th century primarily used the WAIS, a Bender Gestalt and the Rorschach to detect brain damage in psychiatric patients. Brackbill and Fine (1956) recognized how difficult this could be:

> One of the problems that the psychologist is frequently called upon to help solve is the differentiation between a schizophrenic reaction and the presence of central nervous system pathology. In many cases this is very difficult to do on the basis of test performance. The difficulty appears to stem from two sources. Many schizophrenics have the disconcerting tendency to respond to tests in the same way organics do. It is also apparent that quite a heterogeneous group of patients are called schizophrenic. (p. 310)

At this point in time, psychologists working in psychiatric settings already recognized that patients were heterogeneous in presentation, course, and cognitive abilities. For example, process schizophrenia, defined as early onset psychosis with social withdrawal and prominent negative symptoms were more similar to brain damaged patients, versus reactive schizophrenic patients who did not have an obvious prodromal period or long period of subnormal functions. Evidence for similarity with brain damaged individuals came from studies indicating persons with process schizophrenia demonstrating organic signs on the Rorschach which suggested central nervous system pathology (Brackbill & Fine, 1956).

> the difficulty in differential diagnosis of some kinds of schizophrenics and organics results from the involvement of central nervous system pathology in process schizophrenia. (p. 312)

These early observations are consistent with recent research suggesting that negative symptoms of schizophrenia are associated with greater cognitive deficits.

In the 1960s, psychologists continued to explore the cognitive profiles in schizophrenia using precursors of modern intelligence and neuropsychological tests. Lubin, Gieseking, and Williams (1962) compared patients with schizophrenia, brain damage, and controls on the Army Classification Battery which consisted of verbal and visuospatial subtests. They found that patients diagnosed with schizophrenia were less impaired than those with documented brain damage, but that the pattern of deficits was similar.

Neuropsychology began to grow into a well-defined discipline in the 1970s. Standardized neuropsychological test batteries such as the Halstead-Reitan, the Wechsler Adult Intelligence Scale, and the Bender Gestalt were the most commonly used neuropsychological tests as the use of a single test to identifying brain damage became obsolete (Craig, 1979). Several papers were published examining the clinical utility of common neuropsychological batteries such as the Halstead-Reitan and the Luria Nebraska with patients with schizophrenia. Despite the use of more sophisticated tests, findings were astoundingly similar to earlier studies with individuals with schizophrenia generally performing better than brain damaged groups, however, without a distinction in pattern of test results (Chelune, Heaton, Lehman, & Robinson, 1979; Purisch, Golden, & Hammeke, 1978).

Current neuropsychological practice does not consider brain damage to be a unitary concept, nor do we conceive of major mental illnesses such as schizophrenia as being functional or organic. Schizophrenia is conceptualized as a neurodevelopmental brain disease with a strong genetic component. Cognitive dysfunction is one of its core features and a powerful predictor of clinical outcome. Thus, neuropsychological assessment provides key information for the clinical management of schizophrenia (Marcopulos, O'Grady, Shaver, Manley, & Aucone, 2008).

Despite the important function neuropsychological data plays in treatment for persons with schizophrenia, there are relatively few psychiatric hospitals or community mental health centers that staff a full time neuropsychologist (Rabin, Barr, & Burton, 2005). While earlier surveys suggested a growing need for neuropsychologists in psychiatric hospitals (Slick & Craig, 1991), a recent survey still shows very small numbers (less than 3%) of neuropsychologists working in these institutions (Sweet, Meyer, Nelson, & Moberg, 2011). These numbers are surprising given recent findings that that approximately 20% of neuropsychology referrals come from psychiatric services (Sweet et al., 2011).

The goal of this chapter is to address the fundamental elements for conducting a comprehensive, valid, and clinically useful assessment of a person with schizophrenia-spectrum illness, considering the current scientific evidence. The chapter will be organized based on the sections of a typical neuropsychological report: (a) the referral question—what are some common indications for testing? (b) background information—what demographic, developmental, psychosocial and neuro-medical factors are important to consider in interpreting test data? (c) behavioral observations—what was the patient's clinical status at the time of testing? How well was he/she engaged in testing? (d) assessment instruments used—what are some useful measures for assessing cognition in this population? (e) test results/interpretation—how to attribute cognitive impairment to schizophrenia versus other neurocognitive risk factors (i.e., differential diagnoses, signal detection problems); (f) summary of cognitive strengths and weaknesses and how strengths and weaknesses relate to the referral questions—how are impairments likely to impact treatment and outcome? and (g) recommendations—what helpful suggestions can be made for the patient, their family and treatment providers? We provide a conceptual framework, using a developmental life span approach for considering the multiple factors affecting neurocognition in a person with schizophrenia. An illustrative case for how neuropsychological assessment may inform treatment planning in schizophrenia is presented at the end of the chapter.

REFERRAL SOURCES AND QUESTIONS

Persons with schizophrenia very rarely initiate the referral themselves. Instead, family members, primary care physicians, or psychiatrists may request a neuropsychological evaluation, especially at the first episode, to clarify the clinical picture. Patients who are hospitalized are more likely to be referred for testing as they tend to have more severe cognitive impairment compared to patients referred from the community by a primary care physician, or community mental health clinic (Loughland, Lewin, Vaughan, Sheedy, & Harris, 2007). There are numerous reasons why a neuropsychological assessment is indicated for a person diagnosed with schizophrenia. Neuropsychological testing can contribute valuable information to a variety of issues in differential diagnosis, treatment, and prognosis or outcome including: (a) characterizing the nature and extent of cognitive impairment, often as related to the individual's course of illness (e.g., cognitive decline over illness phases or the lifespan); (b) capacity for learning and skill development, particularly as related to rehabilitation and recovery interventions; (c) daily functioning, including educational, community, and vocational skill assessment; (d) cognitive factors in social problem solving; (e) insight into psychotic illness and cognitive problems; and (f) legal issues (e.g., guardianship, competence, sanity).

Referral questions vary depending upon the individual's phase of illness or stage of recovery. For patients who have been hospitalized for an extended period, a common referral question entails assessing cognitive strengths and weaknesses in anticipation of discharge. What kind of supports will they need in the community? For patients acutely admitted, a common referral question involves clarifying diagnosis and symptoms and evaluating how a recent or interval neuro-medical event or process (e.g., brain injury, disease progression) is impacting the current clinical presentation and, in turn, functional outcome. Older patients with a long history of schizophrenia may be referred as part of a work-up for dementia if they are being hospitalized more frequently and present with confusion that does not easily clear after treatment with antipsychotic medication (see Depp, Loughran, & Palmer, this volume). Other common referral questions include determining criteria for intellectual disability for eligibility for specialized community services, providing information as part of a work skills evaluation, deciding whether a person with schizophrenia may require a guardian, or as part of an evaluation to determine competency to stand trial or mental status at time of offense (see Tussey & Marcopulos, this volume). Sometimes referral questions are not clearly formulated, especially in an outpatient psychiatry setting where neuropsychological assessment is not as frequently utilized. These referral sources may need to be educated on how an evaluation can help in the clinical management of their patients and what information can and cannot be provided.

BACKGROUND INFORMATION

Since schizophrenia is a developmental brain disorder, the clinician should consider background history within a developmental life-span perspective, as well as the developmental trajectory of the illness itself (premorbid period, prodromal, first episode, exposure to treatment, and course of the illness). Important factors include early developmental delays in motor or language (Walker, 1994), learning disabilities (LD), educational achievement, behavioral disorders, social functioning, head injury, and Attention Deficit Hyperactivity Disorder (ADHD).

All of these are common in the histories of person with schizophrenia and are associated with certain patterns of cognitive deficits that can have additive or exponential effects on cognition and complicate interpretation of test data. It is often critical to have a collateral informant or other source of information as well as past medical records to clarify this history.

A patient whose psychotic symptoms commenced at an early age is more likely to demonstrate a severe and persistent course, greater cognitive deficits, and a history of developmental delays (Häfner & an der Heiden, 2008). Doody, Johnstone, Sanderson, Owens, and Muir (1998) found that individuals with schizophrenia and learning disability were more likely to have epilepsy, soft neurological signs, and episodic memory deficits. There was a higher genetic risk for illness in their pedigree. Premorbid attention problems in childhood are also common in the histories of individuals diagnosed with schizophrenia and many receive a diagnosis of ADHD prior to their diagnosis of schizophrenia (Cornblatt & Keilp, 1994; Walker, Lewine, & Neumann, 1996). This raises the question of whether this is a comorbidity or more accurately part of the developmental trajectory and prodrome for schizophrenia (see De Marco & Marcopulos, this volume).

As the individual enters early teens, a history of comorbid substance abuse must be taken into consideration when interpreting test results. Over half of adult patients with schizophrenia have comorbid substance abuse (Swartz et al., 2006). Research indicates that their test results do not differ significantly from those patients without substance abuse (Jacobs, Fujii, Schiffman, & Bello, 2008), and counter-intuitively, they may even perform better on testing (see Mueser & McGurk, this volume).

As the individual enters early adulthood, one should consider whether they have had any experience with independent living and competitive employment. Presence of social support and long-term relationships may also reflect the role of cognition in everyday life. This suggests a later onset and milder cognitive deficits which may have some prognostic significance.

History of adherence to treatment is related to insight as well as cognitive impairment. Interestingly, cognitive and clinical insight are dissociable (Aleman, Agrawal, Morgan, & David, 2006; Bayard, Capdevielle, Boulenger, & Raffard, 2009). It is very common for persons with schizophrenia to express very limited or even a total lack of awareness of their clinical symptoms of schizophrenia and disagree with their diagnosis. Consequently, they may refuse treatment. This anosognosia can persist even after many years of significant psychiatric disability and multiple hospitalizations. On the other hand, this same individual may be acutely aware of their difficulties with attention and memory and may accept suggestions for remediation with computer programs or compensation using a day planner.

Psychological and neuropsychological testing may have been performed in the past and must be reviewed and summarized and added to the background section. Practice effects should be considered when planning the assessment (Goldberg et al., 2007; Keefe et al., 2008) with the understanding that practice effects are typically smaller in middle-age schizophrenia samples relative to controls (see Granholm, Link, Fish, Kraemer, & Jeste, 2010).

A common practice for neuropsychological assessment is to estimate premorbid IQ to determine level of cognitive decline in acquired brain dysfunction. However, since schizophrenia is considered a neurodevelopmental disorder, one may argue that "premorbid" IQ may not be a useful construct. Dennis et al. (2009) argue that "any IQ score in a developmental disorder postdates (not predates) the condition, charts the history of the condition, is always confounded with and/or by the condition, and can never be separated from the effects of the condition" (p. 331). In schizophrenia, the premorbid period may not really reflect "normal" functioning per se, but rather less severe deficits in IQ (see Woodberry, Giuliano, & Seidman, 2008). Furthermore, it has been presumed that reading is intact in schizophrenia and, thus, reading tasks are good estimators of premorbid IQ. However, dyslexia and other reading LD may be prevalent in schizophrenia (Revheim et al., 2006). The LD history may be a manifestation of cognitive deficits common in schizophrenia, such as poor verbal working memory, processing speed, and attention.

If there is not a history of dyslexia, word reading has been suggested as a good method as it may be preserved (Kremen et al., 1996). Kremen et al. (1996) and Harvey et al. (2000) recommend estimating IQ with single-word reading tests, such as the WRAT based on the premise that schizophrenia typically starts after reading skills have been established and that the illness does not impact reading. However, more complex reading (such as reading comprehension) often is impaired, and that may be hard to disentangle, particularly in the context of poor verbal working memory, processing speed, and/or verbal memory. One might consider using the parents' IQ or education and occupation as an estimate of what the individual's intellectual level might have been had they not developed schizophrenia.

In addition to historical factors, it is also important to include information regarding current functioning either in the hospital or in the community, as well as a list of current medications which might enhance or reduce cognitive functions (see Sestito & Goldberg, this volume).

Culture and ethnicity are important for appropriate test selection and for conceptualization and interpretation of test data. Some immigrants and ethnic minorities demonstrate a greater risk of developing schizophrenia (Cantor-Graae & Selten, 2005), thus, the neuropsychologist may be more likely to deal with cultural and language issues in assessment with this clinical population (see Fujii, this volume).

BEHAVIORAL OBSERVATIONS AND CLINICAL INTERVIEW

As with all evaluations, the individual being evaluated must provide informed consent to ensure that he/she understands the nature and purpose of evaluation, how the information will be used and who will have access to the report

(APA, 2002; AACN Practice Guidelines, 2007). A statement to this effect can be included in the report for an outpatient or in the patient's medical chart for an inpatient, documenting when testing occurred. If the assessment is being conducted within the hospital setting rather than as an outpatient, the patient may be concerned that their treatment team will use the neuropsychological test results "against them" to postpone or block their discharge from the hospital. The neuropsychologist assessing a hospitalized patient needs to be sensitive to context—these individuals are often civilly committed, thus many of their civil liberties and freedoms have been forfeited (Gardner et al., 1999; Monahan et al., 1996). They may feel coerced to accept treatment and may feel as though the testing is coerced as well. It is important to inform them that participation in neuropsychological assessment is voluntary and they have the right to decline participation. Even very suspicious and paranoid consumers may be more likely to agree if it is clear that their participation is voluntary. Ideally, assessments should be a collaborative effort between the patient/client and the neuropsychologist which support engagement in their recovery. Extra care needs to be taken to put psychiatrically hospitalized persons at ease: answering all their questions, addressing their valid concerns, and explaining how the test results will be used to ensure optimal participation in the assessment process.

Neuropsychological testing, and any psychological testing for that matter, involves developing a working relationship with the individual being tested (rapport) and eliciting his/her best effort. Rapport development can be very challenging with an individual who has prominent negative symptoms such as asociality, disorganization and avolition dominating the clinical picture. Acute paranoia also disrupts rapport building. The neuropsychologist should collaborate with the patient's treatment providers and family to support the patient's participation and to establish a set of reinforcers or incentives to enhance engagement and motivation for the assessment, if necessary. Use of incentives/reinforcers and positive verbal feedback may be employed as a strategy to enhance engagement in testing to facilitate cognitive performance in schizophrenia (Schmand et al., 1994). Shortening the test sessions may also be helpful, and completing testing over multiple short sessions may be necessary to complete the assessment, especially when working with hospitalized patients.

Tests of effort and other indices of engagement are recommended to ascertain whether the assessment data is valid (Heilbronner et al., 2009). Marcopulos et al. (2008) recommend administration of formal, standardized symptom validity tests as a routine part of the assessment battery to index motivational variables explicitly. There are many hypotheses to explain low effort test scores, such as problems with sustained attention, active psychosis, significant paranoia, increased disorganization and other positive symptoms in response to stressful social situations and, if external incentives (secondary gain) are present, deliberate feigning of cognitive deficits or malingering. Many patients in a psychiatric hospital may have incurred legal charges and may have reason to exaggerate or malinger in order to delay or defer their trial (see Tussey & Marcopulos, this volume).

Persons with schizophrenia tend to perform more poorly on tests of effort relative to both neurologically intact and neurologically disordered individuals (Gorissen, de la Torre, & Schmand, 2005; Weinborn, Orr, Woods, Conover, & Feix, 2003). However, there are very limited or non-existent norms for SVTs for schizophrenia so performance must be interpreted with extreme caution. Recently, Schroeder and Marshall (2011) examined performance on imbedded indices of effort in a mixed psychiatric sample with no evidence for secondary gain or lack of cooperation. They found that the majority of psychiatric patients failed fewer than two symptom validity tests. A higher percentage of SVT failures was associated with lower IQs. The researchers recommended adjusting the cut-off score for several measures (Reliable Digit Span and Dot Counting). Clearly, more normative studies are warranted.

There are circumstances in which the clinician might consider further testing even if a patient performs below cutoff on an effort test. For example, an individual with persistent hallucinations, thought disorder, severely impaired attention and no apparent secondary gain for scoring poorly, might still perform below established cut-offs on SVTs. Indeed, our experience suggests that false positives on tests such as the Test of Memory Malingering (TOMM) are not uncommon in an inpatient setting, especially in older chronic patients with negative symptoms and low education (Marcopulos, Bailey, Tussey, Kent, & Grove, 2011). One might consider scores on other neuropsychological measures as an estimate of the individual's current neurocognitive functioning. Ideally, testing may be postponed until psychiatric symptoms can be stabilized. If it may be surmised that the patient is not likely to improve substantially in the foreseeable future, an evaluation of baseline functioning may proceed.

The presentation of schizophrenia is often more variable than other neurological disorders due to active positive symptoms, alertness, mood, medication side effects such as sedation, and motivation. The clinician should describe whether any of these factors appeared to be present and estimate the extent that they may have affected rapport and engagement. Perhaps surprisingly, studies have not shown that active positive symptom significantly affect cognitive test performance. While "state" effects can occur, the core cognitive deficits of schizophrenia are quite robust and relatively impervious to positive symptoms such as hallucinations and delusions and depression (Gladsjo et al., 2004). However, "trait" effects such as negative symptoms and disorganization have been found to correlate with reasoning and problem solving, attention and vigilance (Dominguez, Viechtbauer, Simons, van Os, & Krabbenbaum, 2009). Dominguez et al. (2009) found that only speed of processing correlated with positive symptoms.

Side effects of medications such as sedation can affect testing. It is best to wait for stable medication dosing if possible. Time of day can make a difference in terms of minimizing sedating side effects. Some patients report being more alert in the afternoon, or morning, and these preferences should be honored whenever possible. Other behaviors that can affect the validity of tests and should be noted include presence or extent of disorganized speech, frustration tolerance, non-standardized administration techniques, such as the need to repeat instructions or provide more than ample encouragement or the use of reinforcers such as soda or snacks.

TEST SELECTION

When evaluating a person with schizophrenia, the neuropsychologist should include tests that assess a broad range of cognitive domains, address the referral question, and are appropriate to the functional level of the client, as well as possessing adequate reliability, validity and have norms matching the demographics of the patient. As with all neuropsychological assessments we recommend using tests with demonstrated predictive validity in pertinent functional areas such as work performance or independent living (Bowie, Reichenberg, Patterson, Heaton, & Harvey, 2006; Bryson & Bell, 2003; Evans et al., 2003). Memory, processing speed, attention, and executive functioning, as well as social cognition, have predictive validity for functional status. Processing speed, in particular, has been shown to be most effective in predicting overall cognitive and functional disability and should be included in any test battery (Harvey, Keefe, Patterson, Heaton, & Bowie, 2009). These cognitive functions cans be assessed using individual neuropsychological tests or batteries that were developed specifically for persons with schizophrenia (e.g., MATRICS, BACS).

A longer, comprehensive neuropsychological battery might be appropriate for higher functioning individuals, particularly if there is a legal question to be addressed such as Competency to Stand Trial (CST) or Not Guilty by Reason of Insanity (NGRI) pleas, or for eligibility determinations such as with developmental disability, social security disability, or special services for learning disabilities. In most cases, however, a shorter test battery may be preferred. Abbreviated test batteries have been found to have adequate predictive validity, are better tolerated by patients, and are thus more likely to be completed (Harvey et al., 2009). Harvey et al. (2009) sought the best subset of neuropsychological measures to predict functional capacity, defined as both scores on a performance based skills assessment as well as "real world" outcomes (rating by case managers). Using a sample of older (mean age 57) persons with schizophrenia, they found that the test variable accounting for the most variance in overall cognitive functioning as well as everyday living skills was processing speed (Digit Symbol and Trail Making Test). They concluded that a shorter battery can be just as effective in describing the level of cognitive impairment in persons with schizophrenia.

The MATRICS Consensus Cognitive Battery (MCCB) was developed by a panel of experts to provide a valid, reliable cognitive assessment method for evaluating cognitive enhancing agents in schizophrenia (Kern, Green, Nuechterlein, & Deng, 2004). Criteria for test selection included good test-retest reliability, repeatability, relationship to functional outcome, response to pharmacological agents, practicality, and tolerability. The battery was validated across 5 sites in the Northeast, East, South, Midwest, and West and co-normed on a non-mentally ill community sample with demographic characteristics similar to the 2000 census (Kern et al., 2008). The MCCB takes a little over 60 minutes to administer and includes 10 tests which measure speed of processing, attention and vigilance, working memory, visual and verbal learning, reasoning and problem solving and social cognition (Nuechterlein et al., 2008). Social cognition is important for managing social interactions and predicts success in the community (Couture, Penn, & Roberts, 2006). While the MCCB's advantage is that it covers a broad base of cognitive functions important in schizophrenia, abbreviated forms of validated measures are utilized, so it may not provide a sufficiently comprehensive assessment to answer some legal eligibility determination questions.

The Brief Assessment of Cognition in Schizophrenia (BACS) was developed to assess domains that are most impaired in schizophrenia and associated with functional outcome. The BACS takes only 35 minutes to administer and assesses verbal memory, working memory, motor speed, verbal fluency, reasoning, and problem solving (Keefe et al., 2004, Keefe, Poe, Walker, & Harvey, 2006). In addition to brevity of test administration, an advantage of the BACS is an alternate form which is useful for retesting (Keefe et al., 2008).

Unlike the MATRICS and BACS, the Repeatable Battery for the Assessment of Neuropsychological Status (RBANS; Randolph, 1998) was developed for commercial use and then validated and normed on a sample of patients diagnosed with schizophrenia (Wilk et al., 2004). The test typically takes less than 30 minutes to administer and evaluates for the following cognitive domains: immediate and delayed memory, visuospatial/construction, language, and attention. Individual subtests include measures of verbal learning, verbal working memory, coding, and verbal fluency, which have strong predictive validity of functional outcome in persons with schizophrenia. The RBANS also has an alternate form for repeat testing. Loughland, Lewin, Vaughan, Sheedy, and Harris (2007) found that the RBANS was sensitive to level of severity of cognitive impairment and correlated with Global Assessment of Functioning (GAF) in two samples of out-patients with schizophrenia. The RBANS profile scores identified the core cognitive symptoms of attention and memory.

RESULTS, INTERPRETATION, AND SUMMARY

Cognitive impairment in schizophrenia is usually complex, long-standing, heterogeneous, multi-functional, and characterized by generalized impairment 1 to 2 standard deviations below normal expectations in addition to moderate to severe impairment in several specific cognitive functions (Heinrichs & Zakzanis, 1998). It is difficult to come to any precise conclusions regarding specific etiology or course and for neuropsychological tests to detect the putative additional burden of co-existing neuromedical risk factors (see Stone & Keshavan, this volume). Patients often present with other risk factors for cognitive impairment in addition to schizophrenia, and it may be that our tests do not have sufficient sensitivity to detect the putative additional burden of comorbidity.

Interpretation of test results is complicated by the "signal to noise ratio" issue in these often complex referrals. Frequently, there are so many premorbid risk factors that create noise in the test data which may obscure findings of neuropathological significance. However, referral sources often request information on how the various neurocognitive risk factors are affecting the clinical presentation and outcome. The neuropsychologist should thoughtfully consider multiple diagnoses and myriad plausible risk factors ("embrace the complexity") when describing the relative contribution of these factors in test scores and patterns. For instance Stone and Keshavan (this volume) describe common comorbid medical conditions, such as metabolic syndrome, which impacts test performance and interpretation. Flashman and McAllister (this volume) present the "chicken vs., egg" issue in ascribing deficits as due to mild brain injury and/or schizophrenia. See these chapters for more detail on how to consider these factors in report writing.

Practical implications may be easier to address, such as whether the patient's cognitive strengths and weaknesses suggest that he/she can work effectively and independently towards recovery. It is important to consider where the individual will be living after discharge from the hospital and what cognitive tasks will be required in his/her environment. What kind of supports may be needed to help the client? How can clients be supported to adhere to the recommended treatment and participate in their treatment plan from a cognitive perspective? What can the person's family and treatment providers do to help them remember the details of their treatment plan and carry out tasks related to treatment? It is important to discern whether the client has forgotten to take his/her medications or come to appointments on time or rather assume it is a problem with adherence.

Inaccurate perceptions by treatment providers and/or family of the cognition of an individual with schizophrenia can hinder optimal functioning through placement in inappropriate treatment situations. Without objective neurocognitive data, it is not uncommon for treating staff to under- or overestimate a patient's cognitive ability based on verbal functions. Overestimation may result in placing the client in a situation where social environment demands exceed capacity. For example, a person diagnosed with schizophrenia who is verbally facile may be assumed to be of "average" functioning despite possessing significant memory and executive functioning deficits. This person may be overwhelmed if placed in an independent living situation in which he/she has to monitor his/her own medications and work in a job that requires considerable decision-making. On the other hand, underestimation may preclude optimal/maximal participation in a variety of treatment options. For instance, patients who demonstrate alogia or disorganized speech may erroneously be perceived as cognitively impaired or developmentally disabled when they may possess pockets of average level strengths. These individuals may be placed in living and vocational situations that are overly restrictive and reduce the optimal potential of the individual. Neuropsychological testing can help treatment providers discern when a client "can't" perform a task versus when they "won't" perform a task. This information is critical when considering whether to implement a behavioral strategy.

An important aspect of the neuropsychological report for an individual with schizophrenia is the functional implications of test results. Providing functional implications can assist clinicians in conceptualizing reasons or causes for behavioral deficits associated with difficulties in community functioning, learning in psychosocial rehabilitation, or social cognition (Fujii, 2002). This information can also provide target areas for cognitive remediation.

Attention

Attention is a multifaceted skill that encompasses working memory, vigilance or sustained attention, and processing speed that many argue represents the most salient cognitive deficit in schizophrenia. Performance on attentional tasks has consistently demonstrated predictive validity with functional outcome in meta-analytic studies. Vigilance and working memory have been found to predict moderate social problem solving or social competence (Fett et al., 2010; Green, Kern, Braff, & Mintz, 2000), and response to social skills training cognitive remediation interventions (Kurtz, Seltzer, Fujimoto, Shagan, & Wexler, 2009) while working memory has been associated with psychosocial skill acquisition (Green et al., 2000) and quality of life (Tolman & Kurtz, 2010). Processing speed has been found to predict social competence (Bowie et al., 2008), community functioning (Fett et al., 2010), and quality of life (Tolman & Kurtz, 2010). Tests of processing speed tend to have the highest effect sizes and contribute the most variance to comprehensive batteries. In their meta-analysis on cognitive testing in schizophrenia, Dickinson, Ramsey, and Gold (2007) found that Digit Symbol from the WAIS produced the largest effects size and taps a core cognitive deficit. In terms of psychotic symptomatology, measures of attention and vigilance have been correlated modestly to disorganization (Dominguez et al., 2009). Processing speed has a high effect size and contributes the most variance in batteries such as the BACS and MATRICS (see Harvey et al., 2009).

Intellectual Functioning

Assessment of intelligence is important to rule out co-existing intellectual disability and gauge learning potential. The literature on intelligence in schizophrenia has suggested three trajectories: widespread deficits noted before the onset of symptoms, deficits noted shortly after the onset, and persons without any decrement in intellectual functions (Weickert & Goldberg, 2000). Intelligence has some predictive power as individuals whose IQ was lower prior to the onset of psychosis had more difficulty generalizing their gains made in cognitive remediation (Fiszdon, Choi, Bryson, & Bell, 2006). Intellectual subgroups can be determined by comparing current IQ estimates to estimates of premorbid abilities based upon word reading tests (Kremen et al., 2001).

Academic Skills

Persons with schizophrenia can present with academic skills deficits, as cognitive deficits are often observed in childhood or adolescence (Allen, Franton, Strauss, & van Kammen, 2005) and the onset of symptoms may have caused an interruption or premature end to their education. Assessment of academic skills can be useful to determine reading level for taking self-report personality tests and gauging practical reading for independent living. The Kaufman Functional Academic Skills Test assesses basic real-world skills in arithmetic and reading that are often needed to function independently in the community (Kaufman & Kaufman, 1994). For higher functioning individuals, academic assessment can provide useful information for those who aspire to return to school and finish their degrees that were interrupted at the onset of their illness, as well as persons who would like to pursue job training.

Language

Another important issue for persons with schizophrenia, particularly for those presenting with disorganized speech, is the evaluation of language abilities, including comprehension and abstract reasoning. Vocabulary and Information subtests have been associated with quality of life and social skills in meta-analytic studies (Tolman & Kurtz, 2010; Fett et al., 2010). Performance on these tests can also provide an estimate of premorbid cognitive functioning. Assessing for abstract reasoning is useful for determining simplicity of instructions or explanations when providing directions for everyday functioning such as instrumental activities of daily living (Fujii, 2002). "Schizophasia," which reflects thought disorder rather than a pure language disorder, can be differentiated from true aphasia, but there was a time when some patients with Wernicke's aphasia were mistaken for schizophrenics and hospitalized.

Thought disorder with loose associations, clang associations, neologisms, and word salad can affect verbal tests on the WAIS IV. Loose associations can cause spoiled responses on the Vocabulary, Comprehension, or Similarities subtests. These types of responses should be noted in the behavioral observations section to provide a context to explain the low score. Alogia, long response latencies, and thought blocking can also depress verbal test scores. Prosody, rate, and volume may also be altered and should be differentiated from true speech articulation disorders. Medication side effects causing either dry mouth or excess salivation can affect articulation. Persons with schizophrenia tend to score at least one standard deviation below normative expectations on action, animal or letter based fluency tasks (Woods, Weinborn, Posada, & O'Grady, 2007). On verbal fluency tests, the typical pattern is poorer performance on semantic versus phonological (letter) fluency (Bukat & Goldberg, 2003; Gourovitch, Goldberg, & Weinberger, 1996) and seem to be related to the semantic memory deficits. However, this finding was not replicated in a recent meta-analysis (Doughty & Done, 2009).

Memory

Memory is critical to assess as this is often the most impaired cognitive function in schizophrenia as it affects a person's ability to live independently, manage their recovery, and benefit from psychoeducation and psychosocial rehab efforts. Numerous studies and meta-analyses have found that memory is commonly affected in schizophrenia and more impaired than other cognitive functions (Aleman, Hijman, de Haan, & Kahn, 1999). Meta-analytic studies report verbal memory is associated with almost all functional outcome measures including functional competence (Bowie et al., 2008), community functioning, psychosocial skill acquisition, social problem solving (Fett et al., 2010; Green et al., 2000), and quality of life (Tolman & Kurtz, 2010). Memory has found to be predictive of independent functioning and quality of life 15+ years post testing (Fujii & Wylie, 2003;Fujii, Wylie, & Nathan, 2004).

Memory impairment seems to be worse in those patients with prominent negative symptoms, while medications, age, severity of symptoms, illness duration, and positive symptoms were not correlated with memory impairment. However, memory can be impaired in other psychiatric disorders as well (Egeland et al., 2003). For instance, patients diagnosed with schizophrenia and those diagnosed with unipolar depression have memory impairment, especially in working memory. However, individuals with schizophrenia have been found to have acquisition failures while depressed individuals have retrieval difficulties, using the California Verbal Learning Test (CVLT). Paulsen et al. (1995) found that persons with schizophrenia had moderate to severe impairments in free recall, mild to moderate impairments in recognition, and inconsistent recall across trials. They were less likely to utilize semantic information to chunk information to be remembered. The fact that they were more likely to make phonemically related errors on forced choice recall rather than semantic ones again indicated that they fail to encode information on a semantic level. They also make more intrusion errors. This is consistent with the literature showing that persons with schizophrenia do not distinguish words based on their semantic features (Condray, 2005; Minzenberg, Ober, & Vinogradov, 2002).

Visuospatial Abilities

The literature on the functional implications of visuospatial skills in schizophrenia is emerging. One meta-analysis reported performance on visuospatial measures is predictive of social skills (Fett et al., 2010). Other studies have found relationships between visuospatial functioning and aspects of social functioning including facial emotion recognition (Chan, Wong, Wang, & Lee, 2008), and role playing of social situations (Sitzer, Twamley, Patterson, & Jeste, 2008). Assessing visuospatial skills is particularly important for persons with disorganized schizophrenia as their performances on verbal tests are significantly affected by their speech. Thus, verbal tests may not accurate evaluate reasoning and problem solving potential (Fujii, 2002).

Executive Functions

Deficits in executive functioning are among the most commonly reported findings in schizophrenia (Dickinson et al., 2007). Meta-analytic studies report executive functioning, particularly performance on the Wisconsin Card Sort, is predictive of community functioning (Green et al., 2000), quality of life (Tolman & Kurtz, 2010), and social problem solving (Fett et al., 2010). Wisconsin Card Sorting Test scores have also been associated with work skill acquisition (Sergi, Kern, Mintz, & Green, 2005). Reasoning and problem solving have been associated with disorganization in schizophrenia (Dominguez et al., 2009). Verbal fluency has been associated with community functioning (Green et al., 2000; Fett et al., 2010) and negative symptoms (Dominguez et al., 2009).

Psychomotor Skills

Psychomotor skills, which include motor speed and dexterity, as well as reaction time, have been associated with community/daily activities, social problem solving/instrumental skills, and psychosocial skill acquisition (Green et al., 2000).

Social Cognition and Adaptive Functioning

Social cognition is a broad array of skills that includes social perception, emotional perception and processing, as well as theory of mind (Fett et al., 2010). Social cognition skills have been predictive of community functioning, social behavior in an inpatient milieu, and general social skills (Couture et al., 2006; Fett et al., 2010). The Mayer-Salovey-Caruso Emotional Intelligence Test, which is included in the MATRICS Battery, is one of the few commercially available measures of social cognition that is normed on persons with schizophrenia (Nuechterlein et al., 2008; see Kurtz, this volume).

Cognitive deficits on neuropsychological testing are associated with deficits in adaptive behavior. A formal assessment of adaptive behavior is very helpful in deciding what community supports might be needed. Occupational Therapists conduct living skills assessments which include demonstration of the skills necessary for cooking, shopping, managing finances, planning recreational activities, etc. There are also several standardized measures, either performance based or clinician rated, that have been validated with persons with schizophrenia (see Kurtz, this volume).

Recommendations

The most useful aspects of a neuropsychological report are the recommendations to engage cognitive strengths and support or compensate for cognitive weaknesses. Recommendations addressing neurocognitive deficits can generally be classified as medical or psychosocial interventions. Medical recommendations can be diagnostic, such as referring for neuroimaging studies or a neurological examination, various laboratory studies to diagnose a medical condition, or a dementia work-up. These studies would be recommended if there has been an unexpected decline in cognition and/or lateralizing or localizing signs of brain dysfunction. Other recommendations may entail medication suggestions, for example, avoiding medications with strong anticholinergics effects which may further impair memory or managing medical conditions that are risk factors for cognitive impairment.

Individual and group cognitive remediation has been developed for both inpatient and community settings. Principles and methods have been adapted from traditional cognitive rehabilitation from brain injury literature and further modified for a persistently mentally ill population. As in the brain injury literature, a skill-based, compensatory approach to rehab works best and dovetails nicely with other psychosocial rehabilitation program that emphasize skill building techniques. Meta-cognition interventions are also useful as the cognitive symptoms of schizophrenia and other major mental illnesses are emphasized in symptom education groups (see Medalia & Belluci, this volume). Finally, family and caregiver psychoeducation, social and role functioning implications, and supports and cognitive adaptations, such as routine, structure, are important non-pharmacological interventions.

CASE EXAMPLE

Brian is a 34-year-old, Caucasian male who was admitted to a psychiatric hospital after police found him in his car along the side of the road. He refused to speak to police, thus they took him to the community hospital Emergency Department where he was admitted to the Psychiatric Service. Brian was diagnosed with Schizophrenia, Undifferentiated, with Catatonic Features and prescribed Risperidone and p.r.n. Lorazepam. He presented with persistent negative symptoms and was unable to discuss future goals or address discharge planning. His family was contacted to provide additional background information. Brian experienced his initial break approximately 5 years ago and was hospitalized several times, however, was noncompliant with his aftercare in the community. Thus his symptoms progressively worsened and he became more isolative and uncommunicative.

Brian later revealed that he had previously worked with computers and computer customer service and was hoping to return to that work. Thus a vocational evaluation was conducted. Observations indicated that Brain frequently acknowledged he understood a task, but failed to follow through with the instructions and made multiple mistakes. He performed well on clerical numerical tasks and color discrimination, but his performance was below average on tasks involving manual dexterity and he was slower than average. The vocational evaluation suggested that Brian may be able to return to work provided that he is closely supervised and the job did not demand a quick pace. His treatment team decided to refer for a neuropsychological evaluation to help with

TABLE 3.1 Neuropsychological Test Data for Case "Brian"

Test Name	
Wechsler Abbreviated Scale of Intelligence (T score/Standard Score)	
Vocabulary	30/4
Similarities	37/6
Block Design	38/6
Matrix Reasoning	56/12
Verbal IQ	76
Performance IQ	95
Full Scale IQ	84
Wisconsin Card Sorting Test	
# of categories = 4 (percentiles)	6–10%
Perseverative Errors (T Score	35
Tower of London (Standard Scores)	
Total Move Score	74
Total Correct Score	96
Total Problem Solving Time	62
California Verbal Learning Test 2 (T Score/Z Score)	
Learning Trials	35
Distraction List	–1
Recall After Distraction	–.5
Recall After Delay	–1
Recognition	–1.5
Rey Complex Figure Test (percentile)	
Copy	>16
Immediate Recall	16
30 min. Delayed Recall	21
Recognition	4
Controlled Oral Word Association (T Score)	
Total Letter Words	23
Total Semantic Words	20
Trail Making Test (T Scores)	
Trails A	34
Trails B	27
D 2 Test of Attention (Standard Score)	
TN	86
TN-E	86

treatment planning. The team was particularly interested in executive problem-solving deficits and wanted a profile of his strengths and weaknesses.

Brian arrived early for his appointment and waited patiently until his scheduled appointment time. He was polite and cooperative with the interview and testing. He was casually dressed with adequate hygiene, although he had a very long unkempt beard. His eye contact was intense at times. His affect remained flat, and he did not offer any spontaneous conversation. However, he answered all questions that were posed to him. He did not understand why he was referred for testing and gave a very vague explanation on how he came to be hospitalized. He said he was pulled over by the police, but he did not know why he was sitting in his car. He said he has had a diagnosis of schizophrenia for about a year. He denied any hallucinations or delusions. He stated that his current medications are working well. He denied mood, sleep, appetite, or energy problems. He denied suicidal or homicidal ideation. He said he was hospitalized three times in the past for "bipolar illness." He denied alcohol use but admitted to a period of heavy marijuana use during college. Prior to this hospitalization, he was living alone in his apartment for a year. He claimed he saw his family and friends on a daily basis, although this is not what his family reports. He said prior to his illness, he had been working full time in software support at a computer helpdesk for 8 years. In his free time, he likes to watch sports and spend time with his family. Brian's academic history includes a BA in Business Administration. He said he had a GPA of 3.34. He said his plan was to go back working full time and living in his own apartment.

During testing, Brian said he understood the nature and purpose of testing and agreed to complete it. He understood test instructions easily and demonstrated good attention and concentration. He put forth his best effort, which was confirmed with a formal test of effort using the TOMM. He displayed good frustration tolerance, working on items until the test technician stopped him. Testing is believed to be a valid reflection of Brian's current neurocognitive strengths and weaknesses.

Brian received the following tests: California Verbal Learning Test – Second Edition (CVLT-II), Controlled Oral Word Association (COWA), d2 Test of Attention, Rey Complex Figure Test (RCFT), Test of Memory Malingering (TOMM), Tower of London (TOL), Trail Making Test, Wechsler Abbreviated Scale of Intelligence (WASI), and Wisconsin Card Sorting Test (WCST)

Brian's estimated Full Scale IQ is in the low average range (84), with an estimated Verbal IQ of 76 and an estimated Performance IQ of 95. His estimated premorbid IQ was in the average to high average range.

Verbal fluency was moderate to severely impaired. Verbal subtests on the WASI as well as verbal fluency suffered due to his inability to elaborate his answers and some looseness of association.

His performance on the WCST was mildly impaired. He achieved 4 out of 6 categories. On the TOL, total correct was in the average range, but he had difficulty solving the problems according to the rule constraints. His time to complete the problem solving task was well below average, consistent with his prevocational evaluation.

Brian's performance on the CVLT-II was mildly impaired, with mildly impaired delayed recall. His copy of a complex geometric figure was within normal limits, but his recall was below average. Visual attention was low average to mildly impaired.

Executive functions were moderately to severely impaired, using age- and education-corrected norms.

Thus, Brian's intellectual functioning appeared to be a decline based on premorbid estimates. He demonstrated difficulties with attention, memory, executive problem solving, and processing speed, most likely related to schizophrenia-spectrum disorder.

Brian was enrolled in psychosocial rehabilitation groups, including an executive functioning group called "Let's Get Organized" (Revheim & Marcopulos, 2006). He was tasked with creating lists to track the goals he needed to accomplish to return to his apartment and previous job. His clinical status improved. He shaved his beard, cut his hair, and became more focused on specific plans for discharge. By the time he was ready for discharge, he set up his apartment with the help of his family and had specific plans on returning to his job as computer support. He also had specific plans for maintaining his treatment in the community.

REFERENCES

Aleman, A., Hijman, R., de Haan, E., & Kahn, R. (1999). Memory impairment in schizophrenia: A meta-analysis. *American Journal of Psychiatry, 156*, 1358–1366.

Aleman, A., Agrawal, N., Morgan, K. D., & David, A. S. (2006). Insight in psychosis and neuropsychological function: Meta analysis. *British Journal of Psychiatry, 189*, 204–212.

Allen, D., Franton, L., Strauss, G., & van Kammen, D. (2005). Differential patterns of premorbid academic and social deterioration in patients with schizophrenia. *Schizophrenia Research, 75*, 389–397.

American Academy of Clinical Neuropsychology (AACN). (2007). Practice guidelines for neuropsychological assessment and consultation. *The Clinical Neuropsychologist, 21*, 209–231.

American Psychological Association. (2002). Ethical principles of psychologists and code of conduct. *American Psychologist, 57*, 1060–1073.

Barr, W. B. (2008). Historical development of the neuropsychological test battery. In J. E. Morgan & J. H. Ricker (Eds.), *Textbook of clinical neuropsychology* (pp. 3–17). New York: Taylor & Francis.

Bayard, S., Capdevielle, D., Boulenger, J.-P., & Raffard, S. (2009). Dissociating self-reported cognitive complaint from clinical insight in schizophrenia. *European Psychiatry, 24*, 251–258.

Bowie, C., Leung, W., Reichenberg, A., McClure, M., Patterson, T., Heaton, R., et al. (2008). Predicting schizophrenia patients' real-world behavior with specific neuropsychological and functional capacity measures. *Biological Psychiatry, 63*, 505–511.

Bowie, C., Reichenberg, A., Patterson, T., Heaton, R., & Harvey, P. (2006). Determinants of real-world functional performance in schizophrenia subjects: Correlations with cognition, functional capacity, and symptoms. *American Journal of Psychiatry, 163*(3), 418–425.

Brackbill, G. A. (1956). Studies of brain dysfunction in schizophrenia. *Psychological Bulletin, 53*, 210–226.

Brackbill, G. A., & Fine, H. J. (1956). Schizophrenia and central nervous system pathology. *Journal of Abnormal and Social Psychology, 52*, 310–313.

Bryson, G., & Bell, M. D. (2003). Initial and final work performance in schizophrenia: Cognitive and symptom predictors. *Journal of Nervous and Mental Disease, 191*, 87–92.

Bukat, C. E., Goldberg, T. E. (2003). Letter and category fluency in schizophrenic patients: a meta-analysis. *Schizophrenia Research, 64*, 73–78.

Cantor-Graae, E., & Selten, J.-P. (2005). Schizophrenia and migration: A meta-analysis and review. *American Journal of Psychiatry, 162*, 12–24.

Chan, C., Wong, R., Wang, K., & Lee, T. (2008). Emotion recognition in Chinese people with schizophrenia. *Psychiatry Research, 157*, 67–76.

Chelune, G., Heaton, R., Lehman, R., & Robinson. A. (1979). Levels versus pattern of neuropsychological performance among schizophrenic and diffusely brain-damaged patients. *Journal of Consulting and Clinical Psychology, 47*, 155–163.

Condray, R. (2005). Language disorder in schizophrenia as a developmental learning disorder. *Schizoprenia Research, 73*, 5–20.

Cornblatt, B. A., & Keilp, J. G. (1994). Impaired attention, genetics, and the pathophysiology of schizophrenia. *Schizophrenia Bulletin, 20*, 31–46.

Couture, S. M., Penn, D. L., & Roberts, D. L. (2006). The functional significance of social cognition in schizophrenia: A review. *Schizophrenia Bulletin, 32*, S44–S63.

Craig, P. L. (1979). Neuropsychological assessment in public psychiatric hospitals: The current state of the practice. *Clinical Neuropsychology, 1*, 1–7.

Dennis, M., Francis, D. J., Cirino, P. T., Schachar, R., Barnes, M. A., & Fletcher, J. M. (2009). Why IQ is not a covariate in cognitive studies of neurodevelopmental disorders. *Journal of the International Neuropsychological Society, 15*, 331–343.

Dickinson, D., Ramsey, M., & Gold, J. (2007). Overlooking the obvious: A meta-analytic comparison of digit symbol doing tasks and other cognitive measures in schizophrenia. *Archives of General Psychiatry, 64*, 532–542.

Domiguez, M., Viechtbauer, W., Simons, C., van Os, J., & Krabbendaum, L. (2009). Are psychotic psychopathology and neurocognition orthogonal? A systematic review of their associations. *Psychological Bulletin, 135*, 157–171.

Doody, G. A., Johnstone, E. C., Sanderson, T. L., Owens, D. G., & Muir, W. J. (1998). 'Pfropfschizophrenie' revisited. Schizophrenia in people with mild learning disability. *The British Journal of Psychiatry, 173*, 145–153.

Doughty, O. J., & Done, D. J. (2009). Is semantic memory impaired in schizophrenia? A systematic review and meta-analysis of 91 studies. *Cognitive Neuropsychiatry, 14*, 473–509.

Evans, J. D., Heaton, R. K., Paulsen, J. S. Palmer, B. W., Patterson, T. L., & Jeste, D. V. (2003) The relationship of neuropsychological abilities to specific domains of functional capacity in older schizophrenia patients. *Biological Psychiatry, 153*, 321–330.

Egeland, J., Rund, B. R., Sundet, K., Landrø, N. I., Asbjørnsen, A., Lund, A., et al. (2003). Attention profile in schizophrenia compared with depression: differential effects of processing speed, selective attention and vigilance. *Acta Psychiatrica Scandinavia, 108,* 276–284.

Fett, A., Viechtbauer, W., Dominguez, M., Penn, D., van Os, J., & Krabbendam, L. (2010). The relationship between neurocognition and social cognition with functional outcomes in schizophrenia: A meta-analysis. *Neuroscience and Biobehavioral Reviews, 35,* 573–588.

Fiszdon, J., Choi, J., Bryson, G., & Bell, M. (2006). Impact of intellectual status on response to cognitive task training in patients with schizophrenia. *Schizophrenia Research, 87,* 261–269.

Fujii, D. E. (2002). *Hawaii State Hospital neuropsychology training manual.* Unpublished manuscript.

Fujii, D. E., & Wylie, A. M. (2003). Neurocognition and community outcome in schizophrenia: Long-term predictive validity. *Schizophrenia Research, 59,* 219–223.

Fujii, D. E., Wylie, A. M., & Nathan, J. H. (2004). Neurocognition and long-term prediction of quality of life in outpatients with severe and persistent mental illness. *Schizophrenia Research, 69,* 67–73.

Gardner, W., Lidz, C. W., Hoge, S. K., Monahan, J., Eisenberg, M. M., Bennett, N. S., et al. (1999). Patients' revisions of their beliefs about the need for hospitalization. *American Journal of Psychiatry, 156,* 1385–1391.

Gladsjo, J. A, McAdams, L. A., Palmer, B. W., Moore, D. J., Jeste, D. V., & Heaton, R. K. (2004). A six-factor model of cognition in schizophrenia and related psychotic disorders: Relationships with clinical symptoms and functional capacity. *Schizophrenia Bulletin, 30,* 739–754.

Goldberg, T. E., Goldman, R. S., Burdick, K. E., Malhotra, A. K., Lencz, T., Patel, R. C., et al. (2007). Cognitive improvements after treatment with second-generation antipsychotic medications in first-episode schizophrenia: Is it a practice effect? *Archives of General Psychiatry, 64,* 1115–1122.

Gorissen, M., Sanz de la Torre, J. C., & Schmand, B. (2005). Effort and cognition in schizophrenia patients. *Schizophrenia Research, 78,* 199–208.

Gourovitch, M. L., Goldberg, T. E., & Weinbeger, D. R. (1996). Verbal fluency deficits in patients with schizophrenia: Semantic fluency is differentially impaired as compared with phonologic fluency. *Neuropsychology, 10,* 573–577.

Granholm, E., Link, P., Fish, S., Kraemer, H., & Jeste, D. (2010). Age-related practice effects across longitudinal neuropsychological assessments in older persons with schizophrenia. *Neuropsychology, 24,* 616–624.

Green, M., Kern, R., Braff, D., & Mintz, J. (2000). Neurocognitive deficits and functional outcome in schizophrenia: Are we measuring the "right stuff?" *Schizophrenia Bulletin, 26,* 119–136.

Häfner, H., & an der Heiden, W. (2008). Course and outcome. In K. T. Mueser & D. V. Jeste (Eds.), *Clinical handbook of schizophrenia* (pp. 100–113). New York: Guilford Press.

Harvey, P. D., Keefe, R. S. E., Patterson, T. L., Heaton, R. K., & Bowie, C. R. (2009). Abbreviated neuropsychological assessment in schizophrenia: Prediction of different aspects of outcome. *Journal of Clinical and Experimental Neuropsychology, 31,* 462–471.

Harvey, P. Moriarty, P., Friedman, J., White, L. Parrella, M., Mohs, R., et al. (2000). Differential perseveration of cognitive functions in geriatric patients with lifelong chronic schizophrenia: less impairment in reading compared with other skill areas. *BMC Psychiatry, 47,* 962–968.

Heilbronner, R. L., Sweet, J. J., Morgan, J. E., Larrabee, G. J., Millis, S. R., & Conference Participants (2009). American Academy of Clinical Neuropsychology consensus conference statement on the neuropsychological assessment of effort, response bias, and malingering. *The Clinical Neuropsychologist, 23,* 1093–1129.

Heinrichs, R. W., & Zakzanis, K. K. (1998). Neurocognitive deficit in schizophrenia: A quantitative review of the evidence. *Neuropsychology, 12,* 426–445.

Jacobs, E., Fujii, D., Schiffman, J., & Bello, I. (2008). An exploratory analysis of neurocognition in methamphetamine-induced psychotic disorder and paranoid schizophrenia. *Cognitive and Behavioral Neurology, 21,* 98–103.

Kaufman, A. S., & Kaufman, N. L. (1994). The Kaufman Functional Academic Skills Test. Circle Pines, MN: American Guidance Service.

Keefe, R., Goldberg, T., Harvey, P., Gold, J., Poe, M., & Coughenour, L. (2004). The brief assessment of cognition in schizophrenia: Reliablity, sensitivity, and comparison with a standard neurocognitive battery. *Schizophrenia Research, 68,* 283–297.

Keefe, R. S. E., Harvey, P. D., Goldberg, T. E., Gold, J. M., Walker, T.M., Kennel, C., et al. (2008). Norms and standardization of the Brief Assessment of Cognition in Schizophrenia (BACS). *Schizophrenia Research, 102,* 108–115.

Keefe, R. S. E., Poe, M., Walker, T. M., & Harvey, P. D. (2006). The relationship of the Brief Assessment of Cognition in Schizophrenia (BACS) to functional capacity and real-world functional outcome. *Journal of Clinical and Experimental Neuropsychology, 28,* 260–269.

Kern, R. S., Green, M. F., Nuechterlein, K. H., & Deng, B. H. (2004). NIMH-MATRICS survey on assessment of neurocognition in schizophrenia. *Schizophrenia Research, 72,* 11–19.

Kern, R. S., Nuechterlein, K. H., Green, M. F., Baade, L. E., Fenton, W. S., Gold, J. M., et al. (2008). The MATRICS consensus cognitive battery. Part 2: Co-norming and standardization. *American Journal of Psychiatry, 16,* 214–220.

Kraepelin, E. (1920). Dementia praecox and paraphrenia (R. M. Barclay, Trans.). *Dementia Praecox Studies, 3,* 127–132.

Kremen, W. S., Seidman, L. J., Faraone, S. V., Pepple, J. R., Lyons, M. J., & Tsuang, M. T. (1996). The "3 Rs" and neuropsychological function in schizophrenia: An empirical test of the matching fallacy. *Neuropsychology, 10,* 22–31.

Kremen, W. S., Butka, S. L., Seidman, L. J., Goldstein, J.M., Koren, D., & Tsuang, M. T. (1998). IQ decline during childhood and adult psychotic sympotoms in a community sample: A 10-year longitudinal study. *American Journal of Psychitry, 155,* 672–679.

Kremen, W., Seidman, L., Faraone, S., & Tsuang, M. (2001). Intelligence quotient and neuropsychological profiles in patients with schizophrenia and in normal volunteers. *Biological Psychiatry, 50,* 453–462.

Kurtz, M. M., Seltzer, J. C., Fujimoto, M., Shagan, D. S,. Wexler, B. E. (2009). Predictors of change in life skills in schizophrenia after cognitive remediation. *Schizophrenia Research,* 107, 267–274.

Loughland, C. M., Lewin, T. J., Vaughan, J. C., Sheedy, J., & Harris, A. W. (2007). RBANS neuropsychological profiles within schizophrenia samples recruited from non-clinical settings. *Schizophrenia Research, 89,* 232–242.

Lubin, A., Gieseking, C., & Williams, H. (1962). Direct measurement of cognitive deficit in schizophrenia. *Journal of Consulting Psychology, 26,* 139–143.

Marcopulos, B. A., Fujii, D., O'Grady, J., Shaver, G., Manly, J., & Aucone, E. (2008). Providing neuropsychological services for persons with schizophrenia: A review of the literature and prescription for practice. In J. Morgan & J. Ricker (Eds.), *Textbook of Clinical Neuropsychology* (pp. 243-271). London: Psychology Press.

Marcopulos, B. A., Bailey, C. M., Tussey, C. M., Kent, J. A., & Grove, A. (2011, February). *Prevalence of failed TOMM performance in consecutive neuropsychology referrals in a state psychiatric hospital.* Poster presented at the 39th Annual Meeting of the International Neuropsychological Society, Boston, MA.

Minzenberg, M. J., Ober, B. A., & Vinogradov, S. (2002). Semantic priming in schizophrenia: A review and synthesis. *Journal of the International Neuropsychological Society, 8*, 699–720.

Monahan, J., Hoge, S. K., Lidz, C. W., Eisenberg, M. M., Bennett, N. S., Gardner, W. P., et al. (1996). Coercion to inpatient treatment: Initial results and implications for assertive treatment in the community. In D. L. Dennis & J. Monahan (Eds.), *Coercion and aggressive community treatment: A new frontier in mental health law* (pp. 13–28). New York: Plenum Press.

Nuechterlein, K. H., Green, M. F., Kern, R. S., Baade, L. E., Barch, D. M., Cohen, J. D., et al. (2008). The MATRICS consensus cognitive battery, part 1: test selection, reliability, and validity. *American Journal of Psychiatry, 165*, 203–213.

Paulsen, J. S., Heaton, R. K., Sadek, J. R., Perry, W. Delis, D. C., Braff, D., et al. (1995). The nature of learning and memory impairments in schizophrenia. *Journal of the International Neuropsychological Society, 1*, 88–99.

Purisch, A., Golden, C., & Hammeke, T. (1978). Discrimination of schizophrenic and brain-injured patients by a standardized version of Luria's Neuropsychological Tests. *Journal of Consulting and Clinical Psychology, 46*, 1266–1273.

Rabin, L., Barr, W., & Burton, L. (2005). Assessment practices of clinical neuropsychologists in the United States and Canada: A survey of INS, NAN, and APA Division 40 members. *Archives of Clinical Neuropsychology, 20*, 33–65.

Randolph, C. (1998). Repeatable battery for the assessment of neuropsychological status. San Antonio, TX: The Psychological Corporation,

Revheim, N., Butler, P. D., Schechter, I., Jalbrzikowski, Silipo, G., & Javitt, D. C. (2006). Reading impairment and visual processing deficits in schizophrenia. *Schizophrenia Research, 87*, 238–245.

Schmand, B., Kuipers, T., van der Gaag, M., Bosveld, J., Bulthuis, F., & Jellema, M. (1994). Cognitive disorders and negative symptoms as correlates of motivational deficit in psychotic patients. *Psychological Medicine, 24*, 869–884.

Schroeder, R., & Marshall, P. (2011). Evaluation of the appropriateness of multiple symptom validity indices in psychotic and non-psychotic psychiatric populations. *The Clinical Neuropsychologist, 25*, 437–453.

Sergi, M., Kern, R., Mintz, J., & Green, M. (2005). Learning potential and the prediction of work skill acquisition in schizophrenia. *Schizophrenia Bulletin, 31*, 67–72.

Sitzer, D., Twamley, E., Patterson, T., & Jeste, D. (2008). Multivariate predictors of social skills performance in middle-aged and older out-patients with schizophrenia spectrum disorders. *Psychological Medicine, 38*, 755–763.

Slick, D., & Craig, P. (1991). Neuropsychological assessment in public psychiatric hospitals: The changing state of the practice 1979–1989. *Archives of Clinical Neuropsychology, 1-2*, 73–80.

Swartz, M. S., Wagner, H. R., Swanson, J. W., Stroup, T. S., McEvoy, J. P., Canive, J. M., et al. (2006). Substance use in persons with schizophrenia: Baseline prevalence and correlates from the NIMH CATIE study. *Journal of Nervous and Mental Disease, 194*, 164–172.

Sweet, J. J., Meyer, D. G., Nelson, N.W., & Moberg, P. J. (2011). The *TCN/AACN* 2010 "salary survey": Professional practices, beliefs, and incomes of U.S. neuropsychologists. *The Clinical Neuropsychologist, 25*, 12–61.

Tolman, A., & Kurtz, M. (2010). Neurocognitive predictors of objective and subjective quality of life in individuals with schizophrenia: A meta-analytic investigation. *Schizophrenia Bulletin, 33*, 1125–1237.

Walker, E. (1994). Developmentally moderated expression of the neuropathology underlying schizophrenia. *Schizophrenia Bulletin, 20*, 453–480.

Walker, E. F., Lewine, R. R. J., Neumann, C. (1996). Childhood behavioral characteristics and adult brain morphology in schizophrenia. *Schizophrenia Research, 22*, 93–101.

Weickert, T., & Goldberg, T. (2000). The course of cognitive impairment in patients with schizophrenia. In T. Sharma & P. Harvey (Eds.), *Cognition in schizophrenia: impairments, importance, and treatment strategies* (pp. 3–15). Oxford, UK: Oxford University Press.

Weinborn, M., Orr, T., Woods, S. P., Conover, E., & Feix, J. (2003). A validation of the test of memory malingering in a forensic psychiatric setting. *Journal of Clinical and Experimental Neuropsychology, 25*, 979–990.

Wilk, C., Gold, J., Humber, K., Dickerson, F., Fenton, W., & Buchanan, R. (2004). Brief cognitive assessment in schizophrenia: Normative data for the Repeatable Battery for the Assessment of Neuropsychological Status. *Schizophrenia Research, 70*, 175–186.

Woodberry, K. A., Giuliano, A. J., & Seidman, L. J. (2008). Premorbid IQ in schizophrenia: A meta-analytic review. *American Journal of Psychiatry, 165*, 579–587.

Woods, S., Weinborn, M., Posada, C., & O'Grady, J. (2007). Preliminary evidence for impaired rapid verb generation in schizophrenia. *Brain and Language, 102*, 46–51.

BOX 3.1 NEUROPSYCHOLOGICAL TESTING

1. Referrals for neuropsychological testing in persons with schizophrenia are varied and often dependent on the setting. Common referral questions pertain to implications for rehabilitation and recovery, including potential for vocational rehabilitation and independent living, as well as legal issues such as competency, insanity, or capacity, and need for a guardian.
2. Schizophrenia is a developmental brain disorder, thus clinicians should take a developmental perspective for conceptualization. Inquiring about academic achievement and potential childhood learning or attention deficits disorders, academic, work, and independent living history in adulthood, social and intimate relationship history across the lifespan, as well as current functioning are important for determining premorbid functioning and recovery potentials.
3. Informed consent for neuropsychological testing is important to protect the rights of the individual, particularly if findings can be used to postpone or prevent discharge from an institution.

4. Testing the person with schizophrenia if often challenging as trust, rapport, and ability to engage in testing due to prominent positive or negative symptoms are important issues. Testing in shorter session, testing only during optimal levels of motivation and alertness, use of incentives/reinforcers, and measuring engagement through symptom validity tests are techniques to facilitate attaining accurate test data. Any non-standardized or special considerations and procedures should be documented in the report.
5. Using word recognition reading tests for estimating premorbid IQ in persons with schizophrenia may not be appropriate due to early developmental cognitive deficits and possible learning disorder and attention deficit hyperactivity disorder comorbidities that can impact academic and reading achievement. A multi-method approach is recommended to estimate premorbid IQ based upon word recognition reading and personal and family demographics.
6. Clinicians should include tests that assess a broad array of neurocognitive domains, particularly domains that have demonstrated predictive validity for functionality such as attention, memory, processing speed, executive functioning, and social cognition. The MATRICS, BACS, and RBANS, are extensive neurocognitive screens that have been validated with persons with schizophrenia. Symptom validity tests should be included for measuring engagement, exaggeration, or malingering, the latter two when there is potential for secondary gain.
7. Persons with schizophrenia typically score 1 to 2 standard deviations below normal expectations with moderate to severe impairment in specific cognitive areas, although some with high premorbid abilities can present in the normal ranges. Persons with schizophrenia often have several comorbidities contributing to cognitive deficits such as substance abuse, head injury, and medication effects and all should be considered in interpretation.
8. Recommendations from test results should address functional areas such as impact on recovery including academic and vocational potentials, discharge planning including appropriate placement and need for environmental supports, and everyday practical recommendations to maximize everyday functioning, for example, strategies or compensatory mechanisms to address memory deficits. Individual and group cognitive remediation interventions have also been validated to improve cognitive functioning.

CONTINUING EDUCATION QUESTIONS

1. Which issue is **not** a typical referral questions for neuropsychological testing in persons with schizophrenia:
   a. Impact on legal issues (e.g. guardianship, competence, sanity)
   b. Impact on everyday functioning including educational, community, and vocational potential
   c. Impact of positive symptoms on cognition
   d. Potential for learning in psychosocial rehabilitation
2. What statement is **most** true about estimating premorbid IQ in persons with schizophrenia:
   a. Word recognition reading is always indicated as a measure of premorbid IQ
   b. Cognitive deficits typically occur with the onset of psychotic symptoms, thus the usual procedures for estimating premorbid IQ are indicated
   c. Most persons with schizophrenia have a reading disorder, thus word recognition reading should not be used as measure of premorbid IQ
   d. A multi-method approach should be used to estimate premorbid IQ including word recognition reading, level of education, previous occupation, or parent's occupation
3. What statement is true about using symptom validity testing in a person with schizophrenia:
   a. Symptom validity tests can be used as a measure of engagement in testing in persons with schizophrenia
   b. Auditory hallucinations, impairments in sustained attention, negative symptoms, and low education can significantly impact test performance on symptom validity measures
   c. Persons with schizophrenia who have legal charges may exaggerate or malinger to defer or delay a trial
   d. All of the above
4. Which neuropsychological test batteries were validated with individuals with schizophrenia and recommended for routine neuropsychological testing:
   a. MATRICS Consensus Cognitive Battery (MCCS)
   b. Brief Assessment of Cognition in Schizophrenia (BACS)
   c. Halsted-Reitan Neuropsychological Battery (HRNB)
   d. All of the above
   e. A and b only
5. What are some functional implications of neurocognition in persons with schizophrenia:
   a. Potential placement and supports for discharge planning
   b. Appropriateness of treatment plan goals
   c. Potential for independent medication management
   d. All of the above
   e. b and c only

4

Neurocognition and Functional Outcome in Schizophrenia

MATTHEW M. KURTZ, Ph.D.
Department of Psychology, Wesleyan University, Middletown, CT

A defining feature of schizophrenia is its association with poor functional status, often even before formal diagnosis (APA, 1994). This phenomenon has been recognized as a core abnormality of the disorder from Kraepelin's first descriptions of the disease at the turn of the 20th century. Deficits in skills associated with self-care, social interaction, engaging in recreational activities and work function in young, middle-aged and older individuals with schizophrenia are legion (Bellack et al., 1990; Patterson et al, 2001a, b), and are more pronounced than those evident in other forms of severe and persistent mental illness (e.g., Schretlen et al., 2000). In fact, current estimates suggest that 70%–80% of individuals with schizophrenia are unemployed at any one time, and only one half of 1% patients with schizophrenia who receive Social Security Insurance (SSI/SSDI) ever remove themselves from entitlements. With prevalence rates in North America ranging from one half to 1%, the estimated cost of the illness to society, in terms of lost wages and lifelong medical care, is on the order of billions of dollars (Salkever et al., 2007). The effects of chronic social impairment on the sense of self-worth of clients with schizophrenia are incalculable.

Over the past 20 years, a wealth of evidence has revealed impairments on measures of elementary skills in attention, memory, problem solving, and other aspects of neurocognition in schizophrenia, relative to demographically-matched, healthy comparison groups (Heinrichs & Zakzanis, 1998). While there is ongoing controversy over whether these impairments represent discrete areas of deficit, or a common factor of impairment (e.g., Dickinson, Ragland, Gold, & Gur, 2008), it is generally accepted that impaired test performance bears a moderate-strong relationship to a variety of dimensions of functional status in the disorder (Green, 1996; Green, Kern, Braff, & Mintz, 2000; Green, Kern, & Heaton, 2004) with estimates suggesting that neurocognition accounts for from 20%–60% of the variance in outcome depending upon the specific study examined. The goal of the current chapter, then, is to provide greater clarity regarding relationships between neurocognitive skills and functional status in schizophrenia, and highlight the implications of these relationships for the assessment of the client with schizophrenia. The chapter is organized around the four following themes:

1. How can functional status in schizophrenia be measured in clinical settings?
2. Are elementary measures of neurocognition linked to these different methods for assessments of functional status, and how does the magnitude of this association compare with that for psychiatric symptoms?
3. Does the relationship between elementary neurocognitive skills and functional status in schizophrenia differ when intervening treatment reflects uncontrolled and, typically, minimal community support (e.g., monthly psychiatric visits), versus evidence-based, structured behavioral interventions such as skills training, vocational rehabilitation or comprehensive outpatient rehabilitation consisting of a range of integrated therapies?
4. What is the relationship of measures of social cognition, which include the ability to perceive the intentions and dispositions of others, and functional outcome?

The seminal review paper highlighting the literature showing a relationship between neurocognitive test performance and everyday function was by Heaton and Pendleton (1981). The results of this literature review revealed that IQ scores, as well as specific neuropsychological test results, related to a variety of aspects of self-care and independent living, academic achievement and vocational functioning in healthy populations, as well as varied clinical populations (including mental retardation [MR], stroke and severe psychiatric illness). Since this review, there have been a plethora of studies devoted to understanding the relationship between score on neuropsychological measures and dimensions of outcome in schizophrenia.

MEASUREMENT OF FUNCTIONAL OUTCOME IN SCHIZOPHRENIA

From the perspective of clinical assessment, measures of functional status can be grouped into three general domains: (a) role-play, performance-based measures of elementary social skills, and everyday life skills; (b) interview-based measures of objective functioning and quality-of-life (e.g., Heinrichs Quality-of-Life [QLS] scale, Birchwood Social Functioning Scale); and (c) direct measures of community success such as hours worked and wages earned in independent community employment placements, and independence in community living status (e.g., independent living vs. a group home with nursing staff support). Subjective life satisfaction is another important domain of outcome, but is excluded from this review as there is evidence that its relationship to cognition is quite different from other measures of functional status (Brekke, Kohrt, & Green, 2001; Tolman & Kurtz, 2012).

COMMONLY USED FUNCTIONAL OUTCOME MEASURES IN SCHIZOPHRENIA

Performance-Based Measures of Function

Performance-based measures of life skills in which clients are asked to perform specific elements of everyday life function under the observation of a clinician, have the advantage of a lack of rater bias and can be used to capture very specific aspects of functional status. However, performance-based measures are capacity measures providing evidence regarding what the client is capable of, not what they client can actually execute in their environment. Individual characteristics, such as confidence, motivation, and skills in self-monitoring, as well as environmental influences, such as the availability of opportunities to employ clinic-measured skills, have an enormous impact on the expression of clinic observed functional skills. Two commonly used measures of performance-based functional skills are the *UCSD Performance-Based Skills Assessment* (UPSA; Patterson, Goldman, McKibbin, Hughs, & Jeste, 2001a). This standardized, performance-based instrument of everyday function provides information regarding clients' ability to manage information/planning, finance, communication, mobility, and household management in role-play situations. Two week test-retest reliability is .93 (Harvey, Velligan, & Bellack, 2007), while support for criterion validity has been produced (Mausbach et al., 2008) with strong correlations between UPSA scores and level of residential independence.

Social skills Performance Assessment (SSPA; Patterson, Moscona, McKibbin, Davidson, & Jeste 2001b). A standardized, brief, clinic-based assessment of social skill consisting of two 3-minute social role-plays in which the participant plays the role of: (a) a tenant meeting a new neighbor and, (b) a tenant reporting a leak in their household for the second time to a landlord. Interactions are recorded and rated according to a variety of criteria including interest/disinterest, fluency, clarity, focus and affect, and social appropriateness. Inter-rater reliability was reported as .91 while test-retest reliability has been reported at .92. Scores on the SSPA have been related to interpersonal behavior, work skills and community activity participation (Bowie et al., 2008).

Clinician-Rated Measures of Outcome

The advantage of scales that are clinician-rated and use client or informant report is that they generate information on aspects of client life that only the client has access to. These reports may also provide a more accurate assessment of what the client is actually achieving in their community than performance-based measures. However, lack of insight, a key feature of the illness, can make clients' assessment of their own levels of recreational, social and work function problematic. Informant reports may also be biased, and a substantial proportion of middle-aged and older individuals with schizophrenia cannot provide the name of an individual who can report on their functioning.

Two commonly used measures of clinician-rated outcome in schizophrenia are the Heinrichs Quality-of-Life Scale (QLS; Heinrichs, Hanlon, & Carpenter 1984) and The Birchwood Social Functioning Scale (SFS; Birchwood, Smith, Cochrane, Wetton, & Copestake, 1990). The QLS consists of 21 items rated on a 7-point scale. Administered as a semi-structured interview, the intent of the scale is to measure social and vocational limitations attributable to psychopathology. Items include ratings of intimate relationships, active acquaintances, level of social activity and occupational role functioning. The QLS assesses four interdependent theoretical constructs: (a) intrapsychic foundations, consisting of measures related to sense of purpose and motivation; (b) interpersonal relations, examining social experience; (c) instrumental role, related to work functioning; and (d) common objects and activities, which measures engagement in the community by possession of common objects and participation in a range of activities. The validity of these subscales is supported by principal components factor analysis (e.g., Heinrichs et al., 1984).

The SFS (Birchwood et al., 1990) was developed to assess social adjustment in schizophrenia. The 79-item measure assesses social functioning across seven domains: (a) social engagement/withdrawal, (b) interpersonal behavior/communication, (c) prosocial activities, (d) recreation, (e) independence-competence, (f) independence-performance, and (g) employment/occupation. The SFS takes approximately 30–45 minutes to administer and can be used as a self-report or informant interview based instrument. Items are rated on a 4-point scale with higher ratings corresponding to better functioning.

RELATIONSHIP OF NEUROCOGNITION TO PERFORMANCE-BASED MEASURES OF FUNCTIONING

Studies to date have revealed strong relationships between measures of elementary neurocognition and performance-based activities of daily living (ADLs) and social skill that outweigh links between positive symptoms (e.g., delusions and hallucinations) and performance-based functioning For example, in a study of 222 individuals with schizophrenia or schizoaffective disorder, Bowie and colleagues (2008) using factor-analysis derived composite scores of attention/working memory, verbal memory, processing speed, and executive function showed that attention/working memory and processing speed factors predicted both performance-based ADL skill and social skill, while verbal memory, and executive function predicted ADLs, but not social skill. Negative symptoms predicted performance-based social skills at a level similar in magnitude to cognitive factors. Negative symptoms were not linked to the performance-based ADL measure while positive symptoms did not link to either measure of functional capacity.

Other studies have reported similar findings. Twamley et al. (2002) reported non-specific relationships between a cognitive screening measure (Mattis Dementia Rating Scale) and all seven neurocognitive domain scores (verbal ability, attention/working memory, psychomotor ability, motor ability, learning, memory, and abstraction/cognitive flexibility) measured in their study, and a performance-based measure of ADLs. The cognitive screening measure explained over 40% of the variance in ADL performance scores with negative symptoms only contributing an additional 10% of variance.

The importance of cognitive factors in performance-based functional outcome has also been emphasized in another recent study by Sitzer, Twamley, Patterson, & Jeste (2008), which showed that a cognitive screening measure explained 25% of the variance in scores on a measure of social skill in a large sample of 194 clients with schizophrenia, while clinical variables (positive and negative symptoms, depression and insight) explained only an additional 12% of variance. Other studies have shown similar results with some evidence that processing speed may account for the largest proportion of variance in performance-based social skill when compared to other elementary cognitive measures (Dickinson, Bellack, & Gold, 2007).

NEUROCOGNITION AS A PREDICTOR OF CLINICIAN-RATED OUTCOME IN OUTPATIENT SAMPLES

Chronic Samples

Over the past 10 years a growing number of large-sample, longitudinal studies of chronic outpatient samples have supported links between measures of elementary neurocognition and a variety of measures of clinician-rated outcome. While cross-sectional results may suggest potential causative relationships between neurocognitive variables and functional outcome, they may also simply serve as markers of the ability to perform certain social or functional skills at a single time point, and say little about putative causal relations. Several studies have shown that cross-sectional relationships between neurocognition and functional outcome may be quite different from longitudinal relationships in the same sample of clients (e.g., Jaeger & Douglas, 1992; Silverstein, Schenkel, Valone, & Neurnberg 1998). In contrast, longitudinal studies which measure neurocogntive performance at study entry and functional status at a subsequent follow-up provide strongest evidence implicating cognitive deficits as a predictor of functional impairment and are thus highlighted in this section.

An important feature of the studies reviewed in this section is that these are naturalistic studies, in which treatment during the follow-up interval is uncontrolled and thus clients most likely receive a diversity of forms of community care. Kurtz, Moberg, Ragland, Gur, & Gur (2005), investigated the relationship of tests measuring three neurocognitive domains (visual vigilance, verbal learning, and executive function) and three symptom dimensions (reality distortion, disorganization and psychomotor poverty) as measured at entry to the study, to community function as measured by the Heinrich's Quality-of-Life Scale (QLS) at a 1- and 4-year follow-up. A total of 70 stable outpatients were assessed at a 1-year follow-up, and 26 patients were followed at the 4-year follow-up. Results yielded several interesting findings. First, at a 1-year follow-up symptoms of disorganization and psychomotor poverty and performance on measures of card sorting and visual vigilance were related to measures of QLS. Results from a 4-year follow-up were nearly identical except that verbal learning emerged as a significant predictor as well. These findings suggest that the predictive value of neurocognitive measures, for clinician-rated measures of functioning may vary depending upon the duration of the follow-up interval. Stepwise regression revealed that the neurocognitive predictor, visual vigilance, and psychomotor poverty symptom measures explained the largest amount of variance in quality-of-life at both follow-up intervals.

Several studies have also provided evidence that measures of neurocognition predict *change* in clinician-rated outcome over time. For example, Dickerson, Boronow, Ringel, and Parente (1999) in a sample of 72 clients at a 2-year follow-up showed that cognitive measures of vocabulary, visual scanning and set-shifting, predicted change in occupational function on a clinician-rated scale. Symptom factors were not correlated with change in clinician-rated outcome in this study.

We note that not all studies have shown positive results. Several studies have failed to find relationships between any of the neurocognitive measures studies in their sample and clinician-rated psychosocial status (Addington & Addington, 2000), but the balance of findings still support the contention that cognition is related to clinician-rated outcome.

First-Episode Samples

Findings for chronic samples are also consistent with neurocognition-clinician-rated outcome relations in first-episode samples. First-episode studies are of particular import in that they reveal relationships between measures of cognition and functional status in the absence of the effects of prolonged medication treatment, repeated hospitalizations and the long-term impaired functional characteristic of chronic clients.

For example, Keshavan et al. (2003) investigated measures of attention, verbal and visual memory and problem solving, along with demographic and clinical factors as predictors of outcome at a 1- and 2-year follow-up using a measure of global functioning (GAF) and a measure of outcome based on ratings of social functioning, symptoms and occupational function. One-hundred and four clients presenting for psychosis for the first time (70% of the sample was subsequently diagnosed schizophrenia or schizoaffective disorder) served as participants. Results revealed that problem solving, attention, and non-verbal memory had modest correlations with at least one of the two outcome measures at both a 1- and 2-year follow-up. Verbal learning was not linked to outcome at either time point and negative symptoms had only a modest relationship with global functioning. Positive symptoms were not linked to either measure of outcome.

Milev, Ho, Arndt, and Andreasen (2005), in a study of 99 individuals with schizophrenia in their first episode of illness, investigated a comprehensive neuropsychological battery consisting of 27 measures grouped into five cognitive domains based on a priori theoretical considerations, as predictors of outcome 7 years later. Neurocognitive domains (verbal memory, processing speed and attention, language skills, visuospatial skills, and problem solving) were assessed with Cronbach's alpha and were found to have good internal consistency (Cronbach's alpha > 0.75). The Psychiatric Status You Currently Have instrument was used to assess outcome. Global ratings on this scale were on a 1-to-5 scale based on level of functioning in the areas of work, satisfaction, interpersonal relations and sex, as well as whether the level of functioning was consistent with what would be expected from the subject's education and social background. Of the neurocognitive domains, only verbal memory, processing speed and attention were linked to outcome and among symptom variables only negative symptoms, not psychotic or disorganized symptoms, predicted global outcome. Follow-up analyses revealed that when negative symptoms were entered into a stepwise regression they explained 11% of the variance in outcome; processing speed and attention entered second and explained an additional 3.2%. Verbal memory did not enter the equation in the next step, likely due to shared variance with negative symptoms and processing speed and attention. In sum, results have largely supported a modest to moderate association between neurocognitive deficits and subsequent clinician-rated outcome in first-episode samples, with two important reports of negative findings (e.g., Bilder et al., 2000; Stirling et al., 2003).

Summary

A variety of studies have investigated the relationship of neurocognitive deficits, measured at illness onset in schizophrenia, to subsequent outcome. Results have largely supported a modest to moderate association between neurocognitive deficits and subsequent clinician-rated outcome. There is also evidence that neurocognitive factors explain variance in outcome beyond that linked to negative symptoms. Positive and disorganized symptoms have not been typically linked to outcome in these studies. Specific relationships have not emerged to date, with different studies reporting very different cognitive domains (attention, verbal and working memory, executive function) as linked to outcome.

NEUROCOGNITIVE PREDICTORS OF RESPONSE TO EVIDENCE-BASED PSYCHOSOCIAL INTERVENTIONS

Social Skills Training

While skills training programs vary widely in content, duration, and the setting where they are implemented, they share a common set of strategies for teaching new skills based on social learning theory (Bandura, 1969), including goal-setting, role-modeling, behavioral rehearsal, positive reinforcement, corrective feedback, and homework assignments to help promote generalization to the community. Evidence that deficits in neurocognition could impede the acquisition of elemental social skills through comprehension of information presented in social skills training programs was first demonstrated by Bowen et al. (1994). In that study 30 individuals with schizophrenia and 15 healthy controls were evaluated with two measures of sustained visual vigilance, a working memory measure, and a forced-choice test of early iconic memory at baseline, were given a one-session skills training module in medication management, and then tested for comprehension of written information, comprehension of information presented on videotape, and role-play procedures using material derived from this medication-management training session. Results revealed that all neurocognitive measures correlated with acquisition of elementary social skills. Multiple regression analyses revealed that when a measure of visual vigilance was entered into the equation first it explained 43% of the variance in acquisition of social skills, with the working memory measure explaining an additional 11% of the variance. These findings suggest that if elementary neurocognitive operations impact acquisition of elementary social skills in a single session, it is likely they will impact acquisition of social skills across sustained programs of skills training. These results however, do not speak to the role that cognitive deficits may play on the likelihood of expressing skills once learned or the likelihood of generalization of learned skills to other environments.

The seminal study of neurocognitive vs. symptom predictors of response to sustained programs of social skills training (SST) was conducted by Mueser, Bellack, Douglas, and Wade (1991). In that study of 55 individuals diagnosed with schizophrenia or schizoaffective disorder recently admitted to an inpatient unit for an exacerbation of psychiatric symptoms, overall memory and symptoms were measured at study entry as predictors of treatment response to a 2-week, inpatient skills training program. The skills training focused on acquisition of elementary social skills in (a) expressing negative feelings, and (b) compromise and negotiation, each trained in three sessions over a week. Outcome was measured with a role-play test consisting of six role-plays focused on skills taught directly in the SST program. Assessments of overall assertiveness, along with component skills, were rated. Results revealed that the SST program produced improvement in role-play skill measures. Results also revealed that the overall memory quotient from memory measures, and particularly scores on concentration and verbal memory, were strong predictors of improvement in social skill, while no symptom subscales or demographic characteristics predicted improvement in role-play outcome measures. The authors concluded that acute symptoms were only weakly related to social skills at study entry and did not predict response to treatment whereas memory skills, which were linked to social skill at baseline, also impeded acquisition of elementary skills in assertiveness. Interestingly, clients with impaired memory still improved on measures of social skill, suggesting that clients most in need of improvements in social skill can still show some improvement with training.

Neurocognitive deficits have also been shown to impact attendance and engagement in socials-skills training groups. McKee, Hull, and Smith (1997) in a sample of 19 chronic inpatients investigated the relative role of symptoms and neurocognitive measures of processing speed, verbal list learning, attention, verbal fluency, and verbal inhibition on attendance and level of participation in a 16-session, 5-day-per-week program of community re-entry skills (consisting of medication management skills, symptom identification, and collaborative treatment planning). Results revealed that measures of verbal inhibition predicted participation, whereas negative symptoms and attention predicted attendance. Positive symptoms did not relate to either measure of outcome in this study.

In a closely related study, Smith, Hull, Romanelli, Fertuck, and Weiss (1999) investigated the relationship of symptoms and measures of attention and executive function and verbal list-learning, to progress in a 16-session skills training program focused on community re-entry. Progress in skills training was measured with a skills training assessment. Regression equations indicated that the best model explained 79% of the variance in post-treatment skills scores, and found that verbal memory, along with pretreatment skills scores and group membership, predicted post-treatment skills level scores. Other studies have supported these relationships, showing relationships between sustained visual vigilance and verbal learning specifically, and acquisition of elementary social skill in skills training programs (Kern, Green, & Satz, 1992; Silverstein et al., 1998)

A more recent study has investigated the specificity of relationships of specific neurocognitive skills to progress in a combined social skills and cognitive-behavioral therapy (CBT) program for middle-aged and older patients with schizophrenia, relative to a treatment-as-usual (TAU) control condition. Granholm et al. (2008) investigated the utility of a comprehensive battery of neurocognitive tests, grouped into domains of speed of processing, executive function, verbal learning, and memory, and attention and vigilance, for predicting response to their combined intervention. Data from 65 community-dwelling patients with schizophrenia who participated were presented. Outcome was assessed with a direct measure of skills taught in combined CBT and SST, and the Independent Living Skills survey, a self-report measure of basic and social functioning to assess generalization of treatment. Global neurocognition, as well as attention and vigilance, and speed of processing scores were linked to poorer overall psychosocial status for the entire sample (experimental and TAU control group), while global cognitive function, executive control, attention and vigilance, and verbal learning and memory were related to skill acquisition as assessed through content mastery tests. Importantly, however, the group X condition interaction was not significant for either outcome measure, suggesting that levels of neurocognitive impairment had little impact on outcome in the skills training group relative to the TAU control group. Neurocognitive impairment did relate to measures of group engagement, but not attendance.

Vocational Rehabilitation

Work Therapy Studies Other studies have focused on cognitive predictors of response to either supported employment or work-therapy programs. Lysaker, Bell, Zito, and Bioty (1995) investigated the utility of performance on a measure of problem solving, the WCST, for predicting improvement over a 10-week work therapy program for 53 individuals with schizophrenia classified as impaired on a measure of work related social skills. Individuals were chronically ill and middle-aged (mean age = 42.8) and the majority were outpatients. Work therapy consisted of 10 to 20 hours of sheltered job placements, typically on VA hospital grounds, consistent with clients expressed job interests and coupled with a weekly employment skills group for coping successfully with work-related concerns. The results revealed that performance on a measure of problem solving uniquely predicted acquisition of social skills related to work. Symptoms and background variables did not predict improvement in work-related social skills. A limitation of the study was the selection of only one measure of neurocognitive function, making conclusions regarding specificity of cognition-outcome links difficult.

Similar findings, using a broader neuropsychological battery have been reported by Bell and Bryson (2001). They studied 33 middle-aged, chronic outpatients who completed at least 22 weeks of a work rehabilitation program at a variety of supervised job sites on hospital grounds. Performance in these work sites was then evaluated biweekly using a standardized scale of work behaviors over the trial. At study entry clients were administered a comprehensive neuropsychological battery consisting of measures of overall IQ, sustained visual vigilance, verbal and non-verbal memory, verbal list learning, measures of thought disorder and emotion recognition. Results revealed several interesting findings. Four of the five work domains showed improvement over the work rehabilitation trial. Regression analyses using neurocognitive measures to predict slope across the work training period showed that these cognitive measures significantly explained variance in change all five domains of work performance, with strongest relationships between cognitive measures and work habits and personal presentation at work. Symptom ratings did not predict work function with the exception of negative symptoms, which predicted cooperativeness on the job across the trial.

Competitive Vocational Outcomes Gold, Goldberg, McNary, Dixon, and Lehman (2002) evaluated 150 clients with severe mental illness (of who 74%

had a diagnosis of a psychotic disorder) and investigated cognitive predictors of successful outcome after community vocational training, Findings were collapsed across two vocational training conditions: an individual placement and support model emphasizing integration of clinical and employment services, and rapid placement in competitive employment positions, versus more traditional vocational rehabilitation. A comprehensive neuropsychological test battery was administered to provide an assessment of general intellectual ability, language, academic ability, aspects of attention, verbal and non-verbal memory, executive function, working memory, and motor functioning. Forty of the participants obtained employment over the 24-month follow-up period, with a much higher proportion of clients in the individualized placement and support program finding work. Results revealed several interesting findings. First, surprisingly, there were no differences between employed and unemployed groups on measures from the neurocognitive test battery. Measures of oral vocabulary, visuospatial construction, verbal comprehension, set-shifting, and verbal inhibition, sustained attention and working memory were, however, linked to hours worked in the treatment trial at both the 12- and 24-month follow-ups. Much of the strength of these relationships was driven by a small proportion of clients who worked the most hours, with more modest relationships between neurocognitive skills and hours worked for the majority of clients who worked closer to the modal number of hours in the study. The authors concluded that modest, non-specific relationships were evident between specific neurocognitive skills and duration, but not likelihood of obtaining competitive employment.

In a related study, McGurk, Mueser, Harvey, LaPuglia, and Marder (2003), in a 2-year longitudinal follow-along project of 30 clients with schizophrenia in a supported employment program, investigated the degree to which demographic variables, positive and negative symptoms from the Positive and Negative Syndrome Scale (PANSS), and measures of neurocognitive function, including measures of executive function, attention, psychomotor speed, and verbal learning, could be linked to achievement in competitive employment settings and utilization of employment support services. Better executive functioning and verbal learning skills and lower levels of negative symptoms were associated with more hours worked. Evaluation of utilization of supported employment services, as measured by hours of on-the-job support and contact with employment specialists, showed that (a) better executive function, passive auditory attention, verbal learning, and psychomotor speed were associated with fewer hours of on-the-job supports, and (b) higher positive symptoms were associated with more hours of on-job supports. The authors concluded that both symptoms and neurocognitive function impact work outcomes and need for on-the-job support, but the relationship of symptoms and neurocognition to work function on the one hand, and need for employment support services, on the other, was distinct. Thus, clients with higher levels of negative symptoms achieved less in terms of competitive work function but patients with higher levels of positive symptoms needed more on the job support. Executive function and learning related to both sets of outcome measures.

Comprehensive Outpatient Rehabilitation

Three studies to date have investigated neurocognitive predictors of response to multi-modal, intensive outpatient treatment programs that consist of a variety of behavioral interventions. Woonings, Appelo, Kluiter, Sloof, and van der Bosch (2002) in a sample of 44 middle-aged, hospitalized clients with schizophrenia investigated the relationship of measures of immediate memory, verbal list learning, vigilance, and problem solving, along with a measure learning how to learn, on change in functioning after a comprehensive rehabilitation program using the Rehabilitation and Evaluation scale, designed to assess institutionalized patients deviant and more general behaviors. The intervention was an 8-month rehabilitation program consisting of psychoeducation, cognitive remediation training, training in planning everyday activities, social and vocational skills training. Results revealed that vigilance and problem solving but not verbal memory, were linked to change in psychosocial status across the trial.

Kurtz, Wexler, Fujimoto, Shagan, and Seltzer (2008) investigated the relationship between five measures of neurocognitive function, crystallized verbal ability, visual sustained vigilance, verbal learning, problem solving, and processing speed, and two measures of symptoms, total positive and negative symptoms, and change on a performance-based measure of everyday life-skills after a year of outpatient rehabilitation. For the majority of clients, rehabilitation consisted of a three-day per week program including structured group therapy, life-skills training, and exercise, vocational counseling and computer training. Forty-six patients with schizophrenia or schizoaffective disorder were studied. Results of a linear regression model revealed that verbal learning predicted a significant amount of the variance in change in performance-based measures of everyday life skills after outpatient rehabilitation, even when variance for all other variables in the model was accounted for. Measures of crystallized verbal ability, sustained visual vigilance, problem solving, processing speed, and symptoms were not linked to functional status change. These findings emphasized the importance of verbal learning for benefiting from psychosocial interventions, and suggest the need for alternative rehabilitation strategies for those who do not benefit.

In the largest sample study to date, Brekke, Hoe, Long, and Green (2007) studied a composite measure of cognition, including indices of attention, fluency, verbal learning and memory, and problem solving, along with social cognitive and service intensity measures, as a predictor of change in a clinician-rated index of outcome, the Role Functioning Scale, during a 12-month interval of community psychosocial rehabilitation. One-hundred and two chronically ill clients with schizophrenia were enrolled in an intensive outpatient treatment at one of four sites, each consisting of social and vocational rehabilitation services, housing supports, a crisis hotline, and substance abuse and health services. Results revealed that the composite measure of cognition at study entry, along with service intensity during treatment, predicted substantial change in the outcome measure across the 12-month interval.

Summary

Studies of neurocognitive predictors of response to SST interventions in schizophrenia have suggested: (a) verbal memory is a predictor of acquisition of skills taught directly in skills programs; (b) attention, verbal memory, and verbal inhibition may be linked to participation in SST groups; and (c) attention and negative symptoms are linked to attendance at skills training groups. A limitation of the literature to date is that prediction of outcome has rarely been compared between active treatments and control conditions in the same sample of clients. The one study that has evaluated specificity of relationships between cognitive measures and outcome of treatment to date, failed to find that cognitive measures predicted change in outcome across time differently in a treatment versus a control group. Clearly, more research on this topic is necessary. A strength of these studies is that they almost all measured change in functioning over time, rather than a static index of outcome at the termination of treatment.

Studies of neurocognitive function as predictors of response to work-therapy or supported employment programs suggest (a) a variety of measures of neurocognitive function predict change in clinician-rated work behavior in work-therapy programs, and (b) a variety of measures of neurocognition predict hours worked in competitive employment settings obtained through supported employment programs. There is no evidence at this time to support the contentions that (a) neurocognitive skills differentiate between those clients who competitively work and those who do not after vocational rehabilitation, and (b) there are specific relationships between specific domains of neurocognitive function and work outcome.

Lastly, progress in comprehensive programs of rehabilitation has been predicted by a variety of neurocognitive variables (verbal learning, attention, and problem solving, as well as composite neurocognitive measures).

Social Cognition and Functional Outcome

Social cognition has been defined as the human ability to perceive the intentions and dispositions of others and to use this information flexibly to guide social interactions (Couture, Penn, & Roberts, 2006). Researchers and clinicians have theorized that deficits in social cognition in schizophrenia impact the deployment of appropriate social skill directly, and more likely impact school and work functioning indirectly by influencing the development of peer relationships. Social cognition has also been hypothesized to impact the acquisition of daily living skills by impairing the social interactions necessary to develop skills in money management, home-living and other daily life skills. While the types of elementary neurocognitive skills described in previous sections of this chapter typically explain a range of variance in functional outcome (estimated at 20%–60%), with differences between studies most likely linked to differences in measurement of neurocognitive skill and functional outcome, it is important to note that leaves anywhere from 40%–80% of the variance in outcome in these studies unexplained. Social cognition has been posited as a construct accounting for a proportion of this unexplained variance in outcome. Studies have supported the idea that measures of social cognition explain variance in functional outcome beyond that accounted for by elementary neuropsychological measures (e.g., Pinkham & Penn, 2006). Social cognition is typically assessed through measures of: (a) emotion perception, the ability to infer emotional information from facial expressions, vocal expressions or both;(b) social perception, which is the ability of a client to ascertain social cues from behavior offered in a social context; (c) theory-of-mind, which measures the ability to assess whether others have mental states different from one's own, and to make accurate inferences about the contents of those mental states; and (d) attributional style, which is the tendency to blame others, rather than situations. Each of these indices has been linked to a range of functional outcomes in schizophrenia (Couture et al., 2006).

DISCUSSION AND CLINICAL RECOMMENDATIONS

With respect to the organizing themes of this chapter, based on the literature to date, we can make several conclusions:

1. Functional outcome can be measured in schizophrenia with validated and reliable scales. These measures can be grouped into: (a) performance-based measures, that assess specific abilities in the clinic, are observed by a clinician, and typically measures specific ADL functions or social skill in a role-play format; and (b) clinician-rated scales that rely on client and informant report, and assess achieved levels of community function.
2. A variety of measures of neurocognition (e.g., attention, verbal memory, problem solving, and processing speed, as well as global cognitive measures) have been linked cross-sectionally to performance-based measures of ADLs and social skill, and longitudinally to clinician-rated measures of outcome, attendance and participation in SST groups, acquisition of elementary social skills in SST groups, clinician-rated work skills in clients in work therapy programs and competitive employment outcomes after participation in vocational rehabilitation programs. Current findings suggest that anywhere from 20%–60% of variance in these various outcome measures can explained by neurocognitive factors, and that results are consistent for first-episode and chronic client samples. There is evidence that negative symptoms provide an independent contribution to outcome as well. Positive symptoms have not been linked to outcome.
3. There is no consistent experimental support, at this time, for specific relationships between specific domains of neurocognition and outcome in naturalistic studies that do not actively manipulate intervening treatment. The heterogeneity of findings in this area, suggest that differences in patterns of relationships between specific neurocognitive variables and outcome in studies conducted to date may reflect between-task psychometric

differences in task difficulty and reliability, rather than differences in association of underlying measured constructs.

There is evidence for specificity of neurocognitive predictors of treatment response to different evidence-based interventions in schizophrenia. Acquisition of elementary social skills in skills training programs is most frequently related to attention and verbal memory function. There is no evidence that neurocognitive test results predict likelihood of working competitively after vocational rehabilitation, and differences in hours worked, wages earned, and clinical ratings of work behavior in clients who do work all show generalized relationships to a variety of neurocognitive measures.

4. Social cognition, which includes the ability to perceive the intentions and dispositions of others predicts variance in outcome beyond that predicted by elementary neurocognitive measures.

Taken together these findings provide specific recommendations for interpreting the results of clinical neuropsychological assessment for treatment planning in schizophrenia. First, neurocognitive impairment will likely predict poorer psychosocial function, measured through performance-based or clinician-rated indices of outcome, in the short- and long-term future. Second, deficits in attention and memory evident in a neuropsychological evaluation will impact the ability of clients to benefit from structured skills-training programs. We note, however, that even clients with impairments of greatest severity gain benefit from these programs (Mueser et al., 1991). Third, for clients who work after completing vocational rehabilitation, neurocognitive deficits will likely predict the intensity of work and acquisition of work-related social skill. Fourth deficits in social cognition, as measured through attributional style, facial affect recognition, and theory-of-mind, also predict a poorer outcome in clients with schizophrenia.

It is important to recognize that a limitation of extant research is that it has focused on performance in groups of clients with heterogeneous deficits, on neuropsychological measures, clinician-rated indices of number and quality of social contacts, work function and recreational activities and performance-based indices of ADLs and social skill. Thus, findings from research studies do not provide guidance on neurocognitive predictors of successful return-to-school or work, independent functioning in the community, or likelihood of using compensatory strategies, or prosthetics, for bypassing cognitive deficits in individual patients, questions often confronted by practicing clinical neuropsychologists. Very specific real-world indices of outcome, coupled with clients stratified according to their primary neurocognitive deficit (attention deficit, verbal memory deficit, executive function deficits), will be necessary to shed light on these issues. Our own experience suggests that mild deficits in attention, verbal list learning or prose recall on neuropsychological measures do not have profound influences on functioning, but moderate to severe deficits can impair functioning substantially in school or work settings, or in the ability to live independently. Deficits in executive function are often more difficult to detect in their impact on everyday function, but can impair the ability of clients to make use of compensatory strategies such as memory books, or alphanumeric pagers.

REFERENCES

Addington, J., & Addington, D. (2000). Neurocognitive and social functioning in schizophrenia. *Schizophrenia Bulletin,* 25, 173–182.

American Psychiatric Association. (1994). *Diagnostic and statistical manual of mental disorders-IV.* Washington, DC: American Psychiatric Press.

Bandura, A. (1969). *Principles of behavior modification.* New York: Holt, Rinehart and Winston.

Bell, M. D., & Bryson, G. (2001). Work rehabilitation in schizophrenia: Does cognitive impairment limit improvement? *Schizophrenia Bulletin, 27*(2), 269–279.

Bellack, A. S., Morrison, R. L., Wixted, J. T., & Mueser, K. T. (1990). An analysis of social competence in schizophrenia. *British Journal of Psychiatry, 156,* 809–818.

Bilder, R. M., Goldman, R. S., Robinson, D., Reiter, G., Bell, L., Bates, J. A., et al. (2000). Neuropsychology of first-episode schizophrenia: Initial characterization and clinical correlates. *The American Journal of Psychiatry, 157*(4), 549–559.

Birchwood, M., Smith, J., Cochrane, R., Wetton, S., & Copestake, S. (1990). The Social Function Scale. The development and validation of a new scale of social adjustment for use in family intervention programmes with schizophrenic patients. *British Journal of Psychiatry, 157,* 853–859.

Bowie, C. R. Leung, W. W., Reichenberg, A., McClure, M. M., Patterson, T. L., Heaton, R. K., et al. (2008). Predicting schizophrenia patients' real-world behavior with specific neuropsychological and functional capacity measures. *Biological Psychiatry 63,* 505–511.

Bowen, L., Wallace, C. J., Glynn, S. M., Nuechterlein, K. H., Lutzker, J. R., & Kuehnel, T. G. (1994). Schizophrenic individuals' cognitive functioning and performance in interpersonal interactions and skills training procedures. *Journal of Psychiatric Research, 28*(3), 289–301.

Brekke, J. S., Hoe, M., Long, J., & Green, M. F. (2007). How neurocognition and social cognition influence functional change during community-based psychosocial rehabilitation for individuals with schizophrenia. *Schizophrenia Bulletin, 33,* 1247–1256.

Brekke, J. S., Kohrt, B., & Green, M. F. (2001). Neuropsychological functioning as a moderator of the relationship between psychosocial functioning and the subjective experience of self and life. *Schizophrenia Bulletin, 27*(4), 697–708.

Couture, S. M., Penn, D. L., & Roberts, D. L. (2006). The functional significance of social cognition in schizophrenia: a review. *Schizophrenia Bulletin, 32,* S44–63.

Dickerson, F., Boronow, J. J., Ringel, N., & Parente, F. (1999). Social functioning and neurocognitive deficits in outpatients with schizophrenia: a 2-year follow-up. *Schizophrenia Research, 37,* 13–20.

Dickinson, D., Bellack, A. S., & Gold, J.M. (2007). Social/communication skills, cognition and vocational functioning in schizophrenia. *Schizophrenia Bulletin, 33,* 1213–1220.

Dickinson, D., Ragland, J. D., Gold, J. M., & Gur, R. C. (2008). General and specific deficits in schizophrenia: Goliath defeats David? *Biological Psychiatry, 64(9),* 823–827.

Gold, J. M., Goldberg, R. W., McNary, S. W., Dixon, L. B., & Lehman, A. F. (2002). Cognitive correlates of job tenure among patients with severe mental illness. *The American Journal of Psychiatry, 159,* 1395–1402.

Granholm, E., McQuaid, J. R., Link, P. C., Fish, S., Patterson, T., & Jeste, D. V. (2008). Neuropsychological predictors of functional outcome in Cognitive Behavioral Social Skills Training for older people with schizophrenia. *Schizophrenia Research, 100,* 133–143.

Green, M. F. (1996). What are the functional consequences of neurocognitive deficits in schizophrenia? *The American Journal of Psychiatry, 153,* 321–330.

Green, M. F., Kern, R. S., Braff, D. L., & Mintz, J. (2000). Neurocognitive deficits and-functional outcome in schizophrenia: Are we measuring the "right stuff"? *Schizophrenia Bulletin, 26*(1), 119–136.

Green, M. F., Kern, R. S., & Heaton, R. K. (2004). Longitudinal studies of cognition and functional outcome in schizophrenia: Implications for MATRICS. *Schizophrenia Research, 72,* 41–51.

Harvey, P. D., Velligan, D. S., & Bellack, A. S. (2007). Performance-based measures of functional skills: usefulness in clinical treatment studies. *Schizophrenia Bulletin, 33,* 1138–1148.

Heinrichs, D. W., Hanlon, T. E., & Carpenter, W. T. (1984). The Quality of Life Scale: An instrument for assessing the schizophrenic deficit syndrome. *Schizophrenia Bulletin 10,* 388–396.

Heinrichs, R. W., & Zakzanis, K. K. (1998). Neurocognitive deficit in schizophrenia: A quantitative review of the evidence. *Neuropsychology, 12*(3), 426–445.

Heaton, R. K., & Pendleton, M. G. (1981). Use of neuropsychological tests to predict adult patients' everyday functioning. *Journal of Consulting and Clinical Psychology, 49,* 807–821.

Jaeger, J., & Douglas, E. (1992). Neuropsychiatric rehabilitation for persistent mental illness. *Psychiatric Quarterly, 63*(1), 71–94.

Kern, R. S., Green, M. F., & Satz, P. (1992). Neuropsychological predictors of skills training for chronic psychiatric patients. *Psychiatry Research, 43,* 223–230.

Keshavan, M. S., Haas, G., Miewald, J., Montrose, D. M., Reddy, R., Schooler, N. R., et al. (2003). Prolonged untreated illness duration from prodromal onset predicts outcome in first episode psychoses. *Schizophrenia Bulletin, 29*(4), 757–769.

Kurtz, M. M., Moberg, P. J., Ragland, J. D., Gur, R. C., & Gur, R. E. (2005). Symptoms versus neurocognitive test performance as predictors of psychosocial status in schizophrenia: A 1- and 4- year prospective study. *Schizophrenia Bulletin, 31*(1), 167–174.

Kurtz, M. M., Wexler, B.E ., Fujimoto, M., Shagan, D. S., & Seltzer, J. C. (2008). Symptoms versus neurocognition as predictors of change in life skills in schizophrenia after outpatient rehabilitation. *Schizophrenia Research, 102,* 303–311.

Lysaker, P. H., Bell, M. D., Zito, W. S., & Bioty, S. M. (1995). Social skills at work: Deficits and predictors of improvement in schizophrenia. *The Journal of Nervous and Mental Disease, 183*(11), 688–692.

Mausbach, B. T., Bowie, C. R., Harvey, P. D., Twamley, E. W., Goldman, S. R., Jeste, D.V., et al. (2008). Usefulness of the UCSD performance-based skills assessment (UPSA) for predicting residential independence in patients with chronic schizophrenia. *Journal of Psychiatric Research, 42,* 320–327.

McGurk, S. R., Mueser, K. T., Harvey, P. D., LaPuglia, R., & Marder, J. (2003). Cognitive and symptom predictors of work outcomes for clients with schizophrenia in supported employment. *Psychiatric Services, 54*(8), 1129–1135.

McKee, M., Hull, J. W., & Smith, T. E. (1997). Cognitive and symptom correlates in participation of social skills training groups. *Schizophrenia Research, 23*(3), 223–229.

Milev, P., Ho, B. C., Arndt, S., & Andreasen, N. C. (2005). Predictive value of neurocognition and negative symptoms on functional outcome in schizophrenia: A longitudinal first-episode study with 7-year follow up. *The American Journal of Psychiatry, 162*(3), 495–506.

Mueser, K. T., Bellack, A. S., Douglas, M. S., & Wade, J. H. (1991). Prediction of social skill acquisition in schizophrenic and major affective disorder patients from memory and symptomatology. *Psychiatry Research, 37,* 281–296.

Patterson, T. L., Goldman, S., McKibbin, C.L., Hughs, T., & Jeste, D.V. (2001a). USCD Performance-based skills assessment: Development of a new measure of everyday functioning for severely mentally ill adults. *Schizophrenia Bulletin,* 27(2), 235–245

Patterson, T. L., Moscona, S., McKibbin, C. L., Davidson, K., & Jeste, D.V . (2001b). Social skills performance assessment among older patients with schizophrenia. *Schizophrenia Research, 48,* 351–360.

Pinkham, A. E., & Penn, D. L. (2006). Neurocognitive and social cognitive predictors of interpersonal skill in schizophrenia. *Psychiatry Research, 30,* 167–178.

Salkever, D. S., Karakus, M. C., Slade, E. P., Harding, C. M., Hough, R. L., Rosenheck, R.A., et al. (2007). Measures and predictors of community-based employment and earnings of persons with schizophrenia in a multisite study. *Psychiatric Services, 58,* 315–324.

Schretlen, D. J., Jayaram, G., Maki, P., Park, K. Abibe, S., & DiCarlo, M. (2000). Demographic, clinical and neurocognitive correlates of everyday functional impairment in severe mental illness. *Journal of Abnormal Psychology, 109,* 134–138.

Sitzer, D. I., Twamley, E. W., Patterson, T. L., & Jeste, D. V. (2008). Multivariate predictors of social-skills in middle-aged and older outpatients with schizophrenia-spectrum disorders. *Psychological Medicine 38,* 755–763.

Silverstein, S., Schenkel, L. S., Valone, C., & Neurnberger, S. W. (1998). Cognitive deficits and psychiatric rehabilitation outcomes in schizophrenia. *Psychiatric Quarterly, 69*(3), 169–191.

Smith, T. E., Hull, J. W., Romanelli, S., Fertuck, E., & Weiss, K. A. (1999). Symptoms and neurocognition as rate limiters in skills training for psychotic patients. *The American Journal of Psychiatry, 156*(11), 1817–1818.

Stirling, J., White, C., Lewis, S., Hopkins, R., Tantam, D., Huddy, A., et al. (2003). Neurocognitive function and outcome in first-episode schizophrenia: A 10-year follow-up of an epidemiological cohort. *Schizophrenia Research, 65,* 75–86.

Tolman, A., & Kurtz, M.M. (2012). The relationship of neurocognition to objective versus subjective quality-of-life. *Schizophrenia Bulletin, 38,* 304–315.

Twamley, E. W., Doshi, R. R., Nayak, G. V., Palmer, B. W., Golshan, S., Heaton, R. K., et al. (2002). Generalized cognitive impairments, ability to perform everyday tasks and level of independence in community living situations of older patients with psychosis. *The American Journal of Psychiatry, 159,* 2013–2020.

Woonings, F. M. J., Appelo, M. T., Kluiter, H., Sloof, C. J., & Van Den Bosch, R. J. (2002).Learning (potential) and social functioning in schizophrenia. *Schizophrenia Research, 59,* 287–295.

BOX 4.1 FUNCTIONAL OUTCOME IN SCHIZOPHRENIA: OVERVIEW

1. Impairment in self-care, social interaction, engaging in recreational activity and work function are more pronounced in schizophrenia than in other forms of severe and persistent mental illness.
2. A wealth of evidence has revealed impairments on measures of attention, verbal and non-verbal memory, problem solving, and other elementary neurocognitive skills in schizophrenia.
3. These deficits have been linked to the degree of functional impairment in clients with schizophrenia, with estimates indicating that neurocognition explains from 20% to 60% of the variance in outcome.
4. Research to date shows the relationship between neurocognitive deficits and outcome is stronger than symptoms and outcome.

BOX 4.2 MEASUREMENT OF FUNCTIONAL STATUS IN SCHIZOPHRENIA

1. Functional status can be measured with performance-based indices of everyday life skills and social-skill. These types of assessments are typically administered via role-play and have the advantage of limited rater bias and an assessment of functional skills based on what can actually be observed.
2. A limitation of performance-based measures is that they are "capacity" measures and provide information on whether a client *can* perform a specific function, not whether they *will* perform a specific function in their home environment.
3. Functional status can also be assessed with the use of clinician-rated scales that depend upon self- and informant-report. The advantage of these scales is that with accurate reporting the clinician may obtain a more accurate assessment of achieved levels of community function.
4. The limitations of clinician-rated scales is that limited insight may impair a client's ability to accurately report their level of adaptive community function. Informant reports may also be biased, and a substantial proportion of middle-aged and older individuals with schizophrenia cannot provide the name of an individual who can report on their functioning.

BOX 4.3 RELATIONSHIPS BETWEEN NEUROCOGNITION AND PERFORMANCE-BASED MEASURES OF FUNCTIONAL STATUS

1. Cross-sectional studies have indicated that a variety of neurocognitive domains have been linked to performance-based measures of ADLs.
2. There is modest evidence for a small effect (10% of explained variance) of negative symptoms on performance-based measures of ADLs.
3. Attention/working memory and processing speed are most closely tied to performance-based social-skill.
4. Negative, but not positive symptoms, have been linked to performance-based social skill.

BOX 4.4 RELATIONSHIPS BETWEEN NEUROCOGNITION AND CLINICIAN-RATED OUTCOME

1. Multiple studies have supported a moderate-sized longitudinal relationship between deficits in cognition measured at illness onset, or after many years of illness, and subsequent outcome when outcome is measured through clinician-ratings of community function.
2. Different studies support links between different aspects of neurocognition (e.g., attention, verbal memory, executive function, motor speed), and thus it remains unclear which elements of neurocognition are most tightly linked to clinician-rated outcome.
3. Negative symptoms ion have been linked to clinician-rated outcome.

BOX 4.5 RELATIONSHIPS BETWEEN NEUROCOGNITION AND EVIDENCE-BASED BEHAVIORAL INTERVENTIONS

1. Current research suggests that attention and verbal memory impairment impede the acquisition of elementary social-skill in social-skill training programs.
2. A range of neurocognitive measures predicts acquisition of work skills in work therapy programs.
3. A range of neurocognitive measures, along with negative symptoms, predict hours worked and wages earned in competitive employment after vocational rehabilitation training.
4. A range of neurocognitive measures, along with positive symptoms, predicts need for on-the-job supports.

CONTINUING EDUCATION QUESTIONS

1. Current estimates suggests that measures of elementary neurocognition, such as attention, memory, problem solving and language, explain ______ of the variance in functional outcome in schizophrenia.
   a. 5%–10%
   b. 20%–60%
   c. 75%–90%
   d. 100%
2. It is estimated that ______ of clients with schizophrenia are not working at any one time.
   a. 25%
   b. 40%
   c. 50%
   d. 75%
3. Current evidence suggests that acquisition of social skills in skills training programs is mediated most strongly by:
   a. attention
   b. verbal memory
   c. non-verbal memory
   d. problem solving
4. Methods for measuring functional outcome in schizophrenia include:
   a. Performance-based measures of ADLs and social-skill
   b. Clinician-rated, interview-based, or self-report measures of outcome
   c. Standardized symptom assessment
   d. a and b
5. Current research suggests that in schizophrenia measures of cognitive function predict:
   a. Acquisition of work skills in work rehabilitation programs.
   b. Need for on-the-job supports.
   c. Number of hours worked and wages earned in competitive employment settings.
   d. All of the above.

5

Cultural Issues in Neuropsychological Testing in Persons with Schizophrenia

DARYL FUJII, Ph.D.

Veterans Affairs Pacific Island Health Care System

Cross-cultural issues in testing have become increasingly important for clinical neuropsychology research as evidenced by the growing number of articles examining this topic (for a review see Fujii, 2007). Professional organizations such as the American Academy of Clinical Neuropsychology (2007) and American Psychological Association (2003) recognize that competent and ethical neuropsychological assessments of ethnic minorities must consider factors such as acculturation, English proficiency, education, socioeconomic status, as well as other demographic variables. Furthermore, test equivalency, norms, and predictive validity of neuropsychological tests should not be assumed across ethnic groups.

This chapter reviews cross-cultural issues in neuropsychological testing in persons with schizophrenia focusing on the largest ethnic minority groups in the United States: Hispanic, African, and Asian Americans. For each ethnic group, a description of important considerations for test selection, administration, and interpretation will be followed by a review of the literature on norms and test development, and predictive validity of neuropsychological testing in persons with schizophrenia. This review is not exhaustive and its recommendations are not comprehensive; rather this chapter is intended to broadly identify issues with each group and summarize the existing neuropsychological literature in individuals with schizophrenia. For a more comprehensive review of testing issues with each ethnic minority group, see Manly (2005) and Manly and Enchemendia (2007) for African Americans; Artiola i Fortuny (2008), Judd et al. (2009), Ponton and Corona-LoMonaco (2007), and Salazar, Perez-Garcia, and Puente (2007) for Hispanics, and Fujii (2010), Fujii and Wong (2005), Wong and Fujii (2004) for Asian Americans. See also Marcopulos and Fujii (this volume) for a more thorough coverage of testing and report writing in persons with schizophrenia. Finally, implications of cross-cultural neuropsychological findings for conceptualizing neurocognition in schizophrenia will be discussed.

HISPANICS

Hispanic Americans are the largest ethnic minority group in the United States with about 43 million people accounting for 14.8% of the population. There is much ethnic diversity among U.S. Hispanics, with the overwhelming majority being of Mexican heritage (64%), followed by Puerto Rican (9%), Central American (7.6%), South American (5.5%), Cuban (3.4%), and Dominican (2.8%), while (7.7%) are identified as other. About 40% of Hispanic Americans are foreign born and 78% speak Spanish in the home (Ethnicity and Ancestry Branch Population Division U.S. Census Bureau, 2006). Hispanics have the highest percentage of persons over 25 with less than 5 years education (6.9%) and the lowest percentage of high school graduates (60.3%) in comparison to other U.S. ethnic groups (Whites are 0.4% and 90.6%, respectively) (Infoplease, n.d.).

Given the relatively high percentage of foreign-born Hispanic Americans, language and acculturation issues are highly salient for neuropsychological testing with this population and measures have been developed or translated to address these issues. For example, Ponton and Corona-LoMonaco (2007) recommend assessing for language skills qualitatively through open ended questions during conversation and/or quantitatively using the Woodcock Language Proficiency Battery-Revised, Spanish Form (WLPB-R) (Woodcock & Munoz-Sandoval, 1993). The Short Acculturation Scale of Hispanics (Marin, Sabogal, Marin, Otero-Sabogal, & Perez-Stable, 1987) or Cultural Identity Scales (Felix-Ortiz, Newcomb, & Myers, 1994) are recommended measures for acculturation. For persons requiring translated tests, the Bateria Neuropsicologica en Espanol (Artiola i Fortuny, 2000) and Bateria III Woodcock-Munoz (2005) are examples of neuropsychological tests that have been developed for Spanish speakers (for a review see Salazar et al., 2007).

To address the issue of test selection, Ponton and Corona-LoMonaco (2007) developed a decision tree to assist clinicians in determining the need for an interpreter or use of tests translated into Spanish for both monolingual and bilingual Hispanics. In this heuristic, everyone should be assessed for language skill, language spoken at home, and acculturation. Persons scoring below the 25th%ile on the WLPB-R should be tested with a bilingual clinician. Those scoring at or above the 25th%ile with high acculturation and educated in English should be tested in English, whereas those with low acculturation and foreign educated should be tested in Spanish. A bilingual assessment should be considered for those with low to moderate acculturation.

Despite the availability of translated tests, selecting appropriate norms can be problematic given the diversity of the Hispanic population, whereby a

Hispanic client may not match the demographic characteristics of the standardization sample (Salazar et al. 2007). The majority of research on Hispanics is with Mexican Americans with fewer studies on Hispanics from the Caribbean, other Central, and South Americans. Thus, clinicians should be cautious when searching the literature for appropriate norms.

Another important issue for test interpretation is level of education and illiteracy, as many adult immigrant Hispanics have lower levels of educational attainment, although there again is considerable heterogeneity among countries of origin (Ardila & Rosselli, 2007). Thus clinicians should be familiar with the literature on illiteracy which significantly impacts performance on verbal working memory, verbal abstraction, verbal memory, calculations, visuoconstructional skills, and executive functioning (for a review see Ardila & Rosselli, 2007). The use of norms stratified by age and education, the latter at lower levels, are also important for test interpretation (Gasquoine, 2001). By contrast, one study found that Hispanics born in the United States demonstrated test scores comparable to Whites (Bernard, 1989).

The literature on the neuropsychology of Hispanics with schizophrenia is sparse with findings generally mirroring studies with normal Hispanic populations. Similar to efforts by many researchers to translate western neuropsychological tests into Spanish, two neurocognitive batteries have been developed or validated for persons with schizophrenia or other psychiatric disorders: Screen for Cognitive Impairment in Psychiatry (SCIP-S) (Pino et al., 2008) and NEUROPSI (Hilda-Picasso, Ostrosky, & Nicolini, 2005). Construct validity of the tests was demonstrated through correlations with existing neuropsychological tests and discriminating individuals with schizophrenia from normals.

One study provided evidence for the predictive validity of neuropsychological tests. Jeste et al. (2005) found that neurocognition was the strongest predictor of everyday functioning in both Mexican Americans (MA) and Whites, with level of acculturation the second strongest predictor for MA. Furthermore, MA who opted to be tested in English demonstrated similar test scores to Whites.

AFRICAN AMERICANS

According to recent U.S. Census estimates, there are about 41.1 million African Americans living in the United States or approximately 13.5% of the population (U.S. Census Bureau, 2008a). Although most African Americans are born in the United States, a growing minority (approximately 13%) are immigrants, with about 2.5 million or 6.1% originating from the Caribbean (U.S. Census Bureau, 2008b) and 7.1% immigrating from sub-Saharan Africa (U.S. Census Bureau, 2008c). There is considerable diversity within this immigrant population. For example, 55% of Caribbean Blacks come from Jamaica and Haiti with French Creole being their native language (Kent, 2007). Their educational attainment is similar to native African Americans with one study reporting similar neuropsychological profiles. For both Caribbean Blacks and African Americans, reading level was the strongest predictor of test performance (Byrd, Sanchez, &

Manly, 2005). The top five countries of origin for sub-Saharan Africans are Nigeria (18%), Ethiopia (12%), Ghana (9%), Liberia (7%), and Somalia (7%) (Kent, 2007). Although only 17% of African immigrants spoke English at home, two-thirds are reported to be proficient in English. African immigrants tend to be highly educated; 38% have a bachelor's degree or higher, which is higher than Whites and second only to Asians (Kent, 2007).

Studies have generally reported African Americans perform lower than Whites on a broad array of neuropsychological tests with scores ranging from 0.25 (Johnson-Selfridge, Zalewski, & Aboudarham, 1998) to 0.71 standard deviations lower (Gladsjo et al., 1999) (for a review see Gasquione, 2009). Numerous factors have been shown to contribute to lower scores on neuropsychological testing, including acculturation (Manly et al., 1998) and quality of education (as assessed by reading level) (Manly, Jacobs, Touradji, Small, & Stern, 2002), the latter reported to be the most precise indicator for deriving neuropsychological test performance expectations . Stereotypic threat (Steele, 1997) and linguistic variation, for example, speaking African American English (Qualls, 2007) may also be contributing factors. In a related area, social and environmental factors such as mother's socioeconomic status and parenting practices (Phillips, Brooks-Gunn, Duncan, Klebanow, & Crane, 2000), lowered teacher expectations (Ferguson & Brown, 2000), and social retribution for doing well in school can negatively affect academic motivation (Jencks & Phillips, 2000) and have been associated with lower academic achievement.

To accommodate for the lower scores and to reduce false positives, Heaton, Miller, Taylor and Grant (2004) developed raced-based norms for African Americans. Although there are no formal guidelines for using demographically-corrected norms, recommendations from the American Psychological Association sponsored Multicultural Problem Solving Summit indicated that these norms would be *useful* to identify acquired neurocognitive impairments in premorbidly normal adults who are natives with English as a primary language, *sometimes useful* for young adults who have not completed their education and adults with a mild developmental disorder or persons with different linguistic or cultural backgrounds, and *not useful* and *not recommended* for capital punishment cases or for identifying possible acquired impairment in persons with significant development disabilities including schizophrenia (Romero et al., 2009).

Thus when testing African Americans, clinicians should use quality of education as an indicator of expected performance on neuropsychological tests. Measures of acculturation (Snowden & Hines, 1999) can also help in determining expectations for test scores. Assessing English proficiency would be important for immigrant Blacks, and more pertinent for persons from the Caribbean versus sub-Saharan Africa. Proficiency can be evaluated qualitatively through responses to open ended questions during the interview, or quantitatively through measures such as the Bilingual Verbal Abilities Test (BVAT) (Munoz-Sandoval, Cummins, Alvarado, & Ruef, 1998). If a person is not deemed to be proficient in English, then testing should be administered through an interpreter. Clinicians should avoid using race-based norms when testing African Americans with schizophrenia.

The literature on neuropsychological testing in African Americans with schizophrenia is sparse as most studies involve mixed ethnic samples. Similar to the general neuropsychology literature, studies have reported lower scores for African Americans with schizophrenia when compared to Whites on measures including executive functioning, language, spatial memory and visual processing, vigilance, and psychomotor speed (Lewine & Caudle, 2000; Harvey, Fortuny, Vester-Blockland, & Smedt, 2002). However, significant differences disappear when controlling for education. Similarly, African Americans were found to score lower than Whites on perception of emotion, facial recognition, and delayed face memory (Brekke, Nakagami, Kee, & Green, 2005; Pinkham et al., 2008). Again, significant differences disappeared when faces of African Americans were used as stimuli, suggesting a bias in testing materials (Pinkham et al., 2008). Brekke et al. (2005) reported no differences on a composite score of select neuropsychological tests in comparison to Whites.

Genetic loading for neurocognition in African Americans with schizophrenia was examined in a large multicenter study by Calkins et al. (2010). African Americans with schizophrenia, relatives of these patients, and normals were compared on a broad array of neuropsychological tests. The researchers found that the sample of people with schizophrenia performed worse than relatives, who in turn performed worse than normals in all neurocognitive domains except for language. These findings provided evidence for high heritability for general neurocognition which is similar to Whites. Heritabilities were highest for abstraction/flexibility, verbal memory, facial memory, spatial processing, and emotional processing. Taken together, these preliminary findings suggest that neuropsychological test scores between African Americans with schizophrenia and Whites with schizophrenia are comparable when controlling for age and testing biases, and heritability for neurocognitive deficits is also similar.

ASIAN AMERICANS

Asian Americans comprise 4.2% of the U.S. population. They are highly heterogeneous with 24 ethnicities listed in the 2000 U.S. Census. The 10 most populous Asian ethnicities in descending order are (1) Chinese, (2) Filipino, (3) Asian Indian, (4) Vietnamese, (5) Korean, (6) Japanese, (7) Cambodian, (8) Hmong, (9) Laotian, and (10) Pakistani. Although Asian Americans tend to share cultural values such as an emphasis on group versus individual orientation, interpersonal harmony and cooperation, well-defined roles, and status based on age (respect for elders) (Iwamasa, 1997), many differences exist based upon country of origin (Fujii, 2010). For example, it is estimated that 69% of Asian Americans are foreign born (Reeves & Bennett, 2004). Percentages range from a low of 39% for Japanese Americans to 78% of Asian Indians. A related issue is English proficiency. It is estimated that 40% of Asian Americans speak English less than "very well" with a high of 62% for Vietnamese. The percentage of Asian

Americans with a bachelor's degree ranges from 63.9% for Asian Indians to 7.5% for Hmong and Laotian Americans (Reeves & Bennett, 2004).

Given the strong tendency toward recent immigration for many Asian Americans, similar to Hispanics, acculturation, language, and education are important factors when testing, and interpreters may be essential. However, there are some important differences. First, unlike Hispanics originating from different countries who speak dialects of Spanish, there is no universal language spoken by Asians emmigrating from different countries. Each ethnicity speaks a language unique to that country. Related to this diversity of languages spoken, is the difficulty in developing translated tests. Indeed, most translated tests are translated into Korean (Chey & Park, 2010), Chinese (Chan, Leung, & Cheung, 2010), Japanese (Tsushima, Tsushima,& Fujii., 2010), and Asian Indian languages (Kumar, 2010), with very few tests translated into Southeast Asian languages such as Vietnamese, Laotian, Hmong, Thai, Cambodian, and Filipino (Fujii, 2010).

Another important issue with Southeast Asian Americans is screening for Post Traumatic Stress Disorder (PTSD). Many of the older Vietnamese, Laotians, Hmong, and Cambodians have witnessed the atrocities of war first hand or experienced emotional, physical, or sexual abuse while living in refugee camps or immigrating to the United States. Severe PTSD can mimic or contribute to the development of psychosis (Morrison, Frame, & Larkin, 2003) and is also associated with cognitive deficits, particularly memory problems (Bremner, 2006).

The following are guidelines for performing a neuropsychological assessment with Asian Americans. The first step is to evaluate for English proficiency. It can be assumed that most Asian Americans who are born, raised, and educated in the United States are English proficient. For those who are immigrants, it will be important to ask at what age they immigrated, what primary language is spoken at home, and past placement in English as a Second Language (ESL) programs. Command of English can be informally evaluated by asking open ended questions or quantitatively through measures such as the Bilingual Verbal Abilities Test that compares verbal skills in English versus a person's native language (Munoz-Sandoval, Cummins, Alvarado, & Ruef, 1998). Second, the clinician should assess for acculturation, which can be evaluated quantitatively through measures such as the Asian American Multidimensional Acculturation Scale (Gim-Chung, Kim, & Abreu, 2004), or informally by asking questions from the test such as foods eaten and enjoyed, ethnicity of friends, cultural activities, and generation.

If a person is born in the United Stated, English is the primary language spoken at home, or the person is an immigrant, but attending a university, then it is recommended that testing be administered in English. Interpreters and translated tests should be used for first generation Asians who were educated in Asia, and those with partial education in the United States who speak their native language at home, and/or are less acculturated. All persons who immigrated should be asked whether they would prefer an interpreter.

If an interpreter is necessary, then the clinician should administer translated tests that are validated and normed in the person's native language. For a list of translated and normed tests, clinicians can refer to the American Academy of Clinical Neuropsychology (AACN) Multicultural Reference (Fujii, 2007) or *The Neuropsychology of Asian Americans* (Fujii, 2010).

If normed tests are not available, the clinician can still attain useful "ball park" information through administering tests demonstrating cross-cultural validity, such as Color Trails, Digit Span, and the Rey Auditory Verbal Learning Test (RAVLT), which were administered in the World Health Organization (WHO) studies (Maj et al., 1994). Although discouraged by many, "spot" translations of the memory tests such as the RAVLT can provide useful information, particularly if the person scores within the normal range as this type of performance would rule out impairment. "Ball park" test expectation can be determined by IQ scores attained by persons in that country (see Lynn, 2006). When writing reports, the non-standardized nature of the evaluation and test materials should be described and caveats for test interpretation emphasized.

Finally, for Southeast Asian immigrants, PTSD should always be assessed. One way of screening for possible traumatic experiences is to ask the person to describe in detail their immigration experience. Inquiries can then be made about past or current PTSD symptoms using *DSM-IV* criteria.

In comparison to African American and Hispanics with schizophrenia, there are many more studies on neurocognition in Asians with schizophrenia. However, unlike studies on African Americans and Hispanics, this research was conducted in Asian countries. There is only one study on test translation with the Brief Assessment of Cognition in Schizophrenia (BACS-J) translated and validated in Japanese (Kaneda et al., 2007).

Correlations between neuropsychological test scores in Asians with schizophrenia and severity and type of psychotic symptoms generally mirror findings with Whites. For example, neurocognitive deficits have been found to be worse in deficit versus nondeficit Chinese with schizophrenia (Wang, Yao, Kirkpatrick, Shi, & Yi., 2008) and in Indians with schizophrenia versus bipolar disorder (Pradhan, Chakrabarti, Nehra, & Mankotia., 2008), and associated with negative symptoms in Indians with schizophrenia (McCreadie, Latha, Thara, Padmavathi, & Ayankaran, 1997). Impaired executive functioning has been associated with severity of negative symptoms in Japanese with schizophrenia (Ihara, Berrios, & McKenna, 2003) and theory of mind tasks in Koreans with schizophrenia (Chung, Kang, Shin, Yoo, & Kwon, 2008).

Similarly, predictive validity studies correlating neurocognition with functionality in individuals with schizophrenia parallel findings in the United States. For example, neurocognition has been associated with poorer quality of life in Singaporeans and Japanese with schizophrenia (Woon, Chia, Chan, & Sim, 2010; Matsui, Sumiyoshi, Aria, Higuchi, & Kurachi, 2008), and medication adherence in Japanese with schizophrenia (Maeda et al., 2006). Impairments in reading social cues have been correlated with social functioning in Chinese with schizophrenia (Zhu et al., 2007).

IMPLICATIONS OF CROSS-CULTURAL FINDINGS

An integration of findings across different ethnic groups suggests that neurocognitive profiles in persons of color with schizophrenia are consistent with studies conducted primarily on White populations. A multicenter study of African Americans with schizophrenia, their relatives, and normals found worsening neurocognitive functioning with higher genetic loading. Studies in several Asian countries reported associations with deficit and negative symptoms and impaired neurocognition, and more pronounced cognitive impairment in persons with schizophrenia versus bipolar disorder. Studies with both Hispanics and Asians report predictive validity of neurocognition for functional outcome. Taken together, the emerging cross-cultural literature on neurocognition in schizophrenia supports a robust association between neurocognition and genetic loading, severity of symptoms and illness, and functional abilities. The implication is that schizophrenia is indeed a neurocognitive disease with functional outcome mediated by cognition.

CONCLUSIONS

In summary, awareness of cross-cultural issues in testing persons with schizophrenia is both a competency and an ethical issue. Clinicians must be familiar with testing issues for the ethnic group of the individual with schizophrenia and apply this knowledge to perform competent neuropsychological assessments. For both Hispanics and Asians, heterogeneity, language, acculturation, test selection, appropriate norms, illiteracy, and use of interpreters are salient issues. For Asians, test selection is more complicated as each Asian ethnicity speaks a different language, many which do not have translated tests or appropriate norms. For African Americans in general, acculturation, language, and heterogeneity are not as pronounced an issue, although 13.2% are immigrants. The most salient issues are quality of education and selection of norms, although preliminary evidence suggests that the latter may not be an issue for persons with schizophrenia as studies do not report differences when controlling for education or stimuli. The cross-cultural neuropsychological literature on persons with schizophrenia is still emerging. However, preliminary findings are consistent with those found in White populations with neurocognition demonstrating predictive validity for everyday functioning, correlating strongly with severity of symptoms and illness, and being a highly heritable trait in persons with schizophrenia.

REFERENCES

American Academy of Clinical Neuropsychology. (2007). American Academy of Clinical Neuropsychology (AACN) practice guidelines for neuropsychological assessment and consultation. *The Clinical Neuropsychologist, 21*, 209–231.

American Psychological Association. (2003). Guidelines for multicultural education, training, research, practice, and organizational change for psychologists. *American Psychologist, 58*, 377–402.

Ardila, A., & Rosselli, M. (2007). Illiterates and cognition: The impact of education. In B. Uzzell, M. Ponton, & A. Ardila (Eds.), *International handbook of cross-cultural neuropsychology* (pp. 181–198). Mahwah, NJ: Erlbaum.

Artiola i Fortuny, L. (2000). *Manual de normas y procedimientos para la bacteria neuropsicologica en español.* The Netherlands: Swets & Zeitlinger.

Artiola i Fortuny, L. (2008). Research and practice: Ethical issues with immigrant adults and children. In J. Morgan & J Ricker (Eds.), *Textbook of clinical neuropsychology* (pp. 960–982). New York: Psychology Press.

Bernard, L. (1989). Halstead-Reitan neuropsychological test battery of Black, Hispanic, and white young adult males from poor academic backgrounds. *Archives of Clinical Neuropsychology, 4,* 267–274.

Brekke, J., Nakagami, E., Kee, K., & Green, M. (2005). Cross-ethnic differences in perception of emotion in schizophrenia. *Schizophrenia Research, 77,* 289–298.

Bremner, J. (2006). The relationship between cognitive and brain changes in posttraumatic stress disorder. *Annals of the New York Academy of Science, 107,* 80–86.

Byrd, D., Sanchez, D., & Manly, J. (2005). Neuropsychological test performance among Caribbean-born and U.S.-born African American Elderly: the role of age, education and reading level. *Journal of Clinical and Experimental Neuropsychology, 27,* 1056–1069.

Calkins, M., Tepper, P., Gur, R., Ragland, J., Klei, L., Weiner, H., & Gur, R. (2010). Project among African-Americans to explore risks for schizophrenia (PAARTNERS): Evidence for impairment and heritability of neurocognitive functioning in families of schizophrenia patients. *American Journal of Psychiatry, 167,* 459–472.

Chan, A., Leung, W., & Cheung, M. C. (2010). Neuropsychology in China. In D. Fujii (Ed.), *Neuropsychology of Asian-Americans* (pp. 201–218). New York: Psychology Press.

Chey, J., & Park, H. Y. (2010). Neuropsychology in Korea. In D. Fujii (Ed.), *Neuropsychology of Asian-Americans.* (pp. 247–268). New York: Psychology Press.

Chung, Y. S., Kang, D. H., Shin, N. Y., Yoo, S. Y., & Kwon, J. S. (2008). Deficit of theory of mind in individuals at ultra-high-risk for schizophrenia. *Schizophrenia Research, 99(1-3),* 111–118.

Ethnicity and Ancestry Branch Population Division U.S. Census Bureau. (2006). *Hispanics in the U.S.* Retrieved May 15, 2010, from http://www.census.gov/population/www/socdemo/hispanic/files/Internet_Hispanic_in_US_2006

Felix-Ortiz, M., Newcomb, M., & Myers, H. (1994). A multidimensional measure of cultural identity for Latino and Latina adolescents. *Hispanic Journal of Behavioral Science, 16,* 99–115.

Ferguson, R., & Brown, J. (2000). Certification test scores: Teacher quality, and student achievement. In D. W. Grissmer & J. M. Ross (Eds.), *Analytic issues in the assessment of student achievement* (NCES 2000-050; pp. 133–156). Washington, DC: U.S Department of Education National Center for Education Statistics.

Fujii, D. (Ed.). (2010). Introduction. In D. Fujii (Ed.), *The neuropsychology of Asian-Americans* (pp. 1–10). New York: Psychology Press.

Fujii, D. (2007). Multicultural references. Retrieved on July 21, 2010, from http://www.theaacn.org/position_papers/

Fujii, D. E., & Wong, T. M. (2005). Neuropsychological assessment with Asian-Americans immigrants: Recommendations for meeting Daubert standards. *Journal of Forensic Neuropsychology, 4*(4), 3–31.

Gasquione, P. (2001). Research in clinical neuropsychology with Hispanic American participants: A review. *The Clinical Neuropsychologist, 15,* 2–12.

Gasquoine, P. (2009). Race-norming of neuropsychological tests. *Neuropsychology Review, 19,* 250–262.

Gim-Chung, R., Kim, B., & Abreu, J. (2004). Asian American multidimensional acculturation scale: Development, factor analysis reliability, and validity. *Cultural Diversity and Ethnic Minority Psychology, 10,* 66–80.

Gladsjo, J., Schuman, C., Evans, J., Peavy, G., Miller, S., & Heaton, R. (1999). Norms for letter and category fluency: Demographic corrections for age, education, and ethnicity. *Assessment, 6,* 147–178.

Harvey, P., Fortuny, L., Vester-Blockland, E., & Smedt, G. (2002). Cross-national cognitive assessment in schizophrenia clinical trials: A feasibility study. *Schizophrenia Research, 59,* 243–251.

Heaton, R., Miller, S., Taylor, M., & Grant, I. (2004). *Revised comprehensive norms for an expanded Halstead-Reitan battery: Demographically adjusted neuropsychological norms for African American and Caucasian adults.* Odessa, FL: Psychological Assessment Resources.

Hilda-Picasso, H., Ostrosky, F., & Nicolini, H. (2005). Sensitivity and specificity of a neuropsychological instrument in the evaluation of schizophrenia subtypes: A study with a Spanish speaking population. *Acta Espanol Psiquiatry, 33*(2), 87–95.

Ihara, H., Berrios, G., & McKenna. (2003). The association between negative and dysexecutive syndromes in schizophrenia: A cross-cultural study. *Behavioral Neurology, 14,* 63–74.

Infoplease (n.d.). *Educational attainment by race and Hispanic origin, 1940–2007.* Retrieved May 22, 2010, from http://www.infoplease.com/ipa/A0774057.html

Iwamasa, G. (1997). Asian Americans. In S. Friedman (Ed.), *Cultural issues in the treatment of anxiety* (pp. 99–129). New York: Guilford Press.

Jencks, C., & Phillips, M. (Eds.). (2000). *The black-white test score gap.* Washington, DC: Brookings Institution Press.

Jeste, N., Moore, D., Goldman, S., Bucardo, J., Davila-Fraga, W., Golshan, S. Jest, D., & Patterson, T. (2005). Predictors of everyday functioning among older Mexican Americans vs. Anglo-Americans with schizophrenia. *Journal of Clinical Psychiatry, 66,* 1304–1311.

Johnson-Selfridge, M., Zalewski, C., & Aboudarham, J. (1998). The relationship between ethnicity and word fluency. *Archives of Clinical Neuropsychology, 13,* 319–325.

Judd, T., Capetillo, D., Carrion-Baralt, J., Marmol, L., San Miguel-Montes, L., Navarette, M., … Valdes, J., & the NAN Policy and Planning Committee. (2009). Professional considerations for improving the neuropsychological evaluation for Hispanics: A National Academy of Neuropsychology education paper. *Archives of Clinical Neuropsychology, 24,* 127–136.

Kaneda, Y., Sumiyoshi, T., Keefe, R., Ishimoto, Y., Numata, S., & Ohmori, T. (2007). Brief assessment of cognition in schizophrenia: Validation of the Japanese version. *Psychiatry and Clinical Neurosciences, 61,* 602–609.

Kent, M. (2007). Immigration and America's Black population. *Population Bulletin, 62*(4), 1–16.

Kumar, K. (2010). Neuropsychology in India. In D. Fujii (Ed.), *Neuropsychology of Asian-Americans* (pp. 219–236). New York: Psychology Press.

Lewine, R., & Caudle, J. (2000). Racial effects on neuropsychological functioning in schizophrenia. *American Journal of Psychiatry, 157,* 2038–2040.

Lynn, E. (2006). *Race differences in intelligence: An evolutionary analysis.* Augusta, GA: Washington Summit.

Maeda, K., Kasai, K., Watanabe, A., Henomatsu, K., Rogers, & M., Kato, N. (2006). Effects of subjective reasoning and neurocognition on medication adherence for persons with schizophrenia. *Psychiatric Services, 57,* 1203–1205.

Maj, M., Satz, P., Janssen, R., Zaudig, R., Starace, F., D'Elia, L., … Sartorius, N. (1993). WHO neuropsychiatric AIDS study, cross-sectional phase II: Neuropsychological and neurological findings. *Archives of General Psychiatry, 51,* 51–61.

Manly, J. (2005). Advantages and disadvantages of separate norms for African-Americans. *The Clinical Neuropsychologist, 19,* 270–275.

Manly, J., & Enchemendia R. (2007). Race-specific norms: Using the model of hypertension to understand issues of race, culture, and education in neuropsychology. *Archives of Clinical Neuropsychology, 22,* 319–325.

Manly, J., Jacobs, J., Touradji, P., Small, S., & Stern, Y. (2002). Reading level attenuates differences in neuropsychological test performance between African American and White elders. *Journal of the International Neuropsychological Society, 8,* 341–348.

Manly, J., Miller, S., Heaton, R., Byrd, D., Reilly, J., Velasquez, R., … Grant, I., & the HIV Neurobehavioral Research Center (HNRC) Group. (1998). The effect of African-American acculturaltion on neuropsychological test performance in normal and HIV-positive individuals. *Journal of the International Neuropsychological Society, 4,* 291–302.

Marin, G., Sabogal, F., Marin, B,, Otero-Sabogal, R., & Perez-Stable, E. (1987). Development of a short acculturation scale for Hispanics. *Hispanic Journal of Behavioral Sciences, 9,* 183–205.

Matsui, M., Sumiyoshi, T., Arai, H., Higuchi, Y., & Kurachi, M. (2008). Cognitive functioning related to quality of life in schizophrenia. *Progress in Neuro-Psychopharmacology and Biological Psychiatry, 32,* 280–287.

McCreadie, R., Latha, S., Thara, R., Padmavathi, R., & Ayankaran, J. (1997). Poor memory, negative symptoms and abnormal movements in never-treated Indian patients with schizophrenia. *British Journal of Psychiatry, 171,* 360–363.

Morrison, A., Frame, L., & Larkin, W. (2003). Relationships between trauma and psychosis: A review and integration. *British Journal of Clinical Psychology, 42,* 331–353.

Munoz-Sandoval, A., Cummins, J., Alvarado, C., & Ruef, M. (1998). *Bilingual verbal abilities tests.* Itasca, IL: Riverside Publishing.

Phillips, M., Brooks-Gunn, J., Duncan, G., Klebanow, P., & Crane, J. (2000). Family background, parenting practices, and the black-white test score gap. In C. Jencks & M. Phillips (Eds.), *The black-white test score gap* (pp. 103–148). Washington, DC: Brookings Institution Press.

Pinkham, A. E., Sasson, N., Calkins, M., Richard, J., Hughett, P., & Gur, R. (2008). The other-race effect in face processing among African American and Caucasian individuals with schizophrenia. *American Journal of Psychiatry, 165,* 639–645.

Pino, O., Guilera, G. Rojo, J., Gomez-Benito, J., Bernardo, M., Crespo-Facorro, B., … Rejas, J. on behalf of the Spanish Working Group in Cognitive Function. (2008). Spanish version of the screen for cognitive impairment in psychiatry (SCIP-S): Psychometric properties of a brief scale for cognitive evaluation in schizophrenia. *Schizophrenia Research, 99*(1–3), 139–148.

Ponton, M., & Corona-LoMonaco, M. (2007). Cross-cultural issues in neuropsychology:

Assessment of the Hispanic patient. In B. Uzzell, M. Ponton, & A. Ardila (Eds.), *International handbook of cross-cultural neuropsychology* (pp. 265–282). Mahwah, NJ: Erlbaum

Pradhan, B., Chakrabarti, S., Nehra, R., & Mankotia, A. (2008). Cognitive functions in bipolar affective disorder and schizophrenia: Comparison. *Psychiatry and Clinical Neurosciences, 62*, 515–525.

Qualls, C. D. (2007). Speech, language, and neuropsychological testing: Implications for African Americans. In B. Uzzell, M. Ponton & A. Ardila (Eds.), *International handbook of cross-cultural neuropsychology* (pp. 127–144). Mahwah, NJ: Erlbaum.

Reeves, T. J., & Bennett, C. E. (2004). *We the people: Asians in the United States*. Washington, DC: U.S. Census Bureau.

Romero, H., Lageman, S., Kamath, V., Irani, F., Sim, A., Suarez, P., … and the Summit participants (2009). Challenges in the neuropsychological assessment of ethnic minorities: Summit proceedings. *The Clinical Neuropsychologist, 23*, 761–779.

Salazar, G., Perez-Garcia, M., & Puente, A. (2007). Clinical neuropsychology of Spanish speakers: The challenge and pitfalls of a neuropsychology of a heterogeneous population. In B. Uzzell, M. Ponton, & A. Ardila (Eds.), *International handbook of cross-cultural neuropsychology* (pp. 283–302). Mahwah, NJ: Erlbaum.

Snowden, L., & Hines, A. (1999). A scale to assess African American acculturation. *Journal of Black Psychology, 25*, 36–47.

Steele, C. (1997). A threat in the air: How stereotypes shape intellectual identity and performance. *The American Psychologist, 52*, 613–629.

Tsushima, W., Tsushima, V., & Fujii, D. (2010). Neuropsychology of Japanese Americans. In D. Fujii (Ed.), Neuropsychology of Asian-Americans (pp. 107–130). New York: Psychology Press.

U.S. Census Bureau. (2008a). African Americans by the numbers. Retrieved on May 20, 2010, from http://www.infoplease.com/spot/bhmcensus1.html

U.S. Census Bureau. (2008b). United States — Selected Population Profile in the United States (West Indian (excluding Hispanic origin groups . *2008 American Community Survey 1-Year Estimates*. Retrieved on July 21, 2010, from http://factfinder.census.gov/servlet/IPTable?_bm=y&-reg=ACS_2008_1YR_G00_S0201:575;ACS_2008_1YR_G00_S0201PR:575;ACS_2008_1YR_G00_S0201T:575;ACS_2008_1YR_G00_S0201TPR:575&-qr_name=ACS_2008_1YR_G00_S0201&-qr_name=ACS_2008_1YR_G00_S0201PR&-qr_name=ACS_2008_1YR_G00_S0201T&-qr_name=ACS_2008_1YR_G00_S0201TPR&-ds_name=ACS_2008_1YR_G00_&-TABLE_NAMEX=&-ci_type=A&-charIterations=423&-geo_id=01000US&-format=&-_lang=en

U.S. Census Bureau. (2008c). United States — Selected Population Profile in the United States (Subsaharan African). *2008 American Community Survey 1-Year Estimates*. Retrieved July 21, 2010, from http://factfinder.census.gov/servlet/IPTable?_bm=y&-reg=ACS_2008_1YR_G00_S0201:562;ACS_2008_1YR_G00_S0201PR:562;ACS_2008_1YR_G00_S0201T:562;ACS_2008_1YR_G00_S0201TPR:562&-qr_name=ACS_2008_1YR_G00_S0201&-qr_name=ACS_2008_1YR_G00_S0201PR&-qr_name=ACS_2008_1YR_G00_S0201T&-qr_name=ACS_2008_1YR_G00_S0201TPR&-ds_name=ACS_2008_1YR_G00_&-TABLE_NAMEX=&-ci_type=A&-redoLog=true&-charIterations=463&-geo_id=01000US&-format=&-_lang=en

Wang, X., Yao, S., Kirkpatrick, B., Shi, C., & Yi, J. (2008). Psychopathology and neuropsychological impairments in deficit and nondeficit schizophrenia of Chinese origin. *Psychiatry Research, 158*, 195–205.

Wong, T. M., & Fujii, D. E. (2004). Neuropsychological assessment with Asian-Americans: Demographic factors, culture diversity, and practical guidelines. *Applied Neuropsychology, 11*, 23–36.

Woodcock, R., & Munoz-Sandoval, A. (2005). *Bateria III*. Itasca, IL: Riverside.

Woodcock, R., & Munoz-Sandoval, A. (1993). *Woodcock Language Proficiency Battery-Revised, Spanish Form* (Suppl. Manual). Chicago: Riverside.

Woon, P. S., Chia, M. Y., Chan, W. Y., & Sim, K. (2010). Neurocognitive, clinical and functional correlates of subjective quality of life in Asian outpatients with schizophrenia. *Progress in Neuro-Psychopharmacology and Biological Psychiatry, 34*, 463–468.

Zhu, C. Y., Lee, T. M., Li, X. S., Jing, S. C., Wang, Y. G., & Wang, K. (2007). Impairments of social cues recognition and social functioning in Chinese people with schizophrenia. *Psychiatric Clinics in Neurosciences, 61*, 149–158.

BOX 5.1 HISPANIC AMERICANS

1. Hispanic Americans are the largest ethnic minority accounting for about 14.8% of the American population. About 40% are foreign born with most emigrating from Mexico (64%).
2. Compared to other ethnicities, Hispanic Americans have the lowest percentage of high school graduates (60.3%) and highest percentage of adults with less than 5 years of education (6/9%).
3. Given these demographics, English proficiency, acculturation, level of education, and illiteracy are salient issues for many Hispanic Americans.
4. To address these issues, numerous tests have been translated into Spanish and decision-trees have been developed to assist the clinician in determining the need for an interpreter and use of translated tests. Clinicians should have knowledge of a person's country of origin and illiteracy and use of appropriate norms.
5. The neuropsychological literature on Hispanics with schizophrenia is sparse. Several specialized tests have been translated into Spanish and preliminary findings support the validity of neuropsychological tests for predicting everyday functioning.

BOX 5.2 AFRICAN AMERICANS

1. African Americans comprise 13.4% of the U.S. population. Although most are American born, a growing minority (13%) are immigrants originating primarily from sub-Saharan Africa (7.1%) and the Caribbean (6.1%). Caribbean Africans are similar to American Africans in education levels and test scores, while sub-Saharan Africans tend to be highly educated and about two-thirds are proficient in English.
2. Studies consistently report African Americans perform lower than whites on a broad array of neuropsychological tests. Many factors including acculturation and quality of education have been identified or speculated to contribute to lower scores.
3. African American norms have been developed to adjust for lower scores and reduce false-positive rates. Although not formal, general guidelines for using race-based norms have been suggested. Evaluating for quality of education (as assessed by reading level) and acculturation may assist in determining expected test scores.
4. Similar to Hispanics, the neuropsychological literature on African Americans with schizophrenia is sparse. Preliminary findings suggest that race norm differences disappear in the schizophrenic population. Also, there is a high heritability for neurocognition in African Americans with schizophrenia similar to findings with Whites.

BOX 5.3 ASIAN AMERICANS

1. Asian Americans comprise about 4.2% of the U.S. population and are highly diverse. Twenty-four distinct ethnicities are reported in the U.S. Census, each speaking a unique language and sharing a different culture and history. About 69% of Asian Americans are foreign born and 40% are reported to speak English "less than well."
2. Many Southeast Asian Americans are refugees from the Vietnam War, and Post Traumatic Stress Disorder is a highly salient issue.
3. Given the high percentage of immigrants, similar to Hispanics, English proficiency, acculturation, and education levels are important factors for neuropsychological testing. However, unlike Hispanics, there is no universal language, thus there is a paucity of translated tests and norms, particularly for poorer countries. Guidelines for testing Asian Americans have been proposed.

4. The neuropsychological literature on Asians with schizophrenia is growing and generally come from studies conducted in different Asian countries. Findings consistently mirror studies with Whites with schizophrenia, reporting significant associations between neurocognition and negative/deficit symptoms and strong predictive validity for functional outcome.

CONTINUING EDUCATION QUESTIONS

1. Which statement is *not* true about neuropsychological testing with Hispanics:
   a. English-proficiency, acculturation, education levels, and literacy are salient issues for Hispanic Americans.
   b. The majority of Hispanic Americans are of Mexican heritage.
   c. Hispanic neuropsychological norms are appropriate and should be used for all Hispanic Americans.
   d. There is some evidence for the predictive validity of neurocognition in Mexican-Americans with schizophrenia.
2. Which statement is *not* true about neuropsychological testing with African Americans:
   a. Studies suggest that African Americans with schizophrenia perform similarly to whites when controlling for level of education
   b. About 13% of African Americans are foreign born with the majority immigrating from the Caribbean
   c. Quality of education and acculturation are salient issues for neuropsychological testing with African Americans
   d. A large multi-center study provides evidence for a strong heritability of neurocognition in African Americans with schizophrenia similar to whites.
3. Which statement is *not* true about neuropsychological testing with Asian Americans:
   a. Screening for Post Traumatic Stress Disorder is most important for working with Korean and Japanese Americans
   b. The U.S. Census lists 24 different ethnicities for Asian Americans, each associated with at least one unique language or dialect.
   c. The correlative pattern of neurocognition with negative symptoms and functionality in Asians with schizophrenia is similar to findings with whites
   d. Acculturation and English proficiency are salient issues for a majority of Asian Americans

6

Developmental Disabilities and Schizophrenia

ANTHONY P. DE MARCO, Psy.D.
Department of Psychiatry and Neurobehavioral Sciences, University of Virginia Health System

BERNICE A. MARCOPULOS, Ph.D.
Department of Graduate Psychology, James Madison University, Harrisonburg, VA

Neuropsychology plays a vital role in the treatment of persons with schizophrenia, as the field's practitioners are frequently asked to assist with complex differential diagnostic questions and provide useful recommendations for treatment planning. Generally speaking, referral sources are interested in one's current level of functioning relative to an estimated premorbid level of functioning, a characterization of neurocognitive abilities (strengths and weaknesses), and recommendations that can optimize treatment efforts. There is marked heterogeneity concerning the neurocognitive dysfunction found within schizophrenia (Reichenberg & Harvey, 2007), and these cognitive deficits have demonstrated ecological validity in predicting clinical (Green, 1998) and functional outcomes (Twamley et al., 2002). Inherently, these cases are complex as the neurocognitive profiles of individuals with schizophrenia are not only heterogeneous, but also often obfuscated by a host of comorbidities such as substance abuse, affective distress, and neurological and/or medical disorders other than schizophrenia, as covered in this volume. Thus, neuropsychologists are often faced with the daunting task of teasing out, or accounting for, these comorbid factors in their clinical interpretations. One of the more complex, and perhaps less researched, challenges that neuropsychologists working within psychiatric settings are faced with involves accounting for the impact of developmental disabilities on cognitive functioning in schizophrenia. As schizophrenia is itself a neurodevelopmental disorder, the clinician is faced with an etiological conundrum when considering co-existing or historical diagnoses of other developmental disabilities such as learning disorders, intellectual disability, and attention deficit/hyperactivity disorder. Not only do these disorders show a higher prevalence in persons with schizophrenia, but also the prodromal stage of schizophrenia may be phenotypically-similar to the manifestation of these other developmental disorders.

The objective of this chapter is to review relevant literature and provide a theoretical framework to assist clinicians in considering the comorbid manifestation of schizophrenia with other developmental disorders. In order to accomplish this objective, we review the prevalence of such comorbidities, the clinical presentation of comorbid manifestations, neurocognitive distinctions, neuroimaging, and approaches to treatment, all of which can be used to assist in differentials. We then follow with five theoretical models that can serve as a common foundation upon which conceptualizations of the comorbid presentation can be built. Finally, we conclude with a brief summary section that addresses the neuropsychological evaluation of individuals with schizophrenia and a possible comorbid developmental disorder. While theoretical in nature, the information provided within this chapter is intended to provoke thought and assist in grounding our conceptualization of these diagnostically-complex cases, which hopefully will better inform treatment recommendations.

SCHIZOPHRENIA AND LEARNING/INTELLECTUAL DISABILITY

Prevalence of Schizophrenia in Individuals with Learning/ Intellectual Disability

Since the first categorization of schizophrenia, put forth by Emil Kraepelin (Andreasen & Carpenter, 1993), cognitive impairments and language disturbances have been, and remain, a cardinal feature of the disorder. Therefore, it is not necessarily surprising that while the well-documented lifetime prevalence of schizophrenia within the general population is approximately 1%, epidemiological research has estimated the occurrence of schizophrenia among individuals diagnosed with an intellectual disability to be higher, approximately 3% to 5% (Morgan, Leonard, Bourke, & Jablensky, 2008; Turner, 1989). Low intellectual functioning tends to be present before the onset of psychotic symptoms and is considered a risk factor for schizophrenia (Reichenberg et al., 2006; Woodberry, Giuliano, & Seidman, 2008). As stated by Johnstone et al. (2007), intellectual and cognitive deficits may be part of the psychotic illness yet to manifest itself. For example, neuropsychological impairments in executive and memory functions were significant in those children who later became ill in the Edinburgh High Risk study (Johnstone, Ebmeier, Miller, Owens, & Lawrie, 2005). Intellectual deficits have also been found in the relatives of persons with schizophrenia, further supporting a genetic link (Faraone et al., 2000).

In terms of learning disabilities, early literature has documented an increased prevalence of reading disability and dyslexia in the children of persons with schizophrenia, who are biologically more susceptible to developing the illness (Fish, 1987; Marcus, 1974). The point prevalence of schizophrenia in learning disabled populations has been estimated to be triple that of a normal population (Turner, 1989). Therefore, struggling to differentiate the cognitive sequelae of psychotic processes from premorbid learning difficulties is a common dilemma faced by neuropsychologists employed within a psychiatric setting. This is especially challenging since the presence of psychotic symptoms is likely to overshadow any cognitive precursors or longstanding learning difficulties. Likewise, in younger patients with learning disabilities, behavioral difficulties may be dismissed as "acting out" rather than conceptualized as the manifestation of the prodromal phase of a psychotic illness (Gralton, James, & Crocombe, 2000). Nevertheless, while researchers have demonstrated that it is possible to diagnosis schizophrenia in the context of mild intellectual disabilities, doing so becomes increasingly more difficult in the context of more severe intellectual disabilities (IQ < 45) that are typically characterized by extremely low verbal functioning (Reid, 1989). This makes diagnosing schizophrenia in the context of moderate to severe intellectual impairments extremely difficult, especially among adolescents and children who present with an early-onset psychotic disorder (Friedlander & Donnelly, 2004). Given this diagnostic dilemma, the prevalence rate of schizophrenia in individuals with learning/intellectual disabilities is likely an under-representation (Turner, 1989).

SCHIZOPHRENIA IN THE CONTEXT OF LEARNING/INTELLECTUAL DISABILITIES

What can be expected when evaluating a person with schizophrenia and a comorbid learning/intellectual disability? To begin with previous research elucidating the heterogeneity of cognitive profiles in schizophrenia should continue to inform the process of assessment when evaluating individuals with the comorbid condition (Heinrichs & Zakzanis, 1998). There has been, however, some inconsistency among individual studies attempting to characterize the clinical presentation of the comorbid condition consisting of schizophrenia and learning/intellectual disabilities. Some authors have found that individuals diagnosed with schizophrenia and a comorbid learning/intellectual disability present similarly to those individuals without the comorbid diagnosis using a structured diagnostic interview instrument (Meadows et al., 1991). Other authors, on the other hand, have shown that individuals presenting with the comorbid condition tend to exhibit increased negative symptoms (Doody et al., 1998) or positive symptoms (Banerjee, Morgan, Lewis, Rowe, & White, 2001) of schizophrenia. Additionally, these individuals have been shown to demonstrate greater difficulties with memory, higher degrees of negative symptomatology, and neurological soft-signs (Doody et al., 1998). Morgan and colleagues (2008) found that individuals who were diagnosed with the comorbid condition (i.e., psychiatric illness and intellectual disability) demonstrated more severe psychopathology (e.g., earlier age of onset, more frequent and longer duration of hospitalization, increased suicidality) and a higher risk for mortality. In another study, Bouras et al. (2004) examined the differences in clinical presentation, social functioning, and functional status between a group of individuals diagnosed with a schizophrenia-spectrum disorder and a group of individuals diagnosed with the comorbid condition. Based on this group's findings, individuals presenting with the comorbid diagnosis demonstrated a greater level of psychopathology that could be observed, a greater degree of negative symptoms, and greater impairment in functioning (i.e., psychological, social, and occupational). Differences in one's quality of life, as assessed by the Quality of Life Questionnaire (Schalock & Keith, 1993), which was administered during a clinical interview, were not found; however, a subset of individuals in the comorbid group who were not treated with medication reported a lower quality of life. Additionally, study participants within the comorbid group were more likely to suffer from epilepsy. As an aside, from a clinical perspective recurrent seizures and the utilization of anti-epileptic medications places these individuals at greater risk for cognitive sequelae, further complicating the neuropsychologist's mission to determine the etiology of neurocognitive dysfunction. Lastly, neuroimaging studies, examining cortical similarities and differences between schizophrenia, intellectual disability, and a comorbid group, have concluded that there was a greater similarity in focal regions of interest (i.e., amygdalohippocampal volume) between the schizophrenia and comorbid groups when compared to the intellectual disability only group (Sanderson, Best, Doody, Owens, & Johnstone, 1999). Concerning genome analyses, a particular chromosomal abnormality, or copy number variation (CNV), referred to as 22q11 deletion syndrome, which includes velocardiofacial syndrome and DiGeorge syndrome, has been described as a risk factor for both learning disabilities and schizophrenia (Bassett & Chow, 1999). These associations, in concert, provide some support for the notion that the comorbid manifestation of intellectual disability and psychotic processes may stem from a common underlying etiology (e.g., a neurological insult or copy number variation).

During childhood, dysfunction of receptive language (Cannon et al., 2002) and reading disabilities (Crow, Done, & Slacker, 1995) were found in individuals who later developed a schizophrenic-spectrum disorder in early adulthood, while associations between expressive language disturbances in childhood and schizophrenia were not borne out. Condray (2005) hypothesized that a subset of individuals with schizophrenia may, in fact, exhibit a pre-existing reading disorder (i.e., developmental dyslexia), and further noted that the two disorders may demonstrate some etiological overlap. In other studies, as with progressive dementias, reading and spelling ability has been found to remain relatively well-preserved in schizophrenia, and therefore, these abilities have been implicated as fairly accurate predictors of premorbid intellectual functioning (Dalby & Williams, 1986). However, in light of Condray's hypothesis (2005), caution is warranted when solely relying on word reading as an indicator of premorbid intellectual functioning.

Furthermore, when selecting measures of premorbid functioning Russell and colleagues (2000) found that a word-reading measure, the National Adult Reading Test (NART; Nelson, 1982), overestimated the premorbid functioning in lower functioning patients diagnosed with schizophrenia (see discussion of premorbid IQ estimates in Marcopulos & Fujii, this volume). As eloquently stated by Dennis and colleagues (2009), any intelligence score obtained from an individual diagnosed with a neurodevelopmental disorder, by definition postdates the onset of the condition(s), and therefore, is never truly "premorbid."

In conclusion, learning and intellectual disabilities are not uncommon in schizophrenia, and it is the responsibility of the neuropsychologist to account for the comorbid manifestation, or at least the possibility of a comorbid manifestation, within his or her conceptualization. This task becomes more difficult, though more necessary, if the learning/intellectual disability has not been previously diagnosed. While inconsistencies exist within the literature, there is some support for the notion that schizophrenia and a comorbid learning/intellectual disability will present with greater levels of psychopathology, more cognitive impairment, and poorer overall functioning. The amygdalohippocampal volume of individuals diagnosed with schizophrenia has been found to resemble that of individuals with the comorbid diagnosis, which was significantly reduced relative to normal controls and individuals diagnosed with an intellectual disability in isolation. Additionally, individuals with the comorbid diagnosis may be at greater risk for other neurological disorders (e.g., epilepsy), which may further compromise their neurocognitive functioning. Lastly, caution is warranted when attempting to estimate "premorbid functioning" in individuals diagnosed with neurodevelopmental conditions.

SCHIZOPHRENIA AND ATTENTION-DEFICIT/ HYPERACTIVITY DISORDER

Prevalence of Schizophrenia in Individuals with Attention-Deficit/Hyperactivity Disorder

Overall, individuals diagnosed with Attention-Deficit/Hyperactivity Disorder (ADHD) are more likely to have a comorbid psychiatric disorder at some point throughout their lifetime relative to their non-ADHD counterparts (McGough et al., 2005). In fact, distinct profiles of psychiatric comorbidities have differentiated the different symptom subtypes of ADHD (i.e., inattention, hyperactivity-impulsive, and combined subtypes), with the combined subtype reporting the most severe comorbid psychopathology (Sprafkin, Gadow, Weiss, Schneider, & Nolan, 2007). Inattention, the hallmark feature of attention deficit disorders, is also thought to predate the first psychotic episode of schizophrenia (Amminger et al., 1999; Erlenmeyer-Kimling, 2000; Silverstein, Mavrolefteros, & Turnbull, 2003). The estimated heritability of ADHD has been found to be rather high, approximately 77%, and comparable to that of schizophrenia (Banerjee, Middleton, & Faraone, 2007).

In a genome-wide analysis of a cohort of children diagnosed with ADHD, Williams and colleagues (2010) found a high frequency of 16p13.11 duplications, a CNV that has been previously associated with schizophrenia. As the 22q11 deletion syndrome serves as a risk factor for both schizophrenia and learning disabilities, the overlap of the 16p13.11 duplication provides support for the possibility of an underlying neuropathogenesis shared by schizophrenia and ADHD, possibly explaining the increased prevalence of the comorbid presentation. For example, in a sample of individuals diagnosed with a childhood-onset schizophrenia-spectrum disorder, Ross, Heinlien, and Tregellas (2006) found that approximately 84% of individuals who demonstrated a comorbid diagnosis were, in fact, diagnosed with ADHD. Similarly, Keshavan, Sujata, Mehra, Montrose, and Sweeney (2003) found a high prevalence of ADHD symptomatology in a sample of individuals who were biologically at "high risk for developing schizophrenia" (i.e., relatives of persons diagnosed with schizophrenia). In tandem, these findings illustrate the possibility of some overlap between these two clinical disorders, especially from a neurodevelopmental perspective (Barr, 2001; Karatekin, 2001).

COMORBID MANIFESTATION OF SCHIZOPHRENIA AND ADHD

In studying the relatives of persons with schizophrenia, an argument has been made that there is a subgroup of individuals who exhibit ADHD characteristics, and that this group represents an increased susceptibility to developing schizophrenia and its related disorders. However, while theoretically plausible, this assertion needs to be explicated using prospective, longitudinal studies (Keshavan et al., 2003; Keshavan et al., 2008). Nevertheless, this possibility dovetails with Bellak's (1987, 1994) notion of a subgroup of individuals with schizophrenia who subsequently exhibit "ADD-psychosis." Individuals with "ADD-psychosis" were more impaired in terms of symptomatology and cognitive functioning.

Neurocognitive Distinctions

Attention While inattention appears to be at the core of both schizophrenia and ADHD, distinctive attentional patterns have emerged between groups. Utilizing a continuous performance test, Egeland (2007) retrospectively examined the attentional processes and types of errors between three different clinical groups: (a) ADHD-Inattentive type (ADHD-I), (b) ADHD-Combined type, (ADHD-C), and (c) schizophrenia (paranoid type, disorganized type, undifferentiated type, and residual type). Overall, while the three clinical groups exhibited impairments in attention, group differences in overall inattentiveness were not found. What the author did find were three distinct patterns of inattention that appeared to differentiate each clinical group. For instance, increased variability in response time and more omission errors were found among participants with ADHD-I relative to the other two groups. Additionally, the performances of these individuals were characterized by a higher prevalence of omission errors on the latter portion of the test. The ADHD-C group, as a result of their increased level of hyperactivity/impulsivity, demonstrated an overall faster reaction time and became more impulsive as the test proceeded. Differences in commission errors were not observed. Finally, relative to the other two clinical groups, persons with schizophrenia demonstrated fewer omission errors and were more consistent in terms of reaction time, even as the test proceeded. Egeland (2007) concluded that while persons with schizophrenia demonstrated difficulty with initiating attention, they appeared to appreciate some benefit from practice, which attenuated the adverse impact of their attention deficit (e.g., increased consistency in reaction time and less errors).

In another study, Egeland (2010) found that individuals with first-episode schizophrenia demonstrated a comparable frequency of attention deficits relative to the ADHD-C group on measures of focused, divided, and sustained attention. The ADHD-I group, however, demonstrated a greater frequency of attention deficits relative to both the ADHD-C and the schizophrenia groups. Furthermore, the first-episode schizophrenia group exhibited a lower frequency of impulsivity and hyperactivity when compared to ADHD-C, and fewer deficits in sustained attention when compared to the ADHD-I. In conclusion, these findings suggest that while persons with schizophrenia may demonstrate higher degrees of inattention when interpreted in the context of normative data, when compared to another clinical disorder, which by definition is characterized by inattention, individuals with schizophrenia demonstrate less pronounced attention deficits.

Memory Øie, Sunde, and Rund (1999) examined the differences in memory functioning between adolescents either diagnosed with early-onset schizophrenia or ADHD. The two clinical groups were then compared to a control group comprised of aged-peers who were free of developmental abnormalities. Relative to the control group, adolescents diagnosed with early-onset schizophrenia were globally impaired on various measures of memory functioning, namely working memory and long-term episodic memory (i.e., verbal vs. visual domains, and free recall vs. recognition). In comparison to their ADHD counterparts, adolescents with schizophrenia demonstrated poorer performances in visual memory, while the ADHD group yielded poorer performances on tasks of working memory and a higher degree of distractibility. The authors concluded that while adolescents with schizophrenia demonstrated diffuse memory impairments across verbal and visual domains, impairments in visual memory were more specific to adolescents with schizophrenia rather than ADHD. This study aligns with a more recent study, conducted by Palmer and colleagues (2010), demonstrating differential impairment in visual memory (i.e., family pictures and visual reproductions) when examining intra-individual differences in the cognitive performance of individuals diagnosed with schizophrenia relative to a normative control group (i.e., the WAIS-III/WMS-III standardization sample). In another study, Øie and Rund (1999) found that adolescents with early-onset schizophrenia demonstrated greater difficulties on tasks of visual memory, abstraction, and motor functioning. The ADHD sample, however, demonstrated greater difficulties on tasks associated with attention and verbal learning and memory. Based on these findings, the authors concluded that while the ADHD group demonstrated neurocognitive impairments associated with frontal lobe dysfunction, adolescents with early-onset schizophrenia were more likely to exhibit neurocognitive impairments associated with diffuse cortical dysfunction.

Öner and Munir (2005) compared the neurocognitive profiles of genetically high-risk children (i.e., the offspring of persons with schizophrenia) and children diagnosed with ADHD. Among the authors' high-risk sample, approximately 46% of the children also met diagnostic criteria for ADHD. Compared to a healthy control group, the high-risk sample demonstrated significantly lower verbal and performance intelligence scores, while the ADHD group exhibited only lower verbal abilities. While there was a trend for the ADHD group to perform more poorly on the percent correct and total error scores of a card-sorting task relative to the healthy control group, the high-risk group demonstrated a significantly lower abstraction and cognitive flexibility summary score (i.e., a composite of the following scores: categories completed, perseverative responses, and a similarities subtest). When the high-risk group was divided based on ADHD diagnosis, those high-risk children with comorbid ADHD symptomatology yielded lower neurocognitive performance when compared to both the high-risk and the ADHD groups in isolation. Once again, not only are these findings suggestive of poorer neurocognitive performance within the comorbid group, but they also potentially identify a subgroup of individuals that are at a higher risk for developing a schizophrenia-spectrum disorder (Keshavan et al., 2003; Keshavan et al., 2008).

Neuroimaging Distinctions

Along with the neurocognitive distinctions presented above, neuroimaging, to some degree, can assist neuropsychologists with differentiating between schizophrenia and ADHD, or at least can provide some assistance in conceptualizing the comorbid manifestation. Comparing functional imaging studies between ADHD and schizophrenia has yielded corresponding, yet reversed, findings. For instance, within the prefrontal cortices, Rubia (2002) has reported that individuals with schizophrenia tend to demonstrate under-activation in the left dorsolateral prefrontal lobe, while ADHD has been associated with under-activation in the right dorsolateral prefrontal lobe on what was described as a "stop task." When engaged in response inhibition, the author found over-activation in the right caudate in individuals with schizophrenia, while persons with ADHD demonstrated under-activation of the left caudate regions. Along with other clinical disorders, Gordon, Palmer, and Cooper (2010) examined the EEG asymmetries differentiating schizophrenia and ADHD. The authors found that relative to controls, persons with schizophrenia were characterized by left lateralizing alpha waves, while there was a trend for individuals diagnosed with ADHD to exhibit more right lateralizing EGG abnormalities. These findings dovetail with reports of left cerebral hemispheric abnormalities within schizophrenia, and the correspondence of greater right cerebral hemispheric abnormalities within ADHD (Banaschewski et al., 2005; Barr, 2001; Serene, Ashtari, Szeszko, & Kumra, 2007).

Psychopharmacotherapy

Psychopharmacological treatment of these disorders alters or modifies the transmission of dopamine through neurotransmitter-specific neural pathways (i.e., dopaminergic pathways). Along with imaging studies and neurocognitive differences, psychopharmacotherapy has provided us with some of the more certain distinctions between schizophrenia and ADHD. More specifically, two dopaminergic pathways that have been implicated within these illnesses are the mesolimbic and mesocortical pathways. In short, schizophrenia is typically treated with neuroleptics, dopamine antagonists, which primarily act by blocking the effects of dopamine. By blocking the effects of dopamine within the limbic system (mesolimbic pathway) and frontal cortex (mesocortical pathway), psychotic symptoms are typically reduced, although a common side-effect is the exacerbation of negative symptoms (e.g., amotivation). ADHD, on the other hand, is typically treated with psychostimulants, dopamine agonists, which facilitate an increase in the amount of exogenous dopamine (and other neurotransmitters) within the limbic system and frontal cortex. For this very reason psychostimulants have been indicated in treating resistant depression, but have documented side-effects that include inducing and/or exacerbating psychotic symptoms. Understanding the basic mechanisms of action of these medications has clinical implications, as psychopharmacotherapy and the potential cognitive and/or behavioral side-effects may serve as additional confounding variables that neuropsychologists must incorporate into working case formulations and conceptualizations (Diamond, 2002).

In summary, individuals with ADHD are at a high risk for developing a psychiatric comorbidity at some point throughout their lifetime. Likewise, it is not uncommon to observe ADHD symptomatology in individuals diagnosed with early onset-schizophrenia, those individuals who are considered in the prodromal stage of a psychotic illness, or those at elevated genetic risk. While these two disorders share certain neurocognitive deficits, underlying pathogenesis processes, and behavioral commonalities in the general sense (i.e., inattention), several studies presented above have discerned some of the neurocognitive, neuroanatomical and neurophysiological, and treatment distinctions, highlighting the unique features of each disorder. While the literature on the comorbid presentation is rather scant, there is some evidence suggesting poorer cognitive performance among individuals either diagnosed with the comorbid condition or those who are at high-risk for manifesting both disorders. More specifically, there is greater evidence of impulsivity and inattention on attentional tasks and working memory deficits in ADHD relative to schizophrenia, and greater impairments in visual memory, abstraction, and motor functioning in individuals diagnosed with schizophrenia. When a comorbid group was evaluated, these individuals demonstrated more profound neurocognitive impairments relative to each condition in isolation. Concerning neuroimaging, individuals diagnosed with schizophrenia demonstrate less cerebral activation within the left hemisphere, while individuals diagnosed with ADHD exhibit greater right cerebral hemispheric inefficiencies. As illustrated by Barr (2001), differentiating between schizophrenia and attention deficit disorders is crucial as there are critical implications for implementing treatment efficiently and effectively in order to obtain optimal clinical outcome.

MECHANISMS EXPLAINING THE CO-OCCURRENCE OF SCHIZOPHRENIA AND DEVELOPMENTAL DISABILITIES

Are ADHD, learning disabilities, and/or intellectual disabilities prodromal manifestations of schizophrenia, comorbidities, or separate conditions? This section will serve as a reference to assist practitioners in conceptualizing and approaching referral questions involving patients presenting with diagnoses consisting of schizophrenia and developmental disabilities.

Several authors have posited conceptual frameworks to understand the increased prevalence of schizophrenia and other neurodevelopmental and neurocognitive disorders. Doody and colleagues (1998) proposed five possible mechanisms of action to address the increased prevalence of schizophrenia within individuals diagnosed with intellectual disabilities. Harvey, Koren, Reichenberg, and Bowie (2006) developed four theoretical models to address the association between negative symptoms and cognitive deficits seen in schizophrenia. An amalgamation of these two theoretical models will be presented here, highlighting the similarities between the two theories while acknowledging their differences (which is primarily an emphasis on treatment), in order to provide a conceptual framework for understanding the comorbid presentation of schizophrenia and developmental disorders. Additionally, where applicable and available, studies providing empirical support and/or examples will be utilized to emphasize the practical implications of each model. Although these mechanisms of action are primarily theoretical in nature, they are worth reviewing as they can assist in providing a conceptual framework for clinical neuropsychologists when formulating conceptualizations concerning complex comorbid presentations.

A Continuum Model

The first model, as posited by Doody et al. (1998), suggests that learning disabilities and schizophrenia may be on a continuum and that the co-occurrence of the two disorders represents a more severe manifestation of schizophrenia. This model is consistent with the conceptualization of schizophrenia as a disturbance in neurodevelopmental processes. This disturbance first manifests as cognitive/intellectual difficulties with psychotic symptoms following in a developmental fashion. Along these same lines, Harvey et al. (2006) posited a model suggesting that negative symptoms and cognitive deficits, are either the identical or alternate manifestation of an illness with the same underlying etiology. Furthermore, it was implied that treating one condition would improve the co-existing condition. Therefore, perhaps schizophrenia in isolation represents one tail end of the spectrum while the comorbid condition, consisting of schizophrenia and a developmental disability, represents the other extreme. For instance, persons with schizophrenia and a comorbid intellectual disability have demonstrated greater difficulties with memory, higher degrees of negative symptomatology, and neurological soft-signs (Doody et al., 1998). In a study examining the co-occurrence of intellectual disability and schizophrenia and other psychiatric illnesses, Morgan and colleagues (2008) found that when compared to individuals suffering from psychiatric illness alone, individuals diagnosed with a comorbid disability (i.e., psychiatric illness and intellectual disability) demonstrated more severe psychopathology (e.g., earlier age of onset, more frequent and longer duration of hospitalization, increased suicidality), and a higher risk for mortality. Bonnici and colleagues (2007) also concluded that individuals with comorbid low intellectual deficiency and schizophrenia are likely suffering from a severe form of schizophrenia with early onset, rather than schizophrenia developing because of premorbid low IQ. The conclusion was based on the finding that individuals with intellectual disability had significantly lower gyrification index values relative to the comorbid and schizophrenia groups, who were found to possess similar gyrification index values, and healthy controls who demonstrated the highest gyrification index values. The authors found that individuals with schizophrenia demonstrated reduced gyrification independent of intellectual functioning, and they had difficulty differentiating individuals diagnosed with schizophrenia in isolation from their comorbid counterparts based on gyrification index values. Overall, these findings are consistent with the notion put forth by several researchers discussed earlier, such as Bellak (1985, 1994) and Bouras and colleagues (2004), suggesting the possibility that the comorbid condition represents a subset of patients diagnosed with a more severe manifestation of schizophrenia.

Risk Factor and Susceptibility

The second model proposes that developmental disorders serve as a risk factor increasing one's susceptibility of later developing schizophrenia (Doody et al., 1998; Reichenberg et al., 2005, 2006). Essentially, this mechanism of action can be thought of as a diathesis-stress model, with a developmental disability serving as the predisposition, or the diathesis. The overloading or exhausting of already compromised cognitive resources (the stress) would then lead to disordered thought processes and psychotic symptomatology. Support for the idea of a cognitive/developmental marker predisposing individuals to the illness has been provided by Cannon, Tarrant, Hattunen, and Jones (2003), who have found individuals with premorbid intellectual impairment to be at greater risk than their higher functioning counterparts for developing schizophrenia later in life. Early cognitive deficits have been implicated as indicators of neurodevelopmental dysfunction found in schizophrenia (MacCabe & Murray, 2004; Russell, Munro, Jones, Hemsley, & Murray, 1997), as early declines in intelligence functioning, namely between ages four and seven, have been found to be strong predictors of a diagnosis of schizophreniform disorder in young adulthood (i.e., early twenties) (Kremen, et al., 1998). Furthermore, associations between premorbid intelligence level, which is pre-onset of psychotic symptoms, and disease course and prognosis in schizophrenia have been well established.

Two Disorders: A Co-Occurrence

The third model posited by Doody et al. (1998) suggested that both conditions, schizophrenia and learning/intellectual disorders, have a common underlying etiology, but remain as distinct disorders that happen to co-occur. Similarly, Harvey et al.'s (2006) second model suggested that cognitive deficits and negative symptoms are separable but share an underlying etiology (e.g., obstetric complications, meningitis, or injury to the central nervous system), and that treatment of one may affect the other. Applicable to this specific model is the idea that both disorders share commonalities in neuropathogenesis. For instance, a neuroanatomical study conducted by Leonard and colleagues (2008) concluded that biomarkers, such as asymmetries and reductions within the auditory cortex and cerebellum, may not only serve as risk factors that are specific to schizophrenia, but to a host of developmental disorders. Similarly, as mentioned earlier, several CNVs, or chromosomal abnormalities, have been associated with an increased susceptibility to both learning disability and schizophrenia (Bassett & Chow, 1999), and ADHD and schizophrenia (Williams et al., 2010).

Coincidental Occurrence

A fourth possibility is that the co-occurrence of developmental disabilities and schizophrenia is completely unrelated and coincidental. Based on Harvey et al.'s (2006) model, these are two disorders with two separate etiologies. This hypothesis was posited by Doody et al. (1998) based on earlier research that failed to find an increase in prevalence of learning/intellectual disability in the relatives of persons diagnosed with schizophrenia or an increase in schizophrenia among relatives with learning/intellectual disability. As such, it was postulated that the co-occurrence of the two disorders reflected an unrelated, chance co-occurrence rather than the manifestation of a comorbid disorder with a single underlying etiology. However, Doody et al. illustrated that this earlier work failed to include a comorbid group (individuals with both conditions), and that when included, there was a high prevalence of learning/intellectual disability, schizophrenia, and the comorbid manifestation in first and second degree relatives of individuals with the comorbid diagnosis. Therefore, the "chance co-occurrence" model seems somewhat less credible in accounting for the high rate of comorbidity of these two disorders.

A New Condition

A final model, and perhaps the most unlikely of the five mechanisms of action, is the model in which Doody et al. (1998) referred to the comorbid disorder as a *de novo condition*. In this model, it was suggested that the comorbid manifestation of learning/intellectual disabilities and schizophrenic symptoms is a disorder unto itself and separate from both disorders in isolation. Essentially, it was referred to as a new disorder that has yet to be described. This model was thought to be an unlikely explanation in light of the similarity of core features found in schizophrenia and individuals with the comorbid condition.

In summary, while the aforementioned mechanisms of action are primarily theoretical in nature, the neuropsychologist working with an individual presenting with schizophrenia and a comorbid developmental disorder can utilize these models in shaping his or her case formulation and conceptualization. As illustrated, there is some empirical support, although still small in amount, for the first three models outlined above that suggest the comorbidity of schizophrenia and developmental disabilities represents: (a) a more severe manifestation of schizophrenia, (b) an increased susceptibility among individuals with developmental disabilities to develop schizophrenia, and/or (c) a common etiology shared by both disorders. Less support is offered for the remaining two models (i.e., a *de novo condition* and/or a chance co-occurrence). It is important for the reader to bear in mind that these models are not mutually exclusive. It is certainly plausible for a combination of two or more of the aforementioned mechanisms to serve as a better explanation for the underlying association between these two conditions.

NEUROPSYCHOLOGICAL ASSESSMENT OF PERSONS WITH SCHIZOPHRENIA AND DEVELOPMENTAL DISABILITIES

Neuropsychological evaluations of persons with schizophrenia and a comorbid developmental disability are inherently complex and require the integration of information from a variety of sources, if available. See Marcopulos and Fujii, this volume, for a comprehensive review of the neuropsychological evaluation of individuals with schizophrenia.

Clinical interviews, while extremely fruitful, are sometimes problematic for persons with schizophrenia who are symptomatic and/or presenting with disorganized speech and thought processes. These difficulties are likely to be exacerbated by a comorbid developmental disability, as verbal functioning may be significantly reduced and, as suggested earlier, patients are likely to be more symptomatic. Furthermore, in light of the diagnostic and etiological conundrum outlined above, developmental disabilities, especially learning disabilities, may go undiagnosed in schizophrenia, as these difficulties may be overshadowed by psychotic symptoms. In attempting to estimate a premorbid level of functioning, which may be futile in neurodevelopmental disorders since any score will postdate the onset of the condition(s) (Dennis et al., 2009), caution is warranted when relying on single-word reading measures (Condray, 2005), especially when assessing lower functioning individuals (Russell et al., 2000). It is highly recommended that the neuropsychologist faced with these complex cases conduct a thorough record review by examining any and every piece of relevant historical information afforded to her or him. Prior evaluations, school records, educational and occupational histories (e.g., quality of education, behavioral difficulties, nature and maintenance of employment), legal history, and collateral information (e.g., family members, friends, previous providers) are all valuable sources of information that can assist the neuropsychologist in (a) filling in the gaps created by a fruitless clinical interview, and (b) estimating a timeline of functioning. If a comorbid developmental disability has been diagnosed, the patient's medical record is typically characterized by a wealth of historical information including prior evaluations, all of which can serve as a baseline that can be used to monitor changes over time. Review of such records, when available, prior to meeting with the patient is extremely important as any relevant piece of information revealed during the record review could direct the course of the assessment (i.e., test selection, testing accommodations), interpretation of data, conclusions (e.g., whether or not there has been a decline in functioning), and recommendations (e.g. whether or not it would be useful to provide psychoeducation in written format).

CONCLUSIONS

This chapter set out to provide a theoretical framework that can be used by clinicians when conceptualizing the neurocognitive functioning of individuals diagnosed with schizophrenia and a comorbid developmental disorder. These cases are inherently complex from a diagnostic and etiological perspective, especially during the prodromal stage of the disease process when psychotic illnesses are phenotypically-similar to many other neurodevelopmental disorders. Reviewing the prevalence rates of the comorbid conditions revealed that there is a high degree of symptom overlap between schizophrenia and developmental disorders, and that while there is a relatively high point prevalence of schizophrenia within an intellectually/learning-disabled population, it is likely under-represented due to diagnostic challenges (e.g., low verbal functioning). We presented the similarities and distinctions in neurocognitive functioning, neuroimaging, and approaches to treatment between the various disorders, especially in relation to the comorbid condition when available. This was to serve as a reference to assist clinicians in possibly differentiating between disorders and/or conceptualizing the comorbid manifestations.

We then applied previous theoretical models, put forth by Doody et al. (1998) and Harvey et al. (2006), to the comorbid of manifestation of schizophrenia and developmental disorders with the intention of providing a theoretical framework in which case conceptualizations may be grounded. The models outlined above suggest that the comorbid presentation of schizophrenia and a developmental disability may represent: (a) a more severe manifestation of schizophrenia, (b) an increased susceptibility among individuals with developmental disabilities to develop schizophrenia, (c) a common etiology shared by both disorder, (d) a chance co-occurrence of both disorders, and/or (e) an entirely new disorder unto itself. Once again, these models are not mutually exclusive, as it is plausible that a combination of the aforementioned mechanisms serves as a better explanation for the underlying association between these two conditions.

We concluded with a brief section addressing approaches to evaluating the neurocognitive functioning in individuals with a possible comorbid manifestation of schizophrenia and developmental disabilities. It was emphasized that in order to provide a holistic conceptualization to referral sources, it is extremely important to create a timeline of the individual's neurocognitive, behavioral, and emotional functioning. This is best achieved via clinical interviews and through reviewing any and every available piece of relevant historical information (i.e., medical record, prior evaluations, school records, educational and occupational histories, legal history, and collateral information). The record review is an integral component of the evaluation, as (a) "premorbid estimates" may be misleading as they postdate the onset of neurodevelopmental condition(s) and (b) many times clinical interviews with such complex individuals are truncated due to lower functioning and/or symptomatic presentations.

REFERENCES

Amminger, G. P., Paper, S., Rock, D., Roberts, S. A., Ott, S. L., Squires-Wheeler, E., et al. (1999). Relationship between childhood behavioral disturbance and later schizophrenia in New York High-Risk Project. *American Journal of Psychiatry, 156*(4), 525–530.

Andreasen, N. C., & Carpenter, W. T. Jr. (1993). Diagnosis and classification of schizophrenia. *Schizophrenia Bulletin, 19*(2), 199–214.

Banaschewski, T., Hollis, C., Oosterlaan, J., Roeyers, H., Rubia, K., Willcut, E., et al. (2005). Towards and understanding of unique and shared pathways in the psychophathophysiology of ADHD. *Developmental Science, 8*(2), 132–140.

Banerjee, S., Morgan J., Lewis M., Rowe D., & White M. (2001). A survey of clinical care for patients with schizophrenic disorders and learning disability. *Journal of Clinical Excellence, 3*, 125–131.

Banerjee, T. D., Middleton, F., & Faraone, S. V. (2007). Environmental risk factors for attention-deficit hyperactivity disorder. *Acta Paediatrica, 96*(9), 1269–1274.

Barr, W. B. (2001). Schizophrenia and attention deficit disorder: Two complex disorders of attention. *Annals of the New York Academy of Sciences, 931*, 239–250.

Bassett, A. S., & Chow, E. W. C. (1999). 22q11 deletion syndrome: a genetic subtype of schizophrenia. *Biological Psychiatry, 46*(7), 882–891.

Bellak, L. (1985). ADD psychosis as a separate entity. *Schizophrenia Bulletin, 11*(4), 523–527.

Bellak, L. (1994). The schizophrenic syndrome and attention deficit disorder: Thesis, antithesis, and synthesis? *American Psychologist, 49*(1), 25–29.

Bonnici, H. M., Moorhead, T. W. J., Stanfield, A. C., Harris, J. M., Owens, D. G., Johnstone, E. C., et al. (2007). Pre-frontal lobe gyrification index in schizophrenia, mental retardation and co-morbid groups: an automated study. *Neuroimage, 35*(2), 648–654.

Bouras, N., Martin, G., Leese, M., Vanstraelen, M., Holt, G., Thomas, C., et al. (2004). Schizophrenia-spectrum psychoses in people with and without intellectual disability. *Journal of Intellectual Disability Research, 48*(6), 548–555.

Cannon, M., Caspi, A., Moffitt, T. E., Harrington, H., Taylor, A., Murray, R. M., et al. (2002). Evidence from early-childhood, pan-developmental impairment specific to schizophreniform disorder: Results from a longitudinal birth cohort. *Archives of General Psychiatry, 59*(5), 449–456.

Cannon M., Tarrant C. J., Hattunen M. O., & Jones P. B. (2003). Childhood development and later schizophrenia. In R. M. Murray, P. B. Jones, E. Susser, J. Van Os, & M. Cannon (Eds.), *The epidemiology of schizophrenia* (pp. 100–123). Cambridge, UK: Cambridge University Press.

Condray, R. (2005). Language disorder in schizophrenia as a developmental learning disorder. *Schizophrenia Research, 73*(1), 5–20.

Crow, T. J., Done, D. J., & Slacker, A. (1995). Childhood precursors of psychosis as clues to its evolutionary origins. *European Archives of Psychiatry and Clinical Neuroscience, 245*(2), 61–69.

Dalby, J. T., & Williams, R. (1986). Preserved reading and spelling ability in psychotic disorders. *Psychological Medicine, 16*(1), 171–175.

Dennis, M., Francis, D. J., Cirino, P. T., Schachar, R., Barnes, M. A., & Fletcher, J. M. (2009). Why IQ is not a covariate in cognitive studies of neurodevelopmental disorders. *Journal of the International Neuropsychological Society, 15*, 331–343.

Diamond, R. J. (2002). *Instant psychopharmacology: Up-to-date information about the most commonly prescribed drugs for emotional health-2nd edition*. New York, NY: W. W. Norton.

Doody, G. A., Johnstone, E. C., Sanderson, T. L., Cunningham-Owens, D. G., & Muir, W. G. (1998). 'Pfropfschizophrenie' revisited: Schizophrenia in people with mild learning disability. *British Journal of Psychiatry, 173*(2), 145–153.

Egeland, J. (2007). Differentiating attention deficit in adult ADHD and schizophrenia. *Archives of Clinical Neuropsychology, 22*(6), 763–771.

Egeland, J. (2010). Frequency of attention deficit in first-episode schizophrenia compared to ADHD. *Applied Neuropsychology, 17*(2), 125–134.

Erlenmeyer-Kimling, L. (2000). Neurobehavioral deficits in offspring of schizophrenic parents: Liability indicators and predictors of illness. *American Journal of Medical Genetics, 97*(1), 65–71.

Faraone, S. V., Seidman, L. J., Kremen, W. S., Toomey, R., Pepple, J. R., & Tsuang, M. T. (2000). Neuropsychologic functioning among nonpsychotic relatives of schizophrenic patients: the effect of genetic loading. *Biological Psychiatry, 48*, 120–126.

Fish, B. (1987). Infant predictors of the longitudinal course of schizophrenic development. *Schizophrenia Bulletin, 13*(3), 395–409.

Friedlander, R. I., & Donnelly, T. (2004). Early-onset psychosis in youth with intellectual disability. *Journal of Intellectual Disability Research, 48*(6), 540–547.

Gordon, E., Palmer, D. M., & Cooper, N. (2010). EEG alpha asymmetry in schizophrenia,depression, PTSD, panic disorder, ADHD, and conduct disorder. *Clinical EEG and Neuroscience, 41*(4), 178–183.

Gralton, E., James, A., & Crocombe, J. (2000). The diagnosis of schizophrenia in the borderline learning-disabled forensic population: six-case reports. *The Journal of Forensic Psychiatry, 11*(1), 185–197.

Green, M. F. (1998). *Schizophrenia from a neurocognitive perspective: Probing the impenetrable darkness.* Boston, MA: Allyn & Bacon.

Harvey, P. D., Koren, D., Reichenberg, A., & Bowie, C. R. (2006). Negative symptoms and cognitive deficits: What is the nature of their relationship? *Schizophrenia Bulletin, 32*(2), 250–258.

Heinrichs, R. W., & Zakzanis, K. K. (1998). Neurocognitive deficit in schizophrenia: A quantitative review of the evidence. *Neuropsychology, 12*(3), 426–445.

Johnstone, E. C., Ebmeier, K. P., Miller, P., Owens, D. G. C., & Lawrie, S. M. (2005). Predicting schizophrenia: Findings from the Edinburgh High-Risk Study. *British Journal of Psychiatry, 186*, 18–25.

Johnstone, E. C., Owens, D. G. C., Hoare, P., Gaur, S., Spencer, M. D., Harris, J., et al. (2007). Schizotypal cognitions as a predictor of psychopathology in adolescents with mild intellectual impairment. *British Journal of Psychiatry, 191*, 484–492.

Karatekin, C. (2001). Developmental disorders of attention. In C. A. Nelson & M. Luciana (Eds.), *Handbook of developmental cognitive neuroscience* (pp. 561–576). Cambridge, MA: MIT Press.

Keshavan, M. S., Montrose, D. M., Rajarethinam, R., Diwadkar, V., Prasad, K., & Sweeney, J. A. (2008). Psychopathology among offspring of parents with schizophrenia: Relationship to premorbid impairments. *Schizophrenia Research, 103*(1-3), 114–120.

Keshavan, M. S., Sujata, M., Mehra, A., Montrose, D. M., & Sweeney, J. A. (2003). Psychosis proneness and ADHD in young relatives of schizophrenia patients. *SchizophreniaResearch, 59*(1), 85–92.

Kremen, W. S., Buka, S. L., Seidman, L. J., Goldstein, J. M., Koren, D., & Tsuang, M. T. (1998). IQ decline during childhood and adult psychotic symptoms in a community sample: A 19-year longitudinal study. *American Journal of Psychiatry, 155*(5), 672–677.

Leonard, C. M., Kuldau, J. M., Maron, L., Ricciuti, N., Mahoney, B., Bengtson, M., et al. (2008). Identical neural risk factors predict cognitive deficit in dyslexia and schizophrenia. *Neuropsychology, 22*(2) 147–158.

MacCabe, J. H., & Murray, R. M. (2004). Intellectual functioning in schizophrenia: A marker of neurodevelopmental damage? *Journal of Intellectual Disability Research, 48*(6), 519–523.

Marcus, J. (1974). Cerebral functioning in offspring of schizophrenics: A possible genetic factor. *International Journal of Mental Health, 3*, 57–73.

McGough, J. J., Smalley, S .L., McCracken, J. T., Yang, M., Del'Homme, M., Lynn, D. E., et al. (2005). Psychiatric comorbidity in adult attention deficit hyperactivity disorder: Findings from multiplex families. *American Journal of Psychiatry, 162*(9), 1621–1627.

Meadows, G., Turner, T., Campbell, L., Lewis, S. W., Reveley, M. A., & Murray, R. M. (1991). Assessing schizophrenia in adults with mental retardation: A comparison study. *British Journal of Psychiatry, 158*(1), 103–105.

Morgan, V. A., Leonard, H., Bourke, J., & Jablensky, A. (2008). Intellectual disability co-occurring with schizophrenia and other psychiatric illness: Population-based study. *The British Journal of Psychiatry, 193*(5), 364–372.

Nelson, H. E. (1982). *National Adult Reading Test (NART): Test Manual.* Windsor, UK: NFER-Nelson.

Øie, M., & Rund, B.R. (1999). Neuropsychological deficits in adolescents-onset schizophrenia compared with attention deficit hyperactivity disorder. *American Journal of Psychiatry, 156*(8), 1216–1222.

Øie, M., Sunde, K., & Rund, B.R. (1999). Contrasts in memory functions between adolescents with schizophrenia or ADHD. *Neuropsychologia, 37*(12), 1351–1358.

Öner, Ö., & Munir, K. (2005). Attentional and neurocognitive characteristics of high-risk offspring of parents with schizophrenia compared with DSM-IV attention deficit hyperactivity disorder children. *Schizophrenia Research, 76*(2-3), 293–299.

Palmer, B. W., Savla, G. N., Fellows, I. E., Twamley, E.T., Jeste, D. V., & Larco, J. P. (2010). Do people with schizophrenia have differential impairment in episodic memory and/or working memory relative to other cognitive abilities? *Schizophrenia Research, 116*(2-3), 259–273.

Reichenberg, A., & Harvey, P. D. (2007). Neuropsychological impairments in schizophrenia: Integration of performance-based and brain imaging findings. *Psychological Bulletin, 133*(5), 833–858.

Reichenberg, A., Weiser, M., Rapp, M. A., Rabinowitz, J., Caspi, A., Schmeidler, J., et al. (2005). Elaboration on premorbid intellectual performance in schizophrenia: Premorbid intellectual decline and risk for schizophrenia. *Archives of General Psychiatry, 62*(12), 1297–1304.

Reichenberg, A., Weiser, M., Caspi, A., Knobler, H. Y., Lubin, G., Harvey, P. D., Rabiniowitz, J., & Davidson, M. (2006). Premorbid intellectual functioning and risk of schizophrenia and spectrum disorders. *Journal of Clinical and Experimental Neuropsychology, 28,* 193–207.

Reid, A. H. (1989). Psychiatry and mental handicap: A historical perspective. *Journal ofIntellectual Disability Research, 33*(5), 363–368.

Ross, R. G., Heinlein, S., & Tregellas, H. (2006). High rates of comorbidity are found in childhood-onset schizophrenia. *Schizophrenia Research, 88*(1), 90–95.

Rubia, K. (2002). The dynamic approach to neurodevelopmental psychiatric disorders: Use of fMRI combined with neuropsychology to elucidate the dynamics of psychiatric disorders, exemplified in ADHD and schizophrenia. *Behavioural Brain Research, 130*(1-2), 47–56.

Russell, A. J., Munro, J., Jones, P. B., Hayward, P., Hemsley, D. R., et al. (2000). The National Adult Reading Test as a measure of premorbid IQ in schizophrenia. *British Journal of Clinical Psychology, 39,* 297–305.

Russell, A. J., Munro, J. C., Jones, P. B., Hemsley, D. R., & Murray, R. M. (1997). Schizophrenia and the myth of intellectual decline. *American Journal of Psychiatry, 154*(5), 635–639.

Sanderson, T. L., Best, J., Doody, G. A., Owens, D. G. C., & Johnstone, E. C. (1999). Neuroanatomy of co-morbid schizophrenia and learning disability—A controlled study. *Lancet, 354,* 1867–1871.

Schalock R. L., & Keith K. D. (1993). *Quality of Life Questionnaire.* Worthington, OH: IDS Publishers.
Serene, J. A., Ashtari, M., Szeszko, P. R, & Kumra, S. (2007). Neuroimaging studies of children with serious emotional disturbances: A select review. *The Canadian Journal of Psychiatry, 52*(3), 135–145.
Silverstein, M. L., Mavrolefteros, G., & Turnbull, A. (2003). Premorbid factors in relation to motor, memory, and executive functions deficits in adult schizophrenia. *Schizophrenia Research, 6*(2-3), 271–280.
Sprafkin, J., Gadow, K. D., Weiss, M. D., Schneider, J., & Nolan, E. E. (2007). Psychiatric comorbidity in ADHD symptom subtypes in clinic and community adults. *Journal of Attention Disorders, 11*(2), 114–124.
Turner, T. H. (1989). Schizophrenia and mental handicap: An historical review, with implications for further research. *Psychological Medicine, 19*(2), 301–314.
Twamley, E., Doshi, R. R., Nayak, G. V., Palmer, B. W., Golshan, S., Heaton, R. K., et al. (2002). Generalized cognitive impairments, ability to perform everyday tasks, and level of independence in community living situations of older patients with psychosis. *American Journal of Psychiatry, 159*(12), 2013–2020.
Williams, N. M., Zaharieva, I., Martin, A., Langley, K., Mantripagada, K., Fossdal, R., et al. (2010). Rare chromosomal deletions and duplications in attention-deficit hyperactivity disorder: A genome-wide analysis. *Lancet, 376*(9750), 1401–1408.
Woodberry, K. A., Giuliano, A. J., & Seidman, L. J. (2008). Premorbid IQ in schizophrenia: A meta-analytic review. *American Journal of Psychiatry, 165*, 579–587.

BOX 6.1 SCHIZOPHRENIA AND LEARNING/INTELLECTUAL DISABILITY

1. The occurrence of schizophrenia among individuals diagnosed with an intellectual disability is estimated to be between 3% and 5%.
2. Low intellectual functioning tends to be present before the onset of psychotic symptoms and is considered a risk factor for schizophrenia.
3. Intellectual and cognitive deficits may be part of the psychotic illness yet to manifest itself.
4. The point prevalence of schizophrenia in learning disabled populations has been estimated to be triple that of a normal population.
5. There is an increased prevalence of reading disability and dyslexia in the children of persons with schizophrenia.
6. Schizophrenia and a comorbid learning/intellectual disability will present with greater levels of psychopathology, more cognitive impairment, and poorer overall functioning.
7. Individuals with the comorbid diagnosis may be at greater risk for other neurological disorders.

BOX 6.2 SCHIZOPHRENIA AND ATTENTION DEFICIT/ HYPERACTIVITY DISORDER

1. Individuals diagnosed with ADHD are more likely to have a comorbid psychiatric disorder at some point throughout their lifetime relative to their non-ADHD counterparts.
2. Inattention is thought to predate the first psychotic episode of schizophrenia.
3. The 22q11 deletion syndrome serves as a risk factor for schizophrenia, ADHD, and learning disabilities, suggesting the possibility of an underlying neuropathogenesis shared by each disorder.
4. There is greater evidence of impulsivity and inattention on attentional tasks and working memory deficits in ADHD relative to schizophrenia, and greater impairments in visual memory, abstraction, and motor functioning within individuals diagnosed with schizophrenia.
5. When a comorbid group (schizophrenia and ADHD) was evaluated, these individuals demonstrated more profound neurocognitive impairments relative to each condition in isolation.
6. Individuals diagnosed with schizophrenia demonstrate less cerebral activation within the left hemisphere, while individuals diagnosed with ADHD exhibit greater right cerebral hemispheric inefficiencies.

BOX 6.3 MECHANISMS EXPLAINING THE CO-OCCURRENCE OF SCHIZOPHRENIA AND DEVELOPMENTAL DISABILITIES

1. A Continuum Model: Schizophrenia and developmental disabilities may be on a continuum, and that the co-occurrence of the two disorders represents a more severe manifestation of schizophrenia.
2. Risk and Susceptibility Model: A diathesis-stress model, with a developmental disability serving as the predisposition, or the diathesis. The overloading or exhausting of already compromised cognitive resources (the stress) would then lead to disordered thought processes and psychotic symptomatology.
3. Co-Occurrence Model: Both conditions, schizophrenia and developmental disabilities, have a common underlying etiology but remain as distinct disorders that happen to co-occur.

4. Coincidental Occurrence Model: Suggests that the co-occurrence of developmental disabilities and schizophrenia is completely unrelated and coincidental
5. A New Condition Model: Suggests that the comorbid manifestation of schizophrenic symptoms and developmental disabilities is a disorder unto itself and separate from both disorders in isolation.

CONTINUING EDUCATION QUESTIONS

1. The prevalence of learning disorders in persons with schizophrenia is approximately __________.
   a. 35%
   b. 1%
   c. 3%
   d. 57%
2. Of the presented mechanisms of action, which were adapted from Doody et al. (1998) to assist in conceptualizing the co-occurrence of developmental disorders and schizophrenia, which is the least compelling based on the information presented in this chapter?
   a. The Continuum Model
   b. The Risk Factor and Susceptibility Model
   c. The Co-occurrence Model
   d. The Coincidental Model
   e. The New Condition Model
3. Neuroimaging studies typically demonstrate a correspondence between ________ cerebral hemispheric dysfunction in schizophrenia, and ___________ cerebral hemispheric dysfunction in ADHD.
   a. right … left
   b. left … right
   c. posterior … anterior
   d. dorsal … ventral
4. Individuals who later developed a schizophrenic-spectrum disorder in early adulthood were more likely to have a history of
   a. a receptive language disorder
   b. an expressive language disorder
   c. a learning disability in math
   d. a reading disability
   e. a and d

5. Compared with persons with ADHD, persons with schizophrenia are more likely to demonstrate deficits in
   a. Verbal memory
   b. Impulsivity on attentional tasks
   c. Visual memory
   d. Motor functions
   e. c & d

7

Neuropsychological Considerations in Older Adults with Schizophrenia

COLIN A DEPP, Ph.D.
Department of Psychiatry; University of California, San Diego

CASEY LOUGHRAN, B.A.
Department of Psychiatry; University of California, San Diego
Veterans Administration Medical Center, San Diego

BARTON W. PALMER, Ph.D.
Department of Psychiatry; University of California, San Diego
Veterans Administration Medical Center, San Diego

INTRODUCTION

As the absolute number of older adults will double in the Western world over the next two decades, there will be a corresponding growth in the number of older people with schizophrenia (Dickinson, Iannone, Wilk, & Gold, 2004; Jeste et al., 1999; Palmer, Heaton, & Jeste, 1999). The intersection of aging and schizophrenia has been the subject of a number of long-running controversies dating back to Kraepelin's initial formulations of this disorder as a "dementia praecox". However, with some notable exceptions, there had been relatively little empirical data about the phenomenology and treatment of late-life schizophrenia until recent decades. Neuropsychology has proven to be one of the key sciences in fostering better understanding how this illness changes across the lifespan, influences on its course, and interventions to optimize adaptation (Palmer & Savla, 2009). In the present chapter, we provide an overview of late-life schizophrenia. Although our emphasis is on the neuropsychological aspects of schizophrenia and aging, our overview will also include discussion of the prevalence, course, and clinical characteristics of late-life schizophrenia. Essential questions that are addressed in this chapter are how common is late-life schizophrenia? What is the course of the illness into later life in terms of symptoms, neuropsychological and functional deficits? We then provide a practical overview for clinical neuropsychologists in assessing older adults with schizophrenia, addressing how evaluation can aid in differentiating between late-life schizophrenia and other geriatric psychiatric disorders that exhibit similar symptoms. Finally, we address the remediation of the cognitive and functional deficits in these patients.

Prevalence

The prevalence of psychotic symptoms is higher among older adults compared to younger adults (Ostling & Skoog, 2002); approximately 10% of adults older than 85 exhibit some psychotic symptoms. The underlying cause of psychosis in most older adults is secondary to a medical or neurologic condition (particularly dementia), rather than a primary psychotic disorder such as schizophrenia; nonetheless there are older adults who either continue to manifest primary psychotic disorders which first emerged in earlier adulthood, as well as a smaller portion of adults with new onset primary psychotic disorders. The prevalence of schizophrenia among people older than age 65 has been estimated by the Epidemiological Catchment Area (ECA) studies (using *DSM III* Criteria) to be approximately 0.6% (Copeland et al., 1998). Compared with prevalence in younger adults, this figure is much lower (prevalence ages 18 to 45: 1.0% to 1.9%). Other psychotic disorders, including delusional disorder (~0.1%) or schizoaffective disorder are even more rare in older adults; therefore we will focus this chapter on schizophrenia (See Palmer & Savla, 2009, for a recent review of neuropsychological aspects of schizoaffective disorder.) Subsequent authors have cited issues with the methodology of the ECA data in regard to estimating mental illnesses in older adults, in particular that institutionalized individuals were excluded from these studies. In considering differing sources of sampling biases in estimating prevalence of late-life schizophrenia, the best estimate may be approximately 1% (Cohen, 1990). Even with methodological shortcomings, the 'true' prevalence of schizophrenia is lower among older adults compared to younger adults, which has been attributed to the forces of attrition, in which younger adults with schizophrenia (who may also experience more virulent illnesses) have a higher probability of mortality prior to reaching older age. This change in the population due to excess mortality makes it difficult to estimate age effects from cross-sectional data in mixed-age samples of people with schizophrenia.

There is little data to suggest that the gender or ethnic composition of late-life schizophrenia differs by age group. However, as the growth in the older adult population who are ethnic minorities is increasing faster than the Caucasian population, it is highly probable that more older adults with schizophrenia will be ethnic minorities in the coming decades (Jeste et al., 1999; Palmer et al., 1999). About 85% of older adults with schizophrenia reside in the community (including private households and community-based housing) and the remainder reside in long-term care or psychiatric institutions (Cohen, 1990).

Course

Onset The great majority of people with schizophrenia experience onset of their illness during their twenties; and thus the modal older adult with schizophrenia has lived with the illness for 30 to 40 years. However, there is a subgroup of patients with late or very late onset. A 1988 review of studies by Harris and Jeste (1988) found that 13% of patients experienced onset after age 40, 7% after age 50, and 3% after age 60. There is a lack of consistency across studies in the cut-off for late age of onset; yet the modal study defines late-onset as at age 40 and older and very-late onset after age 60. The balance of the evidence indicates that late-onset schizophrenia is not etiologically distinct from early-onset schizophrenia, and thus does not represent a separate disease entity. Nonetheless, there are a number of unique characteristics of late-onset patients. In particular, late-onset patients are more likely to be women, with evidence for a small spike in likelihood of onset of schizophrenia occurring around the time of menopause. Some laboratory work has attempted to link the onset of schizophrenia with the decline in estrogen production at menopause (with the hypothesis that estrogen may be protective). Although, given that most women with schizophrenia experience age of onset prior to menopause, the role of estrogen in onset is not universal.

Among clinical characteristics, our most recent data suggest that those with onset of illness after age 40 are similar to those with earlier onset in regard to severity of depressive symptoms, as well as severity of negative and deficit symptoms. On the other hand, the later-onset patients had less severe positive symptoms and general psychopathology and were maintained on lower doses of antipsychotic medications (Vahia et al., in press). In regard to neuropsychological functions, the late- and early-onset patients have similar levels of crystallized knowledge, but the late-onset patients had better performance on tests of psychomotor/processing speed, abstraction, and verbal memory. In addition, late-onset patients appear more likely to have attained functional milestones (e.g., marriage, occupations); as a result of more disease-free years of life, late-onset patients have more opportunity for social/occupational attainments. Finally, related to age of onset, there is likely an important distinction between the age of onset of symptoms and the age of initiation of treatment. Patients who experience a greater delay in initiation of treatment appear to have long-lasting negative effects (Bangalore et al., 2009).

Symptom Course There are a handful of highly informative long-term longitudinal studies that have followed patients with schizophrenia over 20 years and into later life (McGlashan, 1988). These studies are in sharp contrast with the earlier assumptions about the progressive nature of schizophrenia as described by Kraepelin. Evidence from these studies suggests that community-dwelling patients experience improvement in psychosocial functioning and reductions in positive symptoms, with over 50% of patients exhibiting improvement in symptoms and some restoration of psychosocial functioning. Cross-sectional study of middle-aged and older patients suggests that older age relates to higher ratings on mental health-related quality of life (Folsom et al., 2009). In addition, there appears to be an, albeit smaller, subgroup of patients who have experienced sustained remission; in one study, approximately 10% of patients followed experienced freedom from symptom exacerbations for five years or longer (Granholm et al., 2005).

Although it is difficult to tease apart the influence of survivor effects in cross-sectional studies and changes in the treatment context of older adults (e.g., deinstitutionalization), there are a number of hypotheses as to the mechanisms of the observed improvements in symptoms expression in older people. It may be that typical age-associated reductions in dopaminergic activity in the brain may attenuate the severity of hallucinations and delusions. It may also be that, after years of exposure to the illness, older people are more likely to accept the illness and adhere to treatment regimens, as well as develop coping mechanisms to counteract positive symptoms. Older adults with severe mental illness are also less likely to abuse substances than are younger patients, lessening a significant risk factor for poor outcomes (although the higher rates of substance abuse in the baby boom population may reverse this trend in the future).

However, in contrast to the positive symptoms, the balance of the evidence suggests that negative symptoms and depression do not exhibit marked improvements into later life. Of note, these aspects of schizophrenia are more potent predictors of community functioning than are positive symptoms. In addition, a subset of patients residing in long-stay institutions do not appear to display syndromal improvements (Davidson et al., 1996). Finally, increasing heterogeneity (older adults with schizophrenia are less like each other than are younger adults) is perhaps the strongest trend with age, which is also the case in normal aging.

Phenomenology and Course of Neuropsychological Abilities into Later-Life The majority of people with schizophrenia, but notably not all, manifest cognitive deficits in addition to the primary psychiatric symptoms associated with this condition (reviewed in Palmer, Dawes, & Heaton, 2009). There is substantial heterogeneity among persons with schizophrenia in terms of the level and pattern of cognitive impairment associated with this disorder; indeed, approximately 25% show no discernable cognitive deficits on standard neuropsychological tests, but most patients evidence mild to moderate deficits in multiple cognitive domains. Although efforts to identify specific subdomains of cognitive impairment, and/or cognitive subtypes, are ongoing, there is no specific pattern of cognitive impairment which is common to all persons with schizophrenia, or which consistently distinguishes schizophrenia from other neuropsychiatric conditions (Dickinson et al., 2004; Palmer & Dawes, 2010).

In contrast to the between-patient heterogeneity in level and pattern of cognitive functioning, however, there is substantial within-person stability. Contrary to Kraepelin's initial conceptualization of this disorder as a *dementia praecox* characterized by a progressively deteriorating course of mental functions, a mass of empirical data reported in recent decades has firmly established that the model course of cognitive functioning in schizophrenia is one of remarkable stability (Heaton et al., 2001; Kurtz, 2005; Rund, 1998). Although there tends to be some decline in cognitive functioning associated with first onset of clinical symptoms, the latter may even partially normalize after stabilization of symptoms after first onset (Klingberg, Wittorf, Sickinger, Buchkremer, & Wiedmann, 2008).

An example of the cognitive stability which typifies schizophrenia across the adult life-span was provided in a longitudinal study from our research group comparing 142 middle-aged and older adults with schizophrenia to healthy comparison subjects who completed a comprehensive annual neuropsychological test battery over periods of up to seven years (Heaton et al., 2001). Heaton et al. found no evidence of deterioration beyond that associated with aging in seven different neuropsychological domains. Moreover, there was no evidence that specific subgroups exhibited decline (e.g., early- or late-onset patients), nor was there decline among patients with changes in symptom status in positive or negative domains. The cognitive stability associated with schizophrenia among older patients with schizophrenia (whether they have late-onset or earlier-onset) is comparable to that of healthy comparison subjects, and markedly distinct from the progressive decline associated with Alzhiemer's disease (Nayak-Savla et al., 2006; Palmer et al., 2003).

An exception to the above comments about cognitive stability in the post-onset course of schizophrenia may be chronically institutionalized patients. Some of the earliest longitudinal studies of cognitive functioning in schizophrenia, conducted before the mass de-institutionalization of long-term psychiatric inpatients was in full swing, suggested an association between chronic institutionalization for schizophrenia and cognitive decline (Schwartzman, Douglas, & Muir, 1962). Consistent with such findings, there have been some indications in more recent studies of greater than age-normal risk of dementia in studies of elderly patients who have spent the majority of their adult lives in inpatient care (reviewed in Rajji & Mulsant, 2008). For instance, Harvey and colleagues (1999) have conducted a number of studies in institutionalized patients and found evidence for greater-than-expected decline in neurocognitive abilities over periods as little as 2 years. Among these patients, risk factors for decline included lower education, older age, and more severe positive symptoms. In contrast, gender, antipsychotic treatment, negative symptoms, and age of first psychiatric hospitalization are not associated with cognitive decline. It is notable that even among patients who do decline, post-mortem neuropathological studies suggest the cognitive deterioration among such patients is not a reflection of comorbid neurodegenerative conditions such as Alzheimer's disease (Friedman, Harvey, Kemether, Byne, & Davis, 1999). In short, it is possible that institutionalized patients represent a subgroup with more virulent illnesses associated with greater cognitive decline, or that the institutional milieu is associated with negative effects on cognitive health.

Finally, in considering the phenomenology and course of neuropsychological abilities in later-life schizophrenia, it is important to remember that normal age-associated cognitive decline represents a backdrop. Thus, even if cognitive deficits do not decline more than expected from normal aging, the impact of normal declines in memory, processing speed, and flexibility that accompany aging (see (Palmer & Dawes, 2010; Salthouse, 2004) may reduce functional capacity beyond thresholds necessary for maintaining independence in the community.

Neurobiological Findings in Later-Life Schizophrenia Only a handful of studies have examined the neurobiology of late-life schizophrenia. Among the most consistent findings is that, as with younger adults, older adults with schizophrenia exhibit enlarged ventricles, and the relationship between ventricular size and poor outcome is consistent across the lifespan (Staal, Hulshoff, Hilleke, & Rene, 1999). As with the evidence for stability in cognitive ability described above, there is no clear evidence of progressive deterioration in brain structures beyond that associated with normal aging. Structural magnetic resonance imaging indicates that the prevalence of white matter intensities increases with age, as with normal aging, and that discrepancies in grey matter in comparison with healthy subjects may decline (Bose et al., 2009). The presence of Lewy bodies, neurofibriallary tangles, and amyloid plaques do not appear to be elevated in the brains of people with chronic schizophrenia. In short, the differences between brain structures between older adults with and without schizophrenia may be less salient than at younger ages, largely because there is greater heterogeneity in brain structure in the normal comparison population at older age.

IMPACT OF COGNITIVE ABILITIES ON LATE LIFE FUNCTIONING

There is consistent evidence that cognitive abilities are strong predictors of various indicators of functional status in older adults with schizophrenia (Kurtz, 2006). Global cognitive impairment is more predictive than are positive or negative symptoms in regard to likelihood of placement in supported living or nursing home settings (Andrews, Bartels, Xie, & Peacock, 2009), performance in most Activities of Daily Living/Independent Activities of daily Living (ADLs/IADLs), and occupational functioning. There is little evidence that any one cognitive deficit is more predictive of functional impairment than others (Evans et al., 2003; Velligan, Bow-Thomas, Mahurin, Miller, & Halgunseth, 2000). Recent work has attempted to further elucidate the pathways from cognitive impairment to functional disability. Using confirmatory path analyses to assess the inter-relationships among cognitive ability, functional capacity, and disability in a sample of older adults with schizophrenia, Bowie et al. (2008) concluded that functional capacity mediated the relationship between cognition and work, interpersonal, and social disability. However, depression and negative symptoms were associated with additive and independent effects on work and interpersonal functioning. Therefore, in comparison to other illness features, generalized cognitive impairment is the greatest risk factor for poor functional outcome in schizophrenia, although the pathways from cognitive impairment may depend upon which functional ability is in question.

Assessment and Differential Diagnosis

General Assessment Approach Having described the phenomenology and clinical course of cognition and symptoms in late-life schizophrenia, we next describe a general approach to differential diagnosis of schizophrenia in older adults in consultation settings, as well as specific neuropsychological and functional measures to aid in evaluation. As there are many causes of psychosis in older adults, clinicians are frequently called upon to determine whether acute psychotic symptoms and related alterations in mental status are due to a medical or psychiatric cause. Although the classic distinction between "functional" and "organic" etiologies, which were popular when pure psychogenic models of mental illness predominated American psychiatry, is now generally recognized as, at least in part, a false dichotomy. There is still value in distinguishing primary psychosis from those that may be a secondary manifestation of a medical disorder requiring additional treatment. Even for patients with established diagnoses of schizophrenia, alterations in mental status often require ruling out non-psychiatric etiologies in that addressing the comorbid conditions can help to improve mental and functional status.

General assessment should cover symptom onset, timing, type and concurrence with medical comorbidities and medical treatments. It should not be assumed that mental status changes are a function of underlying psychotic processes, particularly among older adults with medical problems or recent changes in somatic treatment. Over 80% of older adults have at least one chronic condition, and the average older adult takes over seven prescription medications (Hazzard, 1995). Recent review suggests that schizophrenia is associated with increased risk for HIV, pulmonary problems, cardiovascular illnesses, osteoporosis, and thyroid dysfunction. Many of the chronic illnesses in schizophrenia that are evaluated in abundance in schizophrenia accompany lifestyle factors, such as chronically high rates of smoking, substance abuse, and sedentary behavior—these behaviors can produce cumulative effects on health status. Atypical antipsychotics produce metabolic side effects, which older adults are more susceptible to; and first-generation antipsychotics are associated with neurological side effects such as tardive dyskenesia. In addition to greater risk for comorbidities, chronic conditions may also be more severe. Greater severity of medical conditions may stem from diminished access to care, and the tendency for health providers to focus on psychiatric symptoms during clinic visits at the possible exclusion of medical problems. Therefore, a careful review of medications, illnesses, and recent changes in the physical functioning should be conducted. Mental status may be altered by many medications, including steroids, anti-cholingeric medications, opiates, and many others.

Other important considerations in assessing older adults with psychosis include the use of proxy informants, particularly among patients who have significant memory impairment. Professional caretakers and facility staff can be particularly informative in identifying the pattern, antecedents, and responses to psychotic symptoms among patients with poor insight or memory impairment. Prior to initiating testing, clinicians should assess for the presence of sensory impairments. In addition to altering the validity of many neuropsychological tests, visual and hearing deficits are associated with psychosis in community-dwelling elderly people, particularly among those who are extremely socially isolated.

Comprehensive/quality neuropsychological assessment involves much more than simply learning to administer and score standardized neuropsychological tests. Obtaining scores is only a piece of the beginning, not the culmination of the process of neuropsychological assessment, diagnosis, and treatment planning. Therefore, non-specialists are strongly encouraged to consult with neuropsychologists specifically trained and experienced in working with older neuropsychiatric patients. Such consultation can be invaluable in the process of differential diagnosis, as well as developing rehabilitative plans that capitalize on the patients spared cognitive strengths, while limiting the deleterious influence of cognitive deficits (Palmer, 2004; Twamley, Salva, Zurhellen, Heaton, & Jeste, 2008).

Differentiating Delirium versus Psychotic Disorder In hospital settings, neuropsychologists may be called upon to differentiate between delirium and psychosis due to schizophrenia. History and observations by clinical staff are often revealing in differentiating these two conditions. Delirium is a condition characterized by impaired consciousness and is thus a disorder of attention. The symptoms of delirium can include hallucinations, agitation, and bizarre behaviors, which may present similarly to schizophrenia. However, delirium is associated with waxing and waning reality testing within a short period of time, whereas symptoms of schizophrenia are more stable. A sudden onset, visual hallucinations (vs. auditory hallucinations), and recent medical illness (e.g. infection) or intervention (e.g., surgery, new medication) are more indicative of delirium, whereas auditory hallucinations, insidious onset, and previous episodes of psychosis are more consistent with schizophrenia.

Differentiating Alzheimer's Disease versus Psychotic Disorder Approximately 40% of patients with Alzheimer's disease (AD) and 15% to 40% of those with Parkinson's disease exhibit psychotic symptoms, which can include hallucinations, delusions, or illusions. Older adults with schizophrenia can exhibit memory impairments that may be, on the surface, similar to that seen in dementia. However, a key differentiating factor between schizophrenia and AD is "rapid forgetting," or an inability to retain learned information over a short period of time (Heaton et al., 1994; Tröster et al., 1993). As Heaton et. al. (1994b) indicated, memory deficiencies apparent in schizophrenia are more often characterized by the inability to encode or learn new information and are not due to rapid forgetting. In contrast to patients with AD, patients with schizophrenia may perform worse on measures of naming and praxic skills (Carlsson, Papcke-Benson, Carnes, McBride, & Stein 2002; Davidson et al., 1996). Other distinguishing neuropsychological factors between AD and schizophrenia include the rate of cognitive decline, where a more significant rate of decline occurring within one year is more indicative of AD.

Assessing Functional Capacity

Neuropsychologists who assess older adults with schizophrenia are often called upon to make judgments about functional capacity, and thus the assessment of functional status should complement neuropsychological testing. Functional status measures provide an indication of (a) the degree of impairment in functional abilities to aid in determination of the level of support/community placement, (b) the manifestations of cognitive impairments in daily life as targets for rehabilitation programming, and (3) the presence of functional abilities that are preserved and that can be 'leveraged' in developing rehabilitation programs. The measurement of functioning has become increasingly sophisticated in recent years, generally separating what people can do (functional capacity as measured with performance-based instruments) from what people actually do (disability as typically measured with rating scales). Below we provide several examples of instruments that are validated in older adults with schizophrenia.

Performance-based functional capacity measures involve observed performance of simulated tasks that are encountered in daily life, using role-play scenarios that are graded based on standardized criteria, such as the Direct Assessment of Functional Status (DAFS; Loewenstein et al., 1989) and the University of California, San Diego Performance Skills Assessment (UPSA; Patterson, Goldman, McKibbin, Hughs, & Jeste, 2001). The DAFS and UPSA provide general measures of independent living skills (e.g., communication, personal finances, hygiene, cooking tasks) that are commonly encountered as ADL/IADL tasks in maintaining independent functioning by having patients actually perform a set of standardized tasks during the assessment. (The DAFS was originally developed to assess the functional impairments associated with Alzheimer's disease, but has also been employed with schizophrenia patients; the UPSA was designed to more specifically target the types of functional capacity impairments which may characterize patients schizophrenia.) These measures are sensitive to change in interventions designed to enhance functional skills. (For a comprehensive review of performance based measures of functional capacity, see Moore, Palmer, Patterson, and Jeste (2007). There are also a number of clinician-rated scales to assess community functioning in older adults with schizophrenia, which include the Independent Living Skills Survey. Harvey and colleagues have described a measure developed for older adults with severe mental illness, the Social-Adaptive Functioning Evaluation, which is an observer-rated instrument covering independent living, interpersonal, and instrumental abilities that has been validated in older inpatient and outpatient samples (Harvey et al., 1997).

Assessing Decisional Capacity

Another clinical situation in late-life schizophrenia that neuropsychologists are often involved with is the determination of capacity, such as in decisions surrounding need for conservatorship, medical decision-making, disability status, or privileges such as driving. The generalized components of decisional capacity include understanding (Does the individual understand the risks and benefits of the decision?), appreciation (Can the individual apply the decision to their situation?), reasoning (How does the individual arrive at their decision?), and expression of a choice (Can and will the individual express their decision?). As with other domains of functioning described above, cognitive abilities are the strongest determinant of decisional capacity, over and above psychopathologic symptoms of schizophrenia (reviewed in Palmer & Savla, 2007). There are a wide variety of scales available for assessment of capacity to consent to treatment or research (reviewed in Dunn et al., 2006), and the American Psychological Association and American Bar Association have developed a very helpful handbook for assessing decisional capacity and competency in a wide variety of domains relevant to older patients (APA, 2008). In addition, over the past 15 years there have been a number of empirical studies examining the neuropsychological predictors of decisional capacity (reviewed in Palmer & Savla, 2007). There is little evidence from these studies that any one cognitive domain produces more impairment in capacity to make decisions. It is also vital to note that most patients with schizophrenia retain competence to make decisions (even when they have cognitive deficits or psychotic symptom), and that the presence of a diagnosis of schizophrenia should not lead to assumptions about diminished capacity. Additionally, at least in laboratory based studies, decisional capacity can be improved via repeated administrations of information, that is, the manner in which information is presented to patients could enhance or detract from capacity.

Cognitive Remediation

Can the cognitive deficits in later-life schizophrenia be treated? In the late 1990s there had been some suggestions that the newer (atypical or second generation) antipsychotic medication might be effective in improving certain aspects of cognitive functioning among persons with schizophrenia. However, subsequent data raise doubts about any substantive cognitive benefits of second generation antipsychotics over conventional neuroleptics medications, and none has been shown to result in substantial (functionally relevant) levels of cognitive improvement (reviewed in Palmer & Salva, 2009).

Beyond looking to beneficial cognitive side-effects from antipsychotic medications, efforts are ongoing to develop pharmacologic agents that would directly target the cognitive deficits associated with schizophrenia. A number of pharmacologic compounds have been evaluated, some in randomized controlled trials, with no clear evidence in support of any specific agent (Gray & Roth, 2007). So far, agents used to treat cognition in Alzheimer's disease (cholinesterase inhibitors, glutamaterics) have produced little effect in controlled trials. It is unclear whether age is a moderator of the effect of any of these medications. Nonetheless, it will be important for clinicians to follow the developments in this field, in particular whether medications are effective and safe in older adults with schizophrenia.

There are also recent developments in non-pharmacological strategies to enhance cognitive ability in schizophrenia, with a number of studies employing strategy-focused interventions via computerized training, as well as compensatory approaches that mitigate the impact of cognitive impairments on functioning. As with non-pharmacological agents, it remains unclear whether improvements seen associated with these training programs will provide lasting benefits that transfer to real-world behaviors. In meta-analysis of cognitive training for schizophrenia, the effect of training is enhanced when it is linked with functional rehabilitation (e.g., vocational rehabilitation). Functional rehabilitation is effective in enhancing functional capacity in older people with schizophrenia, as evidenced by the Functional Ability Skills Training (FAST). Although it may not be assumed that older people would be appropriate candidates for vocational rehabilitation, many older adults with schizophrenia want to work, and there are effective paradigms for vocational rehabilitation tailored for older people (Twamley, Narvaez, Becker, Bartels, & Jeste, 2008). Thus, cognitive remediation may be a viable augmentative treatment for older people with schizophrenia, particularly when integrated with functional training.

SUMMARY

In this chapter, we have focused on the neuropsychological aspects of late-life schizophrenia. The data that has accumulated over the past 20 years has indicated that older people with schizophrenia typically exhibit neuropsychological defects, and these deficits tend to be quite stable after the period of initial symptom onset. That is, with the exception of those who have been chronically institutionalized (a status which represents a relatively small minority of contemporary elderly patients with schizophrenia), patients' cognitive functioning tends to remains stable over years, even when symptoms fluctuate. Moreover, these cognitive deficits, not psychotic symptoms, appear to most strongly predict level of functional disability among outpatients with this condition. In evaluating older adults with suspected schizophrenia, it is essential to note that there are many illnesses and diagnoses, such as dementia, that can present with symptoms that are similar to the hallmark characteristics of schizophrenia; yet, a careful review of potential systemic causes, illness history, and potential toxicities can generally rule out the presence of dementia and delirium. With consideration for accommodations for older adults, to mitigate against the overriding influence of fatigue and sensory abilities, the components of neuropsychological evaluations in older people are much the same as that in younger adults. Evaluations may be more likely to include determinations of capacity to make decisions or function independently; and neuropsychologists should be aware of the performance-based and interview assessment tools that are validated for this population. Finally, given the recent initiatives to enhance cognitive ability in people with schizophrenia, there is hope for improved cognitive health of future cohorts of older adults.

REFERENCES

American Psychological Association and American Bar Association. (2008). *Assessment of capacity in older adults project working group, Assessment of older adults with diminished capacity: A handbook for psychologists*. Washington, DC : Author.

Andrews, A. O., Bartels, S., Xie, H., & Peacock, W. (2009). Increased risk of nursing home admission among middle aged and older adults with schizophrenia. *American Journal of Geriatric Psychiatry, 17*(8), 697–705.

Bangalore, S. S., Goradia, D. D.., Nutche, J.., Diwadkar, V. A. , Prasad, K. M., & Keshavan, M. S. (2009). Untreated illness duration correlates with gray matter loss in first-episode psychoses. *Neuroreport, 20*(7), 729–734.

Bose, S. K., Mackinnon, T., Mehta, M. A., Turkheimer, F. E., Howes, O. D., Selvaraj, S., et al. (2009). The effect of ageing on grey and white matter reductions in schizophrenia. *Schizophrenia Research, 112*(1-3), 7–13.

Bowie, C. R., Leung, W. W., Reichenberg, A., McClure, M. M., Patterson, T. L., Heaton, R. K., et al. (2008). Predicting schizophrenia patients' real-world behavior with specific neuropsychological and functional capacity measures. *Biological Psychiatry, 63*(5), 505.

Carlsson, C. M., Papcke-Benson, K., Carnes, M., McBride, P. E., & Stein, J. H. (2002). Health-related quality of life and long-term therapy with pravastatin and tocopherol (vitamin e) in older adults. *Drugs Aging, 19*(10), 793–805.

Cohen, C. (1990). Outcome of schizophrenia into later life: An overview. *Gerontologist, 30*, 790–797.

Copeland, J. R. M., Dewey, M. E., Scott, A., Gilmore, C., Larkin, B. A., Cleave, N., et al. (1998). Schizophrenia and delusional disorder in older age: Community prevalence, incidence, comorbidity, and outcome. *Schizophr Bull, 24*(1), 153–161.

Davidson, M., Harvey, P., Welsh, K. A., Powchik, P., Putnam, K. M., & Mohs, R. C. (1996). Cognitive functioning in late-life schizophrenia: A comparison of elderly schizophrenic patients and patients with alzheimer's disease. *American Journal of Psychiatry, 153*(10), 1274–1279.

Dickinson, D., Iannone, V. N., Wilk, C. M., & Gold, J. M. (2004). General and specific cognitive deficits in schizophrenia. *Biol Psychiatry, 55*(8), 826–833.

Dunn, L., Nowrangi, M., Palmer, B. W., Jeste, D. V., & Saks, E. (2006). Assessing decisional capacity for clinical research or treatment: A review of instruments. *American Journal of Psychiatry, 163*(8), 1323–1334.

Evans, J. D., Heaton, R. K., Paulsen, J. S., Palmer, B. W., Patterson, T., & Jeste, D. V. (2003). The relationship of neuropsychological abilities to specific domains of functional capacity in older schizophrenia patients. *Biological Psychiatry, 53*(5), 422–430.

Folsom, D. P., Depp, C., Palmer, B. W., Mausbach, B. T., Golshan, S., Fellows, I., et al. (2009). Physical and mental health-related quality of life among older people with schizophrenia. *Schizophrenia Research, 108*(1-3), 207–213.

Friedman, J. I., Harvey, P. D., Kemether, E., Byne, W., & Davis, K. L. (1999). Cognitive and functional changes with aging in schizophrenia. Biological Psychiatry,, *46*(7), 921–928.

Granholm, E., McQuaid, J. R., McClure, F. S., Auslander, L. A., Perivoliotis, D., Pedrelli, P., et al. (2005). A randomized, controlled trial of cognitive behavioral social skills training for middle-aged and older outpatients with chronic schizophrenia. *American Journal of Psychiatry, 162*(3), 520–529.

Gray, J. A., & Roth, B. L. (2007). Molecular targets for treating cognitive dysfunction in schizophrenia. *Schizophrenia Bulletin, 33*(5), 1100–1119.

Harris, M. J., & Jeste, D. V. (1988). Late-onset schizophrenia: An overview. *Schizophrenia Bulletin, 14*(1), 39–55.

Harvey, P. D., Davidson, M., Mueser, K. T., Parrella, M., White, L., & Powchik, P. (1997). Social-adaptive functioning evaluation (safe): A rating scale for geriatric psychiatric patients. *Schizophrenia Bulletin, 23*(1), 131–145.

Harvey, P. D., Silverman, J. M., Mohs, R. C., Parrella, M., White, L., Powchik, P., et al. (1999). Cognitive decline in late-life schizophrenia: A longitudinal study of geriatric chronically hospitalized patients. *Biological Psychiatry, 45*(1), 32–40.

Hazzard, W. R. (1995). Elder abuse: Definitions and implications for medical education. *Academic Medicine,, 70*(11), 979–981.

Heaton, R. K., Gladsjo, J. A., Palmer, B. W., Kuck, J., Marcotte, T. D., & Jeste, D. V. (2001). The stability and course of neuropsychological deficits in schizophrenia. *Archives of General Psychiatry, 58*(1), 24–32.

Heaton, R. K., Paulsen, J. S., McAdams, L. A., Kuck, J., Zisook, S., Braff, D., et al. (1994). Neuropsychological deficits in schizophrenics. Relationship to age, chronicity, and dementia. *Archives of General Psychiatry, 51*(6), 469–476.

Jeste, D., Alexopoulos, G., Bartels, S., Cummings, J., Gallo, J., Gottlieb, G., et al. (1999). Consensus statement on the upcoming crisis in geriatric mental health: Research agenda for the next 2 decades. *Arch Gen Psychiatry, 56*(9), 848–853.

Klingberg, S., Wittorf, A., Sickinger, S., Buchkremer, G., & Wiedemann, G. (2008). Course of cognitive functioning during the stabilization phase of schizophrenia. *Journal of Psychiatric Research, 42*(4), 259–267.

Kurtz, M. M. (2005). Neurocognitive impairment across the lifespan in schizophrenia: An update. *Schizophrenia Research, 74*(1), 15–26.

Kurtz, M. M. (2006). Symptoms versus neurocognitive skills as correlates of everyday functioning in severe mental illness. *Expert Review of Neurotherapeutics, 6*(1), 47–56.

Loewenstein, D., Amigo, E., Duara, R., Guterman, A., Hurwitz, D., Berkowitz, N., et al. (1989). A new scale for the assessment of functional status in alzheimer's disease and related disorders. *J Gerontol, 44*(4), P114–121.

McGlashan, T. (1988). A selective review of recent North American long-term followup studies of schizophrenia. *Schizophrenia Bulletin, 14*(4), 515–542.

Moore, D. J., Palmer, B. W., Patterson, T. L., & Jeste, D. V. (2007). A review of performance-based measures of functional living skills. *Journal of Psychiatric Research, 41*(1-2), 97–118.

Nayak Savla, G., Moore, D. J., Roesch, S. C., Heaton, R. K., Jeste, D. V., & Palmer, B. W. (2006). An evaluation of longitudinal neurocognitive performance among middle-aged and older schizophrenia patients: Use of mixed-model analyses. *Schizophrenia Research, 83*(2-3), 215–223.

Ostling, S., & Skoog, I. (2002). Psychotic symptoms and paranoid ideation in a nondemented population-based sample of the very old. *Archives of General Psychiatry, 59*(1), 53–59.

Palmer, B. W. (2004). The expanding role of neuropsychology in geriatric psychiatry. *American Journal of Geriatric Psychiatry, 12*(4), 338–341.

Palmer, B. W., Bondi, M., Twamley, E., Thal, L., Golshan, S., & Jeste, D. V. (2003). Are late-onset schizophrenia spectrum disorders neurodegenerative conditions? Annual rates of change on two dementia measures. *Journal of Neuropsychiatry and Clinical Neuroscience, 15*(1), 45–52.

Palmer, B. W., & Dawes, S. E. (2010). Cognitive aging: From basic skills to scripts and schemata. In D. V. Jeste & C. D. Depp (Eds.), *Handbook of successful cognitive and emotional aging* (pp. 37–54). Arlington, VA: American Psychiatric Publishing.

Palmer, B. W., Dawes, S. E. & Heaton, R. K. (2009). What do we know about neuropsychological aspects of schizophrenia? *Neuropsychology Review, 19*, 365–384.

Palmer, B. W., Heaton, S., & Jeste, D. V. (1999). Older patients with schizophrenia: Challenges in the coming decades. *Psychiatric Services, 50*(9), 1178–1183.

Palmer, B. W., & Savla, G. N. (2007). The association of specific neuropsychological deficits with capacity to consent to research or treatment. *Journal of the International Neuropsychological Society, 13*(06), 1047–1059.

Palmer, B. W., & Savla, G. (2009). Neuropsychological deficits in schizoaffective disorder. In K. Yip (Ed.), *Schizoaffective disorders: International perspectives on understanding intervention and rehabilitation* (pp. 115–134). New York: Nova Science Publishers.

Patterson, T. L., Goldman, S., McKibbin, C. L., Hughs, T., & Jeste, D. V. (2001). Ucsd performance-based skills assessment: Development of a new measure of everyday functioning for severely mentally ill adults. *Schizophr Bull, 27*(2), 235–245.

Rajji, T., & Mulsant, B. (2008). Nature and course of cognitive function in late-life schizophrenia: A systematic review. *Schizophrenia Research, 102*(1-3), 122–140.

Rund, B. R. (1998). A review of longitudinal studies of cognitive functions in schizophrenia patients. *Schizophrenia Bulletin, 24*(3), 425–435.

Salthouse, T. (2004). What and when of cognitive aging. *Current Directions in Psychological Science, 13*(4), 140–144.

Schwartzman, A., Douglas, V., & Muir, W. (1962). Inltellectual loss in schizophrenia. *Canadian Journal of Psychology, 16*, 161–168.

Staal, W., Hulshoff, P., Hilleke, E., & Rene, S. (1999). Outcome of schizophrenia in relation to brain abnormalities. *Schizophrenia Bulletin, 25*(2), 337–348.

Tröster, A. I., Butters, N., Salmon, D. P., Cullum, C. M., Jacobs, D., Brandt, J., et al. (1993). The diagnostic utility of savings scores: Differentiating alzheimer's and huntington's diseases with the logical memory and visual reproduction tests. *Journal of Clinical and Experimental Neuropsychology* , *15*(5), 773–788.

Twamley, E. W., Narvaez, J. M., Becker, D. R., Bartels, S. J., & Jeste, D. V. (2008). Supported employment for middle-aged and older people with schizophrenia. *American Journal of Psychiatric Rehabilitation, 11*(1), 76–89.

Twamley, E. W., Salva, G., Zurhellen, C., Heaton, R. K., & Jeste, D. V. (2008). Development and pilot testing of a novel compensatory cognitive training intervention for people with psychosis. *American Journal of Psychiatric Rehabilitation, 11*(2), 144–163.

Vahia, I., Palmer, B., Depp, C. D., Fellows, I., Golshan, S., Kraemer, H. C., et al. (in press). Is late-onset schizophrenia a subtype of schizophrenia. *Acta Psychiatrica Scaninavica.*

Velligan, D., Bow-Thomas, C., Mahurin, R., Miller, A., & Halgunseth, L. (2000). Do specific neurocognitive deficits predict specific domains of community function in schizophrenia? *Journal of Nervous and Mental Disease, 188*(8), 518–524.

BOX 7.1 PREVALENCE AND SUBTYPES

1. The prevalence of schizophrenia is approximately 1% among adults over age 65.
2. Age of onset among people with schizophrenia is generally around 20 years old. An onset after age 40 is considered late-onset, and after age 60 is very-late onset.
3. Late-onset and early-onset schizophrenia are more similar than different.
4. People with late-onset schizophrenia are more often women, less severe deficits in learning and memory, and better community adjustment.

BOX 7.2 COURSE

1. Long-term follow and cross-sectional study suggest that positive symptoms of schizophrenia improve with age, in contrast to early conceptualizations of schizophrenia as a dementia praecox.
2. Clinical presentation of schizophrenia at an older age is more heterogeneous between patients than at a younger age.
3. Among patients who are community dwelling, neuropsychological deficits appear stable and do not deteriorate more than expected from normal aging.
4. Institutionalized patients show a greater rate of cognitive decline than do community-dwelling patients.

BOX 7.3 NEUROBIOLOGY

1. Structural imaging indicates larger-than-normal ventricles that increase with age as in normal aging.
2. The relationship between ventricular size and poor outcome is consistent across the life-span.
3. Neuropathological studies do not show the presence of neurofibriallary tangles nor amyloid plaques that are characteristic of degenerative dementias.

BOX 7.4 ASSESSMENT AND DIFFERENTIAL DIAGNOSIS

1. There are many causes for alterations in mental status in older age, requiring ruling out non-psychiatric etiologies even in people with chronic schizophrenia and even more so among new onset cases.
2. Differentiating diagnoses of schizophrenia and dementia or delirium should cover symptom onset, timing, type, and concurrence with medical comorbidities and medical treatments.
3. Proxy informants are often essential to identify the pattern, antecedents, and responses to psychotic symptoms.
4. A sudden onset, visual hallucinations (vs. auditory hallucinations), and recent medical illness (e.g., infection) or intervention (e.g., surgery, new medication) are more indicative of delirium; whereas auditory hallucinations, insidious onset, and previous episodes of psychosis are more consistent with schizophrenia.
5. Key difference between schizophrenia and Alzheimer's disease is "rapid forgetting," or an inability to retain learned information over a short period of time, present in AD.

BOX, 7.5 ASSESSMENT MEASURES

1. Selection of neuropsychological tests for older adults should be based on the availability of appropriate age norms and may need alteration if visual or hearing deficits are present.
2. Fatigue is more likely to be present in older adults, and so shorter testing periods and frequent breaks are recommended.
3. Because many neuropsychological assessments in older adults surround decisions related to functional capacity, performance-based and clinician-rated measures of functioning are useful adjuncts to neuropsychological assessment.

4. Decisional capacity assessment is a frequent referral in this age group, and there are standardized approaches to assessing capacity to make medical decisions.
5. No one cognitive domain produces more impairment in capacity to make decisions; and the presence of a diagnosis of schizophrenia should not lead to assumptions about diminished capacity.

BOX, 7.6 NEUROCOGNITIVE REMEDIATION

1. There is little evidence that pharmacologic compounds used to treat Alzheimer's disease improve cognitive deficits in schizophrenia.
2. Cognitive training for schizophrenia is enhanced when it is linked with functional rehabilitation, such as vocational rehabilitation.
3. There is little known about whether older adults benefit from cognitive remediation as much as younger adults.

CONTINUING EDUCATION QUESTIONS

1. What is the approximate prevalence of schizophrenia in older age?
   a. 0.1%
   b. 0.5%
   c. 1.0%
   d. 2.0%
2. Which of the following is not a consistent difference between early- and late-onset schizophrenia?
   a. Ratio of women to men
   b. Proportion of patients who are of the paranoid subtype
   c. Performance on tests of learning and memory
   d. Performance on tests of executive function
3. Which early psychiatrist coined the term dementia praecox?
   a. Blueler
   b. Freud
   c. Krapelin
   d. Vygotsky
4. Which statement best describes the course of cognitive deficits in schizophrenia on average?
   a. Both community-dwelling and institutionalized patients evidence deterioration
   b. Neither community-dwelling nor institutionalized patients evidence deterioration

c. Community-dwelling patients, but not institutionalized patients, evidence deterioration
d. Institutionalized, but not community-dwelling patients, evidence deterioration_

5. Neurofibrillary tangles and plaques are found in post-mortem studies in:
    a. Patients with Alzheimer's Disease and late-life schizophrenia
    b. Patients with Alzheimer's Disease only
    c. Patients with late-life schizophrenia only
6. Delirium is best characterized as a disorder of:
    a. Attention
    b. Learning and memory
    c. Processing speed
    d. Executive function
7. Which is not a component of decisional capacity?
    a. Understanding
    b. Comprehension
    c. Expression of a Choice
    d. Appreciation

8

Medical Comorbidity in Schizophrenia

WILLIAM S. STONE, Ph.D.

Massachusetts Mental Health Center Division of Public Sector Psychiatry, Beth Israel Deaconess Medical Center Department of Psychiatry, Harvard Medical School

MATCHERI S. KESHAVAN, M.D.

Department of Psychiatry, Beth Israel Deaconess Medical Center and Massachusetts Mental Health Center, Harvard Medical School

Schizophrenia and other mental disorders are increasingly coming to be understood as multidimensional conditions that include medical dysfunction in addition to clinical, neuropsychological, social, and neurobiological dimensions of disorder. The extent to which medical dysfunctions overlap with clinical problems in schizophrenia is part of an important debate about the conceptualization and treatment of psychotic disorders. Similarly, the extent to which medical disorders contribute to neuropsychological dysfunction has a significant bearing on the extent of cognitive and function deficits, and on the identification of useful measures for therapeutic interventions.

This chapter focuses on relationships between comorbid medical disorders and neuropsychological dysfunction in schizophrenia. We will focus first on the nature and scope of medical comorbidity, and then on representative evidence that rates of certain related physical disorders are elevated in schizophrenia. We will then emphasize contributions of comorbid medical conditions to neuropsychological dysfunction in schizophrenia. Conditions involving poor glucose regulation will be emphasized in this discussion as an example of a physical condition that may be inherent to schizophrenia, may exacerbate neuropsychological function, and may provide a useful treatment target. We will conclude with a discussion of clinical implications for neuropsychology.

PHYSICAL COMORBIDITY IN MAJOR PSYCHIATRIC DISORDERS

Associations between physical problems and mental disorders are not new. Harris and Barraclough (1998) noted, for example, that premature deaths in patients with mental disorders were recorded in English vital statistics for 150 years. Similar observations were reported in the first half of the 20th century (e.g., Philips, 1934), and also more recently (Iacovides & Siamouli, 2008; Leucht, Burkard, Henderson, Maj, & Sartorius, 2007). To illustrate this point, Figure 8.1 shows standardized mortality ratios (SMR) for schizophrenia patients derived from three recent studies, including a meta-analysis that (Saha, Chant, & McGrath, 2007) included 37 studies, a study of regional differences in mortality in Finland over a five-year period (Kiviniemi et al., 2010), and a study of mortality in the United Kingdom (Brown, Kim, Mitchell, & Inskip, 2010). Figure 8.1 emphasizes premature mortality due to natural causes (i.e., medical conditions such as cardiovascular disease), though deaths attributable to unnatural causes (e.g., suicide, accidents, violence) are also elevated in schizophrenia (Brown et al., 2010). Each of these studies shows that individuals with schizophrenia are 2–3 times more likely to die prematurely from one or more medical disorders compared to the general population. The SMRs did not differ significantly by gender in these three studies (and were not presented in Saha et al., 2007). Notably, two of these studies showed that the magnitudes of SMRs are increasing over time (Brown et al., 2010; Saha et al., 2007).

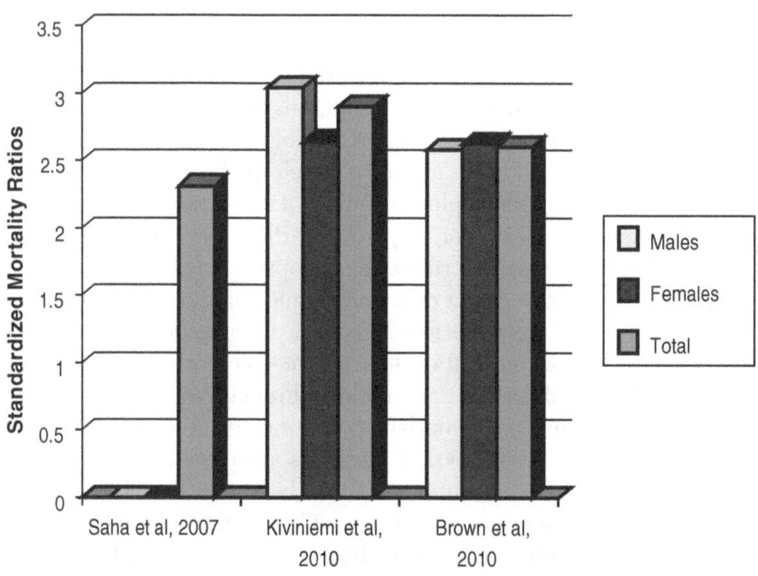

Figure 8.1 Standardized mortality ratios (SMRs) in three representative recent studies show significantly elevated mortality rates for schizophrenia patients due to natural causes. Saha et al did not present SMRs by gender.

Despite the magnitude of these effects, physical problems in major psychiatric conditions have received increased attention only in the last two decades (Brown, 1997; Brown, Inskip, & Barraclough, 2000; Fleischhacker et al., 2008; Ryan & Thakore, 2002), for several reasons. One of the most important of these is a significant reduction in life span. While the extent of the reduction varies, many estimates range from 20% (Marder et al., 2004) to 30% (Fleischhacker et al., 2008) in schizophrenia. Since approximately 38% of this excess mortality is attributable to suicide and to homicide, the remaining 62% is attributable to other medical disorders (i.e., natural causes).

The significance of this phenomenon is underscored by considering the magnitude of this reduction on the average life-span of the general population in the United States. If a 30% reduction is applied to an average life-span of 78 (women would be a few years higher and men would be a few years lower; Fleischhacker et al., 2008), then the span would be reduced to about 55 years of age. A majority of these individuals with serious psychiatric disorders are thus likely to develop significant comorbid medical disorders earlier in life, many of which (e.g., diabetes and cardiovascular disease) are likely to increase cognitive dysfunction. While this does not reflect premature aging per se, it has similarities to aging (Kirkpatrick, Messias, Harvey, Fernandez-Egea, & Bowie, 2008) that have clinical implications for neuropsychological assessment. One of these implications, for example, is that global cognitive deficits will increase as people with these comorbid medical burdens age.

A second reason underlying the increased interest in comorbid medical problems is that they are more likely to go undetected in people with major psychiatric illnesses such as schizophrenia (Subramaniam, Chong, & Pek, 2003), and thus untreated. Many factors contribute to this situation, such as the stigmatization of mental disorders, the suboptimal integration of mental health and other medical services, and interference by the illness itself with the awareness of physical problems and with the capacities to seek out, engage in and adhere to treatment regimens. Even when medical care is obtained, its quality may be substandard (Fagiolini & Goracci, 2009) due to patient problems (e.g., poor treatment compliance), health care provider problems (e.g., a biased focus on psychiatric problems rather than on other medical problems), and to problems involving both patients and providers (e.g., communication problems). Regardless of the causes, however, the outcomes include a growing awareness that many preventable or treatable disorders are missed. Consequently, the burdens of severe mental disorders are increased in individuals, families and societies, while the qualities of their lives are decreased.

A third reason underlying increased interest in comorbid medical problems is that a variety of medical problems may be caused by psychopharmacological treatments (Marder et al., 2004; Newcomer, 2007; Newcomer et al., 2002). In particular, antipsychotic medications contribute to weight gain and to related changes in glucose metabolism, insulin sensitivity and lipid metabolism, which themselves contribute to the development of a variety of disorders, such as diabetes and cardiovascular disease. Consequently, antipsychotic medications may contribute to long-term vulnerabilities for cognitive deficits.

Medical comorbidity in psychiatric illnesses can be viewed in at least two perspectives. First, individuals with schizophrenia may receive less treatment for medical conditions for a variety of reasons, including several listed above. Recognition of this point, in and of itself, could lead to better medical treatment, and to better outcomes for patient's psychiatric conditions. Second, it is possible that, to some extent, excess mortality and comorbid medical problems reflect an inherent relationship to psychiatric conditions. If this latter view is correct, their study may shed light on the nature of the psychiatric disorders themselves, including perhaps the vulnerability to develop them and the types of intervention that might attenuate or even prevent their expression.

MEDICAL CONDITIONS RELATED TO SCHIZOPHRENIA AND/OR ANTIPSYCHOTIC MEDICATIONS

Numerous medical disorders and conditions are elevated in schizophrenia (Brown et al., 2000; Fagiolini & Goracci, 2009; Fleischhacker et al., 2008; Harris & Barraclough, 1998; Leucht et al., 2007; von Hausswolff-Juhlin, Bjartveit, Lindstrom, & Jones, 2009). Table 8.1 provides an overview of several medical disorders related to schizophrenia, again using SMRs from recent representative studies to facilitate comparisons across disorders and studies. In some instances, categories contain types of disease (e.g., respiratory) and also more specific disorders (e.g., chronic obstructive airways disease). The rates in this Table only reflect comorbid medical disorders that resulted in death, and are likely, therefore, to underestimate the total rates of the disorders. Even with this limitation, the table shows that many disorders and classes of disorder occur at elevated rates in individuals with schizophrenia.

While many medical disorders are elevated in schizophrenia, we will emphasize disorders related to the metabolic syndrome because of their medical importance, the relatively high rates at which they occur, and, in most instances, because of their relationships to cognitive dysfunction.

Cardiovascular Disorders

Cardiovascular disease is a heterogeneous class of disorder that shows elevated rates in schizophrenia. Black and Fisher (1992) reported that cardiovascular disease accounted for up to 20% of excess mortality in patients with *DSM-III-R* schizophrenia, with mortality elevated in both genders (Ryan & Thakore, 2002). Recent studies show that patients with schizophrenia are at least twice as likely to die from cardiovascular disease as is the general population, and is a leading medical cause of premature death in this population (Brown et al., 2010; Fleischhacker et al., 2008; Kiviniemi et al., 2010; Saha et al., 2007; von Hausswolff-Juhlin et al., 2009). Many other medical illness or risk factors that increase vulnerability to cardiovascular disease are also elevated in

TABLE 8.1 Representative Total Standardized Mortality Rations (SMRs) for Several Common Comorbid Medical Disorders in Schizophrenia

Disease	SMR	Study
Cardiovascular	2.25	(Brown et al., 2010)
	2.01	(Saha et al., 2007)
Circulatory	2.58	(Brown et al., 2010)
	3.92	(Kiviniemi et al., 2010)
Cerebrovascular	0.87	(Saha et al., 2007)
	3.08	(Brown et al., 2010)
Respiratory	4.01	(Saha et al., 2007)
	3.31	(Kiviniemi et al., 2010)
	4.99	(Brown et al., 2010)
Chronic obstructive airway dis.	3.94	(Brown et al., 2010)
Endocrine disorders (including metabolic problems)	8.01	(Brown et al., 2010)
	3.28	(Kiviniemi et al., 2010)
	5.50	(Saha et al., 2007)
Diabetes Mellitus	6.14	(Brown et al., 2010)
Nervous System	4.27	(Brown et al., 2010)
	3.28	(Kiviniemi et al., 2010)
	4.26	(Saha et al., 2007)
Neoplasms	1.44	(Saha et al., 2007)
	1.20	(Kiviniemi et al., 2010)
	1.49	(Brown et al., 2010)
	1.50	(Tran et al., 2009)
Lung Cancer	2.65	(Brown et al., 2010)
Lung Cancer (men only)	2.20	(Tran et al., 2009)
Breast Cancer (women only)	2.80	(Tran et al., 2009)
	1.96	(Brown et al., 2010)
Digestive	5.28	(Saha et al., 2007)
	1.88	(Kiviniemi et al., 2010)
	2.89	(Brown et al., 2010)

schizophrenia, such as obesity, diabetes, dyslipidemia, hypertension, antipsychotic medications, smoking, diets high in fat, a sedentary lifestyle and the metabolic syndrome, among others (Meyer, 2003; von Hausswolff-Juhlin et al., 2009). Multiple etiologies probably contribute to these problems, such as elongation of Q-T intervals (that are often produced by some antipsychotic medications and may result in arrhythmias), heart failure, syncope and collapse, heart failure, and stroke (Fagiolini & Goracci, 2009).

Dyslipidemia

Dyslipidemias refer to disorders of lipid metabolism, and are risk factors for coronary heart disease, hypertension, diabetes, obesity and the metabolic syndrome (Davidson, 2002). Elevated cholesterol or triglycerides are associated with antipsychotic treatment (Meyer, 2003), though some of those effects may be related to weight gain or obesity (Ryan & Thakore, 2002). While the nature or magnitude of dyslipidemia may reflect an inherent vulnerability to the effects of these medications, it is unclear whether lipid profiles are altered prior to psychosis and to treatment with antipsychotic medications. In one study with drug-naive, first-episode patients with schizophrenia, for example, levels of lipids were normal (Ryan, Collins, & Thakore, 2003). Although altered lipid profiles were highly associated with individual schizophrenia subjects who develop metabolic syndrome (H. J. Koponen et al., 2010), they did not differ between subjects in the Northern Finland 1986 Birth Cohort at ages 15–16 who did or did not develop psychosis (including but not limited to schizophrenia) subsequently at ages 16–21 (H. Koponen, Vuononvirta, et al., 2008). Similarly, lipid profiles did not differ between adolescents in this cohort who were at high familial risk for psychosis, and those who were not (H. Koponen, Maki, et al., 2008).

Obesity

Obesity is a growing epidemic in the general population of the United States, and in other parts of the world (Wirshing & Meyer, 2003). Many environmental factors that predispose the general population to obesity, such as poor diet and/or low levels of physical exercise, also predispose individuals with schizophrenia. In addition, factors such as antipsychotic medications, negative symptoms and other illness-related causes of inactivity, add further to the risk for weight gain in schizophrenia. Interestingly, at least some studies fail to show differences in body mass index (BMI) between patients with schizophrenia who never received antipsychotic medications, and healthy control subjects (Padmavati, McCreadie, & Tirupati, 2010; Strassnig, Miewald, Keshavan, & Ganguli, 2007). Certain types of obesity, however, are expressed more clearly at higher rates. Thakore, Mann, Vlahoos, Martin, and Reznek (2002) showed, for example, that drug-naive patients had a higher BMI than a control group. Although total and subcutaneous body fat did not differ between groups, abdominal fat in the schizophrenic group was over 3.4 times higher than it was in the control group.

Metabolic Syndrome

The medical problems described above, and others such as poor glucose regulation and insulin resistance (discussed below), are each significant individually. They are also important, however, because they tend to cluster together and increase the risk for other components of the cluster. This group of metabolic abnormalities has been referred to in several ways, but is most often called the "metabolic syndrome" (Holt, Pevelert, & Byrne, 2004; Newcomer, 2007; Reaven, 1988). Although definitions of the syndrome vary, components of the syndrome usually include several abnormalities from a list that includes abnormal glucose and/or insulin metabolism, abdominal obesity, dyslipidemia, and cardiovascular disease. The prevalence of the syndrome depends on the precise diagnostic criteria used to define it, but regardless of which definition is used, it is relatively common in the general population. The overall prevalence in the United States was 23.9 % using a definition employed by the National Cholesterol Education Program/Adult Treatment Panel III (Ford & Giles, 2003). Both age (e. g., the rate for 20–29 years of age was 7 %; the rate for over 60 years of age was over 40 %) and ethnicity (e.g., the rate among African American men was 16.5 %; the rate among Mexican American women was 36.3 %) were among the factors that modulated prevalence rates. Similarly, a recent study of occupational groups in the United States showed an overall rate of 20%, but with large differences between groups (Davila et al., 2010). Food preparation workers showed higher rates, for example (29.6%–31.1%) than engineers, architects and scientists (8.5%–9.2%).

The metabolic syndrome occurs more frequently in schizophrenia and other psychiatric disorders than it does in the general population (Newcomer, 2007). One recent study showed that first-episode schizophrenia patients treated with antipsychotic medications showed prevalence rates for the metabolic syndrome that were five times higher than a matched, healthy control group (Saddichha, Manjunatha, Ameen, & Aktar, 2008). Interestingly, medication-naïve subjects in their first episode of schizophrenia showed lower body weight, BMI, and low density lipoprotein (LDL) levels than control subjects (Verma, Subramaniam, Liew, & Poon, 2009), consistent with findings reported by Padmavati et al. (2010) described above. These examples underscore the point that many disorders underlying the metabolic syndrome are associated with the antipsychotic medications used to treat schizophrenia, possibly in addition to other sources of vulnerability. In contrast, Verma et al. also showed that the same drug-naïve patients who had lower BMI's and LDL's showed higher levels of diabetes compared to control subjects.

Glucose/insulin Dysfunction

Schizophrenia has a well-documented association with diabetes and impaired glucose regulation in general. As early as 1919, Kooy reported an association between hyperglycemia and schizophrenia in 10 patients. Since then, the observation of glucose dysregulation in schizophrenia has been repeated many times. Compared to United States general population norms of around 3.4% (Regenold, Thapar, Marano, Gavirneni, & Kondapavuluru, 2002), rates of Type 2 diabetes typically range from about 15% (Dixon et al., 2000; Mukherjee, Decina, Bocola, Saraceni, & Scapicchio, 1996) to 21% (Subramaniam et al., 2003) in patients with schizophrenia. De Hert et al. (2006) reported that rates of diabetes increased at a higher rate with age in patients with schizophrenia than it did in control patients. Patients in the 15- to 25-year-old range showed a 1.6% higher prevalence rate than that of the general population, for example, while patients in the 55- to 65-year-old range showed a 19.2% higher prevalence rate than that of the general population.

Although antipsychotic medications and lifestyle factors (e.g., sedentary behavior, poor diets) contribute to these high rates of diabetes, as they do with the metabolic syndrome (Fagiolini & Goracci, 2009; Leucht et al., 2007; Newcomer, 2007; Nielsen, Skadhede, & Correll, 2010), at least a few studies show elevated rates at the time of the first episode of psychosis, in drug-naïve subjects (Dasgupta, Singh, Rout, Saha, & Mandal, 2010; Kirkpatrick, Miller, Garcia-Rizo, Fernandez-Egea, & Bernardo, 2010; Ryan et al., 2003; Saddichha et al., 2008; Venkatasubramanian et al., 2007; Verma et al., 2009). Ryan et al. (2003), for example, reported impaired glucose tolerance in 15.4% of a first-episode group of subjects compared to 0 % in a control group. More recently, Verma et al. showed elevated levels of diabetes in first-episode psychotic patients, as noted. Kirkpatrick et al. showed abnormal glucose tolerance in antipsychotic-naïve patients, and Fernandez-Egea et al. reported elevated levels of abnormal glucose tolerance in antipsychotic-naïve, psychotic subjects compared to controls (16% versus 0%). It is not clear when abnormal glucose regulation develops, as Koponen et al. showed that adolescents assessed at ages 15–16 who later developed psychosis (again including but not limited to schizophrenia) did not show altered insulin resistance (H. Koponen, Vuononvirta et al., 2008). Nevertheless, these findings raise the possibility that altered glucose metabolism might be related to schizophrenia itself, rather than only to treatments for schizophrenia, or lifestyle factors related to it.

Several converging lines of evidence add to this view, including, among others, elevated rates of diabetes in some families of patients with schizophrenia (Fernandez-Egea et al., 2008; Mukherjee, Schnur, & Reddy, 1989; Spelman, Walsh, Sharifi, Collins, & Thakore, 2007; Wright et al., 1996) (though not all; see H. Koponen, Maki, et al., 2008)), and increased risks for schizophrenia in the offspring of mothers who experienced gestational diabetes during pregnancy (Gunnell, Rasmussen, Fouskakis, Tynelius, & Harrison, 2003). We examined this issue from a different perspective by performing linkage analyses on a pre-selected set of genes that code for enzymes that are involved in the regulation of glucose metabolism (Stone et al., 2004). This approach minimized effects of environmental variables such as medications and diet. Data were utilized from the NIMH Genetics Initiative for Schizophrenia data set (Cloninger et al., 1998), with the genome-wide significance of these genes to schizophrenia assessed using permutation testing procedures. Three genes in the European-American portion of the sample, including 6-phosphofructo-2-kinase/fructose-2,6-bisphosphatase 2 (chromosome 1q32.2), hexokinase 3 (chromosome 5q35.3) and pyruvate kinase 3 (chromosome 15q23) showed significant linkage, while no genes showed significance in the African-American portion of the sample. These findings provide support for the hypothesis that genes involved in glucose regulation might also be involved in schizophrenia. Consistent with this possibility, Lin and Shuldiner (2010) reported that of 338 candidate genes for Type 2 diabetes listed on the Genetic Association Database (http://geneticassociationb.nih.gov), and 268 candidate genes listed for schizophrenia, 37 of these genes were common to both lists (i.e., 11% of the diabetes genes and 14% of the schizophrenia genes; Lin & Shuldiner, 2010).

In summary, schizophrenia is associated with a variety of medical conditions. While a significant portion of these conditions may be exacerbated by environmental factors such as antipsychotic medication and poor lifestyle choices, at least some of them may also reflect inherent vulnerabilities related to schizophrenia itself. We next consider how these medical disorders contribute to neuropsychological dysfunction in schizophrenia.

COMORBID MEDICAL DISORDERS AND NEUROPSYCHOLOGICAL DEFICITS

Medical disorders in schizophrenia have multiple consequences related to mortality and morbidity. They also affect both the course and the functional outcome of illness in other ways, however, including their effects on cognition. The issue may be conceptualized in at least two ways. First, do comorbid medical conditions add to the already substantial cognitive burden in schizophrenia? Second, do they reflect the etiology of schizophrenia in ways that might lead to the development of useful treatment targets?

Comorbid Medical Conditions and Neuropsychological Function in Non-psychiatric Samples

Irrespective of whether schizophrenia or related disorders are present, many of the medical conditions highlighted above demonstrate negative effects on cognition. A few representative examples will be considered from relatively large, recent studies. Among these, Muller et al reported recently on 823 adult subjects who participated in the SMART (Secondary Manifestations of ARTerial disease) study in the Netherlands, and who received tests of verbal and visual learning and memory, visual-spatial function, and executive function (particularly emphasizing problem solving, mental flexibility, and verbal fluency for letters; Muller et al., 2010). All subjects were assessed for other components of the metabolic syndrome in addition to cardiovascular problems. Subjects with atherosclerotic disease particularly showed memory and visual-spatial dysfunction, with a tendency towards greater dysfunction in subjects who demonstrated more components of the metabolic syndrome.

Solomon et al. (2009) reported serum total cholesterol (TC) and neuropsychological data from 1382 non-demented participants in the cardiovascular risk factors, aging and dementia (CAIDE) study, after an average follow-up period of 21 years. Neuropsychological tests included measures of word recall, category fluency and letter digit substitution, in addition to the Purdue Pegboard and Stroop tests. The main findings showed that high midlife TC was associated with poorer word recall and category fluency 21 years later. Notably, declining TC levels in the absence of treatment were associated with poor word recall and slower psychomotor speed, while lipid lowering treatment was associated with better performance in the same measures.

Fergenbaum et al. (2009) assessed obesity and other components of the metabolic syndrome in a Canadian First Nations community. Two hundred and seven mainly young or middle-aged adults received the Clock Drawing Test, and 190 subjects received Trails A and B (which were combined into an executive function score). Subjects who met criteria for either obesity and/or the metabolic syndrome showed significantly poorer performance on these tests emphasizing executive function.

Comorbid Medical Conditions and Cognition in Schizophrenia Samples

The representative studies described above show that non-psychiatric subjects with the metabolic syndrome or with some of its components demonstrate impaired performance on neuropsychological tests. Since most patients with schizophrenia show significant cognitive deficits, it is important to ask whether these medical conditions exacerbate cognitive function. Several studies have addressed this issue. One of these utilized data from the Clinical Antipsychotic Trials of Intervention Effectiveness (CATIE). Chwastiak et al. (2006) analyzed clinical, cognitive and medical data from 1,424 subjects with *DSM-IV* schizophrenia who participated in the study. Fifty-eight percent of the sample had at least one medical condition, while 9% had four or more. The cognitive battery included 11 measures of executive function, verbal learning and memory verbal fluency, working memory, social cognition, motor function, and attention, which were combined into composite scores. Among the major findings, greater numbers of medical conditions were associated with greater levels of cognitive impairment, but not with more severe symptoms of schizophrenia.

Friedman et al. (2010) recently administered a battery of neuropsychological tests to schizophrenia patients with and without two cardiovascular risk factors (hypertension and elevated BMIs). The study also assessed comparison subjects with and without these risk factors. Tests in the neuropsychological battery included The Rey Auditory Verbal Learning Test (RAVLT), Trails A and B, a verbal fluency test (animals), the Letter-Number Sequencing Test from the Wechsler Adult Intelligence Scale, Third Edition (WAIS-III), and a digit span distraction test. After adjustments for age, gender, education and ethnicity, the hypertensive groups performed more poorly on immediate, delayed and recognition memory (RAVLT) than the non-hypertensive groups. Within group analyses showed that hypertensive schizophrenia subjects performed significantly worse than non-hypertensive schizophrenia subjects in delayed memory and in recognition memory. Comparison hypertensive subjects performed worse than comparison non-hypertensive subjects in delayed memory and immediate memory. Hypertension did not affect performance on other cognitive measures.

Elevated BMIs produced a non-significant trend (p = 0.063) towards impairments in delayed memory in both groups.

In another study, Dickinson, Gold, Dickerson, Medoff, and Dixon (2008) administered the Repeatable Battery for the Assessment of Neuropsychological Status (RBANS) to 95 adult subjects with Type 2 diabetes but no psychiatric diagnoses, 575 subjects with schizophrenia who were not screened for diabetes, and 97 subjects with schizophrenia and with Type 2 diabetes. The RBANS provides scaled index scores in Immediate Memory, Visual/Spatial performance, Attention, Language, Digit Span, Coding, Delayed Memory, and Total performance. Figure 8.2 adapted the findings to show that the schizophrenia / diabetes group performed more poorly than the schizophrenia only group on several measures, including the Total Score, Immediate Memory, Visual/Spatial, Delayed Memory, Digit Span, and Coding. Effect sizes were small to moderate, though this may underestimate the effect of diabetes on cognition since an unknown number of subjects with diabetes were not screened out of the schizophrenia only group. Moreover, several markers of diabetes severity correlated significantly with cognitive performance in individual subjects in the schizophrenia / diabetes group, but not in either of the other groups. The group with diabetes alone performed significantly higher than the group with diabetes and schizophrenia on all index scores except Visual/Spatial performance and Digit Span (not shown in Figure 8.2).

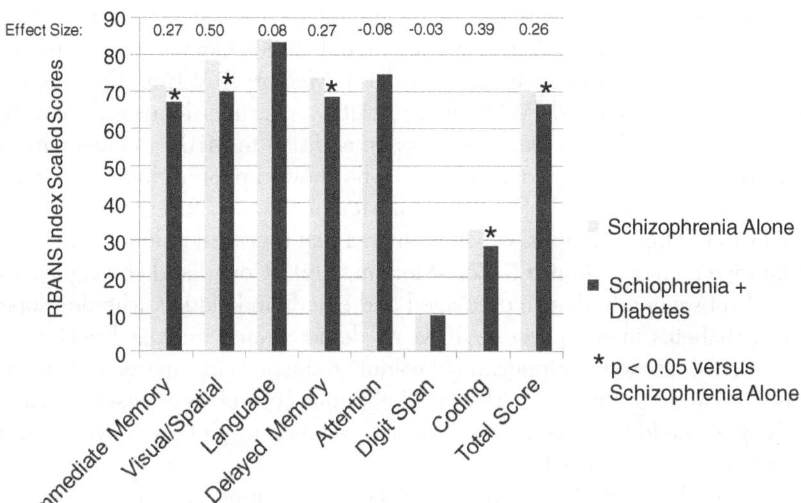

Figure 8.2 Cognitive performance on the Repeatable Battery for the Assessment of Neuropsychological Status (RBANS) index scores in patients with schizophrenia, with and without diabetes. Subjects with schizophrenia and diabetes showed significantly poorer performance in several cognitive domains. Adapted from Dickinson et al, 2008. See text for additional details.

How Do Medical Disorders Impair Cognition in Schizophrenia?

Taken together, these studies show that several medical conditions impair a range of cognitive functions in schizophrenia, as they do in other, non-psychiatric populations. Critical issues concerning the nature of the relationships between comorbid medical disorders and cognitive dysfunction in schizophrenia still need resolution, as do questions concerning the mechanisms by which cognition is impaired. It is likely that different mechanisms underlie dysfunction in different disorders, though common etiological factors may be shared as well. These issues are important conceptually and practically. From neuropsychological and from broader treatment perspectives, understanding the relationships between comorbid medical disorders and schizophrenia could help identify useful treatment targets and strategies. For this reason, we will briefly consider relationships between one medical condition, impaired glucose regulation, and cognition in schizophrenia, in additional detail.

There are several reasons to focus on glucose regulation in schizophrenia. One is that impaired glucose regulation has long been associated with schizophrenia, as noted above, and may reflect common etiological mechanisms (Stone et al., 2004; Stone & Seidman, 2008). Another reason is that both glucose regulation and glucose administration are related to cognition, and particularly to long-term memory, in schizophrenia and in other disorders and conditions. Several studies show, for example, that poor glucose regulation is related to poor memory performance in both rodents and people. Stone et al. demonstrated significant negative correlations between blood glucose levels after glucose injections and performance on an inhibitory avoidance task ($r = -0.89$) in 2-year-old rats (Stone, Wenk, Olton, & Gold, 1990). Convit, Wolf, Tarshish, and de Leon (2003) administered the Logical Memory Test from the Wechsler Memory Scale – Revised (WMS-R) to healthy (e.g., non-demented, non-diabetic), middle-aged and elderly subjects, in addition to MRIs and assessments of glucose tolerance. Individual subjects who showed poorer glucose tolerance also showed poorer recall of the Logical Memory stories, and greater levels of atrophy in the hippocampus, which is an area that is critical to long-term verbal declarative memory (Squire & Zola-Morgan, 1991). Convit and colleagues also showed subsequently that middle-aged and elderly individuals who developed Type 2 diabetes in the previous 10 years demonstrated impaired declarative memory, and also lower hippocampal volume reductions (compared to controls) that correlated significantly with overall glycemic control, as assessed by HbA_{1c} levels (S. M. Gold et al., 2007). Performance on measures of executive function and attention were normal.

A second reason to emphasize glucose regulation in schizophrenia is because glucose administration improves memory deficits in schizophrenia. Newcomer et al. (1999) and Stone, Seidman, Wojcik, and Green (2003) both reported increases in verbal declarative memory performance following glucose administration (compared with saccharin administration) in double-blind, crossover designs. In the latter study, subjects received a brief battery of neuropsychological tests that included the California Verbal Learning Test, the Logical Memory Test from the WMS-R (modified so that only one story was administered in the glucose condition and one story was administered in the saccharin condition), Trails A and B, the Tower of London, and an experimental auditory-verbal continuous performance test. Significant improvement occurred in the glucose condition for a measure of savings (Long-Delay Free Recall /Trial 5 recall). Moreover, we showed subsequently that glucose administration increased brain activation in selective temporal (e.g., left parahippocampus) and frontal lobe regions during a verbal encoding task using an fMRI protocol (Stone, Thermenos, Tarbox, Poldrack, & Seidman, 2005).

These reports are part of broader literature showing glucose facilitation of memory (P. E. Gold, 1995; Korol, 2002; Smith, Riby, van Eekelen, & Foster, 2011). Some of the findings that are most relevant for schizophrenia are described in greater detail elsewhere (Stone & Seidman, 2008), but may be summarized by the following generalizations: (a) glucose administration improves verbal declarative memory in a variety of conditions and paradigms, in people and in rodents; (b) glucose is more effective when the task is difficult or demanding, which may mean that it is most effective when brain regions that process declarative memory are active; (c) poor glucose availability (which may be indexed or estimated through poor peripheral glucose tolerance) to relevant brain regions is associated with poor memory; and (d) additional glucose administration near the time of memory processing (e.g., encoding or retrieval) may compensate for poor glucose availability in memory-impaired subjects, or enhance processing ability in normal subjects.

These findings support the view that declarative memory performance and several of the brain regions that mediate it are sensitive to the effects of circulating glucose. It is likely that this sensitivity reflects, at least in part, deficits in glucose regulation and availability at times when they are needed to support task performance. We hypothesize that other components of the metabolic syndrome in schizophrenia exacerbate this situation further, at least in part by restricting cerebral blood flow. In fact, consistent with a proposal advanced by Convit (2005) to explain relationships between glycemic control, performance on measures of declarative memory and hippocampal volumes, mechanisms related to impaired cerebral blood flow (e.g., endothelial dysfunction that impairs glucose transport across the blood brain barrier) may reflect one common mechanism by which several disorders related to the metabolic syndrome contribute to cognitive dysfunction. In this view, additional glucose administration facilitates memory in schizophrenia by compensating for glucose deficits in brain regions that mediate declarative memory functions (Stone, Glatt, & Faraone, 2004; Stone & Seidman, 2008). It should be emphasized that facilitation of memory by glucose under these sub-optimal circumstances (e.g., administering glucose when glucose regulation is impaired, as in diabetes), while important heuristically, is probably an inefficient way of facilitating neuronal transmission in circuits supporting declarative memory, and one that is contra-indicated in the long-term treatment of insulin insensitivity/diabetes.

Moreover, hyperglycemia is probably a multifactorial problem that can impair cognition through multiple mechanisms. Another pathway from hyperglycemia to cognitive impairment, for example, could involve glutamate toxicity (Lyoo et al., 2009). These findings underscore the potential importance of interventions based on mechanisms that attenuate deficits in glucose regulation, blood flow, glutamate transmission and other medical conditions in improving cognition in schizophrenia.

Implications for Clinical Neuropsychological Assessment and Function

The evidence for elevated rates of multiple medical disorders in schizophrenia is compelling. These disorders add to already high levels of dysfunction to both shorten and to constrict the lives of those they afflict. From a neuropsychological perspective, comorbid medical problems in schizophrenia contribute to poor outcomes in schizophrenia by exacerbating cognitive problems. Consequently, they have important implications for both neuropsychological assessment, and for therapeutic interventions. Several issues should be emphasized in relation to assessment. One of the most important of these involves the question of what portion of the cognitive deficits can be attributed to medical problems, and what portion can be attributed to schizophrenia? The issue is complicated by the large magnitude and range of neuropsychological deficits in schizophrenia (e.g., effect sizes of 1–2 standard deviations by the time of the first psychotic episode (Mesholam-Gately, Giuliano, Faraone, Goff, & Seidman, 2009), which make additional deficits difficult to detect. Since about 50% of the magnitude of deficits in overall cognitive ability (IQ) onset prior to the development of psychosis (Woodberry, Giuliano, & Seidman, 2008) and prior to the onset of many medical disorders, and since the rates of cognitive disorders in schizophrenia exceed the rates of individual medical disorders, it is likely that a majority of the cognitive deficits are related to the schizophrenia.

If this view is correct, however, it does not minimize the importance of additional cognitive problems. Rather, it emphasizes the lack of a 'cognitive reserve' in individuals with schizophrenia, and the potential functional importance of assessing additional sources of deficit that might be amenable to remediation. While there is no straightforward way to accomplish this yet, especially in a single evaluation, the problem is not unique in neuropsychology. One strategy for distinguishing depression from early dementia, for example, involves assessing baseline neuropsychological performance, treating the depression (or otherwise waiting for it to resolve), and then assessing whether cognition improved or continued to deteriorate. A similar strategy for schizophrenia involves obtaining a baseline neuropsychological assessment, referring the patient for medical treatment (as appropriate), and then re-assessing the patient after some degree of symptom reduction and stabilization of the medical condition(s). While not a complete solution (e.g., it is an assumption that reducing symptoms of the medical problem would have the same effect on the resultant cognitive problems), this initial strategy would help establish both the magnitude and the functional importance of the cognitive problems related to various medical etiologies.

Another neuropsychological assessment issue is related to differential diagnosis. The age of the individual is an important variable here. Like the general population, people with schizophrenia develop more medical problems as they age, including disorders that impair cognition. These disorders interact not only with schizophrenia, but also with normal aging. Consequently, people with schizophrenia who are relatively young (e.g. in their late forties or their fifties) are often referred to neuropsychologists for dementia evaluations. While it is certainly possible to develop dementia at those ages (e.g., fronto-temporal dementia), it is uncommon. Changes in other factors, including medical disorders, are more likely to account for declines in cognition in that age range. If earlier neuropsychological testing and a good medical history are available, differences in cognitive performance from a time when the medical condition was not present provides another strategy for assessing the magnitude of the cognitive effects produced by the medical disorder. In this instance, it is essential that the evaluation consider demographic factors including age, level of education, gender, and ethnicity before concluding that cognitive declines have in fact occurred (Harvey, Reichenberg, & Bowie, 2006).

An additional assessment issue may be emphasized by the presence of medical problems in an adolescent or younger adult with psychiatric problems. At least some evidence discussed earlier showed abnormal glucose regulation at the time of the first psychotic episode, elevated rates of diabetes in schizophrenia families, and the possibility of overlapping genetic mechanisms between schizophrenia and glucose regulation. These findings raise the question of whether abnormal glucose condition might be inherently related (i.e., an endophenotype) to schizophrenia. Since most cognitive dysfunction in schizophrenia occurs by the time of the first psychotic episode, the early presence of medical disorders may both contribute to the magnitude of the cognitive decline, and help to confirm the diagnosis of schizophrenia. This also raises the more general question of whether medical disorders have the same significance in schizophrenia when they occur at different stage of the illness.

In addition to functional and diagnostic assessment, neuropsychological evaluations in schizophrenia can play particularly important roles in both cognitive enhancement and in medical care. These roles include encouraging and facilitating general medical care in patients with schizophrenia. Cognition may benefit the most from treatments that minimize symptoms of disorders that more directly impair cognition, but it is also likely to benefit indirectly from treatments for any medical problems that cause physical pain, discomfort and/or disturbed sleep. Moreover, beneficial cognitive effects of treatment for medical problems may be additive with other forms of cognitive enhancement, such as behavioral treatments. A related point is to encourage preventive medical care, along with exercise and healthy eating habits, to minimize or avoid the development of medical problems.

One of the most important types of recommendation the neuropsychologist can make is to map out the steps that patients will need to take to actually make appointments, find their way to physicians, and then communicate their physical problems effectively to physicians and other health care providers. This may mean involving other clinicians or family members. Although follow-up (and initial) appointments may be difficult to keep for some patients with schizophrenia, repeated neuropsychological assessments are among our most effective tools to parse out the effects of more persistent (schizophrenia) and more malleable (treatable medical disorders) problems.

In summary, excess medical problems in schizophrenia are a serious and a growing problem. Many of these conditions that impair cognition, however, are to some extent preventable or subject to remediation. At a time when strategies for cognitive enhancement are coming to be recognized as among the most promising ways to improve functional outcomes in schizophrenia, clinical neuropsychological assessment can advance this goal significantly by identifying treatable forms of cognitive dysfunction in schizophrenia and by assessing the cognitive utility of treatment strategies for medical problems.

ACKNOWLEDGMENTS

Preparation of this chapter was supported in part by the National Institute of Mental Health Grants 1 U01 MH081928-01A1.

REFERENCES

Black, D. W., & Fisher, R. (1992). Mortality in DSM-III-R schizophrenia. *Schizophrenia Research, 7*, 109–116.

Brown, S. (1997). Excess mortality of schizophrenia. A meta-analysis. *British Journal of Psychiatry, 171*, 502–508.

Brown, S., Inskip, H., & Barraclough, B. (2000). Causes of the excess mortality of schizophrenia. *British Journal of Psychiatry, 177*, 212–217.

Brown, S., Kim, M., Mitchell, C., & Inskip, H. (2010). Twenty-five year mortality of a community cohort with schizophrenia. *The British Journal of Psychiatry, 196*, 116–121.

Chwastiak, L. A., Rosenheck, R. A., McEvoy, J. P., Keefe, R. S.; Swartz, M. S., Lieberman, J.y A. (2006). Interrelationships of psychiatric symptom severity, medical comorbidity, and functioning in schizophrenia. *Psychiatric Services, 57*(8), 1102–1109. doi: 10.1176/appi.ps.57.8.1102

Cloninger, C. R., Kaufmann, C. A., Faraone, S. V., Malaspina, D., Svrakic, D. M., Harkavy-Friedman, J., et al. (1998). Genome-wide search for schizophrenia susceptibility loci: the NIMH Genetics Initiative and Millennium Consortium. *American Journal of Medical Genetics (Neuropsychiatric Genetics), 81*(4), 275–281.

Convit, A. (2005). Links between cognitive impairment in insulin resistance: an explanatory model. *Neurobiology of Aging, 26S*, S31–S35.

Convit, A., Wolf, O. T., Tarshish, C., & de Leon, M. J. (2003). Reduced glucose tolerance is associated with poor memory performance and hippocampal atrophy among normal elderly. *Proceedings of the National Academy of Sciences of the United States of America, 100*, 2019–2022.

Dasgupta, A., Singh, O. P., Rout, J. K., Saha, T., & Mandal, S. (2010). Insulin resistance and metabolic profile in antipsychotic naive schizophrenia patients. *Progress in Neuropsychopharmacology and Biological Psychiatry, 34*, 1202–1207.

Davidson, M. (2002). Risk of cardiovscular disease and sudden death in schizophrenia. *Journal of Clinical Psychiatry, 63 (supplement 9)*, 5–11.

Davila, E. P., Florez, H., Fleming, L. E., Lee, D. J., Goodman, E., Leblanc, W. G., et al. (2010). Prevalence of the metabolic syndrome among US workers. *Diabetes Care*, (Epub ahead of print).

De Hert, M., van Winkel, R., Van Eyck, D., Hanssens, L., Wampers, M., Scheen, A., et al. (2006). Prevalence of diabetes, metabolic syndrome and metabolic abnormalities in schizophrenia over the course of the illness: A cross sectional study. *Clinical Practice and Epidemiology in Mental Health, 2*, 14. doi: 10.1186/1745-0179-2-14

Dickinson, D., Gold, J. M., Dickerson, F. B., Medoff, D., & Dixon, L. B. (2008). Evidence of exacerbated cognitive deficits in schizophrenia patients with comorbid diabetes. *Psychosomatics, 49*, 123–131.

Dixon, L., Weiden, P., Delahanty, J., Goldberg, R., Postrado, L., Lucksted, A., et al. (2000). Prevalence and correlates of diabetes in national schizophrenia samples. *Schizophrenia Bulletin, 26*(4), 903–912.

Fagiolini, A., & Goracci, A. (2009). The effects of undertreated chronic medical illnesses in patients with severe mental disorders. *Journal of Clinical Psychiatry, 70 (supplement 3)*, 22–29.

Fergenbaum, J. H., Bruce, S., Lou, W., Hanley, A. J. G., Greenwood, C., & Young, T. K. (2009). Obesity and lowered cognitive performance in a Canadian First Nations population. *Obesity, 17*, 1957–1963.

Fernandez-Egea, E., Bernardo, M., Parellada, E., Justicia, A., Garcia-Rizo, C., Esmatjes, E., et al. (2008). Glucose abnormalities in the siblings of people with schizophrenia. *Schizophrenia Research, 103*, 110–113.

Fleischhacker, W. W., Cetkovich-Bakmas, M., De Hert, M., Hennekens, C. H., Lambert, M., Leucht, S., et al. (2008). Comorbid somatic illnesses in patients with severe mental disorders: clinical, policy and research challenges. *Journal of Clinical Psychiatry, 69*, 514–519.

Ford, E. S., & Giles, W. H. (2003). A comparison of the prevalence of the metabolic syndrome using two proposed definitions. *Diabetes Care, 26*, 575–581.

Friedman, J. I., Wallenstein, S., Moshier, E., Parrella, M., White, L., Bowler, S., et al. (2010). The effects of hypertension and body mass index on cognition in schizophrenia. *American Journal of Psychiatry, 167*, 1232–1239.

Gold, P. E. (1995). Role of glucose in regulating the brain and cognition. *American Journal of Clinical Nutrition, 61 (supplement)*, 987S–995S.

Gold, S. M., Dziobek, I., Sweat, V., Tirsi, A., Rogers, K., Bruehl, H., et al. (2007). Hippocampal damage and memory impairments as possible early brain complications of type 2 diabetes. *Diabetologia, 50*, 711–719.

Gunnell, D., Rasmussen, F., Fouskakis, D., Tynelius, P., & Harrison, G. (2003). Patterns of fetal and childhood growth and the development of psychosis in young males: a cohort study. *American Journal of Epidemiology, 158*, 291–300.

Harris, E., & Barraclough, B. (1998). Excess mortality of mental disorder. *British Journal of Psychiatry, 173*, 11–53.

Harvey, P. D., Reichenberg, A., & Bowie, C. R. (2006). Cognition and aging in psychopathology: focus on schizophrenia and depression. *Annual Review of Clinical Psychology, 2*, 389–409.

Holt, R. I. G., Pevelert, R. C., & Byrne, C. D. (2004). Schizophrenia, the metabolic syndrome and diabetes. *Diabetic Medicine, 21*, 515–523.

Iacovides, A., & Siamouli, M. (2008). Comorbid mental and somatic disorders: am epidemiological perspective. *Current Opinion in Psychiatry, 21*, 417–421.

Kirkpatrick, B., Messias, E., Harvey, P. D., Fernandez-Egea, E., & Bowie, C. R. (2008). Is schizophrenia a syndrome of accelerated aging? *Schizophrenia Bulletin, 34*, 1024–1032.

Kirkpatrick, B., Miller, B. J., Garcia-Rizo, C., Fernandez-Egea, E., & Bernardo, M. (2010). Is abnormal glucose tolerance in antipsychotic-naive patients with nonaffective psychosis confounded by poor health habits? *Schizophrenia Bulletin*, (Epub ahead of print).

Kiviniemi, M., Suvisaari, J., Pirkola, S., Hakkinen, U., Isohanni, M., & Hakko, H. (2010). Regional differences in five-year mortality after a first episode of schizophrenia in Finland. *Psychiatric Services, 61*, 272–279.

Kooy, F. (1919). Hyperglycemia in mental disorders. *Brain, 42*, 214–288.

Koponen, H., Maki, P., Halonen, H., Miettunen, J., Laitinen, J., Tammelin, t., et al. (2008). Insulin resistance and lipid levels in adolescents with familial risk for psychosis. *Acta Psychiatrica Scandinavica, 117*, 337–341.

Koponen, H., Vuononvirta, J., Maki, P., Miettunen, J., Moilanen, I., Taanila, A., et al. (2008). No difference in insulin resistance and lipid levels between controls and adolescent subjects who later develop psychosis. *Schizophrenia Research, 104*, 31–35.

Koponen, H. J., Hakko, H. H., Saari, K. M., Lindeman, S. M., Karvonen, K. M., Isohanni, M. K., et al. (2010). The prevalence and predictive value of individual criteria for metabolic syndrome in schizophrenia: a Northern Finland 1996 Birth Cohort Study. *World Journal of Biological Psychiatry, 11*, 262–267.

Korol, D. L. (2002). Enhancing cognitive function across the life span. *Annals of the New York Academy of Sciences, 959*, 167–179.

Leucht, S., Burkard, T., Henderson, J., Maj, M., & Sartorius, N. (2007). Physical Illness and schizophrenia: a review of the literature. *Acta Pscyhiatrica Scandinavica, 116*, 317–333.

Lin, P. I., & Shuldiner, A. R. (2010). Rethinking the genetic basis for comorbidity of schizophrenia and type 2 diabetes. *Schizophrenia Research, 123*, 234–243.

Lyoo, K., Yoon, S. J., Musen, G., Sominsin, D. C., Weinger, K., Bolo, N., et al. (2009). Altered prefrontal glutamate-glutamine-γ-aminobutyric acid levels and relation to low cognitive performance and depressive symptoms in type 1 diabetes mellitus. *Archives of General Psychiatry, 66*, 878–887.

Marder, S. R., Essock, S., Miller, A. L., Buchanan, R. W., Casey, D. E., Davis, J. M., et al. (2004). Physical health monitoring of patients with schizophrenia. *American Journal of Psychiatry, 161*, 1334–1349.

Mesholam-Gately, R., Giuliano, A. J., Faraone, S. V., Goff, K. P., & Seidman, L. J. (2009). Neurocognition in first-episode schizophrenia: A meta-analytic review. *Neuropsychology, 23*, 315–336.

Meyer, J. M. (2003). Cardiovascular illness and hyperlipidemia in patients with schizophrenia. In J. M. Meyer & H. A. Nasrallah (Eds.), *Medical Illness and Schizophrenia* (pp. 53–80). Washington, DC: American Psychiatric Publishing.

Mukherjee, S., Decina, P., Bocola, V., Saraceni, F., & Scapicchio, P. (1996). Diabetes mellitus in schizophrenic patients. *Comprehensive Psychiatry, 37*(1), 68–73.

Mukherjee, S., Schnur, D. B., & Reddy, R. (1989). Family history of type 2 diabetes in schizophrenic patients. *Lancet, 1*(8636), 495.

Muller, M., van Raamt, F., Visseren, F. L. J., Kalmijn, S., Geerlings, M., Mali, W. P. T. M., et al. (2010). Metabolic syndrome and cognition in patients with manifest atherosclerotic disease: the SMART study. *Neuroepidemiology, 34*, 83–89.

Newcomer, J. W. (2007). Metabolic syndrome and mental illness *American Journal of Managed Care, 13 (supplement 7)*, S170–S177.

Newcomer, J. W., Craft, S., Fucetola, R., Moldin, S. O., Selke, G., Paras, L., et al. (1999). Glucose-induced increase in memory performance in patients with schizophrenia. *Schizophrenia Bulletin, 25*(2), 321–335.

Newcomer, J. W., Haupt, D. W., Fucetola, R., Melson, A. K., Schweiger, J. A., Cooper, B. P., et al. (2002). Abnormalities in glucose regulation during antipsychotic treatment of schizophrenia. *Archives of General Psychiatry, 59*(4), 337–345.

Nielsen, J., Skadhede, S., & Correll, C. U. (2010). Antipsychotics associated with the development of type 2 diabetes in antipsychotic-naive schizophrenia patients *Neuropsychopharmacology*, (Epub ahead of print).

Padmavati, R., McCreadie, R. G., & Tirupati, S. (2010). Low prevalence of obesity and metabolic syndrome in never-treated chronic schizophrenia. *Schizophrenia Research*, (Epub ahead of print).

Philips, R. J. (1934). Physical disorder in 164 consecutive admissions to a mental hospital: The incidence and signifcance. *British Medical Journal, 2*, 363–366.

Reaven, G. (1988). Role of insulin resistance in human disease. *Diabetologia, 30*, 1595–1607.

Regenold, W., Thapar, R., Marano, C., Gavirneni, S., & Kondapavuluru, P. (2002). Increased prevalence of type 2 diabetes mellitus among psychiatric inpatients with bipolar I affective and schizoaffective disorders independent of psychotropic drug use. *Journal of Affective Disorders, 70*(1), 19–26.

Ryan, M. C. M., Collins, P., & Thakore, J. H. (2003). Impaired fasting glucose tolerance in first-episode, drug naive patients with schizophrenia. *American Journal of Psychiatry, 160*, 284–289.

Ryan, M. C. M., & Thakore, J. H. (2002). Physical consequences of schizophrenia and its treatment: The metabolic syndrome. *Life Sciences, 71*, 239–257.

Saddichha, S., Manjunatha, N., Ameen, S., & Aktar, S. (2008). Metabolic syndrome in first episode schizophrenia — A randomized double-blind controlled, short-term prospective study. *Schizophrenia Research, 101*, 266–272.

Saha, S., Chant, D., & McGrath, J. (2007). A systematic review of mortality in schizophrenia. *Archives of General Psychiatry, 64*, 1123–1131.

Smith, M. A., Riby, L. M., van Eekelen, J. A. M., & Foster, J. K. (2011). Glucose enhancement of human memory: A comprehensive research review of the glucose memory facilitation effect. *Neuroscience and Biobehavioral Reviews, 35*, 770–783.

Solomon, A., Kareholt, I., Ngandu, T., Wolozin, B., MacDonald, S. W. S., Winblad, B., et al. (2009). Serum total cholesterol, statins and cognition in non-demented elderly. *Neurobiology of Aging, 30*, 1006–1009.

Spelman, L. M., Walsh, P. I., Sharifi, N., Collins, P., & Thakore, J. H. (2007). Impaired glucose tolerance in first-episode drug-naive patients with schizophrenia. *Diabetic Medicine, 24*, 481–485.

Squire, L. R., & Zola-Morgan, S. (1991). The medial temporal lobe memory system. *Science, 253*(September 20), 1380–1386.

Stone, W. S., Faraone, S. V., Su, J., Tarbox, S. I., Van Eerdewegh, P., & Tsuang, M. T. (2004). Evidence for linkage between regulatory enzymes in glycolysis and schizophrenia in a multiplex sample. *American Journal of Medical Genetics (Neuropsychiatric Genetics), 127B*(1), 5–10.

Stone, W. S., Glatt, S. J., & Faraone, S. V. (2004). The biology of schizotaxia. In W. S. Stone, S. V. Faraone, & M. T. Tsuang (Eds.), *Early clinical intervention and prevention of schizophrenia* (pp. 339–353). Totowa, NJ: Humana Press.

Stone, W. S., & Seidman, L. J. (2008). Towards a model of memory enhancement in schizophrenia: Glucose administration and hippocampal function. *Schizophrenia Bulletin, 34*, 93–108.

Stone, W. S., Seidman, L. J., Wojcik, J. D., & Green, A. I. (2003). Glucose effects on cognition in schizophrenia. *Schizophrenia Research, 62*(1-2), 93–103.

Stone, W. S., Thermenos, H. W., Tarbox, S. I., Poldrack, R. A., & Seidman, L. J. (2005). Medial prefrontal and temporal lobe activation and memory following glucose ingestion: A pilot fMRI study. *Neurobiology of Learning and Memory, 83*, 54–64.

Stone, W. S., Wenk, G. L., Olton, D. S., & Gold, P. E. (1990). Poor blood glucose regulation predicts sleep and memory deficits in normal aged rats. *Journal of Gerontology: Biological sciences, 45*, B169–173.

Strassnig, M., Miewald, J., Keshavan, M. S., & Ganguli, R. (2007). Weight gain in newly diagnosed first-episode psychosis patients and healthy comparisons: One-year analysis. *Schizophrenia Research, 93*, 90–98.

Subramaniam, M., Chong, S. A., & Pek, E. (2003). Diabetes mellitus and impaired glucose tolerance in patients with schizophrenia. *Canadian Journal of Psychiatry, 48*(5), 345–347.

Thakore, J., Mann, J. N., Vlahoos, J., Martin, A. W., R., & Reznek, R. (2002). Increased visceral fat distribution in drug-naive and drug-free patients *International Journal of Obesity Metabolic Disorders, 41*, 137–141.

Tran, E., Rouillon, F., Loze, J. Y., Casadebaig, F., Philippe, A., Vitry, F., et al. (2009). Cancer mortality in patients with schizophrenia: an 11-year prosective cohort study. *Cancer, 115*, 3555–3562.

Venkatasubramanian, G., Chittiprol, S., Neelakantachar, N., Naveen, M. N., thirthall, J., Gangadhar, B. N., et al. (2007). Insulin and insulin-like growth factor-1 abnormalities in antipsychotic-naive schizophrenia. *American Journal of Psychiatry, 164*, 1557–1560.

Verma, S. K., Subramaniam, M., Liew, A., & Poon, L. Y. (2009). Metabolic risk factors in frug-naive patients with first-episode psychosis. *Journal of Clinical Psychiatry, 70*, 997–1000.

von Hausswolff-Juhlin, Y., Bjartveit, M., Lindstrom, E., & Jones, P. (2009). Schizophrenia and physical health problems. *Acta Pscyhiatrica Scandinavica, 119 (supplement 438)*, 15–21.

Wirshing, D. A., & Meyer, J. M. (2003). Obesity in patients with schizophrenia. In J. M. Meyer & H. A. Nasrallah (Eds.), *Medical Illness in Schizophrenia* (pp. 35–51). Washington, DC: American Psychiatric Publishing.

Woodberry, K. A., Giuliano, A. J., & Seidman, L. J. (2008). Premorbid IQ in schizophrenia: A meta-analytic review. *American Journal of Psychiatry, 165*, 579–587.

Wright, P., Sham, P. C., Gilvarry, C. M., Jones, P. B., Cannon, M., Sharma, T., et al. (1996). Autoimmune diseases in the pedigrees of schizophrenic and control subjects. *Schizophrenia Research, 20*(3), 261–267.

BOX 8.1 MEDICAL COMORBIDITIES IN SCHIZOPHRENIA: PREVALENCE

1. Rates of medical comorbidities are elevated among people with schizophrenia relative to healthy populations.
2. These comorbidities contribute to a 20%–30% reduction in lifespan in people with schizophrenia.
3. Rates of cardiovascular disorders, disorders of lipid metabolism, obesity, and glucose dysregulation and insulin dysfunction are highly elevated in schizophrenia.
4. These elevated rates have been linked to antipsychotic medication treatment, poor diet, and a sedentary lifestyle.

BOX 8.2 MEDICAL COMORBIDITIES AND COGNITIVE DYSFUNCTION IN SCHIZOPHRENIA

1. The number of medical comorbidities in schizophrenia has been linked to degree of cognitive dysfunction. Similar relationships have not been shown between symptom severity and medical comorbidities.
2. People with schizophrenia and hypertension have impaired memory relative to people with schizophrenia without hypertension.
3. Individuals with schizophrenia and Type 2 diabetes show greater impairment across a variety of neuropsychological measures, including memory, visuo/spatial skills, attention and working memory and processing speed and severity of Type 2 diabetes correlates with degree of neuropsychological impairment.

BOX 8.3 GLUCOSE REGULATION IN SCHIZOPHRENIA

1. There is some evidence that people with schizophrenia may be predisposed to glucose dysregulation and the co-occurrence of these disorders could reflect shared etiological mechanisms.
2. Glucose administration improves memory in schizophrenia.

BOX 8.4 NEUROPSYCHOLOGICAL ASSESSMENT AND MEDICAL COMORBIDITIES IN SCHIZOPHRENIA

1. One strategy for dissociating neurocognitive effects of schizophrenia from comorbid medical conditions is to assess patients before and after medical intervention and measure change in cognitive status. Any observed improvement can provide insights into the magnitude and functional importance of the effects of the underlying medical disorder on cognition.
2. People with schizophrenia who are middle-aged (40s–50s) may get referred for neuropsychological evaluation for assessment of emergence of dementia due to a change in cognitive status. However, changes associated with medical disorders are much more likely to serve as the culprit for these observed changes in this age range.
3. One of the most important types of recommendations that neuropsychologists can make is to map out steps that patients will need to take to actually make appointments, find their health care provider in the community and communicate their medical issues effectively.

CONTINUING EDUCATION QUESTIONS

1. Among comorbid medical conditions in schizophrenia, some of the very highest estimates for frequency of comorbid conditions are:
   a. Diabetes
   b. Arthritis
   c. Stroke
   d. All of the above
2. Among comorbid medical conditions in schizophrenia there is evidence that ___________ is evident even prior to psychopharmacological treatment and sustained presence of the illness.
   a. Respiratory illness
   b. Headaches
   c. Problems in glucose regulation
   d. None of the above
3. Glucose administration improves ________ deficits in schizophrenia.
   a. Memory
   b. Executive-function
   c. Processing speed
   d. Social cognition
4. BMI has been consistently related to cognition in schizophrenia.
   a. True
   b. False

9

Traumatic Brain Injury and Schizophrenia

LAURA A. FLASHMAN, Ph.D.
THOMAS MCALLISTER, M.D.
RICHARD FERRELL, M.D.

Department of Psychiatry, Dartmouth Medical School, Dartmouth-Hitchcock Medical Center

PSYCHOSIS AFTER TBI

The notion that traumatic brain injury (TBI) can be a relevant etiological factor in the onset of schizophrenia has been an ongoing source of debate in the literature. Despite this, systematic studies have been limited. While a handful of studies have failed to find an increased risk of schizophrenia (see for example, Harrison et al., 2006), a majority of studies support an increased prevalence of psychosis in individuals who have had a TBI. Psychiatric disorders of many types have been reported to be a major cause of disability after TBI. Major depression is the most studied psychiatric disorder, with occurrence rates estimated to be 14%–77% after TBI. Psychotic disorders including schizophrenia and syndromes referred to as schizophrenia-like psychosis (SLP) have been reported to occur more frequently in persons who have had a TBI than in the general population.

Published data on the occurrence of psychosis in individuals who have sustained a TBI vary in their definition of psychosis. This imprecision makes comparing studies difficult and results in a wide range of reported incidence rates. Prevalence rates vary from 0.7% to 9.8%, based on a review by Davison and Bagley (1969) of 8 long-term follow-up studies of individuals with brain injuries published between1917 and 1960. The period of study in these reports was 15 to 20 years. More recent studies have confirmed these estimates. Although the lack of appropriate individuals serving as controls makes it hard to put these figures in perspective, a two- to three-fold increase in the risk of SLP has been suggested for individuals after TBI.

This chapter focuses on the relationship between TBI and psychosis, and its implications for clinical assessment and treatment. We begin with a definition of the terms frequently used when describing these disorders individually and together, and then address the challenging questions regarding the concept of psychotic disorder secondary to TBI (PD-TBI), risk factors for this disorder, the overlap of symptoms between TBI and schizophrenia/psychosis, and implications for treatment.

DEFINITION OF TERMS

Traumatic Brain Injury

TBI occurs when an external force traumatically injures the brain. Typically, the injury is manifest by an alteration in the level of neurological function such as a disturbance in the level of consciousness (Menon, Schwab, Wright, & Maas, 2010). TBI can be classified based on severity, mechanism (closed or penetrating head injury), or other features (e.g. focal vs. diffuse injury), and is one of several types of injuries commonly referred to as acquired brain injuries. Causes include falls, vehicle accidents, and violence. Brain trauma can be caused by a direct impact or by acceleration alone. In addition to the damage caused at the moment of injury, brain trauma causes *secondary injury*, a variety of events that take place in the minutes and days following the injury. These processes, which include alterations in cerebral blood flow and increased intracranial pressure, contribute substantially to the damage from the initial injury. TBI can cause a host of physical, cognitive, emotional, and behavioral effects, and outcome can range from complete recovery to permanent disability or death.

Psychosis

The term "psychosis" has been defined in many different ways, with no single definition receiving universal acceptance (*DSM-IV-TR*, 2000). In its narrowest definition, psychosis is restricted to presence of delusions or prominent hallucinations, with absence of insight. A slightly less restrictive definition would include prominent hallucinations that the individual realizes are not real. Other definitions have also included the presence of other positive symptoms, such as disorganized speech or behavior, or catatonic behavior. Definitions used in earlier classification systems such as *DSM-III* and ICD-9 focused on the severity of impairment, requiring "impairment that grossly interferes with the capacity to meet ordinary demands of life" (*DSM-IV-TR*, 2000, p. 297).

Schizophrenia (Referred to in Text as "Primary Schizophrenia")

According to the *DSM-IV-TR* (2000), schizophrenia is a disorder that lasts for at least six months and includes at least one month of active-phase symptoms, which include two or more of the following: delusions, hallucinations, disorganized speech, grossly disorganized or catatonic behavior, negative symptoms. No single symptom is pathognomonic of the disorder. The signs and symptoms must be associated with marked social or occupational dysfunction, and cannot be better accounted for by another diagnosis, the direct physiological effects of a substance, or a general medical condition. The characteristic symptoms involve a range of cognitive and emotional impairments.

Deficit Syndrome Schizophrenia

A presentation of schizophrenia characterized by at least two of the following six negative symptoms: restricted affect, diminished emotional range, poverty of speech, curbing of interests, diminished sense of purpose, diminished social drive. At least two of these symptoms must have been present in some combination for the preceding 12 months, and are always present during periods of clinical stability.

Psychotic Disorder Secondary to Traumatic Brain Injury (PD-TBI)

This term is typically used to describe a psychosis that develops *de novo* following a TBI. It is, of course, difficult to be sure that the psychosis is in fact directly caused by the cerebral injury. The interval between the TBI and the development of psychosis can vary widely with ranges reported from 0 to 34 years. The mean interval between TBI and development of psychosis has been reported to be 4 to 5 years. This variation in interval can complicate attempts to draw causal inferences about a TBI and subsequent development of psychosis.

This chapter focuses on the limited available evidence that TBI is one of several risk factors for developing psychosis, including a chronic debilitating course that very much resembles schizophrenia.

THE CONCEPT OF PSYCHOTIC DISORDERS SECONDARY TO TBI (PD-TBI)

It is helpful to consider the relationship of TBI and psychosis within a broader framework of etiological theories of schizophrenia. The neurodevelopmental theory of schizophrenia posits that early impairments in cerebral development, possibly caused by events such as TBI, could later lead to a schizophrenic disorder. Specifically, this diathesis-stress model suggests that this early risk factor or injury provides a vulnerability to schizophrenia that might increase likelihood of manifestation of the illness if there is a stress that occurs later in life. Thomas, Genets, Walter, and Colic (2009) hypothesized that after a TBI, there can be neuronal reshaping. They suggest that this reshaping could serve as a potential stressor that leads to impairment in individuals at-risk for schizophrenia. Kim (2008) reviewed the literature and found support for the notion of a risk-modifying effect of TBI in individuals who are genetically at risk for schizophrenia. The literature is less supportive of the idea of TBI as an independent risk factor for schizophrenia in individuals without such risk. It should be noted that this is consistent with the observation that TBI increases the relative risk of developing a host of psychiatric disorders (Kim, 2008).

For example, in a comprehensive review of this topic, Davison and Bagley (1969) summarized the results of eight long-term (15 to 20 years) follow-up studies of head injury patients published from 1917 to 1960. Across these studies the percentage of TBI patients developing a schizophrenia-like psychosis varied from 0.7% to 9.8%. Examination of study results suggests an observed incidence of schizophrenia-like psychosis that is 2 to 3 times greater than that expected by chance in the TBI population. Further, according to these authors, up to 15% of schizophrenics have had a significant brain injury before the onset of their first psychotic episode.

More recently, two additional studies (AbdelMalik, Husted, Chow, & Bassett, 2003; Brown, Chadwick, Shaffer, Rutter, & Traub, 1981) have reported an association between a history of previous childhood TBI and schizophrenia. No locus of brain injury was associated with specific psychiatric symptoms. When perinatal insults were examined, using markers such as low birth weight, prematurity, preeclampsia, prolonged labor, hypoxia and fetal distress, the increased risk of schizophrenia was small, increasing risk by only 1%.

Studies of combat veterans with brain injuries have also reported instances of post-traumatic psychosis, although the authors did not control for the presence of comorbid post-traumatic stress disorder. Participants in these studies may have a higher percentage of penetrating brain injuries, and this may result in a different profile of injury than that of the more typical acceleration and deceleration TBI. Lishman (1968) reported psychotic syndromes in 0.7% of soldiers with penetrating brain injuries who were followed for 4 years post-injury; this is close to the NIMH reported prevalence rate of approximately 1.1% of the population over the age of 18. Hillbom (1960) found that almost 8% of Finnish veterans with brain injuries had psychotic syndromes, although only one third of these had chronic psychoses resembling schizophrenia. Individuals with chronic psychosis had more severe injuries and more frequent left hemisphere injury. Interestingly, 40% of the individuals with TBI and psychotic syndromes had temporal lobe lesions.

The mechanisms underlying these associations are not completely clear; however, several factors have been proposed.

Genetics

Early work by Davison and Bagley (1969) found no evidence of increased genetic loading for schizophrenia in individuals with PD-TBI. In fact, in those studies where adequate family history was available, the incidence of schizophrenia in relatives of TBI patients with psychosis did not exceed the incidence of schizophrenia in the general population, and was considerably less than the incidence of schizophrenia in relatives of schizophrenics without a history of TBI.

In more recent work, however, there does appear to be a relationship between genetic factors and PD-TBI. In a study by Sachdev, Smith, and Cathcart (2001), a genetic vulnerability to psychosis as reflected in the family history was the most significant risk factor for PD-TBI; this was found despite the fact that a positive family history of schizophrenia was present in only a small percentage of the participants included in the study. The lifetime risk of psychosis in first-degree relatives of patients with schizophrenia has been reported to be from 3% to 17%. Sachdev et al. (2001) reported a 24% risk in first-degree relatives in individuals with PD-TBI, vs. 3% for control individuals. This rate is higher than the risk of schizophrenia reported in association with other neurologic disorders, including epilepsy, where the risk is typically found to be similar to that of the general population (with the exception of temporal lobe epilepsy, which has a higher rate than other forms of epilepsy).

Malaspina et al. (2001) found a positive relationship between schizophrenia and brain injury, such that first-degree relatives of probands with schizophrenia who also had a history of TBI were at significantly greater risk for developing schizophrenia compared to other first-degree relatives with similar genetic vulnerabilities. These authors proposed an interaction between genetic risk/predisposition for schizophrenia and TBI. Given similar genetic risk for developing schizophrenia, individuals who also suffered a TBI significantly increased their risk of developing the disorder, consistent with a "two hit" model of disease (schizophrenia) risk.

Clinical/Injury Features

Fujii and Ahmed (2001) compared patients with PD-TBI with individuals who had a history of TBI but no psychosis. They concluded that those with psychosis were more likely to be male, were more likely to have a history of congenital disorders, and were more likely to have suffered a TBI in childhood. Characteristics of the injury itself such as left hemispheric and temporal lobe lesions, closed head injury, increased severity of injury with more diffuse brain damage, and coma of greater than 24 hours duration, may also play a role (Davison & Bagley, 1969; Lishman, 1968; Sachdev et al., 2001). Most patients who develop symptoms of psychosis after moderate to severe TBI have lesions of the frontal and temporal lobes (Fujii & Ahmed, 2002; Sachdev et al., 2001), although the right parietal region has also been implicated (Sachdev et al., 2001). Other studies have reported more severe and diffuse brain injury as the most prominent risk factor (e.g., Zhang & Sachdev, 2003). Overall, neuroimaging findings evaluating anatomical localization of psychosis after TBI have not been consistent, and no convincing theoretical framework has emerged. Similarly, laterality has not emerged as a significant factor in the development of psychosis, although a suggestion has been made that left temporal lesions may be more common (Sachdev et al., 2001).

TBI After Psychosis

There is also evidence suggesting that individuals with psychiatric illness might be at an increased risk for TBI. In a 30-year follow-up study of Axis I and II psychiatric disorders after TBI (Koponen et al., 2002), 22% of the participants met criteria for an Axis I disorder with onset before the TBI. This phenomenon could be influenced by a number of factors, including increased vulnerability to trauma, increased substance use, homelessness, and risk of victimization.

Malaspina et al. (2001) studied almost 2,000 individuals who were first-degree relatives of people with schizophrenia or bipolar disorder, searching for any possible relationship between these illnesses and TBI. They reported that rates of TBI were significantly higher for those with diagnoses of schizophrenia, bipolar disorder and depression than for those with no mental illness. Multivariate analysis of within-pedigree data, however, showed that mental illness was related to TBI only in the schizophrenia pedigree. First-degree relatives of individuals with schizophrenia were more likely to have had a TBI than were first-degree relatives of individuals with bipolar disorder. In other words, members of the schizophrenia pedigree, even those without a diagnosis of schizophrenia, had a greater incidence of TBI compared to members of the bipolar disorder pedigrees, and there was a greater association between TBI and risk of developing schizophrenia.

MANIFESTATIONS OF PSYCHOTIC SYNDROMES AFTER TBI

It is important to state that although an increase in the relative risk of psychosis is associated with a TBI, the phenomenology of the psychotic syndrome can vary, and the clinician should be alert to several patterns. For example, psychotic syndromes after TBI can occur during the period of post-traumatic amnesia, as a complication of chronic post-traumatic epilepsy, or be associated with a TBI induced mood disorder (e.g., a manic psychosis).

Psychotic Syndromes During Post-traumatic Amnesia

In the initial period after injury, during the period of post-traumatic amnesia (PTA), numerous features of delirium are likely to occur including restlessness, a fluctuating level of consciousness, agitation, combativeness, emotional liability, emotional withdrawal or excessive dependency, confusion, distractibility, disorientation, and amnesia. Hallucinations and delusions may also occur during this period, although delusions are seldom well organized. Expressive and receptive speech and language disturbances, including perseveration, are frequently present during this period and can produce a clinical picture similar to the disorder of thought and language found in schizophrenia. Many of these symptoms are likely to improve as the period of PTA resolves.

Case Vignette 1

Mr. C was a 22-year-old man with no prior psychiatric history, who was transferred to our psychiatric hospital from his rehabilitation hospital, secondary to hostile and threatening behaviors and delusions, in the aftermath of a recently sustained traumatic brain injury. He had a prolonged coma and at the time of transfer to our facility, was awake but had persistent confusion, disorientation, and short-term memory deficits consistent with continued post-traumatic amnesia. In addition to the cognitive problems, he had impulse control problems (such as punching walls, kicking things, and being sexually inappropriate towards female staff) and delusions (including that a famous person is in love with him). Over the subsequent month, his confusion resolved and his impulse control improved. Associated with that was a gradual diminution in the expressed delusions, and at the time of discharge, they were no longer evident.

Psychotic Syndromes Related to Post-traumatic Epilepsy

Seizure disorders are a relatively common complication of TBI. Psychotic syndromes associated with post-traumatic epilepsy can occur either in the periictal period (either during seizures or in the immediate post-ictal period), or inter-ictally, in which case the psychotic symptoms are more likely to be chronic than episodic. The most common syndrome is the *post-ictal acute confusional state*, which is characterized by generalized confusion, fluctuating sensorium, agitation, hallucinations, and delusions. This syndrome will generally resolve within a few hours after the seizure, although in rare cases it may persist for up to several days. Inter-ictal psychoses can present with features consistent with a schizophreniform illness, a delusional disorder, or mood disorder with psychotic features.

Epileptic psychosis is associated primarily with complex partial seizures due to temporal lobe epilepsy; psychosis has been reported to occur 4 to 12 times more frequently in temporal lobe epilepsy than in other types of epilepsy. Psychotic syndromes, particularly the schizophrenia-like and paranoid states, are most likely to occur in conjunction with left-sided temporal lobe lesions.

Case Vignette 2

Mr. M sustained a severe TBI secondary to a motor vehicle accident at age 17. He had no psychiatric problems prior to his TBI. He was in a coma for 6 weeks, and was initially dysarthric with a right hemiplegia that eventually resolved to right-sided weakness. Recovery was complicated by ongoing cognitive deficits as well as the development of a persistent, poorly controlled post-traumatic seizure disorder. Eight years after his injury, his family noted the onset of progressive paranoid ideation that eventually evolved into an elaborate delusional system involving a complex government plot to harm him. Caregivers were frequently incorporated into these delusions. Although antipsychotic medications were somewhat effective, he frequently discontinued taking them for fear that they were poisoning him.

Mood-related Psychotic Disorders

A significant body of evidence suggests that TBI results in an increased risk of developing psychiatric disorders, including mood and anxiety disorders, substance abuse, and psychotic syndromes (Deb, Lyons & Koutzoukis, 1998; Hibbard, Uysal, Kepler, Bogdany, & Silver, 1998; Koponon et al., 2002; van Reekum, Cohen & Wong, 2000). For example, Koponon et al. (2002) studied 60 individuals 30 years after their TBI and found that almost half (48%) developed a new Axis I psychiatric disorder after their injury. The most common diagnoses were depression, substance abuse, and anxiety disorders. Major depressive episodes and manic episodes can have psychotic symptoms as part of the clinical presentation. Thus from a clinical standpoint, it is important to recognize that although the most apparent symptoms evident in a person with TBI and psychosis may be hallucinations or delusions, these are actually a component of a major depressive or manic episode.

Case Vignette 3

Mr. K is a 37-year-old, right-handed veteran with a B.S. in Biochemistry and Molecular Biology. He suffered a TBI in a motor vehicle accident, with a loss of consciousness of approximately 20 minutes, as well as a post-traumatic amnesia of approximately one week's duration. Six months after his injury, he developed a depressive episode and was treated with antidepressants. Within 2 weeks, he exhibited signs of mania, characterized by hyperactivity, decreased sleep, reckless spending, and grandiose and paranoid delusions. He has had several subsequent manic episodes, usually in the context of discontinuing his medications, each associated with the recurrence of psychotic symptoms.

The above case examples illustrate the different contexts in which psychosis can be seen in an individual with TBI, and highlight the importance of detailed history, exam, and appreciation for the context in which the symptoms manifest. However, there is also a clinical presentation that most closely resembles that of primary schizophrenia. The clinical features of PD-TBI, in the absence of any identifiable context such as those described above, are very similar to those reported in primary schizophrenia (see Box 1 for base rates for symptom occurrence). As with primary schizophrenia, auditory hallucinations and paranoid delusions occur more commonly than other positive symptoms such as formal thought disorder and bizarre behavior. Visual hallucinations, catatonia, and negative symptoms are less often observed. Psychotic symptoms are associated with more extensive brain damage seen on neuroimaging, especially in the left temporal and right parietal lobes and symptoms are also associated with more severe cognitive impairment (Sachdev et al., 2001).

Prodromal features are common in PD-TBI, and often last for several months. The primary symptoms during the prodrome are bizarre or antisocial behavior, social withdrawal, affective instability, and deterioration in work performance. Symptoms of depression may be seen, but confusion is unusual. The psychotic symptoms most frequently observed in PD-TBI are delusions and hallucinations. In a study by Sachdev et al. (2001), one or more delusions were present in all participants with PD-TBI (see Box 2 for common types of delusions reported). Persecutory delusions are the most frequent type of delusion reported in other studies as well. Delusions related to misidentification, stealing, or hiding, occur somewhat frequently in dementia patients with psychosis, but these types of delusions are not generally described in PD-TBI. Hallucinations are more likely to be auditory, although visual hallucinations are also reported. Formal thought disorder and catatonia are not typical. Agitated behavior and aggression are frequently reported. Negative symptoms are reported in only 15%–22% of cases, which is much lower than the base rates reported in primary schizophrenia.

Little is known about the long-term course of PD-TBI. In one study (Fujii & Amhed, 2002), follow-up was available on 56% of the initial cases reviewed. Of those, 64% showed improvement (as defined by a reduction in psychotic symptoms), 28% had not improved, and 8% were worse. Patients were not followed systematically, and follow-up intervals varied. However, there was some evidence to suggest that PD-TBI, despite the prominence of positive symptoms, may respond poorly to neuroleptic medication.

SIGNIFICANCE OF OVERLAP OF SYMPTOMS: TBI AND SCHIZOPHRENIA

Examination of various manifestations of TBI and schizophrenia indicate that there can be significant overlap in each of these domains. It is important to understand the "typical" presentations of each disorder separately, to understand the combined effects in those individuals who develop PD-TBI.

Age

There is significant overlap between the age of peak risk for both onset of schizophrenia and TBI (see Box 3). In schizophrenia, there is a gender difference for age of onset, with the peak ages of onset at 20–28 years for males, and a slightly later peak onset (26–32 years of age) for females (Castle, Wessely, Der, & Murray, 1991). The disorder occurs 1.4 times more frequently in males than females. Onset of schizophrenia in childhood is much rarer, as is onset in middle-age or later. The peak risk for TBI is between the ages of 15 and 30, with the risk being highest for individuals aged 15–24 years (Kraus et al., 1984). Peak age is similar for males and females, although more males than females sustain TBIs. The highest mortality rate (32.8 cases per 100,000 people) is also found in persons aged 15–24 years. There is a second peak risk period for TBI in the elderly, who primarily sustain their TBIs as a result of falls; the mortality rate in these individuals (65 years or older) is about 31.4 individuals per 100,000 people.

Cognition

The cognitive deficits associated with schizophrenia are described in Chapter 3 of this volume. In general, while the neuropsychological deficits noted in schizophrenia are heterogeneous, schizophrenia has been associated with lower intellectual abilities and more pronounced cognitive deficits in executive functioning, memory, and attention than TBI. Cognitive disability, even more than the positive and negative symptoms of schizophrenia, is often the factor which limits functional independence. Similarly, the cognitive difficulties experienced by people after TBI, especially mild TBI, often have more impact on their recovery and outcome than do their physical limitations.

There are several predictable areas of impairment reported after TBI, including problems in memory, speed of information processing, and attention. These deficits are similar to those frequently reported in individuals with schizophrenia (see Box 4). Attentional skills are complex, and include the ability to select what is important in the environment, and the ability to direct one's attention to what is important. One must also be able to maintain attention and focus. Then as changes occur in the environment, one must be able to shift attention to what is now newly most important. All of these components of attention can be disrupted by a brain injury, and impairments of attention and concentration can contribute to the deficits found in a variety of other cognitive functions.

Many dimensions of memory can be impaired in individuals with TBI, including difficulties with encoding and retrieving new information. Working memory is the ability to hold information in mind, or "online" while retrieving or processing other relevant information, and this skill is very commonly disrupted in individuals after a TBI. There are several reasons why memory problems occur in individuals with TBI. Declarative memory, including problems with encoding and retrieval, and deficits in verbal learning are common and disabling after TBI in both adults and children, and may relate to injury to the hippocampus and related mesial temporal structures. Significant impairment of episodic memory has been reported with hippocampal damage from vascular insult, hypoxia, or surgery, frequent complications of TBI. Episodic memory deficits include inability to learn and remember new contextual information. These deficits can be characterized as a failure of consolidation and/or of rapid forgetting. Individuals with TBI also show deficits in semantic memory; i.e., long-term memory for the culturally shared general knowledge about words, concepts, and symbols, their associations, and rules for their manipulation.

In addition, while individuals with TBI are frequently able to perform well on cognitive tests and to do their work at a level that does not appear to be significantly poorer than what they would have done before their injury, they often report that they have to work much harder, invest more effort, and take more time to perform their work. This added effort results in an inability to maintain performance without significant fatigue, and also means they must allocate additional time to complete tasks.

Other cognitive deficits that might be reported include impairment in reasoning skills, problem solving difficulties, and subtle language problems, such as word finding difficulties. They may have trouble reading social cues, monitoring or inhibiting responses appropriately, shifting strategies when their current one is not working, and being flexible.

Behavioral and Emotional Difficulties

Behavioral and emotional difficulties are frequently seen after TBI, and may be exacerbated by the cognitive difficulties that accompany TBI. There is also significant overlap between these behavioral problems and those frequently described in individuals with schizophrenia.

Restlessness and agitation are common problems, particularly early in recovery. Along with these symptoms, individuals with TBI may have significant problems with attention or reasoning. Family members frequently describe emotional lability and irritability. This is likely the result of damage to the frontal lobes, as one of the functions of the frontal lobes is to inhibit actions that are not consistent with a person's goals. Impulsivity and socially inappropriate behavior can result from diminished reasoning ability and from lack of inhibition. Individuals with TBI may be described as saying hurtful things, being blunt, or acting without consideration of the social norms or consequences in a given situation. With frontal lobe damage, an individual may not be able to inhibit behavior as well as they could prior to the injury. Confabulation is also sometimes reported; this is believed to be due to problems with organization and retrieval of memories which results in inaccurate temporal recall, or "filling in" of missing information by describing things that might have happened to them in the past.

Impaired or diminished insight in individuals with TBI is a frequent complaint among caregivers, just as it is for individuals with schizophrenia. Self-awareness involves being able to process information at a very high level, requiring attention, memory, and reasoning abilities. An individual with a TBI often does not have a very good understanding of their physical, cognitive, or behavioral challenges, or of the impact of their deficits on daily life. They will deny difficulties that are obvious to others or feel they can engage in activities, such as working or driving, even while acknowledging significant problems that might impact on those abilities.

Individuals with TBI are also described as having a number of symptoms considered to be "negative symptoms" in individuals with schizophrenia. These include decreased initiative, decreased emotional responsiveness, and depressed affect. These may be due to frontal lobe injury, resulting in impaired ability to plan and organize, self-start or initiate behavior, or problems with attention.

People with schizophrenia are likely to have additional (comorbid) conditions, including major depression and anxiety disorders. In addition, the lifetime occurrence of substance abuse is almost 50% (Buckley, Miller, Lehrer, & Castle, 2009). Social problems, such as long-term unemployment, poverty and homelessness, are common. The average life expectancy of people is 12 to 15 years less than healthy individuals, due to both increased physical health problems and a higher suicide rate (about 5%; van Os & Kapur, 2009). As has been noted, individuals with TBI are also at increased risk for psychiatric disorders including depression, mania, anxiety, and substance abuse (Silver, Kramer, Greenwald, & Weissman, 2001). There are also increased rates of unemployment, divorce and suicide.

Distinguishing Characteristics

Despite the overlapping and sometimes additive effect that can be seen in deficits in individuals with PD-TBI, there are several features that have been identified that may assist in the differentiation between those with primary schizophrenia and those who have PD-TBI. Individuals with PD-TBI are less likely to demonstrate negative symptoms than individuals with schizophrenia. They are, however, more likely to have positive findings on CT or MRI (65% vs. 12%–35% in schizophrenia). Typical findings include atrophy and focal signs, both at a rate of approximately 60%. As noted above, focal lesions in individuals with PD-TBI are most likely to be found in the frontal and temporal lobes. The most frequently reported neuroimaging findings in individuals with schizophrenia are enlarged ventricles and atrophy or volume loss in the temporal lobes; in contrast, enlarged ventricles were reported only in approximately 20% of individuals with PD-TBI.

EEG abnormalities are reported in approximately 70% of persons with PD-TBI; EEG abnormalities occur in only about 20%–60% of individuals with schizophrenia. In the group of individuals with PD-TBI, one half of the EEG findings were localized, with the most common finding being temporal slowing. In individuals with schizophrenia, the most frequently reported EEG findings were delta and theta waves in the frontal areas, a decreased mean frequency in alpha, and increased beta power.

In summary, there is significant overlap in cognitive, behavioral, and emotional problems in individuals with TBI and individuals with schizophrenia. Although there is no single profile of deficits for either disorder, problems with attention, processing speed, and memory are commonly identified in both, and these cognitive deficits often have a significant impact on their recovery and functional ability. Individuals with TBI more often describe the need to work harder or longer, or the need to put forth additional effort, in order to do what they were able to do prior to their injury; fatigue is also a very frequent symptom.

Individuals with both TBI and schizophrenia may have trouble reading social cues, or responding appropriately in social situations. Restlessness, agitation, irritability and impulsivity are frequently associated with both disorders, as are "negative symptoms" such as decreased initiation and depressed affect. Diminished insight is also frequently described, although this is more likely to resolve over time after a TBI, and appears to be a more stable phenomenon when it occurs in schizophrenia. This overlap of symptoms is not surprising, given the frontal lobe involvement in both TBI and schizophrenia, but it does raise challenges for a clinician trying to ascertain the etiology of particular deficits in an individual with PD-TBI.

CONVERGENCE OF NEURAL SUBSTRATES IN TBI AND SCHIZOPHRENIA

There is also considerable overlap between the neural substrates that have been determined to underlie TBI and those believed to contribute to the occurrence of psychotic disorders, such as schizophrenia, as well as the substrates of specific symptoms characterizing psychotic disorders, such as hallucinations and delusions. Regions most commonly affected in TBI include the frontal lobes, including dorsolateral cortex and orbitofrontal cortex, the anterior and inferior temporal regions. Intracerebral hemorrhages are seen in a variety of regions including the basal ganglia. In moderate and severe TBI, diffuse axonal injury occurs. This type of injury is often especially evident in the corpus callosum, in the superior cerebellar peduncle, in the basal ganglia, and in the periventricular white matter. Thalamic damage has also been reported. Further, not all injury occurs at the time of impact. Secondary injury, or injury that is set in motion by the primary impact but evolves over the subsequent minutes, hours, or even days, also plays a crucial role in the post injury sequelae. The various cascades involved in secondary injury can result in significant and far reaching sequelae removed in location and time from the primary injury. The hippocampal formation is particularly vulnerable, not only to mechanical forces in TBI, but also to the common complications of increased intracranial pressure, hypoxia, and the secondary injury cascades.

As discussed in Chapter 1 of this volume, while no single brain region has been identified as the site or cause of schizophrenia, several brain regions appear to play important roles in the disorder, and these regions overlap with those vulnerable to injury in the typical TBI. Brain changes consistently implicated in schizophrenia include enlarged lateral and third ventricles, reduced frontal and temporal lobe volumes, reduced thalamic volumes, and enlargement of basal ganglia, particularly the caudate and globus pallidus, which could be related to medication effects. More recent neuropathological studies have reported abnormalities in regions of the dorsolateral prefrontal cortex and the hippocampus, based on reduced manually traced volumes, a reduced number, size, or orientation of hippocampal neurons, abnormal expression of cytoskeletal proteins in selected hippocampal regions, and altered distribution of D2 dopamine receptors in the temporal lobe. Functional imaging studies have also focused on frontal, temporolimbic, and basal ganglia areas. In addition, positron-emission tomography studies of drug-free schizophrenics have suggested reduced metabolism in the cingulate gyrus and the hippocampus, plus reduced metabolism in the basal ganglia.

In at least some studies of individuals with schizophrenia, many of the regions that have been found to be abnormal, such as prefrontal cortex, temporolimbic cortex, hippocampal formation, basal ganglia, cingulate gyrus, and thalamus, are interconnected. This raises the interesting possibility that neuroanatomic disruptions in any of the way stations of these circuits may have the capacity to cause psychotic disturbances. This suggestion is supported by the observation that the frontal cortex, sub-cortical white matter, basal ganglia, thalamus, and temporolimbic areas are most consistently affected in those individuals who develop psychotic syndromes in the context of various neurological disorders.

Thus, it is not surprising that psychotic syndromes occur with increased frequency in patients after a TBI. There is significant overlap not only between cognitive, behavioral and clinical symptoms, but also between the regions implicated in the etiology of schizophrenia and its prominent symptoms, and those regions that are commonly affected in TBI, including the frontal and temporal lobes, the basal ganglia, and the thalamus. The hippocampal formation is particularly vulnerable, not only to mechanical forces in TBI, but also to the common complications of increased intracranial pressure, hypoxia, and the secondary injury cascades. In some respects, it is surprising that psychotic syndromes are not seen more commonly after TBI.

ASSESSMENT ISSUES

There have been a small number of studies looking at differences in cognitive performance between individuals with TBI, individuals with schizophrenia, and individuals with both PD-TBI. Fujii and Ahmed (2002) examined data from 69 published case studies of individuals with psychotic disorder due to traumatic brain injury. They found that 88% of cases with neuropsychological test data described cognitive deficits, with 59% demonstrating memory deficits and 41% demonstrating executive and spatial deficits. Specific neuropsychological tests used were not reported. Sachdev et al. (2001) also conducted a chart-based study comparing individuals with PD-TBI to those with TBI and no psychosis, and found poorer performance in the PD-TBI group on tests of executive functioning, memory, parietal lobe functioning, and language. Again, specific tests used to identify these deficits were not described.

In a study examining individuals with TBI, individuals with schizophrenia, and individuals with PD-TBI matched for gender, intellectual functioning, age and education (Fujii, Ahmed, & Hishinuma, 2004), both individuals with schizophrenia and those with PD-TBI performed significantly worse than healthy controls on a number of different tests. Individuals with schizophrenia performed worse than controls on tests of intelligence (WAIS FSIQ), working memory (Digit Span), verbal memory (Anna Thompson story from the WMS-R Logical Memory), visual spatial abilities (Block Design), and executive functioning (WCST, Trails, verbal fluency). Individuals with PD-TBI performed worse than controls on tests of intelligence, vocabulary, verbal memory, and executive functioning (WCST only). No differences were found between healthy controls and the TBI only group. While the PD-TBI group demonstrated a similar pattern of deficits to that of the schizophrenia group, the PD-TBI group was not as globally impaired as those with schizophrenia, who demonstrated deficits in working memory, visual spatial functioning, and more global executive deficits than those with PD-TBI.

Verbal Fluency

Individuals with schizophrenia are likely to have greater impairment on tests of verbal fluency than individuals with PD-TBI. This could be related to differences in symptom presentation between the two disorders. In schizophrenia, deficits in fluency have been associated with severity of negative symptoms. Again, negative symptoms are relatively rare in PD-TBI.

Other individual tests have been examined, most usually examining differences between individuals with TBI only and individuals with schizophrenia only. These are briefly discussed below.

Trail Making Test (TMT)

TMT performance was found to be poorer in individuals with TBI than in individuals with schizophrenia, except for the B:A and B-A/A scores. This suggests a similar underlying executive deficit in both disorders (Perianez et al., 2007).

Tower of Hanoi

Overall, both individuals with TBI and those with schizophrenia demonstrated impaired performance on the Tower of Hanoi. Individuals with schizophrenia perform more poorly than do individuals with TBI and healthy controls on this test of planning and problem solving. Specifically, individuals with schizophrenia had lower scores on the total profile score, more rule breaking behavior, and longer mean execution times than did the TBI or the healthy control group. The three groups did not differ significantly in terms of mean planning time; however, for the planning time of the first initiation, both the participants with TBI and those with schizophrenia demonstrated longer planning times than the healthy control group. Relative to the healthy control group, more moves were required to solve the problems for both the TBI and the schizophrenia group.

Visual Memory

Gorissen, Sanz, and Schmand (2005) examined performance on neuropsychological tests assessing memory, attention, and executive functioning, including WAIS or WAIS-III Digit Span, the Stroop Color Word Test, Trail Making Test, RAVLT or the CVLT, and WMS-R or WMS-III Visual Reproduction in individuals with schizophrenia, individuals with non-psychotic psychiatric disorders, individuals with neurological disorders only (TBI, degenerative disorders, tumors, epilepsy, meningitis, multiple sclerosis), and healthy controls. Individuals with schizophrenia performed significantly more poorly than the individuals with neurological disorders on Visual Reproduction I subtest (immediate figural memory) only. On all other tests except word list recognition and Digit Span (where there were no significant differences between groups), and Trail Making Test, Part A and Stroop Color Word Interference (where individuals with schizophrenia performed worse than controls but not individuals with neurologic disorders), healthy controls performed significantly better than the other three groups, who did not perform significantly differently than each other.

Social Cognition

Social cognition deficits are often reported in individuals with schizophrenia. The deficit has been posited to be related to the structural and functional abnormalities of the frontal lobe. Individuals with schizophrenia have been reported to show impaired performance when compared to healthy controls on an emotion intensity recognition test that is sensitive to amygdala function and emotion attribution tasks, which mainly rely on frontal lobe function (Yamada et al., 2009). A group with frontal lobe damage demonstrated impairment on the emotion attribution tasks but not on the emotion intensity recognition task. Other work has found impairments in both emotion recognition and theory of mind (understanding other people's intentions) in individuals after TBI (Milders, Ietswarrt, Crawford, & Currie, 2008), although deficits were not associated with severity of behavioral problems following TBI. Involvement of the frontal lobes, noted in both disorders, is believed to be responsible for the social cognition deficits observed.

Apathy

Apathy can be seen after both TBI and schizophrenia. While severity of apathy is often similar, individuals with deficit syndrome schizophrenia are typically reported to have more severe anhedonia, blunted affect and alogia, as measured by the Scale for Assessment of Negative Symptoms (SANS; Andreasen, 1984).

SUMMARY

Based on the limited literature in this area, individuals with PD-TBI show more impairment in the domains of verbal memory, executive functioning, and vocabulary than do individuals with TBI and no psychosis. The pattern of deficits seen in PD-TBI suggests frontal-temporal dysfunction, possibly greater in the left hemisphere, which parallels the deficits reported in other psychotic conditions secondary to neurological disorders such as Alzheimer's disease, temporal lobe epilepsy, cerebral vascular accidents, and brain tumors. This suggests a nonspecificity of both cognitive deficits and localization of cerebral abnormalities in psychotic disorders of different etiologies, and raises concern regarding inaccurate attribution when interpreting certain neuropsychological deficits as being specific to schizophrenic spectrum disorders. In general, individuals with TBI and schizophrenia have similar types of cognitive deficits. Those with PD-TBI tend to have more significant deficits than individuals with TBI and no psychosis, but have less severe deficits than individuals with schizophrenia.

TREATMENT ISSUES

McAllister and Ferrell (2002) reviewed many of the complex and important considerations around medication treatment in PD-TBI; these will be discussed briefly below. The first step in the evaluation and treatment of psychotic symptoms is making an accurate diagnosis and determining the etiology of the psychotic symptoms. This necessitates clearly and carefully distinguishing psychotic symptoms from other TBI-related symptoms such as confabulation, misidentification syndromes, and illusions; this can be difficult because of the similarities in clinical presentation described above. Once the presence of psychotic symptoms has been established, identification of potential underlying causes is necessary. It is very important to determine whether there is a history of psychiatric illness that predates the TBI. In addition, identifying a positive family history of psychiatric illness may help provide insight into an individual's current diagnosis. Malaspina et al. (2001) have suggested that TBI can interact with genetic vulnerability to increase the risk of developing schizophrenia and other psychiatric disorders.

Treatment approaches then follow logically from the outcome of this careful evaluation. *Seizure-related symptoms* are best managed with adjustment of the anticonvulsant regimen or, in cases where an individual is considered to be treatment-refractory, with surgical intervention. *Mood disorders with psychotic features* are most successfully treated with antidepressants or anti-cycling agents. While single agents should be tried initially, a combination of drugs may be necessary. Antipsychotic agents may be needed in the initial phases of treatment of a mood disorder with psychotic features, but these can often be tapered and discontinued once the mood disturbance has been successfully treated. When a *schizophrenia-like psychosis* is the primary psychopathology, then antipsychotic agents are indicated. Antipsychotic drugs carry significant risk of adverse effects including metabolic syndrome and movement disorder. Their use should be carefully monitored with circumspect attention to the risk/benefit analysis.

Cholinergic abnormalities have been implicated in both TBI and schizophrenia, and cholinergic dysfunction may be related to the cognitive impairments reported in both of these disorders. Some evidence suggests that antipsychotic medication may help enhance cognitive function as a result of an increase in acetylcholine in the medial frontal cortex. Thus, acetylcholinesterase inhibitors such as galantamine might be useful in the treatment of PD-TBI because of a dual mechanism of action. First, it results in selective competitive inhibition of acetylcholinesterase. Second, it results in allosteric potentialization of nicotinic receptor response. Galantamine has been demonstrated to be helpful as an adjunct therapy to risperdal in one individual with PD-TBI and three case reports of schizophrenia (see Bennouna, Greene, & Defranoux, 2007). Donepezil has also been reported to be effective in treating cognitive deficits in individuals with TBI and in individuals with schizophrenia. Further systematic research is needed to confirm that acetylcholinesterase inhibitors may have efficacy in PD-TBI.

Several physical and cognitive problems, including impaired motor function, gait disturbances, decreased arousal, and slowed speed of information processing, occur commonly after TBI. These difficulties are often exacerbated by the sedation, psychomotor slowing, parkinsonism, and anticholinergic side effects associated with typical antipsychotic agents. The risk of tardive dyskinesia may be increased after TBI. Clinicians and individuals with TBI often report an increased sensitivity to side effects of these medications. To avoid increasing the cognitive and physical difficulties, and to attempt to minimize medication side effects, typical dosing in individuals with PD-TBI starts at a much lower dosage than would be used in individuals with uncomplicated schizophrenia or psychotic disorder. In addition, the titration rate should be adjusted, with slower increases in dosage at longer intervals between increases. Prescribing practices used for geriatric patients are often appropriate. In a review of the pharmacotherapy of psychiatric disorders associated with TBI, Newburn (1998) proposed caution in using drugs having prominent anticholinergic, antihistaminic, or antidopaminergic effects in PD-TBI because of the risk of adverse effects on cognition.

Another point to consider when using pharmacological intervention is that the effects of psychoactive medicines in individuals with TBI may be unusual, paradoxical, or exaggerated. At least one study has shown that discontinuation of medication in individuals with TBI results in an improvement in cognition, relative to testing done before being started on antipsychotic medication, done while on the medication, and done during tapering of antipsychotic medications. Any decisions regarding use of psychoactive agents, including antipsychotic medications, in individuals with TBI must be made only after careful consideration of likely risks and benefits because psychotic symptoms cause suffering and negatively affect nearly all aspects of a person's functioning. An attempt at pharmacotherapy for persons with PD-TBI with severe symptoms will almost always be indicated.

Finally, non-pharmacologic approaches, such as *cognitive remediation*, can also be considered to treat the cognitive impairment noted in PD-TBI.

CONCLUSION

This chapter has explored the manifestations of psychosis in individuals who have also sustained a TBI. While general assessment and treatment practices do not dramatically differ, there are several reasons to carefully consider the role that a TBI is playing in a particular individual with a psychotic disorder. As noted above, the presence of a TBI will likely impact on medication management with respect to starting dose, rate of titration, and discontinuation of the medication. Clinicians may want to be more cautious in their pharmacological approach if there are concerns. In addition, there will likely be an impact on the approach to nonpharmacologic interventions. The combination of cognitive deficits related to the trauma, as well as the ongoing psychotic disorder, may require modification for cognitive remediation or other psychotherapeutic interventions.

In addition, for some people, it is important to understand the role that their TBI has played in the development of what can be a devastating psychiatric disorder. Providing information and education regarding the relationship between TBI and an increased risk of psychosis can be comforting and reassuring to individuals and their families.

The neuropsychologist can play an important role in providing information to individuals, family members and treatment providers about the current cognitive status of the individual and how that might accentuate the need for modifications of the pharmacological regimen, and inform the need for and type of modifications that are necessary for group and individual cognitive remediation and other interventions. Finally, a careful neuropsychological assessment can provide input on the role that the injury has played in causing the psychotic disorder and its impact on every day functioning.

In summary, the relationship between TBI and psychosis/schizophrenia is complex. Psychotic symptoms can occur shortly after injury or years afterward. It is reasonable to view the new onset of hallucinations and delusions during the period of post-traumatic amnesia as likely caused by neurophysiological disruption brought about by the brain injury. In patients without a personal or family history of psychiatric disease, psychotic symptoms occurring in the first weeks or months subsequent to a significant brain injury could be closely linked to damage to critical brain areas. The etiologic significance of a TBI occurring years before the onset of psychotic symptoms is less clear. Genetic vulnerabilities or psychosocial stressors could play an equal or more important role in determining who becomes symptomatic. The body of research on the role of early life central nervous system injury and subsequent development of schizophrenia is intriguing and suggests that the timing of the injury with respect to the neurodevelopmental phase may be an important variable. Psychosis has also been reported in a group of people prior to acquisition of a TBI, suggesting a possible vulnerability to brain injury in at least some individuals with severe mental illness. The exact nature of the relationship between psychosis and TBI will not be elucidated until more is known about the cellular and biochemical events underlying both processes.

Several risk factors have been identified for PD-TBI. Clinical characteristics include male gender and younger age. Injury characteristics include left hemispheric and frontal and temporal lobe lesions or injury, increased severity of injury, and unilateral damage. Typical presentation includes delusions and auditory hallucinations, with agitated behavior and aggression. Negative symptoms and confusion are rare. There is some evidence for a role for a genetic vulnerability.

There can be significant overlap in terms of the cognitive, behavioral, and emotional symptoms associated with both TBI and psychosis. The most frequently reported cognitive deficits include impairment in attention, memory, and executive functioning. These can impact on the behavioral difficulties described, which include restlessness, agitation, emotional lability, irritability, impulsivity, and socially inappropriate behavior. Impaired insight is also commonly described in both TBI and schizophrenia. Psychotic symptoms occur rarely in TBI, but more frequently than in the general population, and they have a very significant impact on the quality of life and functional independence of these individuals. There is considerable overlap in the brain regions implicated in schizophrenia and its psychotic symptoms and the areas most sensitive to damage after TBI.

There are some characteristics that differentiate between individuals with PD-TBI and individuals with psychotic disorder but no history of TBI. Negative symptoms are reported less commonly in PD-TBI. Positive findings, including atrophy and focal frontal and temporal lobe lesions, on CT and MRI are more common in PD-TBI than in schizophrenia. EEG abnormalities are reported in approximately 70% of individuals with PD-TBI; in individuals with schizophrenia, EEG abnormalities are less common. Temporal slowing is the most common EEG finding in PD-TBI. While there has been very little work examining differences in cognitive performance in individuals with TBI, schizophrenia, and PD-TBI, the limited results suggest that individuals with PD-TBI show more impairments in verbal memory, executive functioning and vocabulary than do individuals with TBI only, but typically show similar or less severe deficits in cognitive functioning than do individuals with schizophrenia only.

Understanding the nature of the psychosis in PD-TBI is important in order to develop an appropriate treatment plan. As with any group of individuals with neurological compromise, the treatment approach needs to be developed rationally and implemented cautiously. Use of lower dosages of medication, with slower increases and longer intervals during medication titration, and constant monitoring for side effects and impact on cognition and physical status are recommended. In general, medications used are the same as those which would be used if there weren't a TBI. Recent work suggests there may be also some benefit on cognition with use of acetylcholinesterase inhibitors.

REFERENCES

AbdelMalik P., Husted, J., Chow, E. W. C., & Bassett, A. S. (2003). Childhood head injury and expression of schizophrenia in multiply affected families, *Archives of General Psychiatry, 60*, 231–236.

American Psychiatric Association. (2000). *Diagnostic and statistical manual of mental disorders* (4th ed., text rev.). Washington, DC: Author.

Andreasen, N. C. (1984). *Scale for the Assessment of Negative Symptoms*. Iowa City: Iowa University Press.

Andreasen, N. C., & Flaum, M.A. (1991). Schizophrenia: The characteristic symptoms, *Schizophrenia Bulletin, 17*(1), 27–49.

Bennouna, M., Greene, V. B., & Defranoux, L. (2007). Cholinergic hypothesis in psychosis following traumatic brain injury and cholinergic hypothesis in schizophrenia: A link? *Encephale, 33*, 616–620.

Brown, G., Chadwick, O., Shaffer, D., Rutter, M., & Traub, M. (1981). A prospective study of children with head injuries, III: Psychiatric sequelae. *Psychological Medicine, 11*, 63–78.

Buckley, P. F., Miller, B. J., Lehrer, D. S., & Castle, D. J. (2009). Psychiatric comorbidities and schizophrenia, *Schizophrenia Bulletin. 35*(2), 383–402.

Castle, D., Wessely, S., Der, G., & Murray, R. M. (1991). The incidence of operationally defined schizophrenia in Camberwell, 1965–84. *The British Journal of Psychiatry. 159*, 790–794.

Davison, K., & C. R. Bagley. (1969). Schizophrenia-like psychosis associated with organic disorders of the central nervous system. *British Journal of Psychiatry.114*, 113–184.

Deb, S., Lyons, I., & Koutzoukis, C. (1998). Neuropsychiatric sequelae one year after a minor head injury. *Journal of Neurology, Neurosurgery & Psychiatry, 65*(6), 899–902.

Fujii, D., & Ahmed, I. (2001). Risk factors in psychosis secondary to traumatic brain injury. *Journal of Neuropsychiatry and Clinical Neuroscience, 13*, 61–69.

Fujii, D., & Ahmed, I. (2002). Characteristics of psychotic disorder due to traumatic brain injury: An analysis of case studies in the literature. *Journal of Neuropsychiatry and Clinical Neuroscience, 14*, 130–140.

Fujii, D., Ahmed, I., & Hishinuma, E. (2004). A neuropsychological comparison of psychotic disorder following traumatic brain injury, traumatic brain injury without psychotic disorder, and schizophrenia, *Journal of Neuropsychiatry and Clinical Neuroscience, 16*, 306–314.

Gorissen, M., Sanz, J. C., & Schmand, B. (2005). Effort and cognition in schizophrenia patients, *Schizophrenia Research, 78*, 199–208.

Harrison, G., Whitley, E., Rasmussen, F., Lewis, G., Dalman, C., & Gunnell, D. (2006). Risk of schizophrenia and other non-affective psychosis among individuals exposed to head injury: Case control study, *Schizophrenia Research, 88*, 119–126.

Hibbard, M. R., Uysal, S., Kepler, K., Bogdany, J., & Silver, J. (1998). Axis I psychopathology in individuals with traumatic brain injury. *Journal of Head Trauma Rehabilitation, 13*(4), 24–39.

Hillbom, E. (1960). After-effects of brain injuries. *Acta Psychiatrica Scandinavia Supplement, 142*, 1–95.

Kim, E. (2008). Does traumatic brain injury predispose individuals to develop schizophrenia? *Current Opinion in Psychiatry, 21*, 286–289.

Koponon, S., Taiminen, T., Portin, R., Himanen, L., Isoniemi, H., Heinonen, H., et al. (2002). Axis I and Axis II psychiatric disorders after traumatic brain injury: A 30-year follow-up study. *American Journal of Psychiatry, 159*, 1315–1321.

Kraus, J. F., Black, M. A., Hessol, N., Ley, P., Rokaw, W., Sullivan, C., et al. (1984). The incidence of acute brain injury and serious impairment in a defined population. *American Journal of Epidemiology, 119(2)*, 186–201.

Lishman, W. A. (1968). Brain damage in relation to psychiatric disability after head injury. *British Journal of Psychiatry, 114*, 373– 410.

Malaspina, D., Goetz, R. R., Friedman, J. H., Kaufmann, C. A., Faraone, S. V., Tsuang, M., et al. (2001). Traumatic brain injury and schizophrenia in members of schizophrenia and bipolar disorder pedigrees, *American Journal of Psychiatry, 158*, 440–446.

Menon, D. K., Schwab, K., Wright, D.W., & Maas, A. I. (2010). on behalf of The Demographics and Clinical Assessment Working Group of the International and Interagency Initiative toward Common Data Elements for Research on Traumatic Brain Injury and Psychological Health. Position statement: Definition of traumatic brain injury. *Archives of Physical Medicine and Rehabilitation, 91*,1637–1640.

McAllister, T. W., & Ferrell, R. B. (2002). Evaluation and treatment of psychosis after traumatic brain injury, *NeuroRehabilitation, 17*, 357–368.

Milders, M., Ietswarrt, M., Crawford, J. R., & Currie, D. (2008). Social behavior following traumatic brain injury and its association with emotion recognition, understanding of intentions, and cognitive flexibility, *Journal of the International Neuropsychological Society, 14*, 318–326.

Newburn, G. (1998) Psychiatric disorders associated with traumatic brain injury, optimal treatment. *CNS Drugs, 9*, 441–456.

Perianez, J. A., Rios-Lago, M., Rodriguez-Sanchez, J. M., Adrover-Roig, D., Sanchez-Cubillo, I., Crespo-Facorro, B., et al. (2007). Trail Making Test in traumatic brain injury, schizophrenia, and normal ageing: Sample comparisons and normative data. *Archives of Clinical Neuropsychology, 22*, 433–447.

Sachdev, P., Smith, J. S., & Cathcart, S. (2001). Schizophrenia-like psychosis following traumatic brain injury: A chart-based descriptive and case-control study, *Psychological Medicine, 31*, 231–239.

Silver, J. M., Kramer, R., Greenwald, S., & Weissman, M. (2001). The association between head injuries and psychiatric disorders: findings from the New Haven NIMH Epidemiologic Catchment Area Study.*Brain Injury, 15*(11), 935–945.

Thomas, G., Genest, P., Walter, M., & Cozic, J. Y. (2009). Can concepts of neurodevelopment and neuroplasticity explain post-traumatic psychoses? *Neuro-Chirurgie, 55*, 36–39.

van Os, J., & Kapur, S. (2009). Schizophrenia, *Lancet, 374(9690)*, 635–645.

van Reekum, R., Cohen, T., & Wong, J. (2000). Can traumatic brain injury cause psychiatric disorders? *Journal of Neuropsychiatry and Clinical Neuroscience, 12*, 316–327.

Yamada, M., Ueda, K., Namiki, C., Hirao, K., Hayashi, T., Ohigashi, Y., & Murai, T. (2009). Social cognition in schizophrenia: Similarities and differences of emotional perception from patients with focal frontal lesions.*European Archives of Psychiatry & Clinical Neuroscience, 259*, 227–233.

Zhang, Q., & Sachdev, P. S. (2003). Psychotic disorder and traumatic brain injury, *Current Psychiatry Reports, 5*(3), 197–201.

BOX 9.1 BASE RATE OF SYMPTOMS REPORTED IN PRIMARY SCHIZOPHRENIA (FROM ANDREASEN & FLAUM, 1991)

Positive symptoms	*Frequency*
• Delusions	85–89%
• Hallucinations	35–50%
• Thought Disorder	19–24%
• Catatonic behaviors	0–15%
Negative symptoms	
• Affective Flattening	86–88%
• Inappropriate Affect	37–50%

BOX 8.2 MOST COMMON TYPES OF DELUSIONS SEEN IN PD-TBI (SACHDEV ET AL, 2001, BASED ON SAMPLE OF 45 INDIVIDUALS)

Type of Delusion	*Frequency*
Persecutory	55.5%
Referential	22.2%
Delusions of control	22.2%
Grandiose	20%
Religious	15.4%
Thought alienation/insertion/ withdrawal/broadcasting	13.3%

BOX 9.3 OVERLAPPING AGES OF PEAK RISK FOR TBI AND SCHIZOPHRENIA

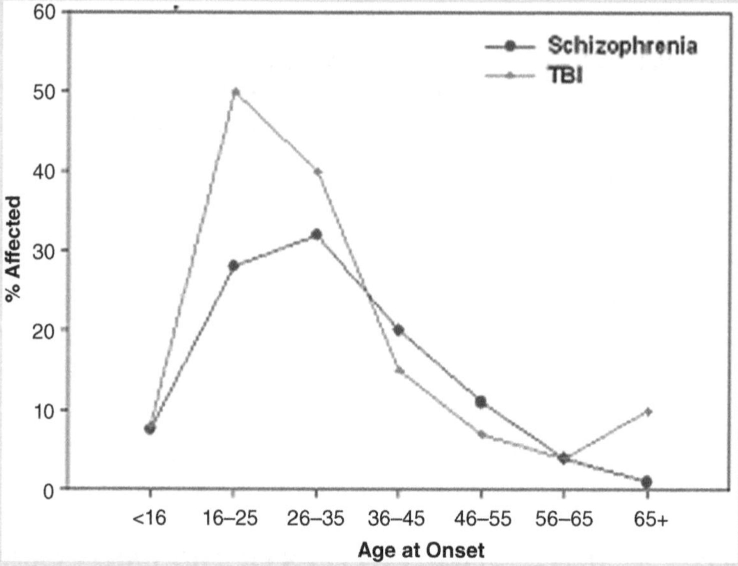

BOX 9.4 MOST COMMON OVERLAPPING SYMPTOMS IN TBI AND SCHIZOPHRENIA

Cognitive:

- Attention
- Memory (encoding/retrieval)
- Working Memory
- Processing Speed

Behavioral:

- Restlessness/Agitation
- Impulsivity
- Socially inappropriate behavior
- Decreased initiation

Emotional:

- Lability
- Decreased emotional responsivity
- Depressed affect

CE QUESTIONS

1. While PD-TBI can occur any time after a TBI, at what time point do recent studies suggest that onset occurs most frequently?
   a. in the first 3 months post-injury
   b. 1 to 2 years after injury
   c. 4 to 5 years after injury
   d. more than 10 years after injury
2. What are the most common psychotic symptoms observed in PD-TBI?
   a. auditory hallucinations
   b. bizarre behavior
   c. catatonia
   d. formal thought disorder
3. Which of the following are clinical risk factors for the development of PD-TBI?
   a. female gender and older age
   b. female gender and younger age
   c. male gender and older age
   d. male gender and younger age
4. Which of the following symptoms is NOT frequently reported in both individuals with TBI and those with schizophrenia?
   a. agitation, irritability, and impulsivity
   b. headaches and dizziness
   c. impairment in attention, memory and executive functioning.
   d. socially inappropriate behavior
5. In what cognitive domains do individuals with PD-TBI show more impairment relative to individuals with TBI without psychosis?
   a. motor speed
   b. receptive language
   c. verbal memory
   d. visuoconstructional ability
6. Which of the following considerations is NOT TRUE when prescribing medication for individuals with PD-TBI?
   a. Antipsychotic medication should not be used when an individual has also sustained a TBI.
   b. Constant monitoring for side effects and impact on cognition and physical status is necessary.
   c. Use of lower dosages of medication, with slower increases and longer intervals during medication titration are recommended.
   d. The treatment approach needs to be developed rationally and implemented cautiously.

10

Influence of Comorbid Substance Use Disorders on Cognition in Schizophrenia

KIM T. MUESER, Ph.D.

Executive Director of the Center for Psychiatric Rehabilitation, and Professor of Occupational Therapy at Boston University

SUSAN R. MCGURK, Ph.D.

Associate Professor of Occupational Therapy at Boston University

Substance use disorders, including substance abuse and substance dependence, are the most common comorbid disorders in schizophrenia. Substance use disorders tend to have an early age of onset often preceding the development of major psychiatric disorders, can precipitate an earlier age of onset of psychosis, and contribute to a worse course of psychiatric illness, especially if they are not successfully treated. The accurate identification of substance use problems presents a major challenge to clinicians assessing and treating schizophrenia. All commonly used psychoactive substances can influence cognitive functioning, depending on drug type, duration of use, and nutrition status while abusing. Thus, the failure to accurately detect substance abuse in a person with schizophrenia can lead to inaccurate interpretation of neurocognitive performance. Clinicians working with clients with schizophrenia need to be familiar with the problem of substance abuse, have the skills and tools for assessing substance use and related problems in this population, and for incorporating relevant information about substance use into their interpretation of clients' cognitive strengths and weaknesses.

We begin this chapter with a review of the epidemiology of substance abuse in schizophrenia, including incidence and prevalence rates and demographic and clinical correlates. Next, we discuss the impact of substance use disorders (abuse or dependence) on schizophrenia, and the course of these disorders in schizophrenia. We then describe methods for assessing substance abuse in schizophrenia, a critical issue because many clients never have their comorbid substance use disorder detected or treated. Next, we summarize the effects of substance abuse on cognitive functioning in schizophrenia, including both acute and chronic effects. We then describe the principles of integrated treatment of substance use disorders in people with schizophrenia, followed by consideration of treatment adaptations for clients with significant neurocognitive impairment.

EPIDEMIOLOGY

Substance abuse refers to a pattern of alcohol or drug use over at least a one month period of time that results in significant impairment in social functioning, role functioning (e.g., work, school, parenting), worsening of a medical condition (including a psychiatric disorder), or that occurs in dangerous situations (e.g., driving, operating heavy machinery) (American Psychiatric Association, 1994). *Substance dependence* refers to alcohol or drug use over at least a one month period characterized by either physical dependence or psychological dependence (American Psychiatric Association, 1994). *Physical dependence* is defined by development of marked tolerance to substance effects (i.e., requiring use of greater amounts of substance to achieve the same effect), the experience of withdrawal effects if the person stops using, or the use of substances to prevent withdrawal effects. *Psychological dependence* is characterized by a significant preoccupation with using substances, defined as giving up important other activities in order to use, spending inordinate amounts of time obtaining and using substances, using more substances than intended, or making repeated unsuccessful attempts to cut down on substance use. In this chapter, we use the term "substance use disorder" to refer to people who meet *DSM-IV* criteria for either substance abuse or dependence.

There is a high prevalence of smoking in schizophrenia (de Leon & Diaz, 2005), as well as other severe mental illnesses (Kotov, Guey, Bromet, & Schwartz, 2010; Venable, Carey, Carey, & Maisto, 2003), which is already present at the first onset of psychosis Berk et al. (2010).In contrast to other commonly used substances, nicotine use in schizophrenia has not been found to contribute to worse symptoms or outcomes (Herran et al., 2000; Liao, Yang, Lee, Chen, & Tsai, 2002; Tang, George, Mao, Cai, & Chen, 2007). In fact, there is some evidence that nicotine use has normalizing effects on psychophysiological and cognitive impairments in schizophrenia (Adler, Hoffer, Wiser, & Freedman, 1993; Dulude, Labelle, & Knott, 2010; Olincy, Johnson, & Ross, 2003; Segarra et al., 2011). Because smoking does not appear to interact with or worsen the course of schizophrenia, and different interventions are effective for the treatment of smoking in schizophrenia (Tsoi, Porwal, & Webster, 2010), we do not consider it further in this chapter.

PREVALENCE OF SUBSTANCE USE DISORDERS

Estimates of the lifetime prevalence of substance use disorders in people with schizophrenia are drawn from two primary sources: community-based surveys of the prevalence of psychiatric and substance use disorders, and clinical surveys of people in treatment for one of those disorders. Although fewer community-based surveys have been conducted, the findings from these studies indicate high rates of lifetime substance use disorders in people with schizophrenia, typically ranging between 40% and 60%, compared to rates of approximately 15% in the general population, and 20% to 35% for people with an anxiety disorder (Kessler et al., 1996; Regier et al., 1990; Teeson, Hall, Lynskey, & Degenhardt, 2000). Clinical surveys of people in treatment for schizophrenia have indicated similarly high rates, with approximately 50% of individuals with a lifetime substance use disorder (Dixon, 1999; Graham et al., 2001; Mueser, Yarnold, & Bellack, 1992; Mueser et al., 1990; Mueser et al., 2000; Weaver et al., 2003). Interestingly, the studies cited above indicate that the high rate of substance use disorders is not unique to schizophrenia, but shared by other people with severe mental illnesses such as bipolar disorder and treatment-refractory major depression. Therefore, severe mental illness is associated with an increased rate of substance use disorders across a range of different psychiatric diagnoses.

While approximately 50% of people with schizophrenia have a lifetime substance use disorder, between 25% and 35% of clients have a recent (past six months) or current substance use disorder (Mueser, Bennett, & Kushner, 1995). In some settings, the prevalence of substance abuse in schizophrenia is even higher (Galanter, Castaneda, & Ferman, 1988), such as people presenting for treatment in an emergency room (Barbee, Clark, Craqanzano, Heintz, & Kehoe, 1989; Barry et al., 2006), homeless individuals (Caton et al., 1995; Caton, Shrout, Eagle, Opler, & Felix, 1994; Susser, Struening, & Conover, 1989), or people who are involved in the criminal justice system (Edens, Peters, & Hills, 1997; Peters, Kearns, Murrin, & Dolente, 1992). Thus, in some subpopulations of people with schizophrenia the presence of substance abuse can be regarded as the norm rather than the exception.

The substances most commonly used by people with schizophrenia are the same as the substances most often used in the general population; thus, access to substances is the primary determinant of the type of substance used, and there is little evidence that people with schizophrenia demonstrate preferences for specific types of substances (Mueser et al., 1992; Mueser et al., 1990). Alcohol is usually the most commonly abused substance, followed by cannabis or cocaine (Cuffel, 1996; Mueser et al., 1990; Mueser et al., 2000; Regier et al., 1990). However, in younger populations, such as persons with a first break psychosis, marijuana can surpass alcohol use as it may be a more attainable substance (Addington & Addington, 2007; Grech, van Os, Jones, Lewis, & Murray, 2005). The use of two, three or more substances (i.e., polysubstance abuse) is very common in schizophrenia, either simultaneously, serially, or both (Chen et al., 1992; Mueser et al., 1990).

DEMOGRAPHICS AND FAMILY HISTORY

The same demographic characteristics related to substance use disorders in the general population tend to be related to substance abuse in schizophrenia (Dixon, Haas, Weiden, Sweeney, & Frances, 1991; Kavanagh et al., 2004; Montross et al., 2005; Mueser et al., 1992; Mueser et al., 1990; Mueser et al., 2000). Men are more likely to have a substance use disorder than women, as are younger individuals than older ones. Race is often related to the types of substances that are abused, but not to overall rates of substance use disorder in schizophrenia, probably reflecting variations in access to different substances between racial groups rather than differences in preference for specific types of substances. Individuals with a drug use disorder tend to have lower levels of education than those who do not, although an alcohol use disorder is not related to educational level. This association appears to reflect the fact that the use of illegal substances is more likely to precipitate dropping out or being expelled from school than use of legal substances such as alcohol. Also similar to the general population (Anthony & Helzer, 1991), single or divorced individuals are more likely to have substance use disorders than those who are married.

A family history of substance use disorder is a well-established predictor of substance abuse in the general population (Knopik et al., 2004). Similarly, among persons with schizophrenia, substance abuse is associated with a stronger family history of substance use disorders (Gershon et al., 1988; Noordsy, Drake, Biesanz, & McHugo, 1994; Vardy & Kay, 1983). Antisocial personality disorder is also a strong clinical correlate of substance use disorders in the general population (Babor, Hesselbrock, Meyer, & Shoemaker, 1994; Hesselbrock, 1986), as well as in people with schizophrenia (Moran & Hodgins, 2004; Mueser et al., 1999; Tengström, Hodgins, Grann, Långström, & Kullgren, 2004). Furthermore, antisocial personality disorder, and its precursor conduct disorder, are more common in schizophrenia than in the general population (Hodgins, Hiscoke, & Freese, 2002; Mueser et al., 1999; Robins, Tipp, & Przybeck, 1991; Schug & Raine, 2009), suggesting that it may account for some of the increased rate of comorbid substance use disorders in schizophrenia (Mueser, Kavanagh, & Brunette, 2007).

Overall, there are few consistent clinical correlates of substance abuse in schizophrenia. Substance abuse tends to be associated with more severe depression in schizophrenia (Blanchard et al., 1999; Brunette, Mueser, Xie, & Drake, 1997; Drake & Brunette, 1998), which is consistent with reports of substance abuse increasing the risk of suicide attempts and competed suicide in schizophrenia (Bartels, Drake, & McHugo, 1992; Caldwell & Gottesman, 1990; Rush & Koegl, 2008). People with co-occurring disorders also tend to have milder negative symptoms than those who do not abuse substances (Kirkpatrick et al., 1996; Mueser et al., 1990; Salyers & Mueser, 2001), which may reflect the relationship between better premorbid functioning and increased vulnerability to substance use disorders (Arndt, Tyrrell, Flaum, & Andreasen, 1992), as discussed in the following section.

ONSET AND COURSE

Substance use disorders in people with schizophrenia frequently develop prior to the onset of the psychotic disorder, although onset after the diagnosis of schizophrenia is not rare, and often the two disorders develop around the same time (Hambrecht & Häfner, 1996, 2000; Silver & Abboud, 1994). In one recent review (Archie & Gyömörey, 2009), estimates of substance use disorder for first episode psychosis varied from 15% (Sobara, Liraud, Assens, Abalan, & Verdoux, 2003) to 53% (Wade et al., 2006), with a median of 37%. These findings suggest that having a substance use disorder increases the risk of developing schizophrenia, and that once a psychosis has developed there is a further risk of developing a substance use disorder.

In the United States, clients with good premorbid social functioning, including better quality social relationships and more frequent success at reaching social developmental milestones, are more likely to develop drug use disorders then clients with poor premorbid functioning, although the rates of alcohol use disorder are comparable between the two groups (Arndt et al., 1992; Cohen & Klein, 1970). This may be due to the fact that alcohol is legal and readily obtained with a minimum of skills, whereas the purchase of illicit drugs is likely mediated by social skills and relationships (Cohen & Klein, 1970). However, one study from Norway indicated the opposite—that schizophrenia clients with drug use disorders had worse premorbid social functioning (Ringen et al., 2008). Good premorbid functioning is a robust predictor of a better course of schizophrenia, including fewer hospitalizations and better psychosocial functioning (Erickson, Beiser, Iacono, Fleming, & Lin, 1989; Harrow, Carone, & Westermeyer, 1985; Zigler & Glick, 1986). Therefore, it may seem counterintuitive that clients with better premorbid functioning in the United States are also more vulnerable to developing substance use disorders. The primary reason for this increased vulnerability is that drug use most frequently occurs in social settings, and people are most likely to be introduced to drugs by other people in social situations, such as at parties, spending time with friends, or in other leisure activities (Dixon et al., 1991; Laudet, Magura, Vogel, & Knight, 2004; Warner et al., 1994). Because illicit drug use is relatively normative in the general U.S. population (especially cannabis use, and even cocaine use in some settings), people with better premorbid social functioning are more likely to be introduced to drugs because they spend more time with other people. In countries in which illicit drug use is much less common in the general population, such as Norway, drug abuse may reflect deviance from normative social behavior, and thus is associated with poor premorbid social functioning.

Drug abuse, especially stimulant and cannabis abuse, is associated with an earlier age of onset of schizophrenia (Barnes, Mutsatsa, Hutton, Watt, & Joyce, 2006; Leeson, Harrison, Ron, Barnes, & Joyce, 2011; Mueser et al., 1990; Salyers & Mueser, 2001; Sugranyes et al., 2009; Tsuang, Simpson, & Kronfol, 1982). Individuals who develop schizophrenia following drug abuse tend to have a stronger family history of psychosis than people with a drug use disorder only

(Tsuang et al., 1982; Vardy & Kay, 1983). The results suggest that drug use precipitates the onset of schizophrenia in vulnerable individuals. The findings from these studies could also suggest that individuals with a high genetic load for schizophrenia may be more likely to experience psychological distress premorbidly, and seek relief by using substances, which could then precipitate the onset of psychosis.

There is also evidence that cannabis use in adolescence is predictive of the subsequent onset of schizophrenia. Andréasson et al. (1987) reported a large 15-year prospective follow-up study of young men conscripted into the Swedish army. There was a strong association between history of cannabis use at conscription, but not other types of drug use, and later diagnosis of schizophrenia. Subsequent analyses of the subgroup with schizophrenia indicated that the cannabis users had a more rapid onset of illness characterized by positive symptoms, which the authors interpreted as supporting an etiologically distinct subgroup (Allebeck, Adamsson, Engström, & Rydberg, 1993; Andréasson, Allebeck, & Rydberg, 1989). Since this study, several other population-based studies have demonstrated a relationship between cannabis use and the development of schizophrenia, controlling for possible confounders (Arseneault et al., 2002; Fergusson, Horwood, & Swain-Campbell, 2003; Henquet et al., 2005; van Os et al., 2002), and between the potency of the cannabis used and risk of psychosis (Di Forti et al., 2009). The relationship between cannabis use and schizophrenia is dose-dependent, is stronger for cannabis use at an earlier age, and is not modified by other drug use. One interpretation of these findings is that cannabis use may precipitate the onset of schizophrenia in vulnerable individuals who would not otherwise have developed the disorder (Barkus & Murray, 2010; Hall & Degenhardt, 2008). If this were the case, one might expect increases in the prevalence of schizophrenia in places where cannabis use has increased. However, two studies that examined this in birth cohorts in Australia between 1940 and 1979 (Degenhardt, Hall, & Lynskey, 2003) and in the United Kingdom from 1996 to 2005 (Frisher, Crome, Martino, & Croft, 2009), failed to find such an association. Research on changes in the prevalence of schizophrenia in these studies may be thwarted by changes in the stringency of the definition of schizophrenia employed (Castle & Morgan, 2008).

The long-term course of substance use disorder in schizophrenia is relatively stable over time in the absence of integrated treatment (i.e., concurrent treatment of the psychiatric and substance use disorder by the same clinician or team of clinicians) (Cuffel & Chase, 1994). Some individuals with a first episode of psychosis demonstrate significant reductions in cannabis use following relatively limited treatment for their co-occurring disorders (Edwards et al., 2006). Rates of sustained substance abuse remission are significantly higher over both intermediate (e.g., 1–3 years) and long-term (e.g., 10 years) periods of time in clients with co-occurring disorder who receive integrated treatment for their disorders (Drake, O'Neal, & Wallach, 2008; Xie, Drake, & McHugo, 2009).

One important precursor to the development of substance use disorder for people with schizophrenia is conduct disorder in childhood (Mueser et al.,

1999; Tengström et al., 2004), which is characterized by a pattern of deceitfulness, aggression towards others, blatant disregard for the truth, and/or cruelty to animals, and is a required precursor for a diagnosis of antisocial personality disorder in adulthood (American Psychiatric Association, 1994). Conduct disorder is a well-established predictor of substance abuse in the general population (Hesselbrock, 1986) and in people with schizophrenia (Hodgins, Tiihonen, & Ross, 2005; Mueser et al., 1999). Furthermore, similar to within the population of people with a primary addiction (Babor et al., 1994), conduct disorder and antisocial personality disorder in people with schizophrenia and co-occurring substance use disorder have an earlier age of onset of the substance abuse, are more likely to engage in polysubstance abuse, have a more rapid progression of their addiction to physical dependence, and experience more severe psychosocial consequences (e.g., homelessness, involvement in the criminal justice system) of their substance use (Mueser et al., 2006; Mueser et al., 1997). Increased levels of impulsivity and risk-taking, which are strongly associated with conduct disorder and antisocial personality disorder (Schalling, Edman, & Åsberg, 1983), may account for this association with substance use disorder in people with schizophrenia (Dervaux et al., 2001; Duva, Silverstein, & Spiga, 2011; Rogers, Moeller, Swann, & Clark, 2010; Schiffer et al., 2010).

CONSEQUENCES OF SUBSTANCE ABUSE

Substance abuse is associated with a wide range of negative clinical consequences in schizophrenia (Drake & Brunette, 1998). Substance abuse frequently precipitates relapses and rehospitalizations (Gupta, Hendricks, Kenkel, Bhatia, & Haffke, 1996; Linszen, Dingemans, & Lenior, 1994; Schmidt, Hesse, & Lykke, 2011). At least some of the precipitation of relapses and rehospitalizations is due to the fact that clients with co-occurring disorders are often not adherent to prescribed medications (Miller et al., 2009; Miner, Rosenthal, Hellerstein, & Muenz, 1997; Swartz et al., 1998; Yamada et al., 2006), further increasing their risk of relapse and rehospitalization. While non-adherence to medication can occur for a wide range of different reasons (Weiden, Mott, & Curcio, 1995; Zygmunt, Olfson, Boyer, & Mechanic, 2002), one factor is that clients are often warned against using drugs or alcohol when they are taking prescribed medications, which may result in them not adhering to their medication rather than not using substances (Mueser, Noordsy, Drake, & Fox, 2003). Alcohol and drugs can either counteract the protective effects of medication, or act directly by increasing dopaminergic neurotransmission believed to underlie psychotic symptoms in schizophrenia. In general, substance abuse in schizophrenia exacerbates symptoms, including psychotic symptoms, depression, and suicidality (Drake & Brunette, 1998).

A wide range of negative social consequences are common, including conflict with family members (Dixon, McNary, & Lehman, 1995; Kashner et al., 1991; Salyers & Mueser, 2001), loss of housing (Drake, Osher, & Wallach, 1991), legal problems (Peters, Greenbaum, Edens, Carter, & Ortiz, 1998), and money problems (Shaner et al., 1995). Substance abuse is also associated with increased exposure to interpersonal trauma and engagement in high risk behaviors for infectious diseases (Rosenberg, Trumbetta, et al., 2001). Thus, health problems are another common consequence of substance abuse in schizophrenia, especially infectious diseases such as the hepatitis C virus (Rosenberg, Goodman, et al., 2001). The net result of the many consequences of substance abuse in schizophrenia is increased morbidity and premature mortality (Xie et al., 2009).

Assessment of Substance Use Disorders

The assessment of substance use disorders is of critical importance to the neuropsychological assessment and interpretation in people with schizophrenia. However, the assessment of substance use problems is complicated by several barriers in this population.

Barriers to Accurate Assessment

A range of barriers may interfere with accurate assessment of substance abuse in schizophrenia. Common complications to assessment include: denial and minimization, fear of sanctions, confusion about the effects of substance abuse vs. the mental illness, and increased sensitivity to substance effects Each of these factors is briefly described below.

Denial and Minimization

Denial and minimization of the effects of substance use are a common feature of substance use disorders in the general population (Babor, Stephens, & Marlatt, 1987). However, among people with schizophrenia, for whom lack of insight into the psychiatric disorder is often a profound clinical feature that interferes with effective treatment, the denial and minimization of the effects of substance use are often even more marked. As a consequence of this lack of insight, people with schizophrenia often fail to report negative consequences of substance use or minimize any negative effects they are aware of (Barbee et al., 1989; Carey, 2002). This means that the assessor must often play the role of a detective, gathering information about the person's use of substances and possible consequences, without the individual fully acknowledging and reporting such effects.

Fear of Sanctions

In the general population, the illegal status of many commonly abused drugs, combined with fear of vocational, educational, or legal consequences of alcohol abuse, often contribute to the minimization or denial of substance use. In addition to these concerns, people with schizophrenia may have further reservations about talking openly about their substance use. Many people with schizophrenia receive disability income and housing subsidies, which may be used to support their substance use habits (Shaner et al., 1995), leading to concerns that disclosure of their substance use could threaten this source of income. These concerns are not unfounded. Individuals with schizophrenia and co-occurring substance use disorders may be appointed a representative payee to manage their disability income with the hope of reducing their access to substances (Ries & Comtois, 1997; Rosen & Rosenheck, 1999; Rosen et al., 2002). Clients may also be concerned about other undesirable consequences of acknowledging their substance use, such as alienating their relationships with treatment providers or family members, who often hold people with schizophrenia responsible for both their substance use and psychiatric problems (Niv, Lopez, Glynn, & Mueser, 2007).

CONFUSION ABOUT SUBSTANCE ABUSE EFFECTS

The criteria for establishing a substance abuse diagnosis is that the person's use of substances interferes with social, occupational, or self-care, or that the individual uses substances in dangerous situations, such as driving a car or operating heavy machinery. Determining these consequences of substance use in schizophrenia can be challenging because impaired social functioning, work or school functioning, and self-care are part of the diagnostic criteria for schizophrenia. Furthermore, many people with the illness do not own and drive cars, and many are unemployed, and those who are employed rarely operate heavy machinery. Consequently, determining whether an individual's use of substances is problematic can be difficult due to the overlap in the defining characteristics of the two disorders. The psychosocial effects of substance use can be evaluated by comparing functioning during periods when the client is using substances with periods when the client is not using (Mueser et al., 2003). However, this can only be done for clients with an episodic history of substance use and for whom there is good longitudinal information about their functioning.

Increased Sensitivity to Substance Effects

Another challenge with assessing substance abuse in schizophrenia is the increased sensitivity of people with this disorder to the effects of modest amounts of substances compared to people in the general population (Mueser, Drake, & Wallach, 1998). People with schizophrenia demonstrate more pronounced effects (e.g., euphoria) to the administration of low doses of psychoactive substances such as amphetamines, marijuana, and alcohol compared to people without schizophrenia (D'Souza et al., 2005; D'Souza et al., 2006; Lieberman, Kane, & Alvir, 1987). This heightened sensitivity may also result in clients experiencing negative consequences related to the use of much lower quantities of substances, and meeting diagnostic criteria for a substance use disorder, compared to the general population (Corse, Hirschinger, & Zanis, 1995). As a result, many screening instruments for substance use disorder in the general population fail to identify people with schizophrenia with substance use problems (Rosenberg et al., 1998), and clinicians expecting the typical pattern of substance abuse may not recognize the negative effects if their clients are abusing only moderate quantities of substances.

The increased sensitivity, or *supersensitivity*, to substance effects in people with schizophrenia likely reflects the biological vulnerability believed to underlie the disorder (Mueser et al., 2007). For example, commonly abused substances can activate dopaminergic mesocorticolimbic tracks involved in reward (Boileau et al., 2003). The brain reward system appears to be dysregulated in schizophrenia, but may be transiently ameliorated by the use of substances (Chambers, Krystal, & Self, 2001; Chau, Roth, & Green, 2004). Repeated use of psychoactive substances may increase biologic sensitivity to their rewarding effects, while also increasing the risk of psychosic exacerbations due to stimulation of the mesolimbic circuit. As would be expected from this supersensitivity to substance effects, people with schizophrenia are less able to sustain active substance use over time without developing a substance use disorder (Drake & Wallach, 1993). From the perspective of assessment, the supersensitivity that characterizes schizophrenia means that the consequences of any substance use in this population need to be carefully evaluated.

PRINCIPLES OF SUBSTANCE USE DISORDER ASSESSMENT

Adherence to several principles can yield accurate and reliable evaluations of substance use problems in schizophrenia (Mueser et al., 2003). These principles are briefly described below, and outlined in Table 10.1.

Routinely Assess Substance Use in All Clients

Because substance use is common in schizophrenia, and its impact can vary considerably from one person to the next, routine assessment of substance use in all persons with schizophrenia is critical to detection and treatment. Assessments of substance use should include both reports of current use as well as past use. Some research suggests that clients are more willing to acknowledge past substance use than current use (Fowler, Carr, Carter, & Lewin, 1998). In addition, past substance use is an important predictor of current substance, since relatively few people with schizophrenia stop using substances in the absence of concerted treatment efforts (Cuffel & Chase, 1994). Therefore, information about lifetime history of substance use is beneficial for identifying clients who are actively using substances, including those who are covertly using and deny use.

TABLE 10.1 Assessment of Substance Use Disorders in Schizophrenia

- Be aware of client characteristics associated with substance use disorders:
  - Male
  - Young
  - Lower level of education (drugs)
  - Intact peer group (drugs)
  - Family history of substance use disorder
  - History of conduct disorder/antisocial personality disorder traits
  - Higher depression/suicidality
  - Lower negative symptoms
- Evaluate all clients with established screening instruments:
  - Dartmouth Assessment of Lifestyle Instrument (DALI)
  - Drug Abuse Screening Test (DAST)
  - Michigan Alcoholism Screening Test (MAST)
  - Substance Abuse Subtle Screening Inventory (SASSI)
- Tap multiple sources of information:
  - Client
  - Clinicians
  - Family members or other significant persons
  - Medical records
  - Results of toxicology screens
- Explore past and present use of specific substances:
  - Alcohol
  - Cannabis
  - Cocaine
  - Amphetamines
  - Heroin and other narcotics
  - Hallucinogens
  - Sedatives
  - Inhalants
  - Over-the-counter medications
- For each substance used, evaluate:
  - Route of administration
  - Pattern of use (e.g., steady use, binging)
  - Situations in which substances are used (e.g., social, alone, on street)
  - Motives for use (e.g., social facilitation, coping, fun/boredom, escape)

TABLE 10.1 Continued

- Evaluate consequences of substance use
  - Exacerbation of symptoms/relapses
  - Social problems (e.g., family, friends)
  - Legal problems
  - Medical problems (e.g., hepatitis C)
  - Violence
  - Victimization
  - Use in hazardous situations
  - Physical tolerance to substance effects
  - Psychological dependence (e.g., unsuccessful quit attempts)
- Examine social facilitators of substance use and support for abstinence
  - Family
  - Friends
  - Co-workers
- Explore personal goals
  - Improved housing
  - Improved social relationships
  - Desire for work or resumption of education
  - Spirituality
  - Health
  - Desire to be a better parent
  - Greater independence
  - Better psychiatric illness management
- Determine motivation to change
  - Negligible awareness of problem or motivation to change
  - Awareness of substance use problems but ambivalent about change
  - Awareness of substance use problems and some reduction in use or concerted attempts to reduce
  - Successful reduction of substance use or abstinence for at least 1 month
  - Has not met criteria for substance abuse for 6 months or more

Use Multiple Sources of Information

All measures of substance use problems have their limitations; in the absence of a single gold standard measure, obtaining information from multiple sources is necessary for an accurate diagnosis (Drake, Rosenberg, & Mueser, 1996). Client self-reports of substance use are often the most accurate single measure, although as discussed they are prone to denial and minimization. The reports of significant others, such as family members, can also provide valuable information, depending on the amount of time they spend with the client, and whether the client attempts to conceal his or her substance use from that person. Clinician reports and medical records can also provide useful information about possible substance use problems. Finally, toxicology reports from laboratory tests of substance use, such as Breathalyzer, urine, or hair analysis can provide important information about substance use, but not abuse or dependence. Combining all the different sources of information allows the clinician to triangulate data and to arrive at an informed evaluation of whether the client has a substance use disorder.

Use Screening Instruments for Substance Abuse

Several standardized self-report instruments have been shown to be accurate in the detection of substance use problems in people with schizophrenia and other severe mental illnesses, including the Alcohol Use Identification Test (Maisto, Carey, Carey, Gordon, & Gleason, 2000), the Dartmouth Assessment of Lifestyle Instrument (Rosenberg et al., 1998), the Drug Abuse Screening Test (Maisto et al., 2000), the Michigan Alcoholism Screening Test (McHugo, Paskus, & Drake, 1993), and the Substance Abuse Subtle Screening Inventory (Lazowski, Miller, Boye, & Miller, 1998). Using these screening instruments on a routine basis with new clients admitted to a service can identify people who may be having substance use problems, and for whom a more refined assessment is needed. These instruments can be administered in a variety of ways, including using self-reported questionnaires, computer administered screens, or by clinical interview (Wolford et al., 1999).

Maintain a High Index of Suspicion

Substance use in schizophrenia should be considered the "norm" rather than the exception (Mueser et al., 2003). Thus, clinicians working with clients who have (or recently have had) access to substances (e.g., people living in the community or presenting for treatment in emergency rooms or acute care psychiatric settings) should assume that many of them are using substances, and maintain a high index of suspicion regarding their use, even in the absence of clear corroborating data. Familiarity with client characteristics associated with substance use and the common consequences of substance use (e.g., relapses and hospitalizations, problems with housing, money, relationships, health, or the legal system) can facilitate the identification of clients who may be covertly using substances.

Diagnosis of Substance Use Disorders

When a screening instrument indicates a high probability that a client has a substance use disorder, subsequent diagnostic assessment should be conducted to verify this, and to evaluate the specific nature of the disorder. Structured clinical interviews are highly reliable for establishing a diagnosis of substance use disorder, such as the Structured Clinical Interview for *DSM-IV* (First, Spitzer, Gibbon, & Williams, 1996) and the Addiction Severity Index (McLellan et al., 1992). Structured diagnostic interviews require significant interviewer training, and can be time-consuming to administer in routine clinical practice. An alternative is to use a clinical rating scale developed for the purposes of establishing a substance use diagnosis.

Two clinician administered diagnostic measures are the Alcohol Use Scale-Revised (AUS) and the Drug Use Scale-Revised (DUS) (Drake et al., 1990; Mueser et al., 2003). These scales are completed based on all the available information about the client's use of substances, including self-reports, collateral reports, input from other treatment team members, and medical records, including toxicology reports. Each scale systematically reviews the *DSM-IV* criteria for substance use disorder, with the assessment focusing on the worst one-month period over the past six months. After reviewing the diagnostic criteria for substance abuse and dependence, the AUD and DUS are summarized with a single five-point scale (i.e., 1 = no substance use over the past six months, 2 = substance use without significant impairment, 3 = substance abuse, 4 = substance dependence, and 5 = substance dependence and institutionalization). The institutionalization part of the highest rating on the AUS or DUS refers to whether clients who meet criteria for substance dependence also experienced repeated or prolonged hospitalizations, emergency room visits, and/or incarcerations due to their substance abuse.

SUBSTANCE ABUSE AND COGNITIVE FUNCTIONING

Substance abuse has unique relevance to schizophrenia because of its potential to further impair the compromised cognitive functioning associated with schizophrenia. However, despite the expectation that substance abuse, especially chronic abuse, will exacerbate cognitive impairment in schizophrenia, the evidence for such effects is mixed. This section addresses the acute and longer term effects of substance abuse on cognitive functioning in schizophrenia, with an emphasis on putative factors that may serve to mitigate the cognitive impairing effects of substances in schizophrenia.

Acute Effects of Substance Abuse on Cognitive Functioning

Given the high prevalence of substance abuse in schizophrenia, the acute effects of substances should be considered during routine cognitive assessment. Prominent cognitive, mood, and perceptual effects of commonly abused substances in schizophrenia are summarized in Table 10.2. The active cognitive effects of substances are wide ranging, and there is evidence of both direct and indirect effects on cognitive performance (Evert & Oscar-Berman, 1995; Payer & London, 2009; Pope, Gruber, Hudson, Huestis, & Yurgelun-Todd, 2001; Schuckit,

TABLE 10.2 Cognitive, Mood, and Perceptual Effects of Commonly Abused Substances

Type of Substance	Effects
Alcohol: Beer, wine, "hard" liquor	• Drowsiness • Slurred speech • Loss of motor coordination • Slowed reaction time • Relaxation • Depression
Cannabis: Marijuana, hash, THC	• Mild euphoria • Relaxation • Anxiety or panic • Perceptual distortions • Racing or paranoid thoughts • Slowed reaction time • Reduced memory
Stimulants: Cocaine, "speed" (amphetamine)	• Alertness • Energy • Feeling "high" • Anxiety • Nervousness • Psychotic symptoms
Hallucinogens: LSD ,ecstasy, PCP, MDA, mescaline, peyote	• Perceptual distortions or hallucinations • Impaired judgment • Feelings of unreality
Sedatives: Benzodiazepines, hypnotics	• Drowsiness • Slurred speech • Reduced motor coordination • Slowed reaction time • Relaxation • Depression
Narcotics: Heroin, morphine, codeine	• Euphoria • Drowsiness • Relaxation • Feeling "high" or "spacey" • Slowed reaction time

2009). It should be noted that the range and severity of acute effects of substances on cognition depend upon the amount of substances ingested and the individual's response to, and experience with, the substance(s). Cognitive effects of commonly abused substances include slowed reaction time (alcohol, cannabis, sedatives, narcotics), impaired attention (stimulants), and reduced memory functioning (cannabis). Indirect effects of substances on ability to participate in cognitive assessment include cravings for substances and compromised reality testing, which can be associated with all illicit substances and alcohol, and which contribute to problems in comprehension of task instructions and overall level of engagement in the assessment.

Cognitive performance can also be impaired by the acute sedating effects associated with alcohol, sedatives, and narcotics, and cannabis. Acute use of substances can be associated with fluctuating levels of arousal, which can range from hyper-alertness to stupor, and which can contribute to diminished persistence of effort. Fluctuating levels of arousal and diminished effort can be reflected in a high degree of variability in cognitive performance both within a specific task (e.g., across learning trials), and across a battery of tests. Substantial fluctuations in task performance can be an indication that performance is adversely impacted by substances. A diminished level of cooperation with the cognitive assessment can also occur with acute effects of substances. An examinee may be irritable, or more easily frustrated with testing demands, which may contribute to limited cooperation, or outright refusal to complete the assessment.

Because of the adverse impact of substances on cognitive task performance, testing should not occur if a person is suspected of using drugs or alcohol, and the assessment should be rescheduled for another time when the person has abstinent for a sufficient period of time. If the client has substance abuse but not physical dependence, one to three days of abstinence is sufficient to commence testing. If the person is physically dependent on a substance and is being detoxified, testing should be postponed for at least a week until the most acute withdrawal symptoms and cravings have been ceased.

Under some circumstances, it may be clinically useful to administer a briefer cognitive test battery to a client who is actively using substances. Assuming sufficient engagement of the client in the task, the results of the cognitive testing could be interpreted as reflecting the combined influences of the mental illness and the substance use disorder. If a subsequent assessment can be conducted when the client is abstinent, then the difference in performance between the two assessments can be reviewed with the client using the principles of motivational interviewing (e.g., empathic listening, Socratic questioning, developing discrepancy between continued use and personal goals) in order to instill motivation to work on substance use problems. Even if subsequent testing when the client is abstinent is not feasible, the results of the testing can be discussed with the client, and the possible deleterious effects of substance use on cognitive performance explored in order to educate and potentially motivate the client to address his or her substance use habits.

Long-term Effects of Substance Abuse on Cognitive Functioning

Despite the high rates of substance use disorder in schizophrenia, there is little consensus regarding the effects of longer term substance use on cognition. This is surprising given the evidence of impairing effects of substance abuse in nonpsychiatric populations (Schuckit, 2009), most notably alcohol (Bates, Bowden, & Barry, 2002; Goodwin, 1992). Additionally, because schizophrenia is associated with substantial and broad-based cognitive impairments, there is an expectation that this population has enhanced vulnerability to the potential brain damaging effects of substance abuse. Thus, the expectations are that the presence of a substance use disorder would be associated with cognitive impairment in schizophrenia that would exceed levels of impairment commonly observed.

Meta-analyses of cognition in schizophrenia have been unable to discern the impact of substance use disorder on performance due to lack of information about substance abuse in research studies (Heinrichs & Zakzanis, 1998). Studies of the long-term effects of substance use on cognition in schizophrenia have yielded mixed results. In some studies, clients with substance use disorders have demonstrated better cognitive performance than those without, whereas other studies have no differences or worse performance (Addington & Addington, 1996; Allen et al., 1999; Cleghorn et al., 1991; Copersino et al., 2004; Coulston, Perdices, & Tennant, 2007; DeRosse, Kaplan, Burdick, Lencz, & Malhotra, 2010; Joyal, Hallé, Lapierre, & Hodgins, 2003; Leeson et al., 2011; Manning et al., 2009; Manning et al., 2007; McCleery, Addington, & Addington, 2006; Nixon, Hallford, & Tivis, 1996; Potvin, Joyal, Pelletier, & Stip, 2008; Ringen et al., 2010; Rodriguez-Jimenez et al., 2010; Rodriguez-Sanchez et al., 2010; Scholes & Martin-Iverson, 2010; Serper et al., 1995).

A meta-analysis including 23 studies with a total of 1,870 clients evaluated the relationship between substance use disorder and cognitive functioning in schizophrenia, including 789 clients with schizophrenia and substance use disorder and 1,106 clients with schizophrenia only (Potvin et al., 2008). There was no difference in the average age of the two groups (approximately 38 years old in each), although there was a significantly higher proportion of men in the substance use disorder group (84%) than in the schizophrenia only group (76%). The effects of substance use disorder as well as specific substance types (alcohol, cannabis, cocaine, mixed) on a composite measure of cognitive performance and six specific domains of cognitive functioning according to the MATRICS (sustained attention, reasoning and problem-solving, verbal and visual learning and memory, and visual memory, speed of processing) (Nuechterlein et al., 2004) were examined. Age, but not gender, was evaluated as a moderator of effect size estimates. The results indicated no difference between clients with a substance use disorder and clients without a disorder on overall cognitive functioning. Comparisons between the groups on specific cognitive domains indicated that clients with a substance use disorder performed significantly *better* on speed of processing, but did not differ in any of the other domains. Analyses of specific substance types indicated that alcohol use disorder was associated with worse working memory, consistent with research on the effects of alcohol on in the general population (Chanraud, Pitel, Rohlfing, Pfefferbaum, & Sullivan, 2010). In contrast, cannabis use disorder was related to *better* problem solving and reasoning, and visual memory. The association between cannabis use and more preserved cognitive functioning has been replicated in two recent meta-analyses (Rabin, Zakzanis, & George, 2011; Yücel et al., 2012). Age was found to moderate the effect size of overall cognitive functioning, speed of processing, and working memory, with stronger effect sizes (i.e., greater differences between groups) for younger clients. The general findings from Potvin et al.'s (2008) meta-analysis are consistent with more studies on this topic (Potvin, Stavro, & Pelletier, 2012).

Research has attempted to elucidate the puzzling lack of consistent effects of substance abuse, especially drug abuse, on cognitive functioning in schizophrenia. One hypothesis is that the apparently paradoxical association between drug abuse and better cognitive functioning in schizophrenia may be explained by their relationships with premorbid social functioning. As previously noted in this chapter, compared to clients who do not develop substance use disorders, clients with schizophrenia who abuse drugs, especially cannabis, tend to have better premorbid social functioning (Arndt, Hartman, & Mileham, 2001), better social functioning, and less severe negative symptoms (Dervaux et al., 2001; Kirkpatrick et al., 1996; Mueser et al., 1990; Potvin, Sepehry, & Stip, 2006; Salyers & Mueser, 2001), presumably reflecting their higher premorbid exposure to drugs through friends, and their greater social skill and social drive to continue using with friends after the onset of their illness (Cohen & Klein, 1970). Since better premorbid social functioning and less severe negative symptoms are associated with better cognitive functioning in schizophrenia (Addington & Addington, 1993; Schretlen et al., 2007; Ventura, Hellemann, Thames, Koellner, & Nuechterlein, 2009), the association between drug abuse and better cognitive functioning in some studies may be explained by the fact that those clients who are most likely to abuse drugs also tend to have better premorbid (and post-illness onset) cognitive functioning.

For example, a sample of 68 recent onset clients with schizophrenia and comorbid drug abuse (predominantly cannabis) had limited impairment in most aspects of cognitive functioning (verbal fluency, and a trend toward worse working memory as assessed by the Digit Span, backwards) compared to similar clients with no substance abuse, while there was a trend for them to have better performance on measures of executive functioning (such as reasoning and problem solving as measured by the Wisconsin Card Sorting Test) (Wobrock et al., 2007). Furthermore, and consistent with the notion that persons with schizophrenia who have better reasoning and problem solving are more likely to have the requisite social skills for obtaining illicit substances, another study using fMRI indicated more activity in brain areas of social-emotional processing in schizophrenia clients with drug abuse histories than similar clients without (Potvin, Mancini-Marie, Fahim, Mensour, & Stip, 2007). Thus, the inconsistent findings of studies comparing the cognitive functioning of schizophrenia clients with vs. those without drug abuse may in part be due to the tendency for clients with better premorbid cognitive functioning to be more prone to developing drug use disorders. It is possible that drug abuse is compromising superior cognitive functioning in some of the clients so that they perform similar to or only slightly better than clients who do not use drugs but had much worse premorbid cognitive functioning.

Another factor that may contribute to the inconsistent findings regarding the association between substance abuse and cognitive functioning is the lower quantities of substances typically abused by clients with schizophrenia compared to those with addiction alone (see previous section on "Increased Sensitivity to Substance Effects"). This lower exposure to alcohol and drugs among clients with a co-occurring substance use disorder may reduce the likelihood that substance abuse will lead to measurable long-term negative effects on cognitive functioning.

Treatment of Co-Occurring Substance Abuse

Historically, the treatment of schizophrenia and other major psychiatric disorders was provided by the mental health system, while substance use disorders were treated in the substance abuse system, with separate funding, clinical training, and eligibility criteria for receiving services each system. As a result of this division between mental health and substance abuse treatment, people with schizophrenia and co-occurring substance use disorders usually received treatment for their disorders in a parallel or sequential fashion. In *parallel treatment*, individuals receive their mental health and substance abuse treatments from separate clinicians at separate agencies at the same time, with the expectation of some coordination between the different treatment providers. In *sequential treatment*, treatment is first provided for one disorder (e.g., stabilization of symptoms in schizophrenia), and then the person is referred for treatment for the other disorder.

Research reviews of the effectiveness of traditional parallel or sequential treatment approaches for people with severe mental illness indicated numerous problems and poor treatment outcomes (Polcin, 1992; Ridgely, Goldman, & Talbott, 1986). The primary problem with *parallel treatment* is that clients with schizophrenia and substance abuse often lack insight into their substance use problems and motivation to pursue treatment. As a result, the vast majority of people with these co-occurring disorders never receive treatment for their substance abuse problems in parallel treatment systems. Even when clients do follow through on referrals for substance abuse treatment, eligibility criteria for receiving substance abuse treatment often prevent individuals from accessing the services they need (Ridgely, Goldman, & Willenbring, 1990), and when they are able to access both treatments, the treatment providers themselves often fail to coordinate the services, leading to suboptimal treatment outcomes.

The primary problem associated with *sequential treatment* is the difficulty of treating one disorder without simultaneously attending to the other. For example, successfully stabilizing the symptoms of schizophrenia in a client who is actively abusing stimulant drugs is notoriously difficult. Similarly, initiating substance abuse treatment for in a floridly psychotic client who is not receiving antipsychotic medication can be difficult or impossible. Thus, sequential treatment approaches fail to account for the fact that schizophrenia and substance abuse interact and worsen each other in a cyclical fashion.

Integrated Treatment

Awareness of the limitations of traditional parallel or sequential treatment approaches to substance abuse in schizophrenia led to the development of integrated treatment programs for both disorders, beginning about 20 years ago. Although a range of different integrated treatment programs have been developed (Carey, 1996; Drake, Antosca, Noordsy, Bartels, & Osher, 1991; Fox et al., 2010; Minkoff, 1989; Mueser et al., 2003; Ziedonis & Fisher, 1996), they share the common characteristic of providing integrated treatment, defined as the treatment for both the mental illness and the substance use disorder at the same time, by the same clinician or team of clinicians, with the burden of integration falling on the treatment team. Although integrated treatment can be provided by blended teams of clinicians working for either a mental health agency or a substance abuse treatment agency, most integrated treatment programs for schizophrenia have been created by developing expertise in substance abuse treatment among those clinicians working at a mental health agency.

In addition, research on integrated treatment programs indicates several other common characteristics related to improved outcomes (Drake et al., 2008), including comprehensive assessment and treatment, harm-reduction philosophy, long-term perspective, motivational-based, stage-wise interventions, and multiple treatment modalities. We briefly describe each of these characteristics below.

Comprehensive Assessment and Treatment

As previously described, substance abuse can have a negative effect on the broad range of outcomes of people with schizophrenia, such as precipitating relapses, social, legal, medical, and housing problems, and impaired role functioning. In order to address a broad range of needs of people with co-occurring disorders, and to enable individuals to live worthwhile and rewarding lives that are free of dependence on substances, comprehensive assessment and treatment are needed. Pharmacological treatment is important to the stabilization of symptoms and prevention of relapses, even in clients who are actively abusing substances (Green, Noordsy, Brunette, & O'Keefe, 2008). Optimal illness management also requires that clients receive training in illness self-management, including psychoeducation about schizophrenia and its treatment, medication adherence strategies, relapse prevention planning, building social support, and coping strategies for stress and persistent symptoms, such as that provided in the Illness Management and Recovery program (Gingerich & Mueser, 2010; Mueser et al., 2002).

Considering the increased family stress associated with substance abuse in people with schizophrenia (Dixon et al., 1995; Salyers & Mueser, 2001), family psychoeducation is crucial to provide in order to avert loss of social and functional supports that often lead to homelessness in this population (Mueser et al., 2009; Pitschel-Walz, Leucht, Bäuml, Kissling, & Engel, 2001). Housing supports are critical for those individuals who are homeless or tenuously living in the community, as effective treatment of substance abuse is extremely difficult in the absence of stable housing (Tsemberis, Gulcur, & Nakae, 2004). Medical services may be necessary to treat a variety of diseases associated with substance abuse in schizophrenia. Legal assistance may be required because many people with co-occurring disorders are involved in the criminal justice system, but may avoid incarceration if they are engaged in integrated treatment for their disorders (Frisman et al., 2006).

Vocational services such as supported employment are important for helping clients pursue work goals, and for instilling motivation for sobriety (Becker, Drake, & Naughton, 2005; Bond, Drake, & Becker, 2008). Individuals also need to be able to access other effective treatments for schizophrenia, such as cognitive behavioral therapy for persistent psychotic symptoms (Wykes, Steel, Everitt, & Tarrier, 2008), social skills training to improve social competence (Kurtz & Mueser, 2008), assertive community treatment to stem the cycle of relapses and re-hospitalizations (Bond, Drake, Mueser, & Latimer, 2001), and cognitive remediation to address cognitive impairments (McGurk, Twamley, Sitzer, McHugo, & Mueser, 2007).

Harm-Reduction Philosophy

Harm reduction involves minimizing the most negative and costly consequences of substance use, while accepting the fact that the person is continuing to use (Denning, 2000; Marlatt, 1998). Most people with co-occurring disorders are not willing to endorse abstinence as an initial treatment goal. Harm-reduction efforts provide the opportunity for the clinician to reduce some of the most injurious consequences of the person's substance use, which can facilitate the development of a therapeutic relationship without requiring the person to endorse abstinence as a goal. The notion of "allowing the client to hit rock bottom" is not acceptable for people with schizophrenia, for whom "rock bottom" is all too often death. Harm-reduction strategies, similar to gradual reduction of substance use, open the door for many people to changing their substance use behaviors, which in the long run often leads to the person recognizing the value of endorsing abstinence as a goal. Examples of harm reduction strategies include providing clean needles for injection drug users, identifying places where the person can use substances where they are less likely to be victimized, teaching safe sex practices (e.g., requesting a partner to use a condom), and shifting from the use of more harmful substances to less harmful ones (e.g., substituting marijuana for cocaine or amphetamine abuse).

Long-Term Perspective

Schizophrenia is often a chronic, relapsing disorder. Similarly, co-occurring substance use disorders can also be chronic and relapsing. Considering the often persistent nature of co-occurring disorders, it is not realistic to impose time constraints on treatment programs for this population. Integrated treatment programs for co-occurring disorders need to be cognizant of the long-term treatment needs of most people, and provide necessary services on a time unlimited basis. Long-term studies of integrated treatment for co-occurring disorders indicate that there is gradual improvement, with many people experiencing sustained remissions of their substance use disorder after several years of treatment (Drake et al., 2006; Xie et al., 2009).

Motivation-Based, Stage-Wise Interventions

People with schizophrenia and substance use disorders often lack motivation to address their substance use problems, despite its dire consequences. Even among clients who recognize that they have substance use problems, motivation to achieve abstinence is often limited. Therefore, effective integrated treatment needs to take into account the client's level of motivation to work on substance use problems, and incorporate strategies to enhance motivation as needed.

Tailoring integrated treatment to an individual's motivational stage can be informed by the concept of the stages of change (Prochaska & DiClemente, 1984). The *stages of change* are based on the observation that individuals who change a health behavior, such as smoking, reducing weight, or substance use, they do so by progressing through a series of discrete stages. Five stages of change have been identified, including: *pre-contemplation* (the individual is not thinking about change), *contemplation* (the person is thinking about change), *preparation* (the individual is making plans to change), *action* (the person is actively changing his or her behavior), and *maintenance* (the person is maintaining the successfully changes). Awareness of an individual's stage of change can inform treatment providers as to how to help the person move onto the next stage.

The stages of change concept was adapted to formulate the *stages of treatment* to describe the stages that individuals with a co-occurring disorder progress through professional-based treatment for their disorders (Mueser et al., 2003; Osher & Kofoed, 1989). Four different stages of treatment have been identified, including *engagement*, *persuasion*, *active treatment*, and *relapse prevention*. Each stage is associated with a unique goal of treatment, with a variety of treatment options available for achieving each goal. Using the stages of treatment concept to match treatment to the client's motivational state can enhance motivation for change, facilitate treatment retention, and optimize outcomes. The stages of treatment are briefly described below, and elaborated in more detail in Mueser et al. (2003).

Engagement Stage In order for change in substance abuse to occur in the context of professional based treatment, a *therapeutic relationship*, or *working alliance*, must first be established between the clinician and the client. Without this relationship, the client is vulnerable to dropping out of treatment as it may appear on responsive to his or her concerns. Therefore, before attempting to motivate the client to work on his or her substance abuse or directly teaching strategies aimed at reducing substance use, the clinician must establish a therapeutic relationship with the client.

A therapeutic relationship can be assumed to be present when the clinician has regular contact with the client for at least several weeks. A number of interventions can be useful to engage clients in treatment. Assertive outreach is often necessary to meet with clients in the community because they often fail to attend clinic appointments. Early contacts with clients often need to focus on addressing pressing concerns, such as housing problems, conflict with family and other significant persons, health problems, or legal difficulties. Working with clients to address these needs, and demonstrating empathy for the challenges the client is experiencing, are effective strategies for engaging clients therapeutically. At times, coercive strategies such as involuntary inpatient or outpatient commitment can be useful for engaging people and treatment. When coercive strategies are used, clients can often be successfully engaged with the clinician forming an alliance with the client aimed at achieving the long-term goal of reducing or eliminating any coercion that has been applied to get the person in treatment.

Persuasion Stage After a working alliance has been established, the goal of the persuasion stage is to motivate the client to see substance use as a problem that he or she wants to work on. This includes increasing the client's awareness of the nature of his or her substance use problems, instilling hope for change and a better life, and motivating the client to actively participate in treatment. Therefore, the persuasion stage does not directly focus on changing the client's substance use, but rather on creating a dialog about substance use, including both negative and positive aspects, and exploring the potential benefits of reducing or stopping alcohol and drug use. Although the persuasion stage does not directly focus on reducing the client's use of substances, but rather on increasing motivation to work on substance abuse, the strongest indicator that the client is motivated to work on his or her substance use problems is either repeated efforts to cut down or stop using, or with some actual success at reducing substance use.

A wide range of interventions can be used in the persuasion stage. Psychiatric stabilization of symptoms can be important as exacerbated symptoms can interfere with a client's ability to perceive negative consequences of substance use. Educating clients and family members about the nature of substance use problems in their interactions with schizophrenia can often motivate them to begin working on this problem. An especially powerful approach is to educate clients and family members about the *stress-vulnerability model* of schizophrenia (Nuechterlein & Dawson, 1984). This model posits that schizophrenia is caused by a *biological vulnerability* determined by genetic and other biological factors, but which interacts with biological and environmental factors. *Environmental stress* can worsen biological vulnerability, leading to increased symptoms and relapses, but *social support* and *coping skills* can reduce the negative effects of environmental stress. From the biological angle, *antipsychotic medications* can help to correct some of the biological vulnerability believed to cause the symptoms of schizophrenia, whereas *drug and alcohol use* can worsen biological vulnerability or reduce the protective effects of medication. Thus, people with schizophrenia are more vulnerable to the effects of modest amounts of substances (i.e., supersensitivity) (Mueser et al., 1998). Educating clients about the stress-vulnerability model of schizophrenia, and their increased sensitivity to drug and alcohol effects, can motivate clients to work on their substance use problems in order to better manage their disorder without ever having to directly acknowledge that they have an "addiction."

Rehabilitation strategies such as social skills training, supported employment, and teaching skills for coping with stress and symptoms can all play a useful, indirect role in motivating clients to work on their substance use problems. People with schizophrenia often use substances in order to facilitate social connections with other people, to cope with symptoms, or in order to have something to look forward to in their lives (Dixon et al., 1991; Mueser, Nishith, Tracy, DeGirolamo, & Molinaro, 1995; Warner et al., 1994). For clients who are aware of the negative consequences of their substance use, but are ambivalent about stopping use because of the desired effects, psychiatric rehabilitation can be used to teach new skills and identify alternative outlets for getting their social, coping, and leisure needs met in ways other than using substances. Decreased reliance on using substances for getting one's needs met can tip the decisional balance towards reducing and stopping substance use in these individuals.

Persuasion groups that give an opportunity for clients to talk openly about their use of substances, including both positive and negative aspects, without being expected to endorse sobriety as a goal, can provide individuals with feedback from others and insight into their substance use problems, fostering motivation to change (Mueser et al., 2003). While persuasion groups focus on increasing motivation to change substance use habits, they also benefit from including participants from the later stages of treatment, who can serve as role models for clients grappling with their own ambivalence about using. These groups can teach curriculum about co-occurring disorders and their management, but focus mainly on group process in a non-threatening and supportive social milieu.

Motivational interviewing is an important approach that is often used in the persuasion stage. Motivational interviewing is a set of techniques designed to foster change of health-related behaviors by exploring with individuals how a particular health behavior (e.g., smoking, substance abuse) has interfered with their ability to achieve personally meaningful goals or to live in accordance with their personal values, consider how a change in that behavior could help them achieve their goals, and supporting their self-efficacy in order to build their confidence that such change is possible (Miller & Rollnick, 2002). The principles of motivational interviewing have been adapted for individuals with schizophrenia and are frequently incorporated in integrated treatment programs for this population (Barrowclough et al., 2010; Bellack, Bennet, & Gearon, 2007; Carey, Leontieva, Dimmock, Maisto, & Batki, 2007; Mueser et al., 2003).

Active Treatment Stage After the individual has demonstrated motivation to work on his or her substance use problems, as indicated by a reduction in substance use or repeated efforts to cut down, the person enters the active stage of treatment. The goal of this stage is to further reduce the client's use of substances or to achieve stable abstinence from substance use. While reductions in substance use are associated with reduced negative consequences, continued substance use places the individual at a much higher risk for a relapse back into substance abuse than if abstinence is achieved. On the other hand, many clients do not embrace abstinence as a goal, either initially or ever. Therefore, working towards substance use reduction is often an important step towards recovery from the substance use disorder.

Similar to previous stages of treatment, a wide range of different strategies can be employed to achieve the goals of the active stage of treatment. Many interventions that may have been used in the persuasion stage of treatment continue to be useful in the active treatment stage, such as motivational interviewing to increase clients' desire for sobriety, and rehabilitation to help clients develop skills for getting their needs met in ways other than using substances. In addition, interventions that directly focus on substance use reduction play a major role in this stage of treatment. These interventions can be provided in the context of "active treatment groups," in which the shared focus is on substance use reduction or maintenance (Mueser et al., 2003), or in individual or family work.

Social skills training can be useful for teaching interpersonal skills for dealing with a range of substance use social situations, such as being offered or pressured to use substances (Bellack et al., 2007; Bellack, Mueser, Gingerich, & Agresta, 2004). Identifying other high risk situations for using substances, such as distressing symptoms, cravings, or having nothing to do, and developing skills for managing those situations can also help clients reduce or stop using substances. Developing a relapse prevention plan can be a useful treatment strategy for clients who achieve abstinence during active treatment. Social network interventions, such as family psychoeducation, can play a helpful role in supporting clients' efforts to cut down and stop using substances in this stage of treatment, as well as in previous stages. Self-help groups such as Alcoholics Anonymous and Dual Recovery Anonymous (Hamilton & Sample, 1994) may be a useful source of peer support for clients who endorse abstinence from alcohol and drugs.

Relapse Prevention Stage The transition from the active stage of treatment to the relapse prevention stage is defined by the individual achieving a period of six months or more of either abstinence or substance use without significant impairment (i.e., substance abuse or dependence). The goals of the relapse prevention stage are twofold. First, it is important to help the client maintain an awareness of the possibility of a relapse into substance use or abuse in the future, and to ensure that a strong relapse prevention plan is in place that involves monitoring early warning signs of a relapse and taking rapid action in the event that such signs occur. It should be noted that relapse prevention plans need to be viewed as "living documents" that should be modified or updated based on experiences with slips into substance use (minor recurrences of use) or outright relapses (recurrences of use accompanied by significant negative consequences).Thus, relapse prevention plans should be modified based on experience using them in order to make them as effective as possible.

Second, the relapse prevention stage shifts the emphasis of collaborative work with the client to improving other areas of functioning, such as illness self-management, independent living, social relationships, work or school, or health. While these areas of functioning are often the focus in prior stages of treatment, even greater attention is paid during the relapse prevention stage based on the assumption that the better the quality of life achieved by the client, the less vulnerable he or she will be to a relapse. The same rehabilitation approaches described in the previous section on can be used to improve functioning in these areas.

Multiple Treatment Modalities Psychotherapeutic interventions for co-occurring disorders can be provided in a variety of different treatment modalities, including individual, group, and family formats. The choice of treatment modality is determined by a combination of factors, some of which are related to the treatment setting (e.g., rural, urban) and others which are related to the client (e.g., level of psychiatric impairment, degree of contact with family). For many clients, a combination of different treatment modalities is optimal, with the selected modalities potentially changing over time. For example, the individual treatment modality is usually necessary during the engagement stage of treatment because it is not feasible to engage the client in group treatment. However, in some circumstances, family treatment may be the preferred modality for engaging clients, such as when substance abuse has recently precipitated a relapse and hospitalization for a client living at home. Once clients are engaged in treatment, group modalities are often effective and efficient, but may be less beneficial for severely impaired clients. Integrated treatment programs need to have the capability of providing different psychotherapeutic modalities based on individual client needs and their stage of treatment.

Adaptations to Integrated Treatment for Clients with Cognitive Impairments

Clinical observations suggest that clients with severe cognitive impairments may have difficulty fully benefiting from integrated treatment for their co-occurring substance abuse unless appropriate adaptations are made. In this section we consider modifications to integrated treatment to accommodate to the special needs of clients with cognitive impairment. This discussion is organized based on the core components of integrated treatment programs described above.

Comprehensive Assessment and Treatment

The denial and minimization of the effects of substance use that can threaten the validity of self-reports in all clients with schizophrenia. However, significantly impaired cognitive functioning can also limit the ability of motivated clients to accurately report about their substance use. When assessing cognitively impaired individuals, increased attention should be given to evaluating recent substance use (e.g., past several days or weeks), with less attention paid to substance use that occurred longer ago.

While information about clients' use of substances from informants such as family members is always helpful in assessing co-occurring substance abuse, the importance of such collateral reports is even greater when clients have significant cognitive impairments. Such reports can often provide valuable information about both the extent of the client's substance use and the situations in which use is most likely to occur, providing clues about possible motives for using. In addition, since cognitively impaired clients often need more supportive services to live in the community, case managers and residential workers may have higher levels of contact with clients and be a valuable source of information about their substance use.

With respect to the broad range of needs of clients with co-occurring substance abuse, clients with cognitive impairment may require greater assistance to obtain the medical and legal services they need to address health or criminal justice problems. Clinicians, family members, or other natural supports may need to accompany clients to appointments, and help them follow through on the steps needed to treat or manage their health conditions or resolve their legal problems. Such clients may also require closer monitoring to avert further health or legal complications resulting from their substance use.

Impaired cognitive functioning in schizophrenia is strongly associated with worse psychosocial functioning across a range of different domains of functioning, including worse social relationships, self-care and independent living skills, and role functioning (Green, Kern, Braff, & Mintz, 2000). Therefore, the need for comprehensive treatment to address these problems is even greater in clients with significant cognitive impairment. However, impaired cognitive functioning has also been shown to impede response to different psychiatric rehabilitation interventions, including social skills training (Mueser, Bellack, Douglas, & Wade, 1991; Smith, Hull, Romanelli, Fertuck, & Weiss, 1999), supported employment (McGurk & Mueser, 2004), and broad-based rehabilitation approaches (Wykes & Dunn, 1992). Two general approaches may be helpful in compensating for or overcoming the effects of cognitive impairment on response to rehabilitation. First, more intensive rehabilitation efforts, such as more frequent skills training sessions or more extensive vocational supports (McGurk, Mueser, Harvey, Marder, & LaPuglia, 2003), may facilitate response to these rehabilitation methods. Second, cognitive remediation can facilitate response to psychiatric rehabilitation by enhancing cognitive functions necessary for learning and applying new skills (McGurk, Mueser, & Pascaris, 2005; Silverstein et al., 2008; Simon, VonKorff, Wagner, & Barlow, 1993).

Two recent meta-analyses have been conducted evaluating the effects of cognitive remediation for schizophrenia (McGurk et al., 2007; Wykes, Huddy, Cellard, McGurk, & Czobar, 2011), including 26 and 40 studies, respectively. Both meta-analyses revealed similar findings. Cognitive remediation has significant overall effects on improved cognitive functioning (effect sizes = .41 and .45, respectively), psychosocial functioning (effect sizes = .36 and .44, respectively), and symptoms (effect sizes = .28 and .18, respectively). There were no moderators of the effects of cognitive remediation on cognitive performance or symptoms. However, the effects of cognitive remediation on psychosocial functioning were moderated by the provision of adjunctive psychiatric rehabilitation, such as social skills training or vocational rehabilitation; studies that evaluated the benefit of adding cognitive remediation to psychiatric rehabilitation demonstrated significantly improved functional outcomes compared to psychiatric rehabilitation alone (effect sizes = .47 and .59, respectively), whereas the impact of cognitive remediation on functioning was much lower in the absence of adjunctive psychiatric rehabilitation (effect sizes = .05 and .28, respectively). Thus, the impact of cognitive remediation on psychosocial functioning appears to act synergistically when it is provided in the context of specifically targeted psychiatric rehabilitation.

Motivation-Based, Stage-Wise Interventions There are no particular adaptations for persons with cognitive impairments in the engagement stage of treatment, as this stage is primarily focused on establishing a working alliance with the client. Outreach, providing practical assistance to address basic needs, and social network support are all effective strategies for engaging clients with cognitive impairments and co occurring substance abuse in treatment. Empathic and reflective listening are especially helpful in working with clients with cognitive impairments, as they concretely show the client that the clinician understands and cares, and because it can help the client clarify his or her own thoughts.

A number of adaptations can be useful when working with clients with significant cognitive impairment in the persuasion stage of treatment. Information processing deficits may make it more difficult for clients to learn psychoeducational material about schizophrenia and its interactions with substance use unless appropriate adaptations are made. Helpful strategies include breaking information into smaller chunks, frequently pausing to summarize or review previously covered material, adopting the client's use of language whenever possible, frequently pausing to ask questions that require the client to process recently presented information, and periodically asking questions to evaluate the client's retention of previously learned material.

Adaptations can also be made in motivational interviewing methods for clients with cognitive impairment (Bellack et al., 2007). Establishing personally meaningful long-term goals plays a critical role in motivational interviewing, but cognitively impaired clients may have greater difficulty conceptualizing long-term goals and the steps necessary to achieve them, and may feel more frustrated with the slow progress towards such goals. Therefore, it is important to focus on shorter term, highly salient, concrete, and personally desired goals in clients with cognitive impairment to ensure that establishing a discrepancy between these goals and continued substance use is relatively straightforward. Furthermore, the clinician may need to frequently remind clients of their goals in order for them to become a priority for the client. As clients with cognitive impairments have often suffered multiple setbacks during their lives, and lack self-confidence that they are able to achieve their goals, as well as being able to cut down or stop using substances, it is important for the clinician to take every opportunity available to support their self-efficacy and to provide abundant praise for any efforts or progress made by the client, however small.

Families can play an important role in the treatment of all people with co-occurring disorders, but their role is even more critical in clients with significant cognitive impairment. During the persuasion stage, families can be helpful in facilitating the client's understanding about substance use and its interactions with schizophrenia, support and reinforce the client's involvement in treatment and rehabilitation (e.g., helping the client practice skills outside the training sessions), and help to identify personally meaningful short-term goals that can motivate the client to work on his or her substance use problems. In general, the frequent contact that relatives often have with clients puts them in a unique position to collaborate with treatment providers, including participation in treatment planning and monitoring progress, and helping to identify alternative strategies for clients getting needs met related to their substance abuse, such as socialization, coping with symptoms, and leisure and recreational activities.

During the active stage of treatment, when the focus of intervention turns to reducing substance use or maintaining abstinence, several adaptations for persons with cognitive impairment may be necessary. Self-monitoring methods are usually more difficult to implement reliably in such persons, and in most cases should be abandoned. Settings in which there is social support for self-monitoring available, or in which other methods can be used to cue clients to self-report (e.g., digital wristwatch with beeps for prompts) (Henquet et al., 2010), may make self-monitoring feasible with such individuals. Since cognitive impairment may reduce a client's response to psychiatric rehabilitation approaches, such impairment can also pose an obstacle to teaching strategies aimed at reducing clients' use of substances in high risk situations, such as offers to use substances or coping with a distressing symptom. Strategies for compensating for the effects of cognitive impairment on slower learning of social and coping skills for high risk substance abuse situations include: targeting the simplest possible social or coping skill; devoting the majority of training sessions to active modeling and behavioral rehearsal of targeted skills with less time spent on discussion; providing more frequent training sessions; developing opportunities to practice targeted skills in community settings; and enlisting the support of family, other significant persons, or residential staff in helping clients practice skills.

Cognitive impairment can pose an obstacle to participating in some self-help groups, such as Alcoholics Anonymous, as clients may have difficulty following some of the abstract concepts talked about in these groups, they may appear significantly different to other group members, and they may feel more anxious because of the number of people and the pace of discussion in these groups (Noordsy, Schwab, Fox, & Drake, 1996). Dual Recovery Anonymous groups that are specifically tailored to people with co-occurring psychiatric and substance use disorders may be more helpful to clients in the active stage of treatment (Hamilton & Sample, 1994).

As in the persuasion stage, family support can be critical to helping clients with cognitive impairment succeed in reducing and stopping their use of substances in the active treatment stage. Families can help clients learn new and more effective social and coping skills in order to bolster their ability to resist the temptation to use substances. In addition to learning new skills, families can be helpful in identifying alternative social and recreational activities for clients that do not involve substance use. Families are especially important to involve in the development of a relapse prevention plan. They are often in the best position to monitor the client's disorders and to help the client take immediate action at the earliest possible time following a warning sign of relapse, a slip back into substance use, or an outright relapse.

During the relapse prevention stage, when the focus of treatment shifts to both preventing relapses and extending clients' recovery to other areas of functioning, similar adaptations to those previously discussed are useful for people with cognitive impairment. The refinement of a relapse prevention plan is most effective when it involves either family members, significant other persons, or staff members with whom the client has regular contact. This is critical in order to reduce relying entirely on the client for preventing relapses. Rehabilitation-based methods are especially important to continue helping clients improve other areas of their life, such as skills training and supported employment, with adaptations to accommodate cognitive impairment as previously described.

Multiple Treatment Modalities

Clients with severe cognitive impairment may benefit less from group interventions for co-occurring disorders that include less impaired persons, as they may experience difficulty keeping up with the pace of the group. Group interventions with cognitive impaired clients usually require fewer participants to ensure active involvement of each person, less discussion and more role playing, more frequent review of material, and more frequent sessions. In the absence of being able to make these special accommodations, individual sessions can be used either to supplement or as an alternative to group sessions.

The family intervention modality is particularly important to use whenever possible with cognitively impaired clients, as families are often in a unique position to reinforce learning new information and skills outside of formal treatment sessions. Family work can be conducted as an alternative to individual or group treatment modalities, or an adjunct (Mueser et al., 2003). In order to capitalize on the unique role that a family can play in helping a relative recover from co-occurring substance abuse, treatment providers need to reach out and convey to them that they are valued collaborators in treatment, and educate them accordingly in the principles of treatment.

SUMMARY AND CONCLUSIONS

Substance use disorders are the most common comorbid disorder in schizophrenia, with approximately 50% of clients with a lifetime history of substance abuse or dependence, compared to only 15% in the general population. Substance abuse contributes to a worse course of schizophrenia, including precipitating relapses and rehospitalizations, increased depression and suicidality, homelessness, aggression, legal problems, increased medical problems, and premature mortality. Substance abuse is most common in young, unmarried males, with alcohol being the most commonly abused substance, usually followed by either cannabis or cocaine, and with most clients abusing a variety of different substances. Clients with better premorbid social functioning are more likely to abuse illicit substances such as cannabis and cocaine than clients with poor premorbid functioning.

Substance abuse in schizophrenia can produce a range of acute clinical and cognitive effects that mimic or resemble the characteristic symptoms and impairments of schizophrenia, and thus accurate detection of substance use is critical for the administration and interpretation of neuropsychological testing. Research on the long-term cognitive effects of substance abuse in schizophrenia are mixed, although there is evidence of impaired neurocognitive functioning associated with alcohol abuse in older populations. Contradictory findings have been reported regarding the effects of drug abuse, especially cannabis abuse, on cognitive functioning in schizophrenia, with some studies indicating that clients with drug use disorders have more preserved cognitive functioning, and others reporting the opposite. Selection factors, most notably the tendency for clients with better premorbid social functioning and more intact cognitive functioning to be more likely to be exposed to illicit substances and to develop drug use routines, appear to account for this association.

Effective treatment for co-occurring substance abuse in schizophrenia requires integrated treatment in which the same clinicians treat both disorders simultaneously and in an integrated fashion. Core elements of effective integrated treatment include comprehensive assessment and services, a harm-reduction philosophy, motivation-based and stage-wise interventions, multiple treatment modalities, and long-term perspective. As cognitive impairment is a common feature of schizophrenia which impede response to integrated treatment, a wide range of compensatory strategies are available to clinicians to help clients compensate for their reduced cognitive functioning and get the maximal benefit out of treatment.

REFERENCES

Addington, J., & Addington, D. (1993). Premorbid functioning, cognitive functioning, symptoms and outcome in schizophrenia. *Journal of Psychiatry and Neuroscience, 18*, 19–23.

Addington, J., & Addington, D. (1996). Substance abuse and cognitive functioning in schizophrenia. *Journal of Psychiatry and Neuroscience, 22*, 99–104.

Addington, J., & Addington, D. (2007). Patterns, predictors and impact of substance use in early psychosis: A longitudinal study. *Acta Psychiatrica Scandinavica, 115*, 304–309.

Adler, L. E., Hoffer, L. D., Wiser, A., & Freedman, R. (1993). Normalization of auditory physiology by cigarette smoking in schizophrenic patients. *American Journal of Psychiatry, 150*, 1856–1861.

Allebeck, P., Adamsson, C., Engström, A., & Rydberg, U. (1993). Cannabis and schizophrenia: A longitudinal study of cases treated in Stockholm County. *Acta Psychiatrica Scandinavica, 88*, 21–24.

Allen, D. N., Goldstein, G., Forman, S. D., Keshavan, M. S., Van Kammen, D. P., & Sanders, R. D. (1999). Neurologic examination abnormalities in schizophrenia with and without a history of alcoholism. *Neuropsychiatry, Neuropsychology, and Behavioral Neurology, 13*, 184–287.

American Psychiatric Association. (1994). *Diagnostic and statistical manual of mental disorders* (4th ed.). Washington, DC: Author.

Andréasson, S., Allebeck, P., Engström, A., & Rydberg, U. (1987). Cannabis and schizophrenia: A longitudinal study of Swedish conscripts. *The Lancet, December 26*, 1483–1486.

Andréasson, S., Allebeck, P., & Rydberg, U. (1989). Schizophrenia in users and nonusers of cannabis: A longitudinal study in Stockholm County. *Acta Psychiatrica Scandinavica, 79*, 505–510.

Anthony, J. C., & Helzer, J. E. (1991). Syndromes of drug abuse and dependence. In L. N. Robins & D. A. Regier (Eds.), *Psychiatric disorders in America: The Epidemiologic Catchment Area Study* (pp. 116–154). New York: Free Press.

Archie, S., & Gyömörey, K. (2009). First episode psychosis, substance abuse and prognosis: A systematic review. *Current Psychiatry Reviews, 5*, 153–163.

Arndt, S., Hartman, J., & Mileham, J. (Eds.). (2001). *Co-occurring disorders: Agency and staff evaluation tools*. Iowa City: Iowa Consortium for Substance Abuse Research and Evaluation.

Arndt, S., Tyrrell, G., Flaum, M., & Andreasen, N. C. (1992). Comorbidity of substance abuse and schizophrenia: The role of pre-morbid adjustment. *Psychological Medicine, 22*, 379–388.

Arseneault, L., Cannon, M., Poulton, R., Murray, R., Caspi, A., & Moffitt, T. E. (2002). Cannabis use in adolescence and risk for adult psychosis: Longitudinal prospective study. *British Medical Journal, 325*, 1212–1213.

Babor, T. F., Hesselbrock, V., Meyer, R. E., & Shoemaker, W. (Eds.). (1994). *Types of alcoholics: Evidence from clinical, experimental, and genetic research* (Vol. 708). New York: The New York Academy of Sciences.

Babor, T. F., Stephens, R. S., & Marlatt, G. A. (1987). Verbal report methods in clinical research on alcoholism: Response bias and its minimization. *Journal of Studies on Alcohol, 48*(5), 410–424.

Barbee, J. G., Clark, P. D., Craqanzano, M. S., Heintz, G. C., & Kehoe, C. E. (1989).

Alcohol and substance abuse among schizophrenic patients presenting to an emergency service. *Journal of Nervous and Mental Disease, 177*, 400–407.
Barkus, E., & Murray, R. M. (2010). Substance use in adolescence and psychosis: Clarifying the relationship. *Annual Review of Clinical Psychology, 6*, 365–389.
Barnes, T. R. E., Mutsatsa, S. H., Hutton, S. B., Watt, H. C., & Joyce, E. M. (2006). Comorbid substance use and age at onset of schizophrenia. *British Journal of Psychiatry, 188*, 2372–2342.
Barrowclough, C., Haddock, G., Wykes, W., Beardmore, R., Conrod, P., Craig, T., et al. (2010). Integrated motivational interviewing and cognitive behavioural therapy for people with psychosis and comorbid substance misuse: Randomised controlled trial. *British Medical Journal, 341*, c6325.
Barry, K. L., Milner, K., Blow, F. C., Impens, A., Welsh, D., & Amash, J. (2006). Screening psychiatric emergency department patients with major mental illnesses for at-risk drinking. *Psychiatric Services, 57*, 1039–1042.
Bartels, S. J., Drake, R. E., & McHugo, G. (1992). Alcohol use, depression, and suicidal behavior in schizophrenia. *American Journal of Psychiatry, 149*(3), 394–395.
Bates, M. E., Bowden, S. C., & Barry, D. (2002). Neurocognitive impairment associated with alcohol use disorders: Implications for treatment. *Experimental and Clinical Psychopharmacology, 10*, 193–212.
Becker, D. R., Drake, R. E., & Naughton, W. J., Jr. (2005). Supported employment for people with co-occurring disorders. *Psychiatric Rehabilitation Journal, 28*, 332–338.
Bellack, A. S., Bennet, M. E., & Gearon, J. S. (2007). *Behavioral treatment for Substance abuse in people with serious and persistent mental illness: A handbook for mental health professionals.* New York: Taylor and Francis.
Bellack, A. S., Mueser, K. T., Gingerich, S., & Agresta, J. (2004). *Social skills training for schizophrenia: A step-by-step guide* (2nd ed.). New York: Guilford Press.
Berk, M., Henry, L. P., Elkins, K. S., Harrigan, S. M., Harris, M. G., Herrman, H., et al. (2010). The impact of smoking on clinical outcomes after first episode psychosis: Longer-term outcome findings from the EPPIC 800 follow-up study. *Journal of Dual Diagnosis, 6*, 212–234.
Blanchard, J. J., Squires, D., Henry, T., Horan, W. P., Bogenschutz, M., Lauriello, J., et al. (1999). Examining an affect regulation model of substance abuse in schizophrenia: The role of traits and coping. *Journal of Nervous and Mental Disease, 187*, 72–79.
Boileau, I., Assaad, J. M., Pihl, R. O., Benkelfat, C., Leyton, M., Tremblay, R. E., et al. (2003). Alcohol promotes dopamine release in the human nucleus accumbens. *Synapse, 49*, 226–231.
Bond, G. R., Drake, R. E., & Becker, D. R. (2008). An update on randomized controlled trials of evidence-based supported employment. *Psychiatric Rehabilitation Journal, 31*, 280–290.
Bond, G. R., Drake, R. E., Mueser, K. T., & Latimer, E. (2001). Assertive community treatment for people with severe mental illness: Critical ingredients and impact on clients. *Disease Management and Health Outcomes, 9*, 141–159.
Brunette, M. F., Mueser, K. T., Xie, H., & Drake, R. E. (1997). Relationships between symptoms of schizophrenia and substance abuse. *Journal of Nervous and Mental Disease, 185*, 13–20.
Caldwell, C. B., & Gottesman, I. I. (1990). Schizophrenics kill themselves too: A review of risk factors for suicide. *Schizophrenia Bulletin, 16*, 571–589.

Carey, K. B. (1996). Substance use reduction in the context of outpatient psychiatric treatment: A collaborative, motivational, harm reduction approach. *Community Mental Health Journal*, *32*, 291–306.

Carey, K. B. (2002). Clinically useful assessments: Substance use and comorbid psychiatric disorders. *Behaviour Research and Therapy*, *40*, 1345–1361.

Carey, K. B., Leontieva, L., Dimmock, J., Maisto, S. A., & Batki, S. L. (2007). Adapting motivational interviewing interventions for comorbid schizophrenia and alcohol use disorders. *Clinical Psychology and Psychotherapy*, *14*, 39–57.

Castle, D. J., & Morgan, V. (2008). Epidemiology. In K. T. Mueser & D. V. Jeste (Eds.), *Clinical Handbook of Schizophrenia* (pp. 14–24). New York: Guilford Press.

Caton, C. L. M., Shrout, P. E., Dominguez, B., Eagle, P. F., Opler, L. A., & Cournos, F. (1995). Risk factors for homelessness among women with schizophrenia. *American Journal of Public Health*, *85*, 1153–1156.

Caton, C. L. M., Shrout, P. E., Eagle, P. F., Opler, L. A., & Felix, A. (1994). Correlates of codisorders in homeless and never homeless indigent schizophrenic men. *Psychological Medicine*, *24*, 681–688.

Chambers, R. A., Krystal, J. H., & Self, D. W. (2001). A neurobiological basis for substance abuse comorbidity in schizophrenia. *Biological Psychiatry*, *50*, 71–83.

Chanraud, S., Pitel, A. L., Rohlfing, T., Pfefferbaum, A., & Sullivan, E. V. (2010). Dual tasking and working memory in alcoholism: relation to frontocerebellar circuitry. *Neuropsychopharmacology*, *35*, 1868–1878.

Chau, D. T., Roth, R. M., & Green, A. I. (2004). The neural circuitry of reward and its relevance to psychiatric disorders. *Current Psychiatry Reports*, *6*, 391–399.

Chen, C., Balogh, M., Bathija, J., Howanitz, E., Plutchik, R., & Conte, H. R. (1992). Substance abuse among psychiatric inpatients. *Comprehensive Psychiatry*, *33*, 60–64.

Cleghorn, J. M., Kaplan, R. D., Szechtman, B., Szechtman, H., Brown, G. M., & Franco, S. (1991). Substance abuse and schizophrenia: Effect on symptoms but not on neurocognitive function. *Journal of Clinical Psychiatry*, *52*, 26–30.

Cohen, M., & Klein, D. F. (1970). Drug abuse in a young psychiatric population. *American Journal of Orthopsychiatry*, *40*, 448–455.

Copersino, M. L., Serper, M. R., Vadhan, N., Goldberg, B. R., Richarme, D., Chou, J. C.-Y., et al. (2004). Cocaine craving an attentional bias in cocaine-dependent schizophrenic patients. *Schizophrenia Research*, *128*, 209–218.

Corse, S. J., Hirschinger, N. B., & Zanis, D. (1995). The use of the Addiction Severity Index with people with severe mental illness. *Psychiatric Rehabilitation Journal*, *19*, 9–18.

Coulston, C. M., Perdices, M., & Tennant, C. C. (2007). The neuropsychological correlates of cannabis use in schizophrenia: Lifetime abuse/dependence, frequency of use, and recency of use. *Schizophrenia Research*, *96*, 169–184.

Cuffel, B., & Chase, P. (1994). Remission and relapse of substance use disorders in schizophrenia: Results from a one year prospective study. *Journal of Nervous and Mental Disease*, *182*, 704–708.

Cuffel, B. J. (1996). Comorbid substance use disorder: Prevalence, patterns of use, and course. In R. E. Drake & K. T. Mueser (Eds.), *Dual diagnosis of major mental illness and substance abuse volume 2: Recent research and clinical implications. New directions in mental health services* (Vol. 70, pp. 93–105). San Francisco: Jossey-Bass.

D'Souza, D. C., Abi-Saab, W. M., Madonick, S., Forselius-Bielen, K., Doersch, A., Braley,

G., et al. (2005). Delta-9-tetrahydrocannabinol effects in schizophrenia: Implications for cognition, psychosis, and addiction. *Biological Psychiatry, 57*, 594–608.

D'Souza, D. C., Gil, R. B., Madonick, S., Perry, E. B., Forselius-Bielen, K., Braley, G., et al. (2006). Enhanced sensitivity to the euphoric effects of alcohol in schizophrenia. *Neuropsychopharmacology, 31*, 2767–2775.

de Leon, J., & Diaz, F. J. (2005). A meta-analysis of worldwide studies demonstrates an association between schizophrenia and tobacco smoking behaviors. *Schizophrenia Research, 76*, 135–157.

Degenhardt, L., Hall, W., & Lynskey, M. (2003). Testing hypotheses about the relationship between cannabis use and psychosis. *Drug and Alcohol Dependence, 71*, 37–48.

Denning, P. (2000). *Practicing harm reduction psychotherapy: An alternative approach to addictions*. New York: Guilford Press.

DeRosse, P., Kaplan, A., Burdick, K. E., Lencz, T., & Malhotra, A. K. (2010). Cannabis use disorders in schizophrenia: Effects on cognition and symptoms. *Schizophrenia Research, 120*, 95–100.

Dervaux, A., Baylé, F. J., Laqueille, X., Bourdel, M.-C., Le Borgne, M.-H., Olié, J.-P., et al. (2001). Is substance abuse in schizophrenia related to impulsivity, sensation seeking or anhedonia? *American Journal of Psychiatry, 158*, 49249–49244.

Di Forti, M., Morgan, C., Dazzan, P., Pariante, P., Mondelli, V., Marques, T. R., et al. (2009). High-potency cannabis and the risk of psychosis. *British Journal of Psychiatry, 195*, 488–491.

Dixon, L., B. (1999). Dual diagnosis of substance abuse in schizophrenia: Prevalence and impact on outcomes. *Schizophrenia Research, 35*(Suppl), S93–S100.

Dixon, L., Haas, G., Weiden, P. J., Sweeney, J., & Frances, A. J. (1991). Drug abuse in schizophrenic patients: Clinical correlates and reasons for use. *American Journal of Psychiatry, 148*, 224–230.

Dixon, L., McNary, S., & Lehman, A. (1995). Substance abuse and family relationships of persons with severe mental illness. *American Journal of Psychiatry, 152*, 456–458.

Drake, R. E., Antosca, L. M., Noordsy, D. L., Bartels, S. J., & Osher, F. C. (1991). New Hampshire's specialized services for the dually diagnosed. In K. Minkoff & R. E. Drake (Eds.), *Dual diagnosis of major mental illness and substance disorder new directions for mental health services* (Vol. 50, pp. 57–67). San Francisco: Jossey-Bass.

Drake, R. E., & Brunette, M. F. (1998). Complications of severe mental illness related to alcohol and other drug use disorders. In M. Galanter (Ed.), *Recent developments in alcoholism: Consequences of alcoholism* (Vol. 14, pp. 285–299). New York: Plenum.

Drake, R. E., McHugo, G. J., Xie, H., Fox, M., Packard, J., & Helmstetter, B. (2006). Ten-year recovery outcomes for clients with co-occurring schizophrenia and substance use disorders. *Schizophrenia Bulletin, 32*, 464-473.

Drake, R. E., O'Neal, E., & Wallach, M. A. (2008). A systematic review of psychosocial interventions for people with co-occurring severe mental and substance use disorders. *Journal of Substance Abuse Treatment, 34*, 123–138.

Drake, R. E., Osher, F. C., Noordsy, D. L., Hurlbut, S. C., Teague, G. B., & Beaudett, M. S. (1990). Diagnosis of alcohol use disorders in schizophrenia. *Schizophrenia Bulletin, 16*, 57–67.

Drake, R. E., Osher, F. C., & Wallach, M. A. (1991). Homelessness and dual diagnosis. *American Psychologist, 46*, 1149–1158.

Drake, R. E., Rosenberg, S. D., & Mueser, K. T. (1996). Assessing substance use disorder in persons with severe mental illness. In R. E. Drake & K. T. Mueser (Eds.), *Dual diagnosis of major mental illness and substance abuse volume 2: Recent research and clinical implications. New directions for mental health services* (Vol. 70, pp. 3–17). San Francisco: Jossey-Bass.

Drake, R. E., & Wallach, M. A. (1993). Moderate drinking among people with severe mental illness. *Hospital and Community Psychiatry, 44*, 780–782.

Dulude, L., Labelle, A., & Knott, V. J. (2010). Acute nicotine alteration of sensory memory impairment in smokers with schizophrenia. *Journal of Clinical Psychopharmacology, 30*, 541–548.

Duva, S. M., Silverstein, S. M., & Spiga, R. (2011). Impulsivity and risk-taking in co-occurring psychotic disorders and substance abuse. *Psychiatry Research, 186*, 351–355.

Edens, J. F., Peters, R. H., & Hills, H. A. (1997). Treating prison inmates with co-occurring disorders: An integrative review of existing programs. *Behavioral Sciences and the Law, 15*, 439–457.

Edwards, J., Elkins, K., Hinton, M., Harrigan, S. M., Donovan, K., & Athanasopoulos, O. (2006). Randomized controlled trial of a cannabis-focused intervention for young people with first-episode psychosis. *Acta Psychiatrica Scandanavica, 114*, 109–117.

Erickson, D. H., Beiser, M., Iacono, W. G., Fleming, J. A. E., & Lin, T. (1989). The role of social relationships in the course of first-episode schizophrenia and affective psychosis. *American Journal of Psychiatry, 146*, 1456–1461.

Evert, D. L., & Oscar-Berman, M. (1995). Alcohol-related cognitive impairments: An overview of how alcoholism may affect the workings of the brain. *Alcohol Health & Research World, 19*, 89–96.

Fergusson, D. M., Horwood, L. J., & Swain-Campbell, N. R. (2003). Cannabis dependence and psychotic symptoms in young people. *Psychological Medicine, 33*, 15–21.

First, M. B., Spitzer, R. L., Gibbon, M., & Williams, J. B. W. (1996). *Structured Clinical Interview for DSM-IV Axis-I Disorders — Patient Edition (SCID-I/P, version 2.0)*. New York: Biometrics Research Department, New York State Psychiatric Institute.

Fowler, I. L., Carr, V. J., Carter, N. T., & Lewin, T. J. (1998). Patterns of current and lifetime substance use in schizophrenia. *Schizophrenia Bulletin, 24*, 443–455.

Fox, M. B., Drake, R. E., Mueser, K. T., Brunette, M. F., Becker, D. R., McGovern, M. P., et al. (2010). *Integrated Dual Disorders Treatment Manual: Best Practices, Skills, and Resources for Successful Client Care*. Center City, MN: Hazelden.

Frisher, M., Crome, I., Martino, O., & Croft, P. (2009). Assessing the impact of cannabis use on trends in diagnosed schizophrenia in the United Kingdom from 1996 to 2005. *Schizophrenia Research, 113*, 123–128.

Frisman, L. K., Lin, H.-J., Sturges, G. E., Levinsom, M., Baranoski, M. V., & Pollard, N. M. (2006). Outcomes of court-based jail diversion programs for people with co-occurring disorders. *Journal of Dual Diagnosis, 2*, 5–26.

Galanter, M., Castaneda, R., & Ferman, J. (1988). Substance abuse among general psychiatric patients: Place of presentation, diagnosis and treatment. *American Journal of Drug and Alcohol Abuse, 14*, 211–235.

Gershon, E. S., DeLisi, L. E., Hamovit, J., Nurnberger, J. I., Maxwell, M. E., Schreiber, J., et al. (1988). A controlled family study of chronic psychoses: Schizophrenia and schizoaffective disorder. *Archives of General Psychiatry, 45*, 328–336.

Gingerich, S., & Mueser, K. T. (2010). *Illness management and recovery implementa-*

tion resource kit (Rev. ed.). Rockville, MD: Center for Mental Health Services, Substance Abuse and Mental Health Services Administration.

Goodwin, D. W. (1992). Alcohol: Clinical aspects. In J. H. Lowinson & P. Ruiz & R. B. Millman (Eds.), *Substance Abuse: A comprehensive textbook* (2nd ed., pp. 144–185). Baltimore: Williams & Williams.

Graham, H. L., Maslin, J., Copello, A., Birchwood, M., Mueser, K., McGovern, D., et al. (2001). Drug and alcohol problems amonst individuals with severe mental health problems in an inner city area of the UK. *Social Psychiatry and Psychiatric Epidemiology, 36*, 448–455.

Grech, A., van Os, J., Jones, B., Lewis, S. W., & Murray, R. M. (2005). Cannabis use and outcome of recent onset psychosis. *European Psychiatry, 20*, 349–353.

Green, A. I., Noordsy, D. L., Brunette, M. F., & O'Keefe, C. D. (2008). Substance abuse and schizophrenia: Pharmacotherapeutic intervention. *Journal of Substance Abuse Treatment, 34*, 61–71.

Green, M. F., Kern, R. S., Braff, D. L., & Mintz, J. (2000). Neurocognitive deficits and functional outcome in schizophrenia: Are we measuring the "right stuff"? *Schizophrenia Bulletin, 26*, 119–136.

Gupta, S., Hendricks, S., Kenkel, A. M., Bhatia, S. C., & Haffke, E. A. (1996). Relapse in schizophrenia: Is there a relationship to substance abuse? *Schizophrenia Research, 20*, 153–156.

Hall, W., & Degenhardt, L. (2008). Cannabis use and the risk of developing a psychotic disorder. *World Psychiatry, 7*, 68–71.

Hambrecht, M., & Häfner, H. (1996). Substance abuse and the onset of schizophrenia. *Biological Psychiatry, 40*, 1155–1163.

Hambrecht, M., & Häfner, H. (2000). Cannabis, vulnerability, and the onset of schizophrenia: An epidemiological perspective. *Australian and New Zealand Journal of Psychiatry, 34*, 468–475.

Hamilton, T., & Sample, P. (1994). *The twelve steps and dual recovery: A Framework of recovery for those of us with addiction and an emotional or psychiatric illness.* Center City, MN: Hazelden.

Harrow, M., Carone, B. J., & Westermeyer, J. (1985). The course of psychosis in early phases of schizophrenia. *American Journal of Psychiatry, 142*, 702–707.

Heinrichs, R. W., & Zakzanis, K. K. (1998). Neurocognitive deficit in schizophrenia: A quantitative review of evidence. *Neuropsychology, 12*, 426–445.

Henquet, C., Krabbendam, L., Spauwen, J., Kaplan, C., Lieb, R., Wittchen, H. U., et al. (2005). Prospective cohort study of cannabis use, predisposition for psychosis, and psychotic symptoms in young people. *British Medical Journal, 330*, 11.

Henquet, C., van Os, J., Kuepper, R., Delespaul, P., Smits, M., à Campo, J., et al. (2010). Psychosis reactivity to cannabis use in daily life: An experience sampling study. *British Journal of Psychiatry, 196*, 447–453.

Herran, A., de Santiago, A., Sandoya, M., Fernandez, M. J., Diez-Manrique, J. F., & Vazquez-Barquero, J. L. (2000). Determinants of smoking behaviour in outpatients with schizophrenia. *Schizophrenia Research, 41*, 373–381.

Hesselbrock, M. N. (1986). Childhood behavior problems and adult antisocial personality disorder in alcoholism. In R. E. Meyer (Ed.), *Psychopathology and Addictive Disorders* (pp. 78–94). New York: Guilford Press.

Hodgins, S., Hiscoke, U. L., & Freese, R. (2002). The antecedents of aggressive behavior among men with schizophrenia: A prospective investigation of patients in community treatment. *Behavioral Sciences & the Law, 21*, 523–546.

Hodgins, S., Tiihonen, J., & Ross, D. (2005). The consequences of conduct disorder for males who develop schizophrenia: Associations with criminality, aggressive behavior, substance use, and psychiatric services. *Schizophrenia Research, 78*, 323–335.

Joyal, C. C., Hallé, P., Lapierre, D., & Hodgins, S. (2003). Drug abuse and/or dependence and better neuropsychological performance in patients with schizophrenia. *Schizophrenia Research, 63*, 297–299.

Kashner, M., Rader, L., Rodell, D., Beck, C., Rodell, L., & Muller, K. (1991). Family characteristics, substance abuse, and hospitalization patterns of patients with schizophrenia. *Hospital and Community Psychiatry, 42*, 195–197.

Kavanagh, D. J., Waghorn, G., Jenner, L., Chant, D. C., Carr, V., Evans, M., et al. (2004). Demographic and clinical correlates of comorbid substance use disorders in psychosis: Multivariate analyses from an epidemiological sample. *Schizophrenia Research, 66*, 115–124.

Kessler, R. C., Nelson, C. B., McGonagle, K. A., Edlund, M. J., Frank, R. G., & Leaf, P. J. (1996). The epidemiology of co-occurring addictive and mental disorders: Implications for prevention and service utilization. *American Journal of Orthopsychiatry, 66*, 17–31.

Kirkpatrick, B., Amador, X. F., Flaum, M., Yale, S. A., Gorman, J. M., Carpenter, W. T., Jr., et al. (1996). The deficit syndrome in the DSM-IV field trial: I. Alcohol an other drug abuse. *Schizophrenia Research, 20*, 69–77.

Knopik, V. S., Heath, A. C., Madden, P. A. F., Bucholz, K. K., Slutske, W. S., Nelson, E. C., et al. (2004). Genetic effects on alcohol dependence risk: Re-evaluating the importance of psychiatric and other heritable risk factors. *Psychological Medicine, 34*, 1519–1530.

Kotov, R., Guey, L. T., Bromet, E. J., & Schwartz, J. E. (2010). Smoking in schizophrenia: Diagnostic specificity, symptom correlates, and illness severity. *Schizophrenia Bulletin, 36*, 173–181.

Kurtz, M. M., & Mueser, K. T. (2008). A meta-analysis of controlled research on social skills training for schizophrenia. *Journal of Consulting and Clinical Psychology, 76*, 491–504.

Laudet, A. B., Magura, S., Vogel, H. S., & Knight, E. L. (2004). Perceived reasons for substance misuse among persons with a psychiatric disorder. *American Journal of Orthopsychiatry, 74*, 365–375.

Lazowski, L. E., Miller, F. G., Boye, M. W., & Miller, G. A. (1998). Efficacy of the Substance Abuse Subtle Screening Inventory-3 (SASSI-3) in identifying substance dependence disorders in clinical settings. *Journal of Personality Assessment, 71*, 114–128.

Leeson, V. C., Harrison, I., Ron, M. A., Barnes, T. R. E., & Joyce, E. M. (2011). The effect of cannabis use and cognitive reserve on age at onset and psychosis outcomes in first-episode schizophrenia. *Schizophrenia Bulletin* (Epub ahead of print).

Liao, D. L., Yang, J. Y., Lee, S. M., Chen, H., & Tsai, S. J. (2002). Smoking in chronic schizophrenic inpatients in Taiwan. *Neuropsychobiology, 45*, 172–175.

Lieberman, J. A., Kane, J. M., & Alvir, J. (1987). Provocative tests with psychostimulant drugs in schizophrenia. *Psychopharmacology, 91*, 415–433.

Linszen, D., Dingemans, P., & Lenior, M. (1994). Cannabis abuse and the course of recent onset schizophrenic disorders. *Archives of General Psychiatry, 51*, 273–279.

Maisto, S. A., Carey, M. P., Carey, K. B., Gordon, C. M., & Gleason, J. R. (2000). Use of the AUDIT and the DAST-10 to identify alcohol and drug use disorders among adults with a severe and persistent mental illness. *Psychological Assessment, 12*, 186–192.

Manning, V., Betteridge, S., Wanigaratne, S., Best, D., Strang, J., & Gossop, M. (2009). Cognitive impairment in dual diagnosis inpatients with schizophrenia and alcohol use disorder. *Schizophrenia Research, 114*, 98–104.

Manning, V., Wanigaratne, S., Best, D., Strathdee, G., Schrover, I., & Gossop, M. (2007). Screening for cognitive functioning in psychiatric outpatients with schizophrenia, alcohol dependence, and dual diagnosis. *Schizophrenia Research, 91*, 151–158.

Marlatt, G. A. (Ed.). (1998). *Harm reduction: Pragmatic strategies for managing high-risk behaviors*. New York: Guilford Press.

McCleery, A., Addington, J., & Addington, D. (2006). Substance misuse and cognitive functioning in early psychosis: A 2 year follow-up. *Schizophrenia Research, 88*, 178–191.

McGurk, S. R., & Mueser, K. T. (2004). Cognitive functioning, symptoms, and work in supported employment: A review and heuristic model. *Schizophrenia Research, 70*, 147–174.

McGurk, S. R., Mueser, K. T., Harvey, P. D., Marder, J., & LaPuglia, R. (2003). Cognitive and clinical predictors of work outcomes in clients with schizophrenia. *Psychiatric Services, 54*, 1129–1135.

McGurk, S. R., Mueser, K. T., & Pascaris, A. (2005). Cognitive training and supported employment for persons with severe mental illness: One year results from a randomized controlled trial. *Schizophrenia Bulletin, 31*, 898–909.

McGurk, S. R., Twamley, E. W., Sitzer, D. I., McHugo, G. J., & Mueser, K. T. (2007). A meta-analysis of cognitive remediation in schizophrenia. *American Journal of Psychiatry, 164*, 1791–1802.

McHugo, G. J., Paskus, T. S., & Drake, R. E. (1993). Detection of alcoholism in schizophrenia using the MAST. *Alcoholism: Clinical and Experimental Research, 17*, 187–191.

McLellan, A. T., Kushner, H., Metzger, D., Peters, R., Smith, I., Grissom, G., et al. (1992). The fifth edition of the Addiction Severity Index: Historical critique and normative data. *Journal of Substance Abuse Treatment, 9*, 199–213.

Miller, R., Ream, G., McCormack, J., Gunduz-Bruce, H., Sevy, S., & Robinson, D. (2009). A prospective study of cannabis use as a risk factor for non-adherence and treatment dropout in first-episode schizophrenia. *Schizophrenia Research, 113*, 138–144.

Miller, W. R., & Rollnick, S. (Eds.). (2002). *Motivational interviewing: Preparing people for change* (2nd ed.). New York: Guilford Press.

Miner, C. R., Rosenthal, R. N., Hellerstein, D. J., & Muenz, L. R. (1997). Prediction of compliance with outpatient referral in patients with schizophrenia and psychoactive substance use disorders. *Archives of General Psychiatry, 54*, 706–712.

Minkoff, K. (1989). An integrated treatment model for dual diagnosis of psychosis and addiction. *Hospital and Community Psychiatry, 40*, 1031–1036.

Montross, L. P., Barrio, C., Yamada, A.-M., Lindarner, L., Golshan, S., Garcia, P., et al. (2005). Tri-ethnic variations of co-morbid substance and alcohol use disorders in schizophrenia. *Schizophrenia Research, 79*, 297–305.

Moran, P., & Hodgins, S. (2004). The correlates of comorbid antisocial personality disorder in schizophrenia. *Schizophrenia Bulletin, 30*, 791–802.

Mueser, K. T., Bellack, A. S., Douglas, M. S., & Wade, J. H. (1991). Prediction of social skill acquisition in schizophrenic and major affective disorder patients from memory and symptomatology. *Psychiatry Research, 37*, 281–296.

Mueser, K. T., Bennett, M., & Kushner, M. G. (1995). Epidemiology of substance abuse among persons with chronic mental disorders. In A. F. Lehman & L. Dixon (Eds.),

Double jeopardy: Chronic mental illness and substance abuse (pp. 9–25). New York: Harwood.

Mueser, K. T., Corrigan, P. W., Hilton, D., Tanzman, B., Schaub, A., Gingerich, S., et al. (2002). Illness management and recovery for severe mental illness: A review of the research. *Psychiatric Services, 53*, 1272–1284.

Mueser, K. T., Crocker, A. G., Frisman, L. B., Drake, R. E., Covell, N. H., & Essock, S. M. (2006). Conduct disorder and antisocial personality disorder in persons with severe psychiatric and substance use disorders. *Schizophrenia Bulletin, 32*, 626–636.

Mueser, K. T., Drake, R. E., Ackerson, T. H., Alterman, A. I., Miles, K. M., & Noordsy, D. L. (1997). Antisocial personality disorder, conduct disorder, and substance abuse in schizophrenia. *Journal of Abnormal Psychology, 106*, 473–477.

Mueser, K. T., Drake, R. E., & Wallach, M. A. (1998). Dual diagnosis: A review of etiological theories. *Addictive Behaviors, 23*, 717–734.

Mueser, K. T., Glynn, S. M., Cather, C., Zarate, R., Fox, M. B., Feldman, J., et al. (2009). Family intervention for co-occurring substance use and severe psychiatric disorders: Participant characteristics and correlates of initial engagement and more extended exposure in a randomized controlled trial. *Addictive Behaviors, 34*, 867–877.

Mueser, K. T., Kavanagh, D. J., & Brunette, M. F. (2007). Implications of research on comorbidity for the nature and management of substance misuse. In P. M. Miller & D. J. Kavanagh (Eds.), *Translation of addictions science into practice* (pp. 277–320). Amsterdam: Elsevier.

Mueser, K. T., Nishith, P., Tracy, J. I., DeGirolamo, J., & Molinaro, M. (1995). Expectations and motives for substance use in schizophrenia. *Schizophrenia Bulletin, 21*, 367–378.

Mueser, K. T., Noordsy, D. L., Drake, R. E., & Fox, L. (2003). *Integrated Treatment for Dual Disorders: A Guide to Effective Practice*. New York: Guilford Press.

Mueser, K. T., Rosenberg, S. D., Drake, R. E., Miles, K. M., Wolford, G., Vidaver, R., et al. (1999). Conduct disorder, antisocial personality disorder, and substance use disorders in schizophrenia and major affective disorders. *Journal of Studies on Alcohol, 60*, 278–284.

Mueser, K. T., Yarnold, P. R., & Bellack, A. S. (1992). Diagnostic and demographic correlates of substance abuse in schizophrenia and major affective disorder. *Acta Psychiatrica Scandinavica, 85*, 48–55.

Mueser, K. T., Yarnold, P. R., Levinson, D. F., Singh, H., Bellack, A. S., Kee, K., et al. (1990). Prevalence of substance abuse in schizophrenia: Demographic and clinical correlates. *Schizophrenia Bulletin, 16*, 31–56.

Mueser, K. T., Yarnold, P. R., Rosenberg, S. D., Swett, C., Miles, K. M., & Hill, D. (2000). Substance use disorder in hospitalized severely mentally ill psychiatric patients: Prevalence, correlates, and subgroups. *Schizophrenia Bulletin, 26*, 179–192.

Niv, N., Lopez, S. R., Glynn, S. M., & Mueser, K. T. (2007). The role of substance use in families, attributions and affective reactions to their relative with severe mental illness. *Journal Nervous and Mental Disease, 195*, 307–314.

Nixon, S., Hallford, H. G., & Tivis, R. D. (1996). Neurocognitive function in alcoholic, schizphrenic, and dually diagnosed patients. *Psychiatry Research, 64*, 35–45.

Noordsy, D. L., Drake, R. E., Biesanz, J. C., & McHugo, G. J. (1994). Family history of alcoholism in schizophrenia. *Journal of Nervous and Mental Disease, 186*, 651–655.

Noordsy, D. L., Schwab, B., Fox, L., & Drake, R. E. (1996). The role of self-help programs in the rehabilitation of persons with severe mental illness and substance use disorders. *Community Mental Health Journal, 32,* 71–81.

Nuechterlein, K. H., Barch, D. M., Gold, J. M., Goldberg, T. E., Green, M. F., & Heaton, R. K. (2004). Identification of separable cognitive factors in schizophrenia. *Schizophrenia Research, 72,* 29–39.

Nuechterlein, K. H., & Dawson, M. E. (1984). Information processing and attentional functioning in the developmental course of schizophrenic disorders. *Schizophrenia Bulletin, 10,* 160–203.

Olincy, A., Johnson, L. L., & Ross, R. G. (2003). Differential effects of cigarette smoking on performance of a smooth pursuit and a saccadic eye movement task in schizophrenia. *Psychiatry Research, 117,* 223–236.

Osher, F. C., & Kofoed, L. L. (1989). Treatment of patients with psychiatric and psychoactive substance use disorders. *Hospital and Community Psychiatry, 40,* 1025–1030.

Payer, D., & London, E. D. (2009). Methamphetamine and the brain: Findings from brain imaging studies. In J. M. Roll, R. A. Rawso, W. Ling, & S. Shoptaw (Eds.), *Methamphetamine addiction: From basic science to treatment* (pp. 61–91). New York: Guilford Press.

Peters, R. H., Greenbaum, P. E., Edens, J. F., Carter, C. R., & Ortiz, M. M. (1998). Prevalence of DSM-IV substance abuse and dependence disorders among prison inmates. *American Journal of Drug and Alcohol Abuse, 24,* 573–587.

Peters, R. H., Kearns, W. D., Murrin, M. R., & Dolente, A. S. (1992). Psychopathology and mental health needs among drug-involved inmates. *Journal of Prison and Jail Health, 111,* 3–25.

Pitschel-Walz, G., Leucht, S., Bäuml, J., Kissling, W., & Engel, R. R. (2001). The effect of family interventions on relapse and rehospitalization in schizophrenia: A meta-analysis. *Schizophrenia Bulletin, 27,* 73–92.

Polcin, D. L. (1992). Issues in the treatment of dual diagnosis clients who have chronic mental illness. *Professional Psychology: Research and Practice, 23,* 30–37.

Pope, H. G., Gruber, A. J., Hudson, J. I., Huestis, M., & Yurgelun-Todd, D. (2001). Neuropsychological performance in long-term cannabis users. *Archives of General Psychiatry, 58,* 909–915.

Potvin, S., Joyal, C. C., Pelletier, J., & Stip, E. (2008). Contradictory cognitive capacities among substance-abusing patients with schizophrenia: A meta-analysis. *Schizophrenia Research, 100,* 242–251.

Potvin, S., Mancini-Marie, A., Fahim, C., Mensour, B., & Stip, E. (2007). Processing of social emotion in patients with schizophrenia and substance use disorder: An fMRI study. *Society for Neuroscience, 2,* 106–116.

Potvin, S., Sepehry, A. A., & Stip, E. (2006). Negative symptoms in dual diagnosis schizophrenia: A meta-analysis. *Psychological Medicine, 36,* 431–440.

Potvin, S., Stavro, K., & Pelletier, J. (2012). Paradoxical cognitive capacities in dual-diagnosis schizophrenia: The quest for explanatory factors. *Journal of Dual Diagnosis, 8,* 35–47.

Prochaska, J. O., & DiClemente, C. C. (1984). *The Transtheoretical Approach: Crossing the Traditional Boundaries of Therapy.* Homewood, IL: Dow-Jones/Irwin.

Rabin, R. A., Zakzanis, K. K., & George, T. P. (2011). The effects of cannabis use on neurocognition in schizophrenia: A meta-analysis. *Schizophrenia Research, 128,* 111–116.

Regier, D. A., Farmer, M. E., Rae, D. S., Locke, B. Z., Keith, S. J., Judd, L. L., et al. (1990). Comorbidity of mental disorders with alcohol and other drug abuse: Results from the Epidemiologic Catchment Area (ECA) study. *Journal of the American Medical Association, 264*, 2511–2518.

Ridgely, M. S., Goldman, H. H., & Talbott, J. A. (1986). *Chronically mentally ill young adults with substance abuse problems: A review of the literature and creation of a research agenda.* Baltimore, MD: University of Maryland Mental Health Policy Studies Center.

Ridgely, M. S., Goldman, H. H., & Willenbring, M. (1990). Barriers to the care of persons with dual diagnoses: Organizational and financing issues. *Schizophrenia Bulletin, 16*, 123–132.

Ries, R. K., & Comtois, K. A. (1997). Managing disability benefits as part of treatment for persons with severe mental illness and comorbid drug/alcohol disorders: A comparative study of payees and non-payee participants. *American Journal on Addictions, 6*, 330–338.

Ringen, P. A., Melle, I., Birkenaes, A. B., Engh, J. A., Faerden, A., Vaskinn, A., et al. (2008). The level of illicit drug use is related to symptoms and premorbid functioning in severe mental illness. *Acta Psychiatrica Scandinavica, 118*, 297–304.

Ringen, P. A., Vaskinn, A., Sundet, K., Engh, J. A., Jónsdóttir, H., Simonsen, C., et al. (2010). Opposite relationships between cannabis use and neurocognitive functioning in bipolar disorder and schizophrenia. *Psychological Medicine, 40*, 1337–1347.

Robins, L. N., Tipp, J., & Przybeck, T. R. (1991). Antisocial personality disorder. In L. N. Robins & D. A. Regier (Eds.), *Psychiatric Disorders in America: The Epidemiologic Catchment Area Study* (pp. 258–290). New York: Free Press.

Rodriguez-Jimenez, R., Bagney, A., Martinez-Gras, I., Ponce, G., Sanchez-Morla, E. M., Aragües, M. et al. (2010). Executive function in schizophrenia: Influence of substance use disorder history. *Schizophrenia Research, 118*, 34–40.

Rodriguez-Sanchez, J. M., Ayesa-Arriola, R., Mata, I., Moreno-Calle, T., Perez-Iglesias, R., Gonzalez-Blanch, et al. (2010). Cannabis use and cognitive functioning in first-episode schizophrenia patients. *Schizophrenia Research, 124*, 142–151.

Rogers, R. D., Moeller, F. G., Swann, A. C., & Clark, L. (2010). Recent research on impulsivity in individuals with drug use and mental health disorders: Implications for alcoholism. *Alcoholism: Clinical and Experimental Research, 34*, 1319–1333.

Rosen, M. I., & Rosenheck, R. (1999). Substance use and assignment of representative payees. *Psychiatric Services, 50*, 95–98.

Rosen, M. I., Rosenheck, R. A., Shaner, A., Eckman, T., Gamache, G., & Krebs, C. (2002). Veterans who may need a payee to prevent misuse of funds for drugs. *Psychiatric Services, 53*, 995–1000.

Rosenberg, S. D., Drake, R. E., Wolford, G. L., Mueser, K. T., Oxman, T. E., Vidaver, R. M., et al. (1998). The Dartmouth Assessment of Lifestyle Instrument (DALI): A substance use disorder screen for people with severe mental illness. *American Journal of Psychiatry, 155*, 232–238.

Rosenberg, S. D., Goodman, L. A., Osher, F. C., Swartz, M. S., Essock, S. M., Butterfield, M. I., et al. (2001). Prevalence of HIV, hepatitis B and hepatitis C in people with severe mental illness. *American Journal of Public Health, 91*, 31–37.

Rosenberg, S. D., Trumbetta, S. L., Mueser, K. T., Goodman, L. A., Osher, F. C., Vidaver, R. M., et al. (2001). Determinants of risk behavior for HIV/AIDS in people with severe and persistent mental illness. *Comprehensive Psychiatry, 42*, 263–271.

Rush, B., & Koegl, C. J. (2008). Prevalence and profile of people with co-occurring mental and substance use disorders within a comprehensive mental health system. *Canadian Journal of Psychiatry, 53*, 810–821.

Salyers, M. P., & Mueser, K. T. (2001). Social functioning, psychopathology, and medication side effects in relation to substance use and abuse in schizophrenia. *Schizophrenia Research, 48*, 109–123.

Schalling, D., Edman, G., & Åsberg, M. (1983). Impulsive cognitive style and inability to tolerate boredom: Psychobiological studies of temperamental vulnerability. In M. Zuckerman (Ed.), *Biological Bases of Sensation Seeking, Impulsivity, and Anxiety* (pp. 123–145). Hillsdale, NJ: Erlbaum.

Schiffer, B., Müller, B. W., Scherbaum, N., Forsting, M., Wiltfang, J., Leygraf, N., et al. (2010). Impulsivity-related brain volume deficits in schizophrenia-addiction comorbidity. *Brain, 133*, 3093–3103.

Schmidt, L. M., Hesse, M., & Lykke, J. (2011). The impact of substance use disorders on the course of schizophrenia — A 15-year follow-up study. *Schizophrenia Research, 130*, 228–233.

Scholes, K. E., & Martin-Iverson, M. T. (2010). Cannabis use and neuropsychological performance in healthy individuals and patients with schizophrenia. *Psychological Medicine, 40*, 1635–1646.

Schretlen, D. J., Cascella, N. G., Meyer, S. M., Kingery, L. R., Testa, S. M., Munro, C. A., et al. (2007). Neuropsychological functioning in bipolar disorder and schizophrenia. *Biological Psychiatry, 62*, 176–186.

Schuckit, M. A. (2009). *Drug and alcohol Abuse, 3rd edition* (6th ed.). New York: Plenum Press.

Schug, R. A., & Raine, A. (2009). Comparative meta-analyses of neuropsychological functioning in antisocial schizophrenic persons. *Clinical Psychology Review, 29*, 230–242.

Segarra, R., Zabala, A., Eguíluz, J. I., Ojeda, N., Elizagarate, E., Sánchez, P., et al. (2011). Cognitive performance and smoking in first-episode psychosis: The self-medication hypothesis. *European Archives of Psychiatry and Clinical Neuroscience, 26*, 241–250.

Serper, M. R., Alpert, M., Richardson, N. A., Dickson, S., Allen, M. H., & Werner, A. (1995). Clinical effects of recent cocaine use on patients with acute schizophrenia. *American Journal of Psychiatry, 152*, 1464–1469.

Shaner, A., Eckman, T. A., Roberts, L. J., Wilkins, J. N., Tucker, D. E., Tsuang, J. W., et al. (1995). Disability income, cocaine use, and repeated hospitalization among schizophrenic cocaine abusers. *The New England Journal of Medicine, 333*, 777–783.

Silver, H., & Abboud, E. (1994). Drug abuse in schizophrenia: Comparison of patients who began drug abuse before their first admission with those who began abusing drugs after their first admission. *Schizophrenia Research, 13*, 57–63.

Silverstein, S. M., Spaulding, W. D., Menditto, A. A., Savitz, A., Liberman, R. P., Berten, S., et al. (2008). Attention shaping: A reward-based learning method to enhance skills training outcomes in schizophrenia. *Schizophrenia Bulletin, 35*, 222–232.

Simon, G. E., VonKorff, M., Wagner, E. H., & Barlow, W. (1993). Patterns of antidepressant use in community practice. *General Hospital Psychiatry, 15*(6), 399–408.

Smith, T. E., Hull, J. W., Romanelli, S., Fertuck, E., & Weiss, K. A. (1999). Symptoms and neurocognition as rate limiters in skills training for psychotic patients. *American Journal of Psychiatry, 156*, 1817–1818.

Sobara, F., Liraud, F., Assens, F., Abalan, F., & Verdoux, H. (2003). Substance use and the course of early psychosis: A 2-year follow-up of first admitted subjects. *European Psychiatry, 18*, 133–136.

Sugranyes, G., Flamarique, I., Parellada, E., Baeza, I., Goti, J., Fermandez-Egea, E., et al. (2009). Cannabis use and age of diagnosis of schizophrenia. *European Psychiatry, 24*, 282–286.

Susser, E., Struening, E. L., & Conover, S. (1989). Psychiatric problems in homeless men: Lifetime psychosis, substance use, and current distress in new arrivals at New York City shelters. *Archives of General Psychiatry, 46*, 845–850.

Swartz, M. S., Swanson, J. W., Hiday, V. A., Borum, R., Wagner, H. R., & Burns, B. J. (1998). Taking the wrong drugs: The role of substance abuse and medication noncompliance in violence among severely mentally ill individuals. *Social Psychiatry and Psychiatric Epidemiology, 33*, S75–S80.

Tang, Y. L., George, T. P., Mao, P. X., Cai, Z. J., & Chen, Q. (2007). Cigarette smoking in Chinese male inpatients with schizophrenia: A cross-sectional analysis. *Journal of Psychiatric Research, 41*, 43–48.

Teeson, M., Hall, W., Lynskey, M., & Degenhardt, L. (2000). Alcohol and drug use disorders in Australia: Implications of the National Survey of Mental Health and Wellbeing. *Australian and New Zealand Journal of Psychiatry, 34*, 206–213.

Tengström, A., Hodgins, S., Grann, M., Långström, N., & Kullgren, G. (2004). Schizophrenia and criminal offending: The role of psychopathy and substance misuse. *Criminal Justice and Behavior, 31*, 1–25.

Tsemberis, S., Gulcur, L., & Nakae, M. (2004). Housing first, consumer choice, and harm reduction for homeless individuals with a dual diagnosis. *American Journal of Public Health, 94*, 651–656.

Tsoi, D. T., Porwal, M., & Webster, A. C. (2010). Interventions for smoking cessation and reduction in individuals with schizophrenia. *Cochrane Database of Systematic Reviews, 6*, 1–72.

Tsuang, M. T., Simpson, J. C., & Kronfol, Z. (1982). Subtypes of drug abuse with psychosis. *Archives of General Psychiatry, 39*, 141–147.

van Os, J., Bak, M., Hanssen, M., Vijl, R. V., de Graaf, R., & Verdoux, H. (2002). Cannabis use and psychosis: A longitudinal population-based study. *American Journal of Epidemiology, 156*, 319–327.

Vardy, M. M., & Kay, S. R. (1983). LSD psychosis or LSD-induced schizophrenia?: A multimethod inquiry. *Archives of General Psychiatry, 40*, 877–883.

Venable, P. A., Carey, M. P., Carey, K. B., & Maisto, S. A. (2003). Smoking among psychiatric outpatients: Relationship to substance use, diagnosis, and illness severity. *Psychology of Addictive Behaviors, 17*, 259–265.

Ventura, J., Hellemann, G. S., Thames, A. D., Koellner, V., & Nuechterlein, K. H. (2009). Symptoms as mediators of the relationship between neurocognition and functional outcome in schizophrenia: A meta-analysis. *Schizophrenia Research, 113*, 189–199.

Wade, D., Harrigan, S., Edwards, J., Burgess, P. M., Whelan, G., & McGorry, P. D. (2006). Substance misuse in first-episode psychosis: 15-month prospective follow-up study. *British Journal of Psychiatry, 189*, 229–234.

Warner, R., Taylor, D., Wright, J., Sloat, A., Springett, G., Amold, S., et al. (1994). Substance use among the mentally ill: Prevalence, reasons for use and effects on illness. *American Journal of Orthopsychiatry, 64*, 30–39.

Weaver, T., Madden, P., Charles, V., Stimson, G., Renton, A., Tyrer, P., et al. (2003).

Comorbidity of substance misuse and mental illness in community mental health and substance misuse services. *British Journal of Psychiatry, 183*, 304–313.

Weiden, P. J., Mott, T., & Curcio, N. (1995). Recognition and management of neuroleptic noncompliance. In C. L. Shriqui & H. A. Nasrallah (Eds.), *Contemporary issues in the treatment of schizophrenia* (pp. 411–433). Washington, DC: American Psychiatric Press.

Wobrock, T., Sittinger, H., Behrendt, B., D'Amelio, R., Falkai, P., & Caspari, D. (2007). Comorbid substance abuse and neurocognitive function in recent-onset schizophrenia. *European Archives of Psychiatry and Clinical Neuroscience, 257*, 203–210.

Wolford, G. L., Rosenberg, S. D., Drake, R. E., Mueser, K. T., Oxman, T. E., Hoffman, D., et al. (1999). Evaluation of methods for detecting substance use disorder in persons with severe mental illness. *Psychology of Addictive Behaviors, 13*, 313–326.

Wykes, T., & Dunn, G. (1992). Cognitive deficit and the prediction of rehabilitation success in a chronic psychiatric group. *Psychological Medicine, 22*, 389–398.

Wykes, T., Huddy, V., Cellard, C., McGurk, S. R., & Czobar, P. (2011). A meta-analysis of cognitive remediation for schizophrenia: Methodology and effect sizes. *American Journal of Psychiatry, 168*, 472–485.

Wykes, T., Steel, C., Everitt, B., & Tarrier, N. (2008). Cognitive behavior therapy for schizophrenia: Effect sizes, clinical models and methodological rigor. *Schizophrenia Bulletin, 34*, 523–537.

Xie, H., Drake, R. E., & McHugo, G. J. (2009). The 10-year course of substance use disorder among patients with severe mental illness: An analysis of latent class trajectory groups. *Psychiatric Services, 60*, 804–811.

Yamada, K., Watanabe, K., Nemoto, N., Fujita, H., Chikaraishi, C., Yamauchi, K., et al, (2006). Prediction of medication noncompliance in outpatients with schizophrenia: 2-year follow-up study. *Psychiatry Research, 141*, 61–69.

Yücel, M., Bora, E., Lubman, D. I., Solowij, N., Brewer, W. J., Cotton, S. M., et al. (2012). The impact of cannabis use on cognitive functioning in patients with schizophrenia: A meta-analysis of existing findings and new data in a first-episode sample. *Schizophrenia Bulletin, 38*, 316–330.

Ziedonis, D. M., & Fisher, W. (1996). Motivation-based assessment and treatment of substance abuse in patients with schizophrenia. *Directions in Psychiatry, 16*, 1–7.

Zigler, E., & Glick, M. (1986). *A Developmental Approach to Adult Psychopathology.* New York: Wiley.

Zygmunt, A., Olfson, M., Boyer, C. A., & Mechanic, D. (2002). Interventions to improve medication adherence in schizophrenia. *American Journal of Psychiatry, 159*, 1653–1664.

BOX 10.1 SUMMARY

About 50% of people with schizophrenia develop a substance use disorder sometime in their lives, and 25-35% have active substance use problems at any point during their illness.

Substance use worsens the course of schizophrenia, including precipitating relapses and rehospitalizations, causing housing instability, medical problems, legal problems, violence and victimization, depression and demoralization, and premature death.

People with schizophrenia are "super-sensitive" to the effects of small amounts of alcohol or drugs, rendering them more vulnerable to developing substance use disorders.

Common motives for using substances include socialization, coping with symptoms and negative feelings, and pleasure-recreation.

The key to accurate assessment of substance use disorders is to tap multiple sources of information about the individual's use of substances and their consequences (e.g., self-report, significant others, clinicians, records).

Alcohol abuse and dependence are associated with impaired cognitive functioning.

Drug abuse, especially cannabis abuse, is associated with less impaired cognitive functioning, presumably due to selection factors rather than the beneficial effects of these substances.

Treating co-occurring psychiatric and substance use disorders with parallel or sequential treatment approaches is ineffective.

Integrated treatment is when co-occurring psychiatric and substance use disorders are treated by the same clinicians at the same time, and in which the providers integrate treatment for both disorders into a seamless package.

Comprehensive treatment for co-occurring disorders includes training in illness self-management, family psychoeducation, vocational rehabilitation, assertive community treatment, and housing services.

Harm reduction places a primary emphasis on first minimizing the harmful consequences of substance use.

The therapeutic relationship is the foundation upon which effective integrated treatment rests.

Enhancing motivation to work on substance use problems is of primary importance when treating someone with co-occurring disorders.

The stages of treatment provide a heuristic to clinicians for matching treatment goals and strategies to the individual's current motivation to work on substance use problems: engagement, persuasion, active treatment, relapse prevention.

Cognitive impairment has been shown to impede response to broad-based rehabilitation approaches for schizophrenia as well as specific evidence-based psychosocial treatments, including social skills training and supported employment.

Cognitive remediation may be useful in reducing impaired cognitive functioning and facilitating the ability of people with schizophrenia to respond to learning-based psychosocial rehabilitation.

CONTINUING EDUCATION QUESTIONS

1. Summarize the lifetime rate of substance use disorder in schizophrenia.
   a. 15%
   b. 25%
   c. 35%
   d. 50%
   e. 75%
2. Which sociodemographic variables are related to substance use disorders in schizophrenia?
   a. Gender and age
   b. Gender and educational level
   c. Marital status and educational level
   d. Age, educational level, and marital status
   e. Gender, age, educational level, and marital status
3. Which of the following is *not* a stage of substance abuse treatment?
   a. Pre-contemplation
   b. Engagement
   c. Persuasion
   d. Active treatment
   e. Relapse prevention
4. Which substance has been paradoxically associated with *better* cognitive functioning in schizophrenia?
   a. Alcohol
   b. Cocaine
   c. Cannabis
   d. Heroin
   e. Amphetamine
5. What are the clinical correlates of substance use disorder in schizophrenia?
   a. Relapse and rehospitalization
   b. Depression
   c. Medical problems
   d. Legal problems
   e. All of the above

11

Medication and Cognition in Schizophrenia

NICOLE SESTITO, Ph.D.
TERRY E. GOLDBERG, Ph.D.
Zucker Hillside Hospital/ Feinstein Institute/AECOM

Cognitive impairments are core features of schizophrenia. Neuropsychological impairments have been demonstrated across multiple areas, including basic cognitive functions such as attention and psychomotor speed, as well as higher order functions including working memory, verbal learning and memory, and executive function (Gold & Harvey, 1993; Saykin et al., 1994). Individuals who have worse cognitive functioning are more likely to be chronically institutionalized, have impaired social skills and social functioning, have poorer self-care skills, and benefit less from psychiatric rehabilitation (Mueser & McGurk, 2004). Cognitive deficits are seen in the earliest stages of the disorder and thus are often present in first episode, antipsychotic naïve individuals, suggesting that these deficits are not merely the byproduct of medication, or chronic, repeated hospitalizations. In regard to treatment, level of cognition is a better predictor of outcome than severity of positive or negative symptoms (Meltzer et al., 1998). The societal effects of cognitive impairments have been well documented. It has been estimated that only about 50% of patients with schizophrenia are employed at any time in any capacity (Cook & Razzano, 2000), and estimates of the yearly direct and indirect cost of schizophrenia in the United States range from to $35 to $65 billion (Sevy & Davidson, 1995).

Given that cognitive impairments have been shown to be a core feature of the disorder, and have a major impact on the social and vocational functioning of individuals with schizophrenia, cognition is increasingly regarded as an important outcome in the assessment of treatment efficacy in this population. Neurocognition has come to be viewed as a key target in clinical trials. While the remission of psychotic symptoms has traditionally been the focus of psychopharmacological treatment in schizophrenia, studies have shown that improvement in psychotic symptoms does not necessarily translate into independent living status (Lauriello, Lenroot, & Bustillo, 2003). Due to the importance of cognitive functioning in schizophrenia, a number of recent studies have examined the effects of first- and second-generation antipsychotics on cognition, and they will be reviewed in this chapter. In addition, this chapter will address current and emerging cognitive enhancing agents. We will also discuss strategies for how to estimate positive drug effects on cognition while considering practice effects as a possible reason for improvement in neuropsychological test performance.

COMMON MEDICATIONS PRESCRIBED IN SCHIZOPHRENIA

First-generation antipsychotic medications (also referred to as typical, conventional, or classic antipsychotics) are a class of antipsychotic drugs that were developed in the 1950s as a way to treat psychosis, particularly in schizophrenia. Some of the more common first-generation drugs include haloperidol (Haldol), thioridazine (Mellaril), chlorpromazine (Thorazine), and mesoridazine (Serentil). Much like newer medications, first-generation antipsychotics block dopamine receptors in the brain (primarily the D2 subtype), particularly in the mesolimbic pathway where an excess of dopamine has been linked to psychotic experiences. However, the first-generation medications are not particularly selective and block dopamine receptors in mesocortical, tuberoinfundibular, and nigrostriatal pathways (see Meltzer, 2002). Blocking of dopamine receptors in these pathways is linked to the unwanted side effects that first-generation medications are known to produce, particularly extrapyramidal symptoms (EPS). These latter include tardive dyskinesia, akathisia, dystonia, akinesia, and parkinsonian symptoms. The most common drug associated with EPS is haloperidol. While neuroleptic malignant syndrome (NMS), a life-threatening neurological disorder, can occur with both first- and second-generation medications, it appears to be more common in individuals using haloperidol or chlorpromazine. These side effects compromise the therapeutic effects of treatment and lead many patients to discontinue their use, increasing the risk of relapse (Kane, 2001).

Second-generation, or atypical antipsychotics, are a group of drugs that also targets psychotic symptoms, but work differently from first-generation antipsychotics. Second-generation medications in general target multiple receptors, including both serotonin and dopamine receptors. They may have less affinity at the D2 receptors, resulting in fewer motor symptoms. These drugs were defined as "atypical" because of the believed absence of EPS. Alternatively, they may be administered at lower doses than traditional dosing of first-generation medications. However, it is now known that second-generation medications can still induce these effects, although to a lesser degree than first-generation medications (Weiden, 2007). The risk of tardive dyskinesia is thought to be lower, but is still recognized as a possible side effect because it can sometimes take years to develop.

Obesity, hyperglycemia, and various other metabolic side effects may also develop when using second-generation medications. It is important to note that these comorbid medical conditions have their own cognitive effects over time, and it is well documented that individuals who suffer from conditions such as obesity and diabetes are at higher risk for dementia and other types of cognitive dysfunction, due to direct effects on brain insulin receptors or glucose processing or cerebrovascular risk (Awad, Gagnon, Messier, 2004; Stone & Keshavan, this volume ;van den Berg et al., 2010;). Clozapine (Clozaril) was the first second-generation medication introduced in the 1950s, but fell out of favor due to concerns over agranulocytosis, an acute condition involving a severe and dangerous low white blood cell count. However, research has indicated its effectiveness in treatment-resistant schizophrenia, and adverse effect monitoring systems have been developed, again making clozapine a viable antipsychotic. Other common second-generation medications, including their year of release into the market, are risperidone (Risperdal, 1994), olanzapine (Zyprexa, 1996), quetiapine (Seroquel, 1997). ziprasidone (Geodon, 2001), and aripiprazole (Abilify, 2002).

EFFECTS OF ANTIPSYCHOTICS ON POSITIVE AND NEGATIVE SYMPTOMS

After their introduction, first-generation antipsychotics were shown to reduce the positive symptoms of schizophrenia, including hallucinations, delusions, and disorganized speech, and prevent their recurrence. While they reduced hospitalizations and/or relapse, they did not positively change the long-term course of the disorder or subsequently improve outcome. They also did not seem to markedly improve the negative symptoms of schizophrenia, such as apathy, alogia, and flat affect. In addition, they were associated with many of the side effects mentioned previously. Second-generation antipsychotics have been widely regarded as a therapeutic advance in the treatment of schizophrenia and related disorders. It has also been widely claimed that improvement in negative symptoms are a core characteristic of second-generation drugs (Sernyak & Rosenheck, 2007). However, the superiority of second-generation antipsychotics has been questioned. There is currently a lack of consensus regarding the effectiveness of first- versus second-generation antipsychotics in schizophrenia (see Lieberman et al., 2003).

Many studies have not found conclusive evidence that second-generation antipsychotics are better as a group in improving positive and negative symptoms. One the largest and most comprehensive independent trials designed to compare the effective of first- and second-generation antipsychotic medications in schizophrenia was the Clinical Antipsychotic Trials of Intervention Effectiveness (CATIE), which was supported by the National Institute of Mental Health. The study was conducted between October 2001 and December 2004 at 57 U.S. clinical sites. Patients were randomly assigned to receive olanzapine, perphenazine (Trilafon; a first-generation drug), quetiapine, or ziprasidone under double-blind conditions and were followed for up to 18 months. Perphenazine was selected as the first-generation medication because it is a midpotency medication with only a moderate incidence of EPS and sedation. The methods and results of the CATIE study have been described in detail multiple times (Stroup et al., 2003; Swartz et al., 2003). To summarize, the key finding in CATIE was that perphenazine (the first-generation medication) was not significantly different in overall effectiveness or efficacy compared with second-generation medications. In addition, it was found that perphenazine was the most cost effective drug. In terms of drug tolerance and side effects, the second-generation drugs did not have any consistent benefits over the first-generation drug (see Swartz et al., 2008).

The results of the CATIE study have been very controversial. However, other studies have supported their conclusion that second-generation drugs do not have the superiority over first-generation drugs as commonly believed. Leucht, Pitschel-Walz, Abraham, and Kissling (1999) conducted a meta-analysis that quantified the efficacy and tolerability of the new antipsychotics risperidone, olanzapine, sertindole (Serdolect), and quetiapine in schizophrenia compared to placebo and conventional antipsychotics. There were differences among the second-generation antipsychotics in terms of how they compared to first-generation medications. Sertindole and quetiapine were found to be as effective as haloperidol, and risperidone and olanzapine were slightly more effective than haloperidol in the treatment of global symptomatology. With respect to negative symptoms, all new antipsychotics were more effective than placebo. However, so was the first-generation drug haloperidol despite widespread opinion to the contrary. Treatment with second-generation antipsychotics was also found to be associated with less adverse effects and lower drop-out rates.

While it is sometimes implied that all second-generation drugs surpass first-generation medications, recent research has found that all second-generation medications may not be equal in this regard. A recent meta-analysis examined the effects of second-generation versus first-generation antipsychotics in schizophrenia across multiple domains (Leucht et al., 2008). The authors compared nine second-generation antipsychotic drugs with first-generation drugs. In terms of the remission of positive and negative symptoms, the authors found that four second-generation antipsychotic drugs—amisulpride (Solian; a selective D2 blocker not available in the U.S.), clozapine, olanzapine, and risperidone—were more efficacious than first-generation drugs in the main domains (i.e., overall change in symptoms, and in positive and negative symptoms). However, the other five second-generation antipsychotic drugs were only as efficacious as first-generation antipsychotic drugs, even in terms of negative symptoms. The second-generation medications also differ amongst themselves in many properties, including costs and side effects (e.g., metabolic effects). Therefore, the second-generation class drugs are not a homogenous group and should not be generally regarded as superior to first-generation drugs.

Despite the lack of strong evidence favoring second-generation medications, the fact remains that second-generation antipsychotics have largely replaced first-generation medications as the treatment of choice (Rosenheck et al., 2006). Even within the literature comparing medications of this class, the results are often contradictory with different medications being found superior in different comparative studies. Recent meta-analyses have revealed several methodological flaws in these studies, including insufficient random assignment, lack of double-blind conditions, inadequate duration of the trial, and small sample size (Keefe, Silva, Perkins, & Lieberman, 1999). In addition, many of these types of studies are sponsored by the pharmaceutical company which manufactured one of the medications.

A meta-analysis by Heres et al. (2006) examined whether or not there was a link between drug sponsorship and study outcome. In 90% of the studies reviewed, the reported overall outcome was in the favor of the sponsor's drug. This resulted in contradictory conclusions across studies when the findings of studies of the same drugs but with different sponsors were compared. The authors also found several sources of bias that may limit the validity of the results of these studies. These sources of bias occurred in the areas of doses and dose escalation, study entry criteria and study populations, statistics and methods, and reporting of results and wording of findings.

In sum, the differential efficacy of first- and second-generation antipsychotics in schizophrenia is still being debated, and there is not strong evidence to state conclusively that second-generation medications are superior. It would be misguided for a neuropsychologist to promote the use of one antipsychotic medication over another in clinical practice on the basis of symptom efficacy or on the basis of impact on cognition (see below). Moreover, because of the inconclusive nature of studies that compare first- and second-generation antipsychotics, and the noted methodological problems, clinicians should review these studies and their findings from a critical perspective.

EFFECTS OF ANTIPSYCHOTICS ON COGNITION

Importance of Targeting Cognition

As discussed by Velligan and Miller (1996), cognitive impairments are important because they predict multiple domains of functioning for patients with schizophrenia, including performance of activities of daily living, social and occupational functioning, and level of independent living the community. Cognitive impairments are also more related to functional outcome than other aspects of the illness, including severity of positive and negative symptoms (Bowie & Harvey, 2006; Green, 1996; Velligan, Mahurin, & Diamond, 1997). In addition, it has been shown that neurocognitive deficits contribute independently to decreased quality of life in schizophrenia (Mohamed et al., 2008) and are central and enduring features of the disorder (Goldberg et al., 1993), independent of psychotic symptoms. Because of the results of these studies, it is thought that cognitive dysfunction is a central feature of schizophrenia and should be viewed as another domain of pathology. In addition, since the social and occupational disabilities seen in schizophrenia are likely associated with the largest indirect costs of the illness, treatment or remediation of cognitive deficits may have a large impact on the disability and cost associated with schizophrenia. Therefore, the benefits of cognitive enhancement to society as a whole could be substantial (see Harvey & Keefe, 2001).

Because of the significant effects of cognitive impairment on people with schizophrenia and society, it is not surprising that cognition has become a key target in clinical trials. Numerous studies in recent years have examined whether second-generation antipsychotics have a greater impact on cognitive symptoms than first-generation drugs. These studies have largely been conducted under the hypothesis that first-generation drugs have little or no impact on cognition. Several longitudinal studies and industry sponsored trials have found that second-generation antipsychotics improve cognition. However, many of these studies have been shown to have substantial methodological problems that may negatively impact the validity of their results.

Support for Cognitive Enhancement with Antipsychotics

There has been no lack of support for second-generation medications and their cognitive enhancing effects in schizophrenia. A large number of studies, including meta-analyses, have shown that second-generation medications have an advantage over first-generation antipsychotics in moderating cognitive impairments. A meta-analysis by Keefe et al. (1999) reviewed the literature on this topic and found that second-generation antipsychotics improve cognitive function in people with schizophrenia compared to first-generation medications. More recently, numerous other studies have yielded results in a similar direction, but not without complications. In a large meta-analysis that encompassed 1,513 patients, 14 studies, and domains of cognitive function that included learning, attention, processing speed, and fluency, Woodward et al. (2005) came to very similar conclusions that second-generation antipsychotics were superior to first- generation drugs. However, the authors also identified specific variables, such as study blind and random assignment, that influenced results supporting cognitive change due to second-generation medications. Along similar lines, Harvey and Keefe (2001) also found that second-generation antipsychotics enhance cognitive functioning in schizophrenia, but that the studies that have shown these positive results have deficient methodologies. Most critically, the methodology between studies can differ in their sample sizes, dosing strategies, treatment duration, and test batteries, among other things, and weaknesses in these areas make results difficult to interpret.

Most of these studies have examined the most commonly used second-generation antipsychotics, including olanzapine, quetiapine, and risperdione. An important study by Bilder et al. (2002) compared clozapine to other second-generation medications. Examining the cognitive enhancement effects of clozapine is important because it is considered the "gold standard" for treatment-resistant schizophrenia. While clozapine has been well-studied in terms of its effect on cognition, only a handful of these studies have directly compared clozapine to other second-generation medications. This study was also the first to use a double-blind design, and also compared clozapine to haloperidol, a first-generation drug. Participants were given a comprehensive neuropsychological battery that focused on measures of general ability, learning and memory, attention, executive function, and motor skills. The results showed that the second-generation medications had an advantage over haloperidol, but clozapine showed no advantage over other second-generation drugs. In addition to having no advantage, clozapine has also been associated with a decline in memory functions. The potent anticholinergic properties of the drug may have been responsible for this (Goldberg et al., 1993; see also Adcock et al. 2009). This is in contrast to clozapine's superiority in treating the positive and negative symptoms in schizophrenia, highlighting that a medication's ability to treat these symptoms of schizophrenia does not generalize to its ability to improve cognitive functioning. As mentioned previously, cognitive impairments have been shown to be more highly correlated to functional outcome than other dimensions of schizophrenia, including severity of positive and negative symptoms. Therefore, it is important to keep in mind that an individual who shows improvement in their distress resulting from reduction in positive or negative symptoms may not show significant improvement in performance in everyday activities (e.g., performance at work or school).

Some theorize that it is not just the case that second-generation antipsychotics have a positive impact on cognition while first-generation antipsychotics do not, but that first-generation antipsychotic medications may even have a negative impact. First-generation drugs primarily work by blocking D_2 receptors in the brain, which may have a negative impact on some aspects of cognition. As discussed previously, first-generation antipsychotics are also thought to have a greater risk of extrapyramidal symptoms (EPS). The EPS seen may significantly impair neurocognitive functions, particularly on tests of motor output, processing speed, and reaction time. In addition, the anticholinergic medications used to treat EPS are found to impair cognition, particularly memory (Velligan & Miller, 1999). These reasons, along with the fact that second-generation drugs are thought to be better tolerated and have higher adherence rates, have led to a large number of studies that focus on the second-generation drugs and their effects on cognition.

Are Second-Generation Antipsychotics Truly Superior?

Though the general consensus may be that first-generation drugs have a negative impact on cognition, some research suggests otherwise. A meta-analysis of 36 studies by Mishara and Goldberg (2004) examined the extent to which first-generation medications have an enhancing effect on cognition. They found that first-generation antipsychotics produced modest to moderate gains in most cognitive domains tested in people with schizophrenia, with an overall effect size of about .20 to .25. Moreover, these medications seemed to differentially enhance cognitive functions. Attention, language, intellectual, memory, and perceptual functions were modestly to moderately enhanced; executive and oculomotor functions were only slightly enhanced. Consistent with a previous critical review (Cassens et al., 1990), motor functioning was adversely impacted. The authors postulated that the relative consistency of the effects across domains might have less to do with the constructs that the individual tests are regarded as measuring than with improvement in cognitive control or attention and its subprocesses. This review suggested that gains associated with first-generation antipsychotics, whatever their cause, were measurable. The authors concluded that the topic of first-generation medications and their effect on cognition should be revisited.

The ability of second-generation antipsychotics to enhance cognitive performance has been questioned directly and recently, particularly in two large-scale studies: CATIE and EUFEST. Data gathered from the CATIE study (described previously) were analyzed to compare the neurocognitive effects of several second-generation antipsychotic medications (olanzapine, quetiapine, or risperidone) and one first-generation medication, perphenazine. The participant sample included over 800 individuals with schizophrenia. The participants were randomly assigned in a double-blind fashion and examined with 11 neuropsychological tests that were combined into a neurocognitive composite score. The participants were again evaluated at 2 months, 6 months, and 18 months. At 2 months, treatment resulted in small neurocognitive improvements for all medications with no significant difference between groups, and results at 6 months were similar. After 18 months of treatment, however, improvement was greater in the perphenazine group, the first-generation drug, than in the olanzapine or risperidone group. Data from this study failed to support previous findings that second-generation medications have an advantage over first-generation drugs in improving neurocognition (Keefe et al., 2007).

The authors in the CATIE study reviewed several reasons why other studies have demonstrated that second-generation drugs have an advantage. First, the authors suggested that the prior studies may not generalize well to the type of everyday clinical practice that was examined in the CATIE trial. The authors provide a detailed description of the methodological differences between the CATIE trial and other published studies. Among the most significant differences is that the CATIE study included neurocognitive data on 817 patients, which was more than twice that of the largest trial previously conducted. It is possible that these smaller studies are susceptible to results that are less stable and generalizable. Furthermore, the CATIE trial used broader inclusion and minimal exclusion criteria, such as allowing for comorbid conditions and past substance abuse history. It was also conducted in a variety of clinical settings where people with schizophrenia are treated. The authors point out that the real-world features of this study were intended to enhance the external validity and applicability of the results.

In addition, previous studies were found to have used unusually high dosages of first-generation antipsychotics, usually haloperidol, creating an unfair comparison because of the increased risk of EPS and anticholinergic treatment which can impair cognition. In the CATIE trial, perphenazine was dosed according to input from scientific experts and leaders from each of the pharmaceutical companies. It should also be noted that perphenazine may have a reduced risk of EPS and anticholinergic treatment when compared to haloperidol and other high-potency first-generation medications.

Another major study, the European First Episode Schizophrenia Trial (EUFEST), also sought to compare the effects of first- and second-generation antipsychotic drugs in individuals with first-episode schizophrenia. The study design has been described in detail elsewhere (Fleischhacker, Keet, & Kahn, 2005; Kahn et al., 2008). The purpose of one study resulting from the EUFEST data compared the effect of haloperidol with that of second-generation antipsychotic drugs on the cognitive performance of this patient group. Participants were 498 patients recruited from Europe or Israel and randomly assigned to open-label haloperidol (a first-generation medication) or amisulpride, olanzapine, quietiapine, or ziprasidone. The Rey Verbal Learning Test, Trail Making Test, WAIS-III Digit-Symbol test, and Purdue Pegboard were administered at baseline and the 6-month follow-up evaluation. The researchers found that when they compared follow-up to baseline, composite cognitive test scores (albeit on this rather limited battery) improved for all five treatment groups. However, there were no overall differences among the treatment groups. The authors concluded that while their study showed moderate improvement in the cognitive performance of these patients, the magnitude of improvement does not differ between treatment with haloperidol and treatment with second-generation drugs. Much like the CATIE study, the authors also postulated that one reason their findings are different from previous studies is because haloperidol was administered in a lower, more appropriate dose.

EFFECTS OF COGNITIVE ENHANCING MEDICATIONS IN SCHIZOPHRENIA

Cognitive enhancing medications have been the subject of much preclinical and clinical research across multiple disorders. Because of the level of cognitive impairments seen in individuals with schizophrenia, and the impact it has on their functional outcomes, the concept of a pharmacological intervention as an adjunctive treatment in this population is particularly appealing. However, the results of several studies that have targeted multiple brain systems have not been promising.

Cognitive impairment, particularly memory impairment, has been associated with abnormal functioning of the cholinergic system (Friedman, 2004). Over the past decade, the use of acetylcholinesterase inhibitors, such as donepezil (Aricept), have become common place in the treatment of Alzheimer's disease and other dementias and are recommended by the American Academy of Neurology (Gauthier, 2004). The benefits of these medications have been examined in schizophrenia, and at first glance would seem to be a reasonable add-on medication in treatment because of the cognitive deficits seen in the disorder. A paper by Stip, Sepehry, and Chouinard (2007) reviewed a number of studies that examined cognitive performance in people with schizophrenia before and after treatment with three cholinesterase inhibitors—donepezil, rivastigmine (Exelon), or galantamine (Razadyne). Statistical analyses revealed a small to medium improvement in short-term and long-term memory when patients were compared with their baseline performance. However, when compared to a placebo-control group at the end of the trial, they performed worse on both short- and long-term memory measures. The patient groups from the studies reviewed were on both first- and second-generation medications. Other studies have replicated the finding that acetylcholinesterase inhibitors do not appear to be effective in the treatment of cognitive impairments in schizophrenia (Keefe et al., 2008).

Glutamatergic interventions have also been examined in schizophrenia. The glutamate system is implicated in schizophrenia both because it is involved in neuroplasticity during learning and because NMDA antagonists have psychotimemic effects. There have been several attempts to improve cognition using a variety of approaches involving the glutamatergic system, including NMDA and AMPA receptor subtypes (Harvey, 2009). The Cognitive and Negative Symptoms in Schizophrenia Trial (CONSIST; Buchanan et al., 2007) used two different agents to influence the NMDA receptor system. In this study, participants were randomized to one of these two active treatment groups or to placebo and examined for 16 weeks in a double-blind protocol. They measured a wide range of neuropsychological domains, including processing speed, verbal fluency, motor speed, vigilance, verbal and visual memory, and executive function. The results were strongly negative, and neither active compound was superior to placebo in improving cognitive performance in schizophrenia. The negative results of this study were replicated when targeting the AMPA receptor system (Goff et al., 2008).

Nicotinic agonists have also been studied in schizophrenia, the impetus involving genetic factors and various sensory gating abnormalities. Two receptor complexes, Alpha-7 and the Alpha4-Beta2 subunits, have been the target of interventions (Harvey, 2009). Again, the results have been negative and showed no detectable effects on cognition (Freedman et al., 2008; Astra-Zeneca, 2008).

Psychostimulants, such as amphetamine (Adderall) and modafinil (Provigil), have shown modest effects at best in improving cognition, despite a great deal of theoretical evidence that they alter frontal-cortical networks modulated by dopamine. The evidence for their effect on cognition is variable in individuals with schizophrenia, and there is some evidence that those with less severe cognitive impairment benefit more (Morein-Zamir et al., 2007). A well-conducted large-scale study of adjunctive modafinil in schizophrenia was negative (Kane et al., 2008). In addition, the use of amphetamines or modafinil is associated with significant safety concerns that include relapse and exacerbation of psychosis.

Despite extensive research, the exact mechanism of action for medications like modafinil remains unclear. It seems that modafinil, like other stimulants, increases norepinephrine and dopamine at or near synaptic terminals by blockading the norepinephrine and dopamine transporters, but research has been inconsistent (Minzenberg & Carter, 2008). Therefore, the possible benefits of these medications need to be balanced by concerns regarding the long-term safety of these interventions for individuals with schizophrenia (e.g., an increase in psychosis) (Harvey, 2009).

ADDRESSING POLYPHARMACY

Many times, people with schizophrenia are not treated with one individual medication, but several medications at a time to treat their symptoms. One of the issues of polypharmacy is determining which medication may be causing a positive result or a negative side effect. Neuropsychologists are frequently asked to tease apart the impact of medications on cognition, a task that can be highly difficult. It is important to note that there is little to no research that shows a strong benefit to using multiple medications to treat psychiatric symptoms in this population. In fact, polypharmacy has been shown to be an important predictor of decreased survival rate in schizophrenia, and increased extrapyramidal symptoms (EPS) and adverse cardiac reactions, which can contribute to poorer outcomes (see Janssen, Weinmann, Berger, & Gaebel, 2004). Despite this evidence, polypharmacy continues to be used in both outpatient and inpatient care settings. Factors such as a high number of past hospitalizations and long illness duration were associated with polypharmacy treatment at hospital discharge, indicating that the most treatment-resistant individuals may be more likely to receive multiple medications, further complicating the clinical picture (Janssen et al., 2004). Based on what is known about the effects of antipsychotic medication on cognition in schizophrenia, it is at best difficult for clinicians to discern which medications among many may be the most likely to produce a given cognitive complaint. In addition, it is important to keep multiple etiological factors in mind when working with individuals with schizophrenia, who have known illness-related cognitive impairments separate from those resulting from medication use.

It is also important to consider the anticholinergic properties of a medication, and that all antipsychotics are not created equally in this sense. Antipsychotic medications such as chlorpromazine, clozapine, olanzapine, and thioridazine are known to have significant anticholinergic properties. The illness-related cognitive impairments seen in schizophrenia can be exacerbated by the presence of what are known as "central side effects" caused by the anticholiergic properties of these antipsychotics. Central side effects are cerebral and include impaired concentration, confusion, attention deficit, and memory impairment (Lieberman, 2004). Studies have also shown that certain forms of cognitive training rely on the engagement of key neuromodulator systems in the brain, which can be negatively impacted by anticholinergic medications. A recent study by Adcock et al. (2009) found that a cognitive training exercise resulted in changes in the brains of individuals with schizophrenia, bringing them closer to the neurophysiological patterns seen in healthy participants. However, they also observed that medication-related serum anticholinergic activity, as measured via radioimmunoassay, was negatively correlated with improvement in global cognition. In addition, anticholinergic activity uniquely accounted for 20% of the variance in global cognition change in the participants who received the training. These results indicated that cholinergic blockade from these medications reduces the brain's ability to adapt in response to the cognitive training. Because of these issues, it is also important to consider the anticholinergic properties of a medication when determining its effect of cognition.

THE ISSUE OF PRACTICE EFFECTS

Many of the methodological problems that occur in studies that have found significant differences between first- and second-generation antipsychotics have been discussed. It is also critical to mention that most of these studies did not include control groups. This is important because it raises the possibility that improvements can be due to practice effects since individuals are tested on multiple occasions and only weeks or months apart. In addition, the studies were not designed to rule out a placebo effect that results from the more general positive effects one can experience while being closely monitored in a treatment study.

A study by Goldberg et al. (2007) examined the results of a randomized comparison of two of the most widely prescribed second-generation antipsychotics, olanzapine and risperidone, in people with first-episode schizophrenia. In addition, to answer the question of whether or not a practice effect was present, they included a healthy control group in their comparisons. Patients were randomly assigned to a medication group for 16 weeks. Both patients and healthy controls received cognitive assessments at baseline and after 6 and 16 weeks. First, the authors found that there was no differential impact of olanzapine and risperidone on cognitive improvement. Both medication groups' cognitive performance improved on most measures. When compared to the healthy control group, all three groups improved on cognitive measures. Of the 16 measures given, the patient group showed greater improvement than the control group on just two measures. Figure 11.1 displays improvement in CVLT performance across treatment groups over time.

Thus, the cognitive improvements observed in the trial were consistent with the practice effects observed in the healthy control group, suggesting that some of the improvements in cognition seen in the individuals with schizophrenia may have been due to practice effects.

In the context of an adjunctive medication study, Keefe et al. (2008) examined the performance of 250 patients who were clinically stable and receiving only a second-generation medication antipsychotic (risperidone, olanzapine, quetiapine, ziprasidone, or aripiprazole). The primary outcome measure was

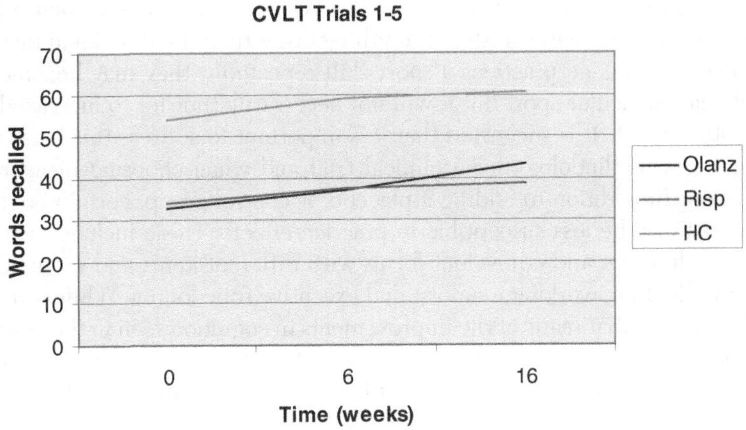

Figure 11.1 Improvement in California Verbal Learning Test (CVLT) performance across treatment groups over time.

the CATIE neurocognitive battery composite score. This group showed large improvements from baseline to a 12-week follow-up, with effect sizes between .41 and .45, despite no change in medication status. As such, gains could only be attributed to practice effects.

A more recent review discussed how practice effects are an underappreciated confound in interpreting cognitive improvement in clinical trials (Goldberg, Keefe, Goldman, Robinson, & Harvey, 2010). The authors point out that at first glance, a practice effect may seem clinically advantageous and even

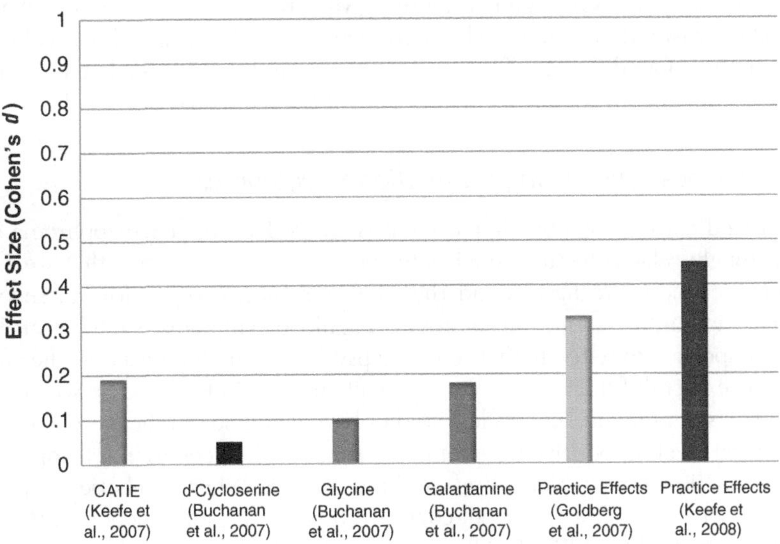

Figure 11.2 Medication treatments have limited efficacy for cognitive deficits.

indicate learning. However, there is little evidence that improvement of this type or magnitude will transfer to anything other than the individual task. For example, if someone practices a sport skill repeatedly, they may become better at that particular sport but it will not necessarily transfer to increased skill in another sport. It is suggested that it is important to address this issue when designing a methodology for a clinical trial and when choosing measures of cognition. In addition to adding a placebo or control group, certain cognitive measures may be less susceptible to practice effects. These include measures that use different and equivalent forms with different items and sequences in tests of attention, working memory, and executive functioning. While it may be a sobering fact that many of the improvements in cognition seen in these studies may be due to practice effects, it is crucial that these issues be addressed, or we risk that the results of these studies will be routinely misinterpreted.

TRACKING CHANGE IN CLINICAL CASES

Despite the issue of practice effects, it may be possible as clinicians to track change in individuals being treated with antipsychotic medication. A methodology exists for this: the Reliable Change Index (RCI), which takes into account the standard deviation of time1-time 2 changes and the magnitude of a practice effect to define a confidence interval. Scores that fall outside the interval reflect real change, i.e., change not due to the effects of practice or "noise." Thus, this change score can be applied at the level of the individual case. Further research is needed to determine an RCI that would identify the level of change that would exceed those expected by reassessment alone for multiple tests. Although no such large scale study exists at this time, Goldberg et al. (2010) used the MATRICS consensus cognitive battery (MCCB) to demonstrate how change can be measured over time. In brief, for many clinical neuropsychological tests, the authors found that an effect size gain of more than 1.0 would be needed to detect nonrandom cognitive enhancement at the individual case level.

What Does This Mean for Functional Outcome?

As noted earlier, cognitive impairment is a core feature of schizophrenia and is strongly related to functional outcome. Based on the issues that we have addressed here, we have found that the presumptive superiority of second-generation antipsychotics in improving cognitive symptoms is equivocal. It is also important to reiterate that reducing psychotic symptoms is not sufficient to improve overall functioning. While patients may be in less distress when their positive symptoms are controlled, studies have found no significant relationship between levels of positive symptoms and functional outcomes in schizophrenia (Green, 1996; Green, Kern, Braff, & Mintz, 2000). When psychotic symptoms have been successfully reduced, cognitive functioning still independently contributes to quality of life (Goldberg et al., 1993; Mohamed et al., 2008). Thus, it is important that clinicians appreciate this and not presume that medications alone will improve patients' everyday functioning or quality of life.

CONCLUSIONS

Cognitive impairment has been found to be strongly related to functional outcomes in schizophrenia; reducing psychotic symptoms is not sufficient to improve patients' everyday functioning and overall quality of life. Though second-generation antipsychotics appeared promising for the treatment of the cognitive impairments seen in schizophrenia, more recent studies have documented that second-generation medications may not be superior to first-generation antipsychotics. Furthermore, several methodological flaws have plagued studies with positive findings, including administration of unusually high doses of first-generation antipsychotics, lack of a control or placebo group, and use of measures that are susceptible to practice effects, making interpretation difficult. Cognitive enhancing medication may seem like an appealing adjunctive treatment choice in schizophrenia, but the results of these studies have not been promising. In addition, while they have not been shown to be effective in improving cognition, some are associated with worsening of psychotic symptoms and relapse. Therefore, their use may have a detrimental effect in this population.

Because of the diminished support for second-generation medications as a line of treatment in improving cognitive dysfunction in schizophrenia, it is important to consider alternatives for treatment of these impairments. Cognitive training has been shown to be a promising tool in the remediation of cognitive deficits, but the results are mixed and it is unclear whether they generalize from improvement in performance on select neuropsychological measures to everyday tasks (Dickinson et al., 2010). Future research on all treatment methods should focus on controlling for practice effects and other methodological problems.

REFERENCES

Adcock, R.A., Dale, C., Fisher, M., Aldebot, S., Genevsky, A., Simpson, G.V., … Vinogradov, S. (2009). When top-down meets bottom-up: Auditory training enhances verbal memory in schizophrenia. *Schizophrenia Bulletin, 35,* 1132–1141.

Astra-Zeneca. (2008). AstraZeneca and Targacept announce top-line results from phase IIb study of AZD3480 in cognitive dysfunction in schizophrenia. Retrieved December 8, 2009, from, http://astrazeneca.com/search/?itemId=4376018

Awad, N., Gagnon, M., & Messier, C. (2004). The relationship between impaired glucose tolerance, type 2 diabetes, and cognitive function. *Journal of Clinical and Experimental Neuropsychology, 26,* 1044–1080.

Bilder, R. B., Goldman, R. S., Volavka, J., Czobor, P., Hoptman, M., Sheitman, B., … Lieberman, J. A. (2002). Neurocognitive effects of clozapine, olanzapine, risperidone, and haloperidol in patients with chronic schizophrenia or schizoaffective disorder. *American Journal of Psychiatry, 159,* 1018–1028.

Bowie, C. R., & Harvey, P. D. (2006). Cognitive deficits and functional outcome in schizophrenia. *Neuropsychiatric Disease and Treatment, 2,* 531–536.

Buchanan, R. W., Javitt, D. C., Marder, S. R., Schooler, N. R., Gold, J. M., McMahon, R. P., … Carpenter, W. T (2007). The Cognitive and Negative Symptoms in Schizophrenia Trials (CONSIST): the efficacy of glutamatergic agents for negative symptoms and cognitive impairments. *American Journal of Psychiatry, 164,* 1593–1602.

Cassens, G., Inglis, A. K., Appelbaum, P. S., & Guthell, T G. (1990). Effects on neuropsychological function in chronic schizophrenic patients. *Schizophrenia Bulletin, 16*, 477–499.

Cook, J. A., & Razzano, L. (2000). Vocational rehabilitation for persons with schizophrenia: recent research and implications for practice. *Schizophrenia Bulletin, 26*, 87–103.

Davidson, M., Galderisi, S., Weiser, M., Werbeloff, N., Fleischhacker, W.W., Keefe, … Kahn, R.S. (2009). Cognitive effects of antipsychotic drugs in first-episode schizophrenia and schizophreniform disorder: a randomized, open-label clinical trial (EUFEST). *American Journal of Psychiatry, 166*, 675–682.

Fleischhacker, W. W., Keet, I. P., & Kahn, R. S. (2005). The European First Episode Schizophrenia Trial (EUFEST): rationale and design of the trial. *Schizophrenia Research, 78*, 147–156.

Freedman, R. Olincy, A., Buchanan, R.W., Harris, J. G., Gold, J. M., Johnson, L., … Kem, W. R. (2008) Initial phase 2 trial of a nicotinic agonist in schizophrenia. *American Journal of Psychiatry, 165*, 1040–1047.

Friedman, J. I. (2004). Cholinergic targets for cognitive enhancement in schizophrenia: focus on cholinesterase inhibitors and muscarinic agonists. *Psychopharmacology, 174*, 45–53.

Gauthier, S. (2004) Treatment of Alzheimer's disease: general methodological aspects. *Revue neurologique, 160*, 261–264.

Goff, D. C., Lamberti, J. S., Leon, A. C., Green, M .F., Miller, A. L., Patel, J., … Johnson, S. A. (2008). A placebo-controlled add-on trials of the Ampakine, CX516, for cognitive deficits in schizophrenia. *Neuropsychopharmacology, 33*, 465–472.

Gold, J. M., & Harvey, P. D. (1993). Cognitive deficits in schizophrenia. *The Psychiatric Clinics of North America, 16*(2), 295–312.

Goldberg, T. E., Greenberg, R. D., Griffin, S. J., Gold, J. M., Kleinman, J. E., Pickar, D., … Weinberger, D. R. (1993). The effect of clozapine on cognition and psychiatric symptoms in patients with schizophrenia. *The British Journal of Psychiatry, 162*, 43–48.

Goldberg, T. E., Goldman, R. S., Burdick, K. E., Malhotra, A. K., Lencz, T., Patel, R.C., V Robinson, D. G. (2007). Cognitive improvement after treatment with second-generation antipsychotic medications in first-episode schizophrenia: Is it a practice effect? *Archives of General Psychiatry, 64*, 1115–1122.

Goldberg, T. E., Keefe, R. S., Goldman, R. S., Robinson, D. G., & Harvey, P. D. (2010). Circumstances under which practice does not make perfect: a review of the practice effect literature in schizophrenia and its relevance to clinical treatment studies. *Neuropsychopharmacology, 35*, 1053–1062.

Green, M. F. (1996). What are the functional consequences of neurocognitive deficits in schizophrenia? *American Journal of Psychiatry, 153*, 321–330.

Harvey, P. D. (2009). Pharmacological cognitive enhancement in schizophrenia. *Neuropsychology Review, 19*, 324–335.

Harvey, P. D., & Keefe, R. S. E. (2001). Studies of cognitive change in patients with schizophrenia following novel antipsychotic treatment. *American Journal of Psychiatry, 158*, 176–184.

Heres, S., Davis, J., Maino, K., Jetzinger, E., Kissling, W., & Leucht, S. (2006). Why olanzapine beats risperidone, risperidone beats quetiapine, and quetapine beats olanzapine: an exploratory analysis of head-to-head comparison studies of second-generation antipsychotics. *American Journal of Psychiatry, 163*, 185–194.

Janssen, B., Weinmann, S., Berger, M., & Gaebel, W. (2004). Validation of polypharmacy process measures in inpatient schizophrenia care. *Schizophrenia Bulletin, 30,* 1023–1033.

Kahn, R. S., Fleischhacker, W. W., Boter, H., Davidson, M., Vergouwe, Y., Keet, I. P., … Grobbee, D. E. (2008). EUFEST Study Group: effectiveness of antipsychotic drugs in first-episode schizophrenia and schizophreniform disorder: An open randomised clinical trial. *Lancet, 371,* 1085–1097.

Kane, J. M. (2001). Extrapyramidal side effects are unacceptable. *Eurpoean Neuropsychopharmacology, 11,* 397–403.

Kane, J. M., D'Souza, D. C., Patkar, A. A., Youakim, J. M., Tiller, J., Yang, R., & Keefe, R. S. E. (2008). *Effects of adjunctive armodafinil in schizophrenia.* Poster presented at the 47th annual meeting of the American College of Neuropsychopharmacology, Scottsdale, AZ.

Keefe, R. S. E., Silva, S. G., Perkins, D. O., & Lieberman, J. A. (1999). The effects of atypical antipsychotic drugs on neurocognitive impairment in schizophrenia: a review and meta-analysis. *Schizophrenia Bulletin, 25,* 201–222.

Keefe, R. S., Bilder, R. M., Davis, S. M., Harvey, P. D., Palmer, B. W., Gold, J. M., … Lieberman, J. A.; CATIE Investigators; Neurocognitive Working Group. (2007) Neurocognitive effects of antipsychotic medications in patients with chronic schizophrenia in the CATIE Trial. *Archives of General Psychiatry, 64,* 633–647.

Keefe, R. S., Malhotra, A. K., Meltzer, H. Y., Kane, J. M., Buchanan, R. W., Murthy, A., … Goldman, R. (2008). Efficacy and safety of donepezil in patients with schizophrenia or schizoaffective disorder: significant placebo/practice effects in a 12-week, randomized, double-blind, placebo-controlled trial. *Neuropsychopharmacology, 33,* 1217–1228.

Lauriello, J., Lenroot, R., & Bustillo, J. R. (2003). Maximizing the synergy between pharmacotherapy and psychosocial therapies for schizophrenia. *The Psychiatric Clinics of North America, 26,* 191–211.

Lieberman, J. A. (2004). Managing anticholinergic side effects. *Primary Care Companion to the Journal of Clinical Psychiatry, 6,* 20–23.

Lieberman, J. A., Tollefson, G., Tohen, M., Green, A.I., Gur, R. E., Kahn, R., … Hamer, R. M. (2003). Comparative efficacy and safety of atypical and conventional antipsychotic drugs in first episode psychosis: a randomized, double-blind trial of olanzapine versus haloperidol. *American Journal of Psychiatry, 160,* 1396–1404.

Leucht, S., Pitschel-Walz, G., Abraham, D., & Kissling, W. (1999). Efficacy and extrapyramidal side-effects of the new antipsychotics olanzapine, quetiapine, risperidone, and sertindole compared to conventional antipsychotics and placebo. A meta-analysis of randomized controlled trials. *Schizophrenia Research, 35,* 51–68.

Leucht, S., Corves, C., Arbter, D., Engel, R. R., Li, C., & Davis, J. M. (2008). Second-generation versus first-generation antipsychotic drugs for schizophrenia: a meta-analysis. *Lancet, 373,* 31–41.

Meltzer, H. . (2002). Mechanism of action of atypical antipsychotic drugs. In K. L. Davis, D. Charney, J. T. Coyle, & C. Nemeroff (Eds.), *Neuropsychopharmacology: The fifth generation of progress* (pp. 819–831). Nashville, TN: American College of Neuropsychopharmacology.

Meltzer, H. Y., Casey, D. E., Garver, D. L., Lasagna, L., Marder, S., Massand, P. S., & Tandon, R. (1998). Evaluating the effects of antipsychotics on cognition in schizophrenia. *Journal of Clinical Psychiatry, 59,* 35–40.

Minzenberg, M. J., & Carter, C. S. (2008). Modafinil: a review of neurochemical actions and effects on cognition. *Neuropsychopharmacology, 33,* 1477–1502.

Mishara, A. L., & Goldberg, T.E. (2004). A meta-analysis and critical review of the effects of conventional neuroleptic treatment on cognition in schizophrenia: Opening a closed book. *Biological Psychiatry, 55,* 1013–1022.

Mohamed, S., Rosenheck, R., Swartz, M., Stroup, S., Lieberman, J.A., & Keefe, R. S. (2008). Relationship of cognition and psychopathology to functional impairment in schizophrenia. *American Journal of Psychiatry, 165,* 978–987.

Morein-Zamir, S., Turner, D. C., & Sahakian, B. (2007). A review of the effects of modafinil on cognition in schizophrenia. *Schizophrenia Bulletin, 33,* 1298–1306.

Mortimer, A. M. (1996). Cognitive function in schizophrenia: do neuroleptics make a difference? *Pharmacology, Biochemistry, and Behavior, 56,* 789–795.

Mueser, K. T., & McGurk, S. R. (2004). Schizophrenia. *Lancet, 363 (9426),* 2063–2072.

Rosenheck, R. A., Leslie, D.L., Sindelar, J., Miller, E. A., Lin, H. Stroup, S., ... Lieberman, J. (2006). Cost-effectiveness of second-generation antipsychotics and perphenazine in a randomized trial of treatment for chronic schizophrenia. *American Journal of Psychiatry, 163,* 2080–2089.

Saykin, A. J., Shtasel, D. L., Gur, R E., Kester, D. B., Mozley, L. H., Stafiniak, P., & Gur, R. C. (1994). Neuropsychological deficits in neuroleptic naive patients with first-episode schizophrenia. *Archives of General Psychiatry, 51,* 124–131.

Sernyak, M., & Rosenheck, R. (2007). Experience of VA psychiatrists with pharmaceutical detailing of antipsychotic medications, *Psychiatry Services, 58,* 1292–1296.

Sevy, S., & Davidson, M. (1995). The cost of cognitive impairment in schizophrenia. *Schizophrenia Research, 17,* 1–3.

Stip, E., Sepehry, A. A., & Chouinard, S. (2007). Add-on therapy with acetylcholinesterase inhibitors for memory dysfunction in schizophrenia: a systematic review, part 2. *Clinical Neuropsychopharmacology, 30,* 218–229.

Stroup, T. S., McEvoy, J. P., Swartz, M. S., Byerly, M. J., Glick, I. D., Canive, J. M.,... Lieberman, J. A. (2003). The National Institute of Mental Health Clinical Antipsychotic Trials of Intervention Effectiveness (CATIE) project: schizophrenia trial design and protocol development. *Schizophrenia Bulletin, 29,* 15–31.

Swartz, M. S., Perkins, D. O., Stroup, T. S., McEvoy, J. P., Nieri, J. M., & Haak, D. C. (2003). Assessing clinical and functional outcomes in the Clinical Antipsychotic Trials of Intervention Effectiveness (CATIE) schizophrenia trial. *Schizophrenia Bulletin, 29,* 33–43.

Van den Berg, E., Rejimer, Y. D., de Bresser, J., Kessels, R. P., Kappelle, L. J., & Biessels, G. J. (2010). A 4 year follow-up study of cognitive functioning in patients with type 2 diabetes mellitus. *Diabetologia, 53,* 58–65.

Velligan, D. I., Mahurin, R. K., & Diamond, P. L. (1997). The functional significance of symptomatology and cognitive function in schizophrenia. *Schizophrenia Research, 25,* 21–31.

Velligan, D. I., & Miller, A. I. (1996). Cognitive dysfunction in schizophrenia and its importance to outcome: the place of atypical antipsychotics in treatment. *Journal of Clinical Psychiatry, 60,* 25–28.

Weiden, P. J. (2007). EPS profiles: the atypical antipsychotics are not all the same. *Journal of Psychiatric Practice, 13,* 13–24.

Woodward, N. D., Purdon, S. E., Metlzer, H. Y., & Zald, D. H. (2005). A meta-analysis of neuropsychological change to clozapine, olanzapine, quetiapine, and risperidone in schizophrenia. *International Journal of Neuropsychopharmacology, 8,* 457–472.

BOX 11.1 COGNITION AS A TREATMENT TARGET IN SCHIZOPHRENIA

- Cognitive impairments predict functional outcome in patients and impacts functional performance more so than psychotic symptoms.
- Cognitive impairments contribute independently to quality of life, regardless of whether psychotic symptoms fully remit.
- Cognitive dysfunction is now considered to be a central part of schizophrenia that endures over time, i.e., is a trait, and is another domain of pathology.
- The specific nature of cognitive impairments (e.g., executive function and cognitive control, episodic memory) may map to neural systems and hence guide drug development.
- It would be misguided for a neuropsychologist to promote the use of one medication over another; furthermore it is important to interpret the results of these studies cautiously in clinical practice due to confounds and biases.

BOX 11.2 EFFECTS OF MEDICATION ON COGNITION IN SCHIZOPHRENIA

- There appears to be smaller differences between first- and second-generation antipsychotics in their treatment of cognitive symptoms than originally thought.
- There does not appear to be a relationship between the effectiveness of an antipsychotic medication in treating positive symptoms of schizophrenia and its ability to improve cognition.
- The effects of various cognitive enhancing medications in schizophrenia to date have not been promising.
- Despite evidence against its use, polypharmacy is widely used in treating psychiatric symptoms in schizophrenia.
- It is difficult at best to determine which medication out of many might cause subtle cognitive impairment. Nevertheless adjunctive anticholinergics and antipsychotics with anticholinergic properties might be especially prone to negative effects.
- In studies that document cognitive improvement with second-generation antipsychotics, a practice effect may account for at least some of the gains.

CONTINUING EDUCATION QUESTIONS

1. Cognitive impairments have been linked to the following:
   a. Chronic institutionalization
   b. Poorer social skills
   c. Impairments in everyday functioning
   d. All of the above
2. Which second-generation medication is considered to be the gold-standard for treatment-resistant schizophrenia?
   a. Olanzapine
   b. Clozapine
   c. Risperidone
   d. Ziprasidone
3. Which of the following is NOT true about second-generation antipsychotics?
   a. They may have less of an affinity for D2 receptors in the brain
   b. They may be given at lower doses than first-generation antipsychotics
   c. There is no risk for the development of EPS while taking them
   d. Their superiority over first-generation medications is in question
4. Studies have shown that many of the positive findings for second-generation antipsychotics may in fact be due to:
   a. Practice effects
   b. Unusually high doses of comparative first-generation medications
   c. Placebo effects
   d. All of the above
5. Cognitive enhancing medications, such as acetylcholinesterase inhibitors, have been studied in schizophrenia. They have been found to:
   a. Improve short-term memory
   b. Improve long-term memory
   c. Be difficult for patients to tolerate
   d. Not be effective in improving cognition

12

Neuropsychologically Informed Interventions to Treat Cognitive Impairment in Schizophrenia

ALICE MEDALIA, Ph.D.

Department of Psychiatry; Columbia University College of Physicians & Surgeons

DONA BELLUCCI, Ph.D.

Department of Psychology; Essex County Hospital Center

INTRODUCTION

Cognitive impairment is considered one of the major reasons that people with schizophrenia have difficulty functioning in everyday life (Green, 1996). In fact, cognitive dysfunction is even more predictive of functional impairment than positive symptoms. Impairments in attention, memory, processing speed, and problem-solving ability are commonly seen in patients with schizophrenia, depression, bipolar disorder, and alcohol and substance abuse (Medalia, Revheim, & Herlands, 2009). While the severity and profile of these deficits varies depending on factors like diagnosis, course of illness, and social-environmental factors, it has been estimated that more than 80% of patients with schizophrenia spectrum disorders score below 84% of the general population on cognitive tests (Keefe & Fenton, 2007). These cognitive deficits are persistent and not simply related to an episode of illness. Even when the person is psychiatrically stable, cognitive impairment is evident.

Cognitive deficits interfere with an individual's ability to work, study, live independently, socialize, and manage one's illness. These daily living tasks all require an ability to attend and remember, to identify goals and the steps to reach them, to prioritize and organize activities, and to integrate feedback to monitor performance. This can be seen in the example of illness management.

Many patients do not take medications as prescribed because they have difficulty organizing their pills, they forget their dosing schedule, and they have difficulty recalling whether or not they took their medication (Heinrichs, Goldberg, Miles, & McDermid, 2008; Jeste et al., 2003).

Difficulties with memory and information processing often interfere with a patient's ability to benefit from psychiatric skills training programs. In the arena of independent living, cognitive deficits interfere with one's ability to remember appointments and schedules, and manage everyday tasks such as remembering where keys and other personal items were placed. People with problem-solving deficits have trouble organizing their living space so that they tend to lose items and may find it challenging to maintain a budget or negotiate public transportation. The behavioral difficulties that result from cognitive impairments often lead to psychiatric patient's being labeled as "unmotivated." However, in reality, it is not they do not *want* to remember but rather lack the underlying cognitive ability to do so.

In order for patients to achieve good functional outcome, cognitive impairments must be addressed by specific therapeutic interventions. At present there are no FDA-approved medications to improve neurocognitive functions in schizophrenia and the affective disorders. Currently used medications to treat psychosis may provide some cognitive benefit, but careful attention should be paid to the potential cognitive toxicity of pharmacotherapeutic regimens (see Sestito & Goldberg, this volume). A crucial starting point in addressing cognitive impairment is education. Psychoeducation about cognitive symptoms should be provided to the patient and his or her family so that they understand the basis of the forgetful, inattentive behaviors and can strategize ways to support improved cognitive functioning (Medalia & Revheim, 2002). Finally, patients may benefit from participation in a cognitive remediation program, which will strengthen the specific cognitive skills that interfere with daily functioning, and teach strategies to compensate for the deficits (Krabbendam & Aleman, 2003; Kurtz, Moberg, Gur, & Gur, 2001; McGurk, Twamley, Sitzer, McHugo, & Mueser 2007; Twamley, Jeste, & Bellack 2003) (see Table 12.1).

COGNITIVE REMEDIATION

Cognitive remediation (CR) is a behavioral treatment that engages the patient in exercises intended to improve the neuropsychological skills that underlie

TABLE 12.1 Typical Components of Cognitive Remediation

1.	Assessment of baseline cognition
2.	Set cognitive goals related to overall recovery and to rehabilitation activities
3.	Provide CR groups at least 2 × week for a minimum of 3–4 months
4.	Work on specific exercises to target cognitive skills
5.	Engage in discussion about the use of cognitive skills in daily life
6.	Monitor and track progress and adjust treatment planning and goals accordingly

thinking. It differs from cognitive behavioral therapy (CBT) in both focus and methodology. The focus of CR is on the neuropsychological processes that underpin thinking, while the focus of CBT is on the form and content of thought. For example, while CBT might focus on a patient's reasoning and attributional style (e.g., jumping to conclusions or being quick to self-blame), CR focuses on improving working memory capacity and ability to sustain attention. CBT might focus on a patient's belief that there is a plot to harm him or her, whereas CR focuses on improving attention, executive functioning, and verbal memory.

While the immediate goal of CR is to improve cognition, the ultimate goal is to improve functioning in daily tasks—including school, work, social interactions, and independent living. CR might be used to help someone become more attentive so that she can better focus on schoolwork, household, or job responsibilities. Narrowly defined, CR is a set of cognitive drills or compensatory interventions designed to enhance cognitive functioning. However, from the vantage of the psychiatric rehabilitation field, CR engages the patient in a learning activity to enhance the neurocognitive skills relevant to overall recovery goals (Anthony, 2008; Medalia et al., 2009). CR programs vary in the extent to which they reflect these narrow or broader perspectives. Several different approaches to CR have been studied as a treatment for schizophrenia and schizoaffective disorder.

CONCEPTUAL APPROACHES TO COGNITIVE TRAINING

While all CR programs focus on cognition, there is considerable diversity in specific approaches. One basic distinction is whether they use a restorative or compensatory approach, or both. Restorative approaches to cognitive remediation attempt to repair impaired cognitive skills directly, whereas compensatory approaches do not attempt to restore impaired cognitive skill but rather attempt to compensate for or circumvent the deficit. The restorative approach directly targets cognitive skills through drill and practice techniques, with the goal being improved cognitive functioning. Restorative models usually gauge outcome by looking at improvements on the cognitive exercise itself and on neuropsychological tests. Although restorative models take into consideration functional gains, in its pure form there is a lack of accompanying interventions directly aimed at applying new cognitive skills to real-world settings. The process of generalization or transfer of skills is assumed. In contrast, the primary objective in compensatory approaches is not improved underlying cognitive skills but rather improved daily functioning with overall rehabilitation as its goal. In this approach, success is typically gauged by measuring functional gains. Compensatory cognitive training programs rely on the patient to initiate and maintain alternate strategies to promote adaptive behavior in real world settings. One type of compensatory approach relies on environmental modification, in order to reduce the cognitive demands on the individual and facilitate optimal functioning. For example, the use of a key hook by the door to reduce misplacing or losing keys is an environmental manipulation. Environmental modifications are highly reliant on therapists, and usually very specific to the unique situation of the patient. In contrast, restorative approaches and compensatory approaches other than environmental manipulation typically require considerable patient participation.

One similarity among approaches to CR is that all are based on the notion of neuroplasticity. Neuroplasticity, also called brain plasticity, brain malleability, or cortical plasticity, refers to the brain's ability to reorganize itself through forming new neural connections or by adding cells. Neuroplasticity allows the neurons in the brain to adjust their activity and organization in response to new situations or to changes in the environment. This process occurs in both children and adults, reflecting that the brain is not "hard-wired" with fixed or immutable neuronal connections. Rather, activities like thinking, learning, and acting stimulate neurons and drive change in both the brain's physical structure and functional organization. Because of neuroplasticity, the brain has the capacity to compensate for damage by reorganizing and forming new connections. In order for plasticity to take place the neurons need to be stimulated through activity. This idea of neural stimulation driving activation of "new" neuron connections is the basis for goal-directed experiential therapeutic rehabilitation programs for individuals with TBI. There is solid evidence that neuroplasticity occurs in adults and such changes persist well into old age (Mahncke, Bronstone, & Merzenich, 2006). Neuroplasticity is central to theories of learning and memory as well. In fact, it can be argued that all learning and memory activities involve neuronal changes in the brain (Bruel-Jungermen & Larochre, 2007; Doidge, 2007). As such, all the CR approaches discussed in this chapter, with the possible exception of therapies that soley rely on changing the environment, have foundations in the neuroplasticity model since they provide new experiences to which the individual brain must respond and adapt. At this level of analysis, the approaches differ only in terms of the "type" or "level" of stimulation they provide. Some approaches such as POSIT Science or Cogpac address these issues at an elemental level and others such as Cognitive Enhancement Therapy (CET) address it on a higher order level. In summary, all are assumed to produce changes in cognitive functioning as a result of the process of neuroplasticity.

Restorative Approaches

Restorative approaches typically address cognitive deficits through drill and practice on cognitive exercises. The software tends to differ depending on the level of neural process it targets, and the extent to which it incorporates learning principles into the game design. There are numerous software companies developing cognitive exercises, and any listing would rapidly become outdated. POSIT Science is an example of a company which produces software designed to target the most basic neural processes, i.e., sensory processing of information. The software exercises aim to strengthen or resuscitate the basic sensory processes thought to underlie all information processing and higher order neuropsychological functions. In this model, cognitive impairment in schizophrenia is viewed as the result of deficits in basic neural processes. That is, impaired perceptual processes and early sensory deficits in schizophrenia underlie higher order cognitive impairment. It is believed that interference or noise in the earliest perceptual representations in the brain leads to poor performance as these faulty representations are processed and used for cognitive tasks. Simply stated, disturbances in elemental perceptual processes, such as speed and accuracy of encoding verbal information, are hindering cognitive functions, such as verbal learning and memory, which lead to deficits in overall functioning, such as in social skills.

Scientific Brain Training and FitBrains are examples of software companies that make restorative cognitive exercises that target higher level cognitive processes. Rather than target basic sensory processing with the assumption that this will generalize to improvements in the higher order processes, many companies develop software exercises that directly target attention, memory, concept formation and other skills. Thus it can be seen that even within the restorative approach there are differences in the way the technique is applied. Some programs remediate the higher order neuropsychological functions, while others focus on training underlying sensory processing. There are a number of studies showing that both approaches are efficacious (Bell, Fiszdon, Greig, Wexler, & Bryson, 2007; Fisher, Holland, Merzenich, & Vinogradov, 2009; McGurk et al., 2007) To date, there has been no study directly comparing the advantages of targeting sensory processes versus neuropsychological functions. A meta-analysis of 40 studies of cognitive remediation in schizophrenia, conducted through June 2009, found that remediation approach was not associated with cognitive outcome (Wykes, Huddy, Cellard, McGurk, & Czobor, 2011). As this meta-analysis included studies of approaches that targeted sensory, molar and complex cognitive functions, the current evidence is that all are effective with no one approach having an advantage over the other.

Compensatory Approaches

The compensatory approach assumes that there are multiple alternative neuropsychological skills that can be engaged to perform any given task. In other words, compensation calls on different cognitive skills to accomplish the same goal. For example, a person with poor memory may use categorization to help remember a shopping list. Compensation strategies may come naturally to those who do not experience cognitive dysfunction, but an individual with cognitive dysfunction may not have the flexibility to see things from different perspectives or shift ideas on how to do things. They may not naturally alter the course of their behavior to fit available cognitive abilities. Therefore, compensatory strategies may need to be taught to individuals with cognitive dysfunction.

Compensatory approaches teach people to use both internal and external coping strategies to work around their deficits. An example of an internal coping strategy would be teaching someone organization strategies, such as chunking information, in order to compensate for poor memory skills. Compensatory approaches assume that the brain can compensate for deficits by engaging other areas of the brain and/or by forming new connections between "healthy neurons" (Diller, 1993). A broad example comes from work with TBI, where it is commonly found that functions once accomplished by a damaged hemisphere can be recovered or compensated for through rehabilitation efforts targeting the undamaged hemisphere (Dirette, Jinojosa, & Carnevale, 1999). In the above example, systematic chunking of information will improve memory by strengthening encoding which results in the strengthening of connections in the neuronal system (Dirette et al., 1999).

An example of an external compensatory strategy is environmental manipulation such as providing someone with a watch that has an alarm that rings at designated appointment or medication times. The alarm acts as a cue for the individual to recall a plan of action that needs to be initiated. Although the alarm itself acts as a prosthetic device and does not directly target underlying cognitive skills, through repeated exposure and pairings with behaviors, new habits may be formed and learning can occur, in some cases, over time. Other examples of environmental manipulation may include the use of signs and lists to aid in memory. Although debatable, even within the external types of compensatory strategies it is possible that new learning takes place and habits are formed. Depending on the type of manipulation and the level of demand on the patient, it is plausible that changes in the brain's neural network could occur.

When teaching compensatory strategies to an individual, the goal is to strive for efficiency so that the least amount of effort is expended. Many individuals with cognitive dysfunction have limited resources to process information and do not respond well to increased demands for performance. One needs to look for the simplest and most direct route to accomplish a goal, one with minimal effort and minimal demands. Observing an individual's behavior over time and analyzing the methods they use to perform tasks are useful when investigating compensatory strategies.

Environmental Modification

Cognitive Adaptive Training (CAT) (Velligan et al., 2000; Velligan et al., 2002) is a manualized, highly individualized, compensatory approach that provides environmental manipulation as the primary intervention. CAT attempts to bypass cognitive impairments and improve adaptive functioning in real world settings (i.e., work, home) by providing individuals with environmental supports such as lists, calendars, and other organizational tools. The therapist works intensely, usually for many hours over several months, with an individual to modify their environment in order to improve their adaptive functioning.

The benefits to working in such an intense individualized manner with patients are evident in the reported improvements in adaptive and global functioning, quality of life, and increased medication adherence (Velligan et al.,

2000; Velligan, 2002; Velligan & Gonzalez, 2007). More research is needed to determine the cost benefit analysis of therapist driven interventions like this, which are very time and labor intensive, and questions remain about ease of application on a large scale in the community.

Integrated Models

CET is an example of a program that utilizes a combination of techniques that are founded in both the compensatory and restorative models (Eack et al., 2009; Hogarty, Greenwald, & Eack, 2006). CET is an integrative approach in that it attempts to restore basic cognitive skills in a step wise fashion through the use of computer drill and practice exercises while at the same time attempting to facilitate higher order cognitive change through compensatory strategies that help patients reduce the amount of cognitive effort expended. Reducing cognitive effort or, in other words, teaching more efficient processing is accomplished through using strategies such as perspective taking and "gistful" thinking as patients are provided with new experiential opportunities. Typically, basic cognitive skills are initially targeted, followed by higher order cognition with particular emphasis on social cognition.

In summary, restorative and compensatory approaches are two conceptual models that inform different cognitive remediation programs. Some programs exclusively use one or another approach (Fisher et al., 2009; Velligan et al., 2002) but many use a combination of techniques that reflect both approaches (Medalia et al., 2009; Hogarty et al., 2006). There is no evidence that one approach is more efficacious than another across inpatient and outpatient settings, although when any cognitive remediation program is provided within the context of a broader psychosocial rehabilitation program the impact on functional outcome is significantly better (McGurk et al., 2007; Wykes et al., 2011).

SPECIFIC APPROACHES TO COGNITIVE REMEDIATION

Computer Assisted Cognitive Remediation

Although there are a few programs that exclusively use paper and pencil tasks and verbal discussion, most CR programs utilize computers. The majority of computer-based CR programs use a designated software package that targets either one or multiple cognitive skills. This practice has the potential disadvantage of ignoring the ever-increasing array of software and web based activities being developed to treat cognition. An alternative to using designated prepackaged software programs is to have a method for analyzing all computer-based exercises. As new programs become available it is possible to assess whether and how they may be suitable for cognitive remediation. It is conceivable, for example, that a software exercise provides an excellent drill and practice of working memory, but is so unappealing to the user that they refuse to engage in the activity. Or, an activity may purport to target one skill but in fact target several others as well. Medalia et al. (2009) developed a rubric for evaluating software exercises that takes into account not only the cognitive skill being targeted but also the range of difficulty level, the goal properties of the task and the degree to which motivational elements are incorporated into the exercise. This system of task analysis, which can be used to evaluate any computer based cognitive exercise, begins with a consideration of five critical components referred to as the 5 Cs: cognitive, client, computer, context, and choice (see Table 12.2). The first area of focus is the cognitive deficits that can be addressed by a particular program, and the evidence of the efficacy of the program to provide cognitive enhancement. It is important to note that many of the programs place multiple simultaneous cognitive demands on the individual and that these are not always sequential or isolated but rather overlapping. When exploring and analyzing software, one must carefully reflect on which cognitive processes are being engaged. The second "C" refers to client variables that should be considered when selecting software, for example, client's level of cognitive functioning, capacity for engaging in proximal versus distal goal pursuits, particular interests, frustration tolerance, and relevance to the individual's treatment goals. "Computer" refers to practical aspects of compatibility of the software requirements and hardware. Increasingly, exercises are becoming web based and require web connectivity. The capacity for computer based monitoring of progress is also a variable to consider. The fourth and fifth "Cs" refer to motivationally enhancing elements. "Context" is the extent to which the activity utilizes the motivationally enhancing technique of contextualization. For example, is the activity contextualized as a real world activity like remembering shopping items or sorting objects in a file cabinet? Finally, "Choice" refers to the amount of learner control in the software, since the more control or adaptability of the program by the learner, the more motivating the exercise will be.

Rubrics for cognitive task analysis provide a tool for systematic consideration of the features of computer based cognitive activities, and also allow for

TABLE 12.2 How to Evaluate Software for Cognitive Remediation

Factors	Considerations	Examples
Cognitive	What specific cognitive deficits are targeted? How proximal is the task goal and how much working memory is needed to hold the goal in mind?	Attention, memory, auditory processing, problem solving Distal goal requires large working memory capacity.
Client	What individual client characteristics play a role in ability to do the task?	Frustration tolerance, motivation, level of deficit, learning style
Computer	Is software compatible with available equipment?	Hardware issues, Internet access, performance tracking
Context	Is the exercise contextualized in a real world activity?	Memory task consists of remembering items on grocery list
Choice	How much choice and control does the software offer the player?	Patient can control difficulty level or can choose features like a timer

Adapted from the 5Cs of evaluating software (Medalia et al., 2009)

some standardization of the task analysis. This enables better comparisons of the activities, which facilitates the task of determining which software to use for particular patients and settings.

Individual Versus Group Treatment

CR programs vary depending on whether they work with individuals or groups. The CRT program which has been researched by Wykes and colleagues (Wykes et al., 2003, Wykes et al., 2007) is an example of an individual based approach. When a group approach is used, there are differences in whether the group does the same activity all together or whether individual participants work independently on an individualized program of exercises. The manualized group program developed by Twamley, Savla, Zurhellen, Heaton, and Jeste (2008) is an example of an effective non computer based program that engages patients in a group activity to work on compensatory strategies to improve cognitive functioning. In this 12-week, two hour per week program, patients are first introduced to strategies targeting the domains of prospective memory, attention and vigilance, learning and memory, and executive functioning. They then receive assistance in planning how to use the strategies in their everyday lives. Two different group approaches are used in the NEAR program (Medalia et al., 2009), where patients meet in a group but work at an individual pace on computerized cognitive exercises, and also meet for the more traditional group activity where everyone works on the same task. These later groups are called "Bridging groups" because all participants work together on exercises that bridge their individual activities to everyday tasks.

Bridging groups offer an important opportunity for generalization to occur. Through discussion of real world experiences group leaders can assist in fostering the transfer of skills from the cognitive exercise to real life. People can share their experiences with each other and apply meta-cognitive skills to their experiences. Furthermore, groups are often comprised of individuals who are functioning and progressing at different levels, which allows for some individuals to serve as mentors or role models while at the same time allowing others to benefit from the experience of more seasoned group members.

Group work provides patients with a forum for discussion about learning, a way to share learning experiences, to hear the learning experiences of other patients and practice applying cognitive skills. Especially for patients with severe and persistent mental illness and accompanying cognitive deficits, intangible benefits like these can make a difference in humanizing cognitive remediation treatment so that treatment is more easily tolerated, patients come to treatment more frequently, stay in treatment longer and ultimately learn more effectively. Finally, group based cognitive remediation programs create a physical space where patients gather weekly. This regularly scheduled assembly creates its own kind of community among patients who may otherwise be living in relative social isolation due to symptoms of their illness. The group therapeutic milieu hopefully provides patients with a sense of safety and support instead of fear or embarrassment. Learning with peers who suffer from illnesses of a similar magnitude or severity level, also helps patients see how their peers struggle with and address some of the same or related issues involved in the process of rehabilitation and recovery.

While groups offer the benefit of social facilitation, not all patients are able to tolerate the group experience. One benefit to providing individualized CR is that a more intensive therapeutic alliance may be possible in this setting. By first fostering trust in the context of a dyadic relationship, the patient may then develop the internal emotional controls to tolerate group membership. Individual work is however rarely consistent with the model of care used in many clinic settings in the United States. Providing CR in a group format is cost and time effective. Several clients can be seen simultaneously (2–8 persons) with relatively low staffing levels (1–2 persons). This allows for maximum utilization of specially trained clinical staff. There is evidence that the level of clinician training has an impact on the effectiveness of CR (Medalia & Richardson, 2005), whereby clients in groups run by clinicians with graduate training in mental health show greater response than clients in groups run by less well trained clinicians. By providing CR in a group, one can offer many patients at the same time the benefit of a highly trained professional.

Some programs, such as NEAR, attempt to capitalize on the benefits of both the individual and group processes. Although CR is provided in a group format, individuals are allowed to progress through the exercises based on their individual level of impairment and improvement. Furthermore patients are encouraged in NEAR to utilize programs that are in concert with their own area of interest.

BEHAVIORAL LEARNING TECHNIQUES

The influence of learning theory on CR approaches is evident in the use of such techniques as positive reinforcement, shaping, prompting, modeling and errorless learning. It is believed that people with schizophrenia have relatively intact implicit learning processes (Danion, Meulemans, Kauffmann-Muller, & Vermaat, 2001). Implicit learning refers to unconscious learning or learning without awareness. It is learning that occurs without conscious effort, usually in response to the environment around us. An example of implicit or procedural memory compared to explicit or declarative memory may be useful to help understand implicit learning. Explicit or declarative memory is intentional recall of previously learned information, such as remembering the capitals of each state or the zip code of your home. In contrast, procedural or implicit memory is memory for responses which we are often unaware of and which are usually in response to something in the environment based on previous experience such as riding a bike or writing. Many approaches to CR attempt to capitalize on the idea that implicit learning appears relatively intact in schizophrenia, by using specific techniques to enhance this process and promote improved cognitive functioning.

Shaping refers to the technique of providing reinforcements for successive approximations of a desired behavior. Through reinforcing the behavior we increase its likelihood of occurring and thus "shape" it toward our desired outcome. Prompting is the technique of providing individuals with a cue or reminder to perform a desired activity and modeling is demonstrating directly a desired behavior in an effort to increase learning.

Silverstein et al. (2009) conducted a multi-site study that utilized a reward based learning method that was based on operant conditioning. By using consequences to teach and modify behavior, they sought to improve attentiveness and functioning in a chronic schizophrenia population. The investigators utilized a group approach where patients who participated in a conversational skills training group received reinforcement for successive approximations of desired attentive behaviors. They utilized individualized reinforcement schedules based on the specific goals of the individual client. The results indicated that attention shaping did have a positive effect on improving patients' attentional abilities as well as improving skill acquisition. That is, compared to the control group who received skills training without attention shaping, the attention shaping group not only learned to attend better but also appeared to display increased learning in terms of conversational skills.

Errorless learning (EL) is a technique that attempts to improve learning by providing a learning experience that minimizes errors. It refers to the careful titration of difficulty level so that the client learns without resorting to trial and error, and has a positive experience with increasing challenge. The client is started at a level that is believed to be easy enough to guarantee success, and then the level of difficulty is slowly increased. The work by Kern et al. (2009) has demonstrated that individuals who received community based vocational training based on principles of errorless learning displayed significant improvement in quality of work performance as compared to the group who received traditional training only. Because of this research, errorless learning is increasingly being incorporated into a number of CR programs.

Techniques to Promote Generalization of Learning

Another distinction between programs is whether they exclusively focus on neuroscience-based drill and practice programs assumed to reactivate and restore specific brain regions, or whether they additionally provide bridging activities to translate neuropsychological gains into real-world change. Bridging is a technique that promotes generalization by making explicit connections between the cognitive skills acquired during sessions and the application of these skills in everyday life (Medalia et al., 2009). Group discussions promote bridging by encouraging patients to talk about the ways in which the skills they are using to complete the software exercises are relevant to daily life. This may be supplemented by in vivo work with a coach, who accompanies the patient into the community to observe and guide application of cognitive skills to everyday tasks.

Techniques to Promote Motivation to Learn

Since cognitive remediation involves learning to remember, pay attention, problem solve, and more generally learn to efficiently use cognitive skills to negotiate daily living, therapeutic approaches should optimally incorporate a consideration of how people learn. Further, to the extent that the programs are designed for people at different levels of development, these learning principles need to be specific to adult learners, or children, or the elderly. Educational psychology has made significant contributions to understanding the factors that play a role in an individual's capacity to learn. Although it was once believed that ability to learn was in direct correlation with intellectual functioning, it is now well understood that learning is a function of a multitude of factors with IQ being just one (Cronbach & Snow, 1977; Schunk, 2001; Schunk & Zimmerman, 2008). In particular, instructional style and motivation have been identified as salient factors that impact the learning process (Choi & Medalia, 2009; Cordova & Lepper, 1996). By considering the factors that mediate learning, it becomes possible to maximize the benefits of CR.

Motivation has long been recognized as a key predictor of learning in students enrolled in formal education programs. Research with students has shown that they learn the most, learn the fastest, and retain knowledge the longest when they are excited and motivated for the pleasure of learning, exploring, seeking challenge and testing their abilities (Deci & Ryan, 2008; Wigfield & Eccles, 2002, Zimmerman & Schunk, 2004). This type of excitement about learning is called intrinsic motivation and it has consistently been associated with greater learning outcomes. Without apparent need for external or extrinsic rewards, persuasion or pressure, intrinsically motivated individuals find performance of the task rewarding in and of itself.

Motivation is increasingly appreciated as playing a significant role in the learning process of people with schizophrenia who participate in cognitive remediation. Apathy, anhedonia, and avolition are frequent symptoms in schizophrenia. These motivational problems can compromise engagement in treatment in general and can compromise engagement in learning activities (Medalia & Richardson, 2005). Motivated patients are more likely to complete the tasks within a specified therapeutic time period rather than become disengaged and at risk for attrition and/or insufficient treatment intensity (Choi & Medalia, 2005). Furthermore, motivated patients seem to benefit more from the treatment , i.e., they make greater cognitive improvement (Choi & Medalia, 2009).

Given the role that motivation plays in treatment outcome, it is important to consider how best to teach neurocognitive skills to people whose illness can lead to a lack of motivation and insight. Since participants are not always intrinsically motivated when they enroll in cognitive remediation programs, it is important for clinicians to know that intrinsic motivation can be manipulated by applying certain instructional techniques, and that when these techniques are used, learning outcomes are increased. There is now evidence that people with schizophrenia respond to some of the same instructional techniques known to enhance intrinsic motivation in healthy students (Choi & Medalia, 2009). The adaptable nature of intrinsic motivational processes in schizophrenia provides a platform from which to design effective cognitive remediation programs to enhance not only cognition but functional outcome.

One way to promote intrinsic motivation and task engagement is to use tasks that are contextualized, personalized and allow for learner control (Cordova & Lepper, 1996). Contextualization means that rather than presenting material in the abstract, information is instead put in a context whereby the practical utility and link to everyday life activities are obvious to the patient. Personalization refers to the tailoring of a learning activity to coincide with topics of high interest value for the patient. Learner control can be gained by offering the patient the opportunity to choose from among a forced-choice menu of activities. For example, a person exerts control over a learning situation when they chose auditory over visual presentation, or when they chose the difficulty level. Incorporating opportunities for personalization, learner control and contextualization of the activity are just a few of the techniques that can be used to enhance motivation to learn. Motivational systems are responsive to a number of parameters in the environmental learning milieu, giving cognitive remediation programs an opportunity to address motivational deficits at multiple levels (Medalia & Choi, 2009).

ASSESSMENT APPROACHES IN COGNITIVE REMEDIATION

Cognitive impairments are prevalent, persistent and evident at every stage of the illness, as such, all patients, regardless of disease chronicity and age, should be considered candidates for CR. Ideally, all patients should be referred to CR therapy if there is evidence that cognitive deficits are interfering with functional outcome. Once referred, an assessment will facilitate development of a treatment plan. While not essential to starting a course of cognitive remediation, especially given the increasing array of web based remediation packages that allow choice of exercises based on subjective complaints (e.g., POSIT, Scientific Brain Training Pro, Lumosity, Brain Fitness, etc.), neuropsychological assessments are extremely useful because they allow for a more finely tuned approach to treatment planning and give a baseline measure against which to compare post-treatment outcome. Assessments can be done in two ways: (a) psychometric measures administered by a trained professional and (b) computer administered software or web-based assessment packages. The type of neuropsychological assessment available will likely depend, in part, on the level and qualifications of the staff available, program structure and financial resources. Computerized assessments validated in schizophrenia samples, such as those from Cambridge Cognition Ltd. Cantab (www.camcog.com), are designed for use in research trials, while clinician administered assessments were designed for both clinical and research use. When formal cognitive testing is available, brief 30–45-minute assessments, like the Brief Assessment of Cognition in Schizophrenia (BACS) or the MATRICS Consensus Cognitive Battery (MCCB), would identify whether CR is indicated, and what aspects of cognition should be targeted. These shorter assessment protocols have been shown to lead to higher completion rates and fewer missing data (Keefe et al., 2004) than long neuropsychological test batteries. Furthermore, research has suggested that, in schizophrenia, a brief neuropsychological assessment battery can more reliably predict performance than the longer traditional neuropsychological assessment battery (Keefe et al., 2004). For these reasons, the brief neuropsychological test batteries that were developed specifically for use in assessing cognition in schizophrenia are recommended for use whenever possible.

However, there are several issues to consider when providing formal neuropsychological assessments. Formal testing is often not available and/or affordable, and it can be time-consuming especially in programs that are structured to be exclusively group based. Furthermore, while the BACS and MCCB can be administered by trained non psychologists, interpretation of the results and development of a personalized treatment plan requires training in neuropsychology. Formal testing can sometimes be anxiety provoking for the patient and may hinder or prevent participation in a CR program, unless it is done in a way that engages the patient. Patients who are sensitive to being judged may prefer to have assessments done by someone other than the CR therapist, or they may prefer to wait to take the assessment until they have participated in several sessions, and understand why they need an assessment.

Informal assessments can combine brief measures, interviews, self-report questionnaires and team feedback. It is a fluid process based on observations and reactions over time, with the aim of identifying areas of strength and weakness so as to inform potential treatment strategies. Assessments typically include a determination of reading level, which is important not only to gauge appropriateness of materials used in the treatment, but because reading level is highly correlated with intellectual level and may give clues to learning potential. Attention and concentration should also be assessed with a brief measure and/or through naturalistic observations of the individual's ability to stay on task. A problem-solving exercise can be given to provide some assessment of critical thinking and preferred learning style. Interviews with patients as well as significant others can be extremely valuable. Unfortunately, because about half of the people with schizophrenia have significant cognitive impairments but are not aware of them, it is ill advised to only rely on a patient's self-report (Medalia & Thysen, 2008). A careful interview designed to uncover problems following schedules, sustaining attention, or following instructions can also be useful.

Whether a standardized or more informal assessment is used, some assessment is needed to guide the treatment process. Once the assessment is completed, patients typically want an opportunity to review results and discuss concerns and questions. This can facilitate their engagement in the treatment process and increase their commitment to improving their cognitive skills.

EFFICACY OF COGNITIVE REMEDIATION

Numerous randomized controlled trials of a variety of CR techniques have been performed in both laboratory and clinical settings around the world. Most of these studies have been comprised of people who have cognitive deficits secondary to psychotic disorders, such as schizophrenia. These studies have been reviewed in several meta-analyses that, while differing in focus, have generally showed moderate to large effect sizes (Krabbendam & Aleman, 2003; Kurtz et al., 2001; McGurk et al., 2007; Twamley et al., 2003; Wykes et al., 2011). For example, the 2007 meta-analysis done by McGurk and colleagues, which included data from 26 randomized controlled trials of CR in schizophrenia including 1,151 patients, found moderate effect sizes for impact on both cognition and psycho-social functioning. These findings were confirmed in the 2011 meta-analysis by Wykes et al., which evaluated 109 reports of 40 randomized trials of CR that enrolled over 2,100 schizophrenia patients. Despite variability in methodological rigor, trial methodology did not moderate any of the therapy effects, leading the authors to conclude that the benefits of cognitive remediation reported in the reviewed research cannot be attributed to poor study methods.

As can be seen in Figure 12.1, the effect sizes vary in accordance with the goals of treatment. When the studies had a highly proximal goal of improvement on a training task, the effect size was large. When the goals of training became more distal and accordingly affected by a multiplicity of variables, the effect sizes diminished. Still, moderate range effect sizes were found both for CR studies that used neuropsychological test results as an outcome measure, and for the studies with the most distal goal of improving daily functioning.

It is also of interest to know which cognitive functions are best impacted by cognitive remediation. In the meta-analyses by McGurk et al. (2007) and

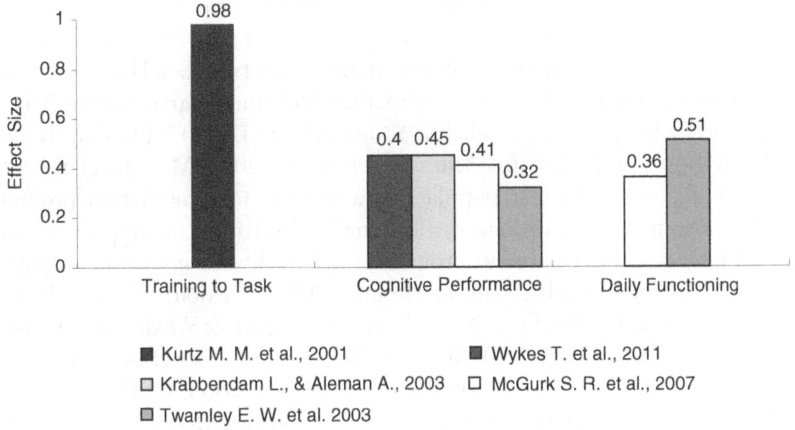

Figure 12.1 Meta-analyses of cognitive remediation outcomes

Wykes et al (2011), the results indicated a medium range effect size for overall cognition (0.41–.45), and low medium to medium effect sizes for other domains of cognitive performance. The six domains which demonstrated significant improvement following CR were: attention/vigilance, speed of processing, verbal working memory, visual learning and memory, reasoning/problem solving, and social cognition (McGurk et al., 2007; Wykes et al., 2011). The effect size for visual learning and memory was not significant in either the McGurk et al. (2007) or Wykes et al. (2011) meta-analyses. These results provide strong support for the effects of cognitive remediation on improving the cognitive functioning in schizophrenia. The results are particularly impressive in light of the fact that robust improvements were demonstrated across studies which included a variety of program and patient conditions.

The effects of CR on psychosocial functioning are extremely important since the ultimate goal of almost all psychiatric interventions is to improve overall functioning and quality of life. Psychosocial functioning includes such abilities as caring for one's needs on a daily basis, managing independent living, obtaining and sustaining employment and engaging in and enjoying interpersonal relationships. Three meta-analytic reviews provide strong evidence of the ecological validity of CR. Twamley et al. (2003) conducted a meta-analysis on 17 randomized controlled studies of CR which included investigation of the effects of CR on psychosocial functioning. The studies included varied greatly in terms of setting, patient population, and duration and type of intervention. Patients who received CR displayed significant improvements in everyday functioning (effect size of 0. 51). In the McGurk et al. (2007) and Wykes et al, (2011) meta-analyses, it was also found that CR had a significant effect on improving psychosocial functioning (average effect size of 0.35). Compared to controls, individuals who participated in CR displayed greater improvement in obtaining and working competitive jobs, the quality of and satisfaction with interpersonal relationships and the ability to solve interpersonal problems.

Taken together, the studies on efficacy of CR inform us that remediation effects on cognition are of moderate size, persist up to 8 months after CR stops, and that the cognitive gains generalize to improvements in social behaviors, real-world problem-solving ability, and occupational outcome, particularly when CR is combined with psychiatric rehabilitation (Bell et al., 2007; Fiszdon, Bryson, Wexler, & Bell, 2004; McGurk, Mueser, & Pascaris, 2005; Medalia et al., 2002; Wykes et al., 2011). Patient populations amenable to remediation programs include those in acute care and institutionalized settings, in supportive housing and intensive day treatment programs, and to those who are in outpatient treatment (Bellucci, Glaberman, & Haslam, 2003; Fiszdon, Whelan, Bryson, Wexler, & Bell, 2005; Kurtz, Seltzer, Fujimoto, Shagan, & Wexler, 2009; Medalia, Dorn, & Watras Gans 2000; Medalia, Revheim, & Casey, 2002; Medalia et al., 2003; Medalia & Revheim, 2002; Silverstein et al., 2009; Wykes et al, 2007).

Findings from randomized controlled trials indicate that integration of CR with other psychiatric rehabilitation interventions, such as supported employment and social-skills training, is more effective than isolated CR approaches in achieving overall psychiatric rehabilitation (Bell et al., 2007; Greig, Zito, Wexler, Fiszdon, & Bell, 2007; Spaulding, Reed, Sullivan, Richardson, & Weiler, 1999; Wexler & Bell, 2005; Wykes et al., 2011). Patients in work therapy programs that incorporated CR maintained greater vocational benefits (more likely to work, worked longer, and earned more) even at 3-year follow-up than did those who received work therapy alone (McGurk et al., 2007). This suggests that CR may enable individuals to more effectively participate in and benefit from other forms of rehabilitative efforts such as vocational training and social skills training.

PREDICTORS OF POSITIVE RESPONSE

Although the majority of research and results from meta-analytic studies indicate that CR is efficacious there is great variability in response in response to this treatment. Multiple factors come into play when discussing response to treatment and investigators have begun to examine what factors may moderate outcome in CR (Choi & Medalia 2005; Fiszdon, Choi, Bryson, & Bell, 2006; Kurtz et al., 2009; Medalia & Richardson 2005). There is interest in defining the issues that potentially affect the success of CR programs, as the efficacy of a treatment largely depends on the appropriate selection of individuals and treatment modalities which can demonstrate the most gains. Treatment controlled studies of the efficacy of CR provide important information about the impact of the intervention on a group of individuals, however, group data often obscures information about individual response. In any group of individuals exposed to a treatment some may have a largely positive response while others may have no response at all. The question then arises: What was different about the patients and the treatment experience for those who showed a treatment response? A delineation of those factors can elucidate the mechanisms of a positive treatment outcome.

Fiszdon et al. (2006) examined the impact of intellectual status on response to CR. The authors examined the role of the neurodevelopmental schema of Weickert and colleagues (2000) in predicting response to a 6-month course of CR. The authors divided subjects into three distinct subgroups based on the pattern of change in cognitive functioning since the onset of illness: patients whose intellectual functioning did not change from premorbid levels (intellectually preserved group), patients whose cognitive functioning declined after onset of the disorder (intellectually deteriorated group), and those with consistently low intellectual functioning (intellectually compromised group). They found that response to CR differed by intellectual group. Participants classified as having preserved or deteriorated intellect who received CR displayed significantly greater improvement from pre to post neuropsychological test performance compared to those who did not receive CR. Participants classified as premorbidly intellectually compromised were able to improve on the training tasks but did not display significantly higher pre-post improvement on neuropsychological tests following CR compared to those who did not receive

CR. These results suggest that level of premorbid intellect does play a role in response to CR. Those with compromised intellect did not benefit meaningfully from CR while those with higher premorbid intelligence had greater success with generalization of training.

Level of cognitive impairment is also an obvious candidate to consider when predicting success of CR. Fiszdon et al. (2005) found that measures of vigilance and immediate verbal memory at intake were predictive of cognitive remediation outcomes and were also strong predictors of success on a trained memory task. Kurtz et al (2009) examined which neurocognitive variables would predict change in everyday life skills following cognitive remediation and they found that auditory attention and working memory predicted a significant amount of the variance in change scores. Medalia and Richardson (2005) found that to a small extent the baseline level of cognitive skill was also relevant to treatment outcomes. The majority of analyses of the baseline cognitive data did not reveal them to be important but there was a cluster of results that indicated that for the most cognitively disorganized chronic patients, especially those hospitalized for more than two years and with earlier onset, a brief course of treatment was not sufficient.

Motivation, which was discussed earlier, has been investigated as a potential moderator of CR outcome. Medalia and Richardson (2005) used voluntary attendance rate as a measure of motivation. They found that individuals who had better attendance were far more likely to display improvement following CR. Choi and Medalia (2005) utilized the same measure of motivation with similar results. Furthermore, the authors propose that motivation and treatment intensity are intertwined to create an environment that improves the chances of success. Fiszdon et al. (2005) also found motivation, as measured by a cooperative attitude, was predictive of a positive response to CR. A study by Choi and Medalia (2009), which directly manipulated the engaging qualities of the cognitive exercises, found that when cognitive remediation exercises included motivationally enhancing features, clients became more motivated and showed significantly better cognitive and functional outcomes.

Other client characteristics have been investigated as moderators of CR outcome. Wykes et al. (2011) concluded that cognitive remediation was more effective when patients were clinically stable; symptoms did not prevent improvements in cognition, but at high levels the effect size was modest. There is little evidence from the meta-analytic studies (McGurk et al., 2007; Wykes et al., 2011) to suggest that age of the client moderates treatment response, although the limited diversity of age in the controlled randomized trials might mask adequate assessment of this variable.

Treatment intensity has been considered as a factor that might impact effectiveness of CR interventions. Common sense would assume that increased exposure to an intervention would result in increased improvements. However, the limited evidence to date does not support this. CR sessions are typically held two to three times a week with ranges between one and ten hours a week. Active treatment typically lasts three to six months, but can range from several weeks to two years, depending on the treatment setting, goals, and/or severity of deficits. The meta-analysis by Krabbendam and Aleman (2003) found the duration of treatment did not have an influence on effect size. Similarly, the meta-analyses conducted by McGurk et al. (2007) and Wykes et al. (2011) found that the number of program hours spent in CR was not related to overall cognitive improvement. The studies included in these meta-analyses varied greatly in terms of training method and duration of training. The authors suggested that it may be possible that even a relatively moderate amount of CR may produce significant immediate improvement.

One consideration is that the effects of intensity on outcome cannot be compared across different CR approaches since a variety of factors may vary with each approach. Choi and Medalia (2005) found that less than twice a week is insufficient to lead to cognitive and functional improvement for people attending the NEAR CR program. In contrast, Roder, Mueller, Mueser, and Brenner (2006) reported that treatment intensity was not significantly related to outcome of IPT therapy. It is likely that level of intensity is involved in a reciprocal relationship with several additional variables such as level of motivation. In a clinic setting where, unlike the research settings, CR participants pay as opposed to being paid to participate, attendance at sessions requires motivation. If treatment intensity is important for a positive outcome, then it is all the more reason for treatments to actively engage participants so that they are motivated to attend.

Finally, there has been some effort to examine the role of treatment variables in response to CR. While there is no consensus on who is qualified to serve as a CR clinician and in community clinic settings there is in fact considerable diversity in credentialing practices, level of clinician training appears to be an important and complex aspect. Medalia and Richardson (2005) found that level of clinician training was a significant predictor of improvement in NEAR programs. Patients were more likely to display improvement if they worked with a clinician with more graduate level training in mental health. They hypothesized that a more highly trained therapist may be more adept at recognizing the subtler aspects of cognitive deficits and therefore may address them in a more effective manner. Furthermore, highly trained clinicians have invested more effort in their careers and may have more intrinsic motivation and commitment themselves to provide effective treatment. This in turn might influence outcome, just as the motivation of teachers has been shown to impact learning outcomes in students (Schunk & Zimmerman, 2008).

Another treatment related variable that has been shown to impact outcome concerns the framework of the CR program. CR programs vary in the extent to which they narrowly define their scope, with some making explicit links to broader rehabilitation goals, and others more narrowly focusing on cognition as it impacts neuropsychological test performance. In the meta-analyses by McGurk et al. (2007) and Wykes et al. (2011), it was shown that CR was more successful with greater functional outcomes, when provided in conjunction with psychiatric rehabilitative programs. For example, effect sizes of CR were higher when the CR was linked with supportive employment and participants who attended both programs had better vocational outcomes (Bell et al., 2007). This would argue for the implementation of CR programs within the context of broader rehabilitation and skills based interventions so that it is possible to integrate the goals of CR with overall rehabilitation goals (Anthony, 2008). Rehabilitation programs focus on skills development and seek to give patients the tools to function adaptively and independently in society. Patients can more readily understand the need for CR if they link the benefits of improved cognition with attainment of their recovery goals.

SUMMARY

Cognitive remediation is a behavioral treatment which is used to target the neuro-cognitive impairments that are associated with schizophrenia and schizoaffective disorder. While the immediate goal of CR is to improve neurocognitive functioning, the ultimate goal is to improve functioning in daily tasks, including school, work, social interactions, and independent living. A large literature on the efficacy of cognitive remediation indicates that moderate effect sizes can be expected and that remediation effects persist up to eight months after treatment stops. The cognitive gains generalize to improvements in social behaviors, real-world problem-solving ability, and occupational outcome. Multisite clinical implementation trials done around the world (Hodge et al., 2008; Roder et al., 2006) indicate that CR can be successfully implemented in community settings. While many questions remain about dosing, the relative merits of instructional techniques, the value of booster sessions and bridging groups, and the profiles of patients who respond best, there is convincing evidence that cognitive remediation can offer substantial and lasting benefits for the cognitive deficits seen in schizophrenia.

Case Vignette

Anthony is a 25-year-old, single, unemployed man who lives with his parents and younger siblings. He was first treated as an outpatient at the age of 18, when he was a freshman in college, at which point he was diagnosed with schizophrenia. Because he often did not make it to class and had difficulty organizing and completing assignments, he left college after his first year. He was able to remain in the community under the supportive, but constant, supervision of his family who secured him sporadic manual jobs in family businesses. Even when stable on medication, Anthony's level of functioning was significantly impaired, with poor ADLs and marked social withdrawal. He was first hospitalized at the age of 21.

Following three brief acute hospitalizations for medication nonadherence, Anthony presented to an intermediate stay county facility which offered him CR in the context of a rehabilitative model that included pharmacotherapy, recreational and vocational services, psychoeducation, and family education and therapy. The treatment team, which included Anthony and his parents, worked together to establish the treatment goals. Anthony very much wanted to return to work and eventually school, and wanted to return to live with his family.

Education on CR was provided to Anthony, his family, and the treatment team members who were not as familiar with CR. As part of the education, everyone received a copy of the handbook, *Dealing with Cognitive Dysfunction in the Psychiatric Disorders, A Handbook for Family and Friends* (Medalia & Revheim, 2002). It was clear from discussions with Anthony and his family, as well as staff reports, that Anthony was experiencing cognitive impairments. Interestingly, Anthony was quite aware of how his problems with memory and attention were interfering with his functioning. A computer-based neuropsychological assessment battery (Mindstream's Neurotrax Schizophrenia Assessment Battery) found Anthony was most impaired on measures of memory and information processing speed. Using the NEAR framework of CR (Medalia et al., 2009), computer based cognitive training exercises were selected based on the areas of deficit in addition to considering Anthony's interests and motivation. Anthony was scheduled for twice weekly one hour sessions of CR during his three month hospitalization. He appeared to enjoy the CR sessions from the start and was often noted in the bridging discussions to make comments such as "this really helps me to think better and my reaction time is much better." Anthony's attendance to groups, other than CR, began to improve, as did his overall functioning. Anthony was discharged home to his family with partial day programming. On discharge, neuropsychological testing was repeated and Anthony displayed some improvement on measures of information processing speed, attention, and executive functioning, however, memory remained unchanged. The most significant improvement noted was on information processing speed where Anthony's score went from 79. 8 (1 SD below normal range of functioning) to 87.9 (which falls within normal range of functioning). Obviously, with so many active ingredients of treatment being supplied simultaneously it is difficult to tease out the sole effect of one. However, Anthony's story demonstrates that within an intermediate inpatient setting, CR is feasible and that clients and their families are quite receptive to this approach.

REFERENCES

Anthony, W. A. (2008). Cognitive remediation and psychiatric rehabilitation. *Journal of Psychiatric Rehabilitation, 32*, 87–88.

Bell, M. D., Fiszdon, J. M., Greig, T., Wexler, B. W., & Bryson, G. (2007a). Neurocognitive enhancement therapy with work therapy in schizophrenia: A six month follow-up of neuropsychological performance. *Journal of Rehabilitation Research and Development 44*, 761–770.

Bellucci, D. M., Glaberman, K., & Haslam, N. (2003). Computer-assisted cognitive rehabilitation reduces negative symptoms in the severely mentally ill. *Schizophrenia Research, 59*, 225–232.

Bruel-Jungerman, E., & Larochre, D. S. (2007). Brain plasticity mechanisms and memory: A part of four. *Neuroscientist, 13,* 492–505.

Choi, J., & Medalia, A. (2005). Factors associated with a positive response to cognitive remediation in a community psychiatric sample. *Psychiatric Services, 56,* 602–224.

Choi, J. ,& Medalia, A. (2009). Intrinsic Motivation and Learning in a Schizophrenia Spectrum Sample. *Schizophrenia Research, 118*(1), 12–19.

Cordova, D. I., & Lepper, M. R. (1996). Intrinsic motivation and the process of learning: Beneficial effects of contextualization, personalization, and choice. *Journal of Educational Psychology, 88,* 715–730.

Cronbach, L. J., & Snow, R. E. (1977). *Aptitudes and instructional methods.* New York: Irvington/Naiburg.

Danion, J. M., Meulemans, T., Kauffmann-Muller, F., & Vermaat, H. (2001). Intact implicit learning in schizophrenia. *American Journal of Psychiatry, 158,* 944–948.

Deci, E. L., & Ryan, R. M. (2008). Facilitating optimal motivation and psychological well- being across life's domains. *Canadian Psychology/Psychologie Canadienne, 49,* 14–23.

Diller L. (1993). An introduction to cognitive rehabilitation.In C. B. Royeen (Ed.), *AOTA self-study series: Cognitive rehabilitation* (pp. 7–19). Rockville, MD: American Occupational Therapy Association.

Dirette, D. K., Jinojosa, J., & Carnevale, G. J. (1999) Comparison of remedial and compensatory interventions for adults with acquired brain injuries. *Journal Head Trauma Rehabilitation, 14,* 595–601.

Doidge, N. (2007). *The brain that changes itself: Stories of personal triumph from the frontiers of brain science.* New York: Penguin Group.

Eack, S. M., Greenwald, D. P., Hogarty, S. S., Cooley, S. J., DiBarry, A. L., Montrose, D. M., et al. (2009). Cognitive enhancement therapy for early course schizophrenia: effects of a two-year randomized control trial. *Psychiatric Services, 60,* 1468–1476.

Fisher, M., Holland, C., Merzenich, M., & Vinogradov, S. (2009). Using neuroplasticity-based auditory training to improve verbal memory in schizophrenia. *American Journal of Psychiatry, 166* (7), 805–811.

Fiszdon, J. M., Bryson, G. J., Wexler, B. E., & Bell, M. D. (2004). Durability of cognitive remediation training in schizophrenia: performance on two memory tasks at 6-month and 12-month follow-up. *Psychiatry Research, 125,* 1–7.

Fiszdon, J. M., Whelan, H., Bryson, G. J., Wexler, B. E., & Bell, M. D. (2005). Cognitive training of verbal memory using a dichotic listening paradigm: impact on symptoms and cognition. *Acta Psychiatrica Scandinavica, 112,* 187–193.

Fiszdon, J. M., Choi, J., Bryson, G. J., & Bell, M. D. (2006). Impact of intellectual status on response to cognitive task training in patients with schizophrenia. *Schizophrenia Research, 87,* 261–269.

Green, M. F. (1996). What are the functional consequences of neurocognitive deficits in schizophrenia? *American Journal of Psychiatry, 153,* 321–330.

Greig, T. C., Zito, W., Wexler, B. E., Fiszdon, J., & Bell, M. D. (2007). Improved cognitive function in schizophrenia after one year of cognitive training and vocational services. *Schizophrenia Research, 96,* 156–161.

Heinrichs, R. W., Goldberg, J. O., Miles, A. A., & McDermid, V. S. (2008). Predictors of medication competence in schizophrenia patients. *Psychiatry Research, 157,* 47–52.

Hodge, H. R., Siciliano, D., Whithey, P., Moss, B., Judd, G., Shores, E. A., et al. (2008).

A randomized controlled trial of cognitive remediation in schizophrenia. *Schizophrenia Bulletin*, doi:10.1093/schbul/sbn102.

Hogarty, G. E., Greenwald, D. P., & Eack, S. M. (2006). Durability and mechanism of effects of cognitive enhancement therapy. *Psychiatric Services, 57*, 1751–1757.

Jeste, S. D., Patterson, T. L., Palmer, B. W., Dolder, C. R., Goldman, S., Jeste, D. V. (2003). Cognitive predictors of medication adherence among middle-aged and older outpatients with schizophrenia. *Schizophrenia Research, 63*, 49–58.

Keefe R. S,, & Fenton, W. S. (2007) How should DSM-V criteria for schizophrenia include cognitive impairment? *Schizophrenia Bulletin, 33*, 912–920.

Keefe, R. S., Goldberg, T. E., Harvey, P. D., Gold, J. M., Poe, M. P., & Coughenour, L. (2004). The brief assessment of cognition in schizophrenia: reliability, sensitivity, and comparison with a standard neurocognitive battery. *Schizophrenia Research, 68*, 283–297.

Kern, R. S., Liberman, R. P., Becker, D. R., Drake, R. E., Sugar, C. A., & Green, M. F. (2009). Errorless learning for training individuals with schizophrenia at a community mental health setting providing work experience. *Schizophrenia Bulletin, 35*, 807–815.

Krabbendam, L., & Aleman, A. (2003). Cognitive rehabilitation in schizophrenia: A quantitative analysis of controlled studies. *Psychopharmacology, 169*, 376–382.

Kurtz, M. M., Moberg, P. J., Gur, R. C., & Gur, R. E. (2001). Approaches to cognitive remediation of neuropsychological deficits in schizophrenia: a review and meta-analysis. *Neuropsychology Review, 11*, 197–210.

Kurtz, M. M., Moberg, P. J., Gur, R. C., & Gur, R. E. (2004). Results from randomized, controlled trials of the effects of cognitive remediation on neurocognitive deficits in patients with schizophrenia. [comment]. *Psychological Medicine, 34*, 569–570.

Kurtz, M. M., Seltzer, J. C., Fujimoto, M., Shagan, D. S., & Wexler, B .E. (2009). Predictors of change in life skills after cognitive remediation. *Schizophrenia Research, 107* (2-3), 267–274. (Epub 2008 Nov 8.)

Manhncke, H. W., Bronstone, A., & Merzenich, M. M. (2006). Brain plasticity and functional losses in the aged: scientific bases for a novel intervention. *Progress in Brain Research, 157*, 81–109.

McGurk, S. R., Mueser, K. T., & Pascaris, A. (2005). Cognitive training and supported employment for persons with severe mental illness: One-year results from a randomized controlled trial. *Schizophrenia Bulletin, 31*, 898–909.

McGurk, S. R., Twamley, E. W., Sitzer, D. I., McHugo, G. J., & Mueser, K. T. (2007). A meta-analysis of cognitive remediation in schizophrenia. *American Journal of Psychiatry, 164*, 1791–1802.

Medalia, A., Dorn, H., & Watras-Gans, S. (2000). Treating problem-solving deficits on an acute care psychiatric inpatient unit. *Psychiatry Research, 97*, 79–88.

Medalia, A., Revheim, N., & Casey, M. (2002). Remediation of problem-solving skills in schizophrenia: evidence of a persistent effect. *Schizophrenia Research, 57*, 165–171.

Medalia, A., & Revheim, N. (2002). *Dealing with cognitive dysfunction associated with psychiatric disabilities: A handbook for families and friends of individuals with psychiatric disorders.* http://www.omh.state.ny.us/omhweb/cogdys_manual/cog dyshndbk.pdf

Medalia, A., Herlands, T., & Baginsky, C. (2003). Rehab Rounds: cognitive remediation in the supportive housing setting. *Psychiatric Services, 54*, 1219–1220.

Medalia, A., & Richardson, R. (2005). What predicts a good response to cognitive remediation interventions? *Schizophrenia Bulletin, 31*, 942–953.

Medalia, A., & Thysen, J. (2008). Insight into neuro-cognitive dysfunction in Schizophrenia. *Schizophrenia Bulletin, 34,* 1221–1230.

Medalia, A., Revheim, N., & Herlands, T. (2009). *Cognitive remediation for psychological disorders, therapist guide.* New York: Oxford University Press.

Medalia, A., & Choi, J. (2009). The role of motivation and engagement in successful cognitive training with schizophrenia patients. *Schizophrenia Bulletin, 35*(sup. 1), 355.

Roder, V., Mueller, D. R., Mueser, K. T. & Brenner, H. D. (2006). Integrated Psychological Therapy (IPT) for Schizophrenia: Is It Effective? *Schizophrenia Bulletin, 32,* S81–S93.

Schunk, D. H. (2001). *Social cognitive theory and self-regulated learning.* Mahwah, NJ: Erlbaum.

Schunk, D. H., & Zimmerman, B. J. (2008). *Motivation and self-regulated learning: Theory, research, and applications.* Mahwah, NJ: Erlbaum.

Silverstein, S. M., Spaulding, W. D., Menditto, A. A., Savitz, A., Liberman, R. P., Berten, S., et al. (2009). Attention shaping: a reward-based learning method to enhance skills training outcomes in schizophrenia. *Schizophrenia Bulletin, 35,* 222–232.

Spaulding, W. D., Reed, D., Sullivan, M., Richardson, C., & Weiler, M. (1999). Effects of cognitive treatment in psychiatric rehabilitation. *Schizophrenia Bulletin, 25,* 657–676.

Twamley, E. W., Jeste, D. V., & Bellack, A. S. (2003). A review of cognitive training in schizophrenia. *Schizophrenia Bulletin, 29,* 359–382.

Twamley, E. W., Savla, G. N., Zurhellen, C. H., Heaton, R. K., & Jeste, D. V. (2008). Development and pilot testing of a novel compensatory cognitive training intervention for people with psychosis. *American Journal of Psychiatric Rehabilitation, 11,* 144–163.

Velligan, D. I., Bow-Thomas, C. C., Huntzinger, C., Ritch, J., Ledbetter, N., Prihoda, T. J., et al. (2000). Randomized controlled trial of the use of compensatory strategies to enhance adaptive functioning in outpatients with schizophrenia. *American Journal of Psychiatry, 157,* 1317–1323.

Velligan, D. I., Prihoda, T. J., Ritch, J. L., Maples, N., Bow-Thomas, C. C., Dassori, A. (2002). A randomized single-blind pilot study of compensatory strategies in schizophrenia outpatients. *Schizophrenia Bulletin, 28*(2), 283–292.

Velligan, D. I., & Gonzalez, J. M. (2007). Rehabilitation and recovery in schizophrenia. *Psychiatric Clinics of North America, 30,* 535–548.

Velligan, D. I., Diamond, P. M., Mintz, J., Maples, N., Li, X., Zeber, J., et al. (2008). The use of individually tailored environmental supports to improve medication adherence and outcomes in schizophrenia. *Schizophrenia Bulletin, 34,* 483–493.

Weickert, T. W., Goldberg, T. E., Gold, J. M., Bigelow, L. B., Eagan, M. F., Weinberger, D. D. (2000). Cognitive impairments with patients with schizophrenia displaying preserved and compromised intellect. *Archives of General Psychiatry, 57,* 907–913.

Wexler, B. E., & Bell, M. D. (2005). Cognitive remediation and vocational rehabilitation for schizophrenia. *Schizophrenia Bulletin, 31,* 657–676.

Wigfield, A., & Eccles, J. S. (2002). *Development of achievement motivation.* San Diego, CA: Academic Press.

Wykes, T., Reeder, C., Williams, C., Corner, J., Rice, C., & Everitt, B. (2003). Are the effects of cognitive remediation therapy (CRT) durable? Results from an exploratory trial in schizophrenia. *Schizophrenia Research, 61,* 163–174.

Wykes, T., Newton, E., Landau, S., Rice, C., Thompson, N., & Frangou, S. (2007). Cognitive remediation therapy (CRT) for young early onset patients with schizophrenia: An exploratory randomized controlled trial. *Schizophrenia Research, 94*, 221–230.

Wykes, T, Huddy, V., Cellard, C., McGurk, S. R., & Czobor, P. (2011). A meta-analysis of cognitive remediation for schizophrenia: methodology and effect sizes. *American Journal of Psychiatry, 168*(5) , 472-85; doi:10.1176/appi.ajp.2010.10060855

Zimmerman, B. J., & Schunk, D. H. (2004). Self-regulating intellectual processes and outcomes: A social cognitive perspective. In D. Y. Dai & R. J. Sternberg (Eds.), *Motivation, emotion and cognition: Integrative perspectives on intellectual functioning and development* (pp. 323–349). Mahwah, NJ: Erlbaum.

BOX 12.1 DEFINITION OF COGNITIVE REMEDIATION (CR)

1. Narrowly defined, CR is a set of cognitive drills or compensatory interventions designed to enhance cognitive functioning.
2. However, from the vantage of the psychiatric rehabilitation field, CR engages the patient in a learning activity to enhance the neurocognitive skills relevant to overall recovery goals.
3. CR programs vary in the extent to which they reflect these narrow or broader perspectives.

BOX 12.2 MOTIVATION AND CR

1. Motivation is increasingly appreciated as playing a significant role in the learning process of people with schizophrenia who participate in cognitive remediation.
2. In particular, instructional style and motivation have been identified as salient factors that impact the learning process. By considering the factors that mediate learning, it becomes possible to maximize the benefits of CR.
3. One way to promote intrinsic motivation and task engagement is to use tasks that are contextualized, personalized and allow for learner control.

BOX 12.3 META-ANALYSES OF EFFICACY OF CR

1. When studies of CR have a highly proximal goal of improvement on a training task (i.e., performance on the trained task), the effect size was large.
2. When the goals of training became more distal and accordingly affected by a multiplicity of variables, the effect sizes diminished.

3. Still, moderate range effect sizes were found both for CR studies that used neuropsychological test results as an outcome measure, and for studies with the most distal goal of improving daily functioning.

BOX 12.4 PREDICTORS OF POSITIVE RESPONSE TO CR

1. Although the majority of research and results from meta-analytic studies indicate that CR is efficacious there is great variability in response to this treatment.
2. Level of premorbid intellect does play a role in response to CR. Those clients with higher premorbid intelligence have greater success with generalization of training.
3. When cognitive remediation includes motivationally enhancing features, clients became more motivated and show significantly better cognitive and functional outcomes.
4. CR is more successful with greater functional outcomes, when provided in conjunction with psychiatric rehabilitative programs.

CONTINUING EDUCATION QUESTIONS

1. Which of the following statements is true about cognitive remediation (CR)?
   a. It has a moderate effect size on cognition
   b. It has a large effect size on psychotic symptoms
   c. It has persistent effects on cognition for up to 24 months
   d. It can only use one software program
2. Research indicates which variable significantly moderates ability of cognitive remediation (CR) to impact functional outcome?
   a. Treatment intensity
   b. Whether CR is conducted within the context of a broader psychiatric rehabilitation focus
   c. Training level of the clinician
   d. Age of the client
3. In order to proceed with cognitive remediation, assessments of cognitive functioning are
   a. only useful if a comprehensive neuropsychological battery including IQ testing is performed
   b. useful when brief but valid and reliable assessments are performed
   c. not useful
   d. best done using computerized test formats

4. Meta-analyses of cognitive remediation studies find that CR is effective in improving all but which cognitive function
   a. attention and speed of processing
   b. verbal working memory
   c. visual learning and memory
   d. reasoning/problem solving
5. Techniques to improve motivation to learn
   a. are not relevant to schizophrenia populations because their motivational system is impaired
   b. can enhance cognitive remediation outcomes in schizophrenia
   c. are best delivered by clinicians
   d. are most effective when they rely on extrinsic motivation

13

Criminal Forensic Neuropsychological Evaluations

Implications for Schizophrenia

CHRISCELYN M. TUSSEY, Psy.D.
Bellevue Hospital Center, New York University School of Medicine

BERNICE A. MARCOPULOS, Ph.D.
Department of Graduate Psychology, James Madison University, Harrisonburg, VA

Forensic neuropsychology is the practice of providing neuropsychological evidence and opinions to assist the trier of fact in resolving legal issues (Greiffenstein, 2008; Slobogin, 2003). The assessment of cognitive functioning can be crucial for a wide range of psycholegal questions. Although the majority of neuropsychologists' forensic involvement in early years revolved around civil litigation, forensic opportunities have expanded to include the criminal arena (see Denney & Sullivan, 2008). According to Borum and Grisso (1995) for instance, 46%–50% of forensic psychologists reported using some form of neuropsychological assessment in pretrial evaluations. Results of a national survey of board-certified neuropsychologists conducted by Mittenberg, Patton, Canyock, and Condit (2002) revealed that 4%, or 1,341, out of 33,531 annual evaluations completed by 131 survey respondents, fell in the criminal forensic domain. This may, in part, be attributable to the growing awareness of the high rates of neuropathology in the criminal population, an increased understanding of brain-behavior relationships and criminal behavior, and a greater appreciation for related psycholegal implications. Neuropsychological assessment can provide information not only relevant to the trier of fact during trial, but also provide useful information for risk assessment and appropriate community or institutional placement of an individual with schizophrenia to potentially minimize either perpetration or victimization.

The objective of this chapter is two-fold: to provide the reader with a primer on criminal forensic neuropsychological evaluation (for a broader based, more comprehensive review of forensic evaluations, see Melton, Petrila, Poythress, & Slobogin, 2007, and Denney & Sullivan, 2008), and to examine the impact of schizophrenia and related sequelae on forensic evaluation. However, there is a dearth of literature on the latter, with most information only available regarding general forensic neuropsychological assessment. As such, forensic information specific to persons with schizophrenia is included when available; however, portions of this chapter are derived from inferences and generalizations about the forensic evaluation of the severely mentally ill. Given the relative infancy of criminal forensic neuropsychological evaluation of persons with schizophrenia, it is an exciting venture to author this chapter, and it is hoped that it will serve as an impetus for further research and clinical examination.

There has been a dramatic increase in the number of forensic patients at state hospitals across the United States over the past 20 years and, thus, a neuropsychologist working in an inpatient psychiatry setting is quite likely to assess a patient currently facing legal charges (Fisher, Geller, & Pandiani, 2009). Similarly, a neuropsychologist working in corrections is quite likely to evaluate an inmate with a severe mental illness such as schizophrenia. Epidemiologic studies have revealed that 15%–24% of U.S. inmates have a severe mental illness (Diamond, Wang, Holzer, Thomas, & Cruser 2001; National Commission on Correctional Health Care, 2002; Teplin, Abram, & McClelland, 1996). According to Peters, Sherman, and Osher (2008), 6.7% of prisoners reported a history of schizophrenia, whereas only 1.4% of the general population reported a history of this diagnosis. Steadman, Osher, Robbins, Case, and Samuels (2009) found a 14.5% prevalence rate for males and 31% for female inmates with serious mental illness in jails.

Why is there such a high rate of severe mental illness such as schizophrenia in the criminal justice system? As psychiatric hospital beds have dropped dramatically since their peak in the mid-1950s, there has been a shift from psychiatric care in hospitals to jails and prisons (Lamb & Weinberger, 2005). According to Morrissey and Cuddeback, (2008), the relative risk of incarceration for a person with severe mental illness is about 150% greater than the risk of hospitalization. A number of factors account for this phenomenon. Lamb, Weinberger, and Gross (2004) cited deinstitutionalization, changes in civil commitment criteria, inadequate community resources, and the role of law enforcement in managing psychiatric crises, as important factors increasing the numbers of mentally ill in jails and prisons. When defendants exhibit psychotic symptoms in the jails, they are often transferred to psychiatric hospitals for treatment and pre-trial evaluations. Prior to changes in commitment laws and when psychiatric beds were more plentiful, they might have been admitted to the hospital with psychotic symptoms first, and perhaps avoided accruing legal charges. When people with serious mental illness are convicted of crimes, they must receive mental health treatment in prisons, which is likely to be less than adequate. The 2006 Department of Justice (Bureau of Justice Statistics, 2006) study found only approximately one in three state prisoners, one in four federal prisoners, and one in six jail inmates with mental health issues had received treatment since admission. Psychotropic medication was the most common form of treatment administered (27% in state prisons, 19% in federal prisons, and 15% in local jails).

There is a higher prevalence of criminal offenses among persons with schizophrenia and schizoaffective disorder compared with the general population, as well as with other persons with severe mental illness, which includes bipolar disorder, major depression, and other non-alcohol and drug related psychoses (Brennan, Mednick, & Hodgins, 2000; Hodgins, Mednick, Brennan, Schulsinger, & Engberg 1996). For instance, Brennan et al. (2000) found in their Danish community survey that 2.7% of males without a mental illness diagnosis were arrested for a violent crime whereas 11.3 of those with schizophrenia were arrested. Both men and women with schizophrenia are at elevated risk when compared to the general population to be convicted of non-violent offenses. Furthermore, persons with schizophrenia are at a higher risk to be convicted of violent criminal offenses and at even higher risk to be convicted of homicide (Wallace, Mullen, & Burgess, 2004). For many offenders with schizophrenia, their criminal behavior predated the onset of their psychotic symptoms (Munkner, Haastrup, Joergensen, & Kramp, 2003, 2009; Wallace et al., 2004). In a recent study, Hodgins and colleagues (2011) found that 23.6% of their sample of persons with first episode psychosis had previous criminal offenses. Interestingly, the patients with previous offenses were found to be more neuropsychologically impaired with lower premorbid and current IQs and poorer performance on verbal learning and memory, visual memory, visuospatial perception, organization, and processing speed.

Among the severe mental illnesses, schizophrenia-spectrum disorders are the most frequently implicated in aggression and violence. Comorbid substance abuse, psychotropic medication non-adherence, and active psychotic symptoms have been the most common factors implicated in violence in people with schizophrenia (Arsenault, Moffitt, Caspi, Taylor, & Silva, 2000; Cuffel, Shumway, Choujian, & McDonald, 1994; Swanson, Borum, & Swartz, 1996; Swanson, Holzer, Ganju, & Jono, 1990; Tardiff, Marzuk, Leon, & Portera, 1997; Tiihonen, Isohanni, Rasenen, Koiranen, & Moring, 1997). Swanson et al. (2006) examined a sample of 1,410 persons with schizophrenia and found that the 6-month prevalence rate of any violence was 19.1% and 3.6% of the sample was involved in serious violent behavior. They also found that positive psychotic symptoms increased the risk of minor and serious violence whereas negative psychotic symptoms lowered the risk. The research revealed that minor violence was associated with co-occurring substance abuse and interpersonal and social factors, and serious violence was associated with psychotic and depressive symptoms, childhood conduct problems, and history of victimization. Related disorders in the schizophrenia spectrum, such as schizoaffective disorder, are also associated with an increased risk of aggression and violence (Arango, Calcedo-Barba,

González-Salvador, Calcedo-Ordóñez, 1999). Walsh et al. (2004) followed 271 persons with schizophrenia over a 2-year period and found that 25% committed assault. Assault was defined as any physical contact with another person that was reported by the patient, the case manager, or it was noted in the case records. Previous violence, alcohol abuse, and a history of special education predicted violence in this sample. These results are somewhat higher than other community studies such as Swanson et al. (2006) who used patient self-report only and found a 6 month prevalence of any violence 19.1%. More recently, Douglas, Guy, and Hart (2009) performed a meta-analysis on studies looking at psychosis and violence. They found that psychosis was associated with a 49% to 68% increase in risk of violence.

To keep these statistics in perspective, persons with schizophrenia have higher rates of violence than the general population, although most never commit a violent crime. Barr (2008) points out that most of the individuals with schizophrenia considered at risk for violence have the same risk factors for violence as the general population (i.e., substance abuse and previous violence). Medication nonadherence also increases risk of violence in persons with schizophrenia (Torrey, 1994). Schizophrenia is commonly viewed as an unpredictable and dangerous psychiatric condition, despite public fears outweighing the actual risk of being injured by an individual with severe mental illness (Steadman, Mulvey, Monahan, & Robbins, 1998). This public perception of dangerousness, albeit overstated, fosters stigma and negative stereotypes among this population (Link, Cullen, Frank, & Wozniak, 1987). Choe, Teplin, and Abram (2008) reviewed U.S. studies of both perpetration and victimization of violence in severe mental illness. They suggested that the rates of violence perpetration may be overstated because most of the studies were done with patients admitted involuntarily. Involuntary commitment criteria include being dangerous to self and others so these samples have much higher base rates of violence than community out-patient samples. Conversely, they suggested that violence victimization for those with serious mental illness is higher than the general population. Negative symptoms, including cognitive impairment, can make persons with schizophrenia more vulnerable to victimization (Swanson et al., 2006).

FORENSIC NEUROPSYCHOLOGICAL EVALUATION

Types of Forensic Evaluations

The most common forensic referrals in psychiatric settings are: Competence to Stand Trial (CST), Mental Status at Time of Offense (MSO), and risk assessments. These three types of assessments will be the focus of this chapter. As extensively discussed in this volume, persons with schizophrenia have significant cognitive deficits and these deficits, along with other symptoms of psychosis, are relevant to evaluations of trial competence, sanity, or risk assessment.

CST Although there are multiple competence evaluations in which a neuropsychologist may be involved (e.g., competence to proceed in sentencing, to waive one's rights to counsel, to be executed), this chapter will focus on competence evaluations conducted to determine a defendant's ability to stand trial. According to the landmark decision in *Dusky v. United States* (1960), a defendant has a right to a competency evaluation before proceeding to trial. Milton Dusky, a 33-year-old man with schizophrenia, was charged with kidnapping and assisting in the rape of an underage female. Dusky's attorney expressed concerns about his trial competency, and he was subsequently hospitalized and evaluated. Despite his acute psychotic symptoms, he was found Competent to Stand Trial and received a 45-year sentence. The case was appealed to the United States Supreme Court on petition of writ of certiorari, with the petitioner requesting that his conviction be reversed on the grounds that he was not competent to stand trial at the time of the proceedings. The Court ultimately granted the writ and ruled that in order to be competent to stand trial, a defendant must have a "sufficient present ability to consult with his lawyer with a reasonable degree of rational understanding" and a "rational as well as factual understanding of the proceedings against him" (*Dusky v. United States*).

The *Dusky* standard is employed in nearly every state, though some locations have made minor alterations. It is necessary to note that while assessing CST, contrary to common beliefs, education level, intelligence, or an unwillingness to cooperate with one's attorney do not alone preclude trial competence. However, cognitive impairment, particularly in intelligence, memory and attention, increases the likelihood that a defendant will be deemed incompetent (Nestor, Daggett, Haycock, & Price, 1999). Nestor et al. examined 181 defendants at a state psychiatric hospital who were referred for neuropsychological testing and were evaluated for competency to stand trial. As a group the defendants scored in the low average range, but they found that the defendants who were deemed CST by forensic evaluators had higher attention, memory and intelligence tests scores than the ones who were judged incompetent to stand trial (IST). Tests measuring executive functioning and academic skills showed no differences between CST and IST. Nestor et al. concluded that neuropsychological assessment can discern the neurocognitive constructs related to trial competence. Thus, a forensic neuropsychologist can provide unique insight into the impact of cognitive impairment on a defendant's ability to continue with legal proceedings such as documenting intellectual disability, and impairments in attention, memory and language which can impact restoration efforts (Marcopulos, Morgan, & Denney, 2008).

MSO A forensic neuropsychologist's role in an MSO evaluation (also known as "sanity," "insanity," or "criminal responsibility" evaluations) is to determine if a defendant had an altered mental status at the time of an alleged offense due to some form of neuropathology which would mitigate or exculpate him/her from criminal responsibility. Standards for legal insanity in MSO evaluations vary much more from jurisdiction to jurisdiction than do standards for trial competence. Although the exemption of particular individuals from culpability dates back to ancient times, the modern history of the insanity defense is most tied with the Daniel M'Naghten Case (1843) in Britain. Trial evidence suggested that Daniel M'Naghten attempted to assassinate Sir Robert Peel, the British Prime Minister, in response to his delusional belief that the Prime Minister was persecuting him. Mr. M'Naghten mistakenly killed Mr. Peel's secretary and was ultimately ruled insane and spent over 20 years in mental asylums until his death. Queen Victoria responded to outrage about how this case was resolved and requested stricter rules for legal determinations of insanity. Over time, the original M'Naghten standard for invoking the insanity defense was criticized and evolved in a variety of ways across different jurisdictions to respond to the criticism.

Today, in general, the legal term "insanity" often requires the presence of a severe mental illness and often consists of two prongs: a cognitive prong and a "volitional" prong. The cognitive component implies that a defendant is unable to appreciate the nature, character, and consequences of his/her act because of an underlying mental illness. The "volitional" prong is sometimes referred to as the "elbow test," which suggests that the defendant would have committed the act even if a policeman were "at his/her elbow." Jurisdictions often include all of these components or some combination of them. Similar to CST, there are many false beliefs about what constitutes "insanity." For instance, amnesia for an alleged offense or failure to cooperate with an evaluation does not definitively indicate insanity. Indeed, although memory deficits may be present on neuropsychological evaluation, one cannot assume that impairment of the same magnitude, or at all, was present at the time of the alleged offense(s). Rather, such data are only one source of information, and additional considerations, such as the temporal relationship between the alleged offense, testing, and any factors which could have significantly impacted brain functioning in the interim (e.g., traumatic brain injury, progressive neurodegenerative disorder, etc.), deficient effort during testing, and collateral information, must be taken into account.

Risk Assessment These types of evaluations are often completed to determine an individual's risks before transitioning to a new setting. For example, forensic neuropsychologists may examine a Not Guilty by Reason of Insanity (NGRI) acquitee who is being considered for release. The evaluator will examine the role of any potential brain injury that could negatively impact the acquitee's ability to function in a less-structured environment and make recommendations for the conditions of release. A forensic evaluator should also consider whether or not the individual has been violent during his/her hospitalization, whether or not he/she has been adherent with medication and treatment, and if he/she has any insight into the need for continued treatment. In some jurisdictions where Sexual Violent Predator statutes exist, a forensic neuropsychologist may also examine the role of one's neuropathology on his/her ability to be transitioned to a less-structured environment or make recommendations about the need for civil commitment. Risk assessment also occurs in the sentencing phase of a capital trial where a forensic neuropsychologist may examine the potentially mitigating and/or risk factors associated with the defendant's brain dysfunction.

Regardless of the specific risk being assessed, these evaluations typically involve a thorough review of both static and dynamic factors that might impact one's future functioning. Static variables are historical factors which are not susceptible to change, such as age at first offense and prior criminal history. These variables are one factor to examine when assessing long-term recidivism potential. The evaluation of change in offender risk level, however, requires the consideration of dynamic risk factors or those which may be amenable to change via intervention. Although age is sometimes considered a dynamic risk factor, the most useful dynamic risk factors are those amenable to deliberate interventions (e.g., substance abuse, unemployment).

Ethical Considerations for Forensic Neuropsychological Assessment

Forensic neuropsychological evaluation is quite different from traditional psychological evaluation. Unique considerations for forensic neuropsychological evaluation include differing assumptions, roles, alliances, and methodology (Denney & Wynkoop, 2000; Greiffenstein & Cohen, 2005). These differences likely reflect the fundamental difference in goals between clinical and forensic practice. For instance, typically neuropsychological practice in a clinical setting attempts to reduce human suffering and improve functioning through effective intervention (Denney & Sullivan, 2008). In contrast, with few exceptions, the aim of forensic assessment is to determine if a defendant's psychological difficulties meet an identified legal standard.

Neuropsychologists in clinical practice often assume that patients voluntarily seek assessment/treatment because they are concerned about their cognitive deficits and are motivated to get help. Collaboration, shared goals, and joint beliefs are key in this form of service delivery. In contrast, forensic neuropsychological evaluations typically are not voluntary, and a genuine psychological issue may not be present. Due to the potential for secondary gain (e.g., a shorter sentence), individuals in forensic settings have external motivation to manipulate an evaluator (Rogers, 2008). As a result, neuropsychologists conducting forensic evaluations must always consider the possibility of feigning or exaggerating either psychopathology, cognitive impairment, or both.

Due to the different tasks of neuropsychologists in clinical versus forensic settings, divergent roles emerge in each setting. While a treating neuropsychologist may adopt a more traditional helping role and be perceived as an advocate for the patient, a forensic neuropsychologist must be careful to remain objective and unbiased. Thus, the forensic evaluator does not "join" with the evaluee, their attorney, or serve as his/her advocate. Rather, the task of a forensic neuropsychologist is typically to provide information and/or education to the court. Forensic evaluators may find themselves in roles that clinicians may find abhorrent. For example, the opinion of a forensic evaluator typically has substantial weight in judicial proceedings and can result in what may be perceived by non-forensic clinicians as harm to the evaluee. For example, a forensic neuropsychologist may opine that a defendant is competent to be executed, an opinion with implications with which a clinical evaluator may struggle.

Although we emphasize that all defendants should be treated with respect and dignity, it is important to remember that in a forensic setting, the client is often not the person being evaluated; rather, it is typically the court. Neuropsychologists who are employed at a hospital where high volumes of both forensic and non-forensic referrals are made must work hard to remember who the client is in each case. The focus in a clinical setting is to assess and improve the patient's functioning. Typically, a patient's self-report is accepted as true, though collateral information via accompanying family members, etc., is collected when possible. However, in a forensic context, an evaluee's self-report must be examined more critically. An ongoing, systematic method for the assessment of negative response bias and malingering is important. According to Denney and Wynkoop (2000), surreptitious observation of an evaluee can provide volumes of useful information. As with any type of evaluation, a forensic neuropsychologist must synthesize all available information to derive an answer to the referral question(s). In a forensic setting where self-report should ideally be corroborated by external data, collateral information is of upmost importance. For additional information about important sources of data that can be obtained, tailored to the practice of criminal forensic neuropsychology, see Denney and Wynkoop (2000).

Aspirational Standards of Competence for Forensic Neuropsychologists: Some authorities have argued that neuropsychologists are ill prepared to practice in the forensic arena and require specialty training in forensic work (Denney, 2005; Denney & Wynkoop, 2000). Sufficient training and experience in this field are very important, particularly given the impact that forensic opinions can have on a defendant and the many opportunities for error. Grisso (2003) identified five prominent deficits among mental health professionals who practice in the forensic arena, nicknamed the "Five I's": *ignorance* and *irrelevance* in courtroom testimony, psychiatric or psychological *intrusion* into essentially legal matters, and *insufficiency* and *incredibility* of information presented to the courts" (2003, p. 11). Given these potential risks, it is crucial that neuropsychologists have several core areas of forensic competence prior to engaging in practice.

An ethical neuropsychologist conducting forensic work should have fundamental understanding of the legal arena in which he/she will be working. Specifically, it is important that forensic neuropsychologists are familiar with key constitutional amendments relevant to forensic practice. The Fifth, Sixth, Eighth, and Fourteenth Amendments are considered the most relevant for criminal forensic practice (Denney & Sullivan, 2008). Simply stated:

- The Fifth Amendment ensures citizens' privilege against self-incrimination and assures due process.
- The Sixth Amendment states that the accused are entitled a speedy and public trial with representation.
- The Eighth Amendment protects against cruel and unusual punishment.

- The Fourteenth Amendment states that state and federal laws cannot infringe upon citizens' Constitutional rights, and promises due process.

For a comprehensive review of these Amendments and others pertinent to psychologists performing forensic work, please see Melton, Petrila, Poythress, and Slobogin (2007). Also, the competent forensic neuropsychologist should be familiar with key U.S. Supreme Court Landmark Cases, such as *Miranda v. Arizona* (1966) and *Dusky v. United States* (1960; discussed above). Denney and Sullivan (2008) review 12 of the most pertinent landmark cases for forensic practitioners. Forensic neuropsychologists should also be familiar with established rules for the admissibility of evidence (e.g., *Frye v. United States*, 1923, and *Daubert v. Merrell Dow Pharmaceuticals*, 1993) as well as relevant case law. For additional information about guidelines for ethical forensic psychological practice, see the American Psychological Association Ethical Principles of Psychologists and Code of Conduct (2002) and the revised *Specialty Guidelines for Forensic Psychologists* (Committee on the Revision of the Specialty Guidelines for Forensic Psychology, 2011). It is hoped that our sophistication regarding ethical service delivery in the forensic neuropsychological arena will parallel the continued growth of this subspecialty.

PERSONS WITH SCHIZOPHRENIA, COGNITIVE DEFICITS, AND FORENSIC EVALUATION

Now that the role of a forensic neuropsychologist has been briefly renewed, it is appropriate to shift focus to the primary purpose of this chapter—to describe how neuropsychology can be useful in forensic assessment of persons with schizophrenia. Schizophrenia is considered neurodevelopmental in nature with psychiatric symptoms and cognitive deficits of heterogeneous presence and severity. Neuropsychological studies have found some degree of impairment in nearly all areas of cognitive functioning in people with schizophrenia, although some individuals are relatively intact. Cognitive impairments can have direct implications for individuals involved in the judicial system. Historically, the focus of forensic psychological assessment for people with schizophrenia has been on positive, negative, and disorganization symptoms. However, over the past 15 years, the focus on cognitive dysfunction in most people with schizophrenia adds another domain for consideration in the process. Highlighting symptoms of cognitive deficits, which are probably less stigmatizing, provides an alternate context for understanding criminal behavior. It also leads to strategies for restoring competence.

Although a number of studies have attempted to articulate the specific cognitive deficits found in schizophrenia, in general the literature suggests deficits are generalized but prominent in processing speed and learning and memory. Other specific symptoms of impaired cognition may include: deficient abstract reasoning, decision making, and planning; slow processing speed; low intelligence; inhibition/impulsivity problems; perseveration (cognitive inflexibility);

and lack of insight for both clinical and cognitive symptoms (see Kurtz & Marcopulos, this volume). Below is a discussion of some of the ways in which these deficits may influence CST, MSO, and risk assessments.

CST Recall that CST evaluations require a *present* ability to factually and rationally understand legal proceedings and to consult with one's attorney. In the majority of cases, a defendant with schizophrenia will be found incompetent based on acute psychotic symptoms, rather than due to cognitive impairments, unless profound. When a defendant's cognitive symptoms are so severe that they preclude trial competence and perhaps to the point that they cannot be restored, it is usually in the context of a severe negative symptom profile. This profile includes prominent cognitive symptoms, but also paucity of speech and asociality, making it very difficult for them to work effectively with their attorney. Although rarely resulting in an incapacity decision since the bar is set so low, level of cognition may nevertheless inform how to maximize comprehension and participation in proceedings (e.g., slow, concrete communications with check-ins or memory aids).

For example, though not specific to schizophrenia, low vocabulary abilities may result in poor understanding of complex words typically used in legal terminology (Fujii, 2002). As such, a forensic evaluator must take great care to use simple language, keeping in mind that trial competence requires a fairly minimal level of knowledge about legal proceedings. An occasional argument from an evaluee hoping to remain "incompetent" to postpone trial is "I didn't go to law school. How would I know this?" However, given the minimal standards for trial competence, this is a poor argument for continued incompetence.

Poor executive functioning, common in persons with schizophrenia, can affect one's ability to understand the severity of one's crime or impact one's ability to make decisions. For instance, impaired ability to understand complex abstract principles may make it difficult for a defendant to understand, let alone reason through, the decision-making process of plea bargaining. One's ability to consult with an attorney may be impeded by difficulty with thought disorganization, which could also impede recollection of events and strategic planning. This may ultimately preclude a defendant from developing a coherent defense in collaboration with counsel, testifying, or regulating his/her behavior in court. In addition, attention and memory and processing speed are also impacted and may make learning information, as well as consulting with an attorney, very difficult. These deficits may hinder a defendant's ability to mentally "keep up" with judicial proceedings. Poor social skills due to deficits in social cognition can impair the client-attorney relationship (Nestor et al., 1999).

It is important to highlight that persons with schizophrenia often have impaired working memory and difficulty with initial acquisition of information, which may impede a defendant's ability to learn court-related facts. If information is encoded, persons with schizophrenia may require cued or multiple-choice testing may be necessary to assist with recall. The ability to retain information found in schizophrenia contrasts sharply with patterns observed in cortical dementia, such as Dementia of the Alzheimer's Type, where an individual has difficulty both learning and rapidly recalling information (Heaton et al., 1994). A neuropsychologist could help discern whether the defendant has a condition that is progressive, such as a dementia, or if it is a static deficit (e.g., schizophrenia, TBI). Differential diagnoses such as these are essential in CST evaluations where cognitive factors are thought to preclude trial competence (Heck & Herrick, 2007). This is especially pertinent given the relevance of such a diagnosis for restorability to competence which is discussed further below (e.g., an individual with dementia may never be able to learn and retain the requisite trial information particulary given that their cognitive deficits progress over time).

An important factor in the assessment of trial competence is the temporal relationship between the forensic evaluation and the court hearing. Trial competence requires a defendant's *present* ability to stand trial. However, sometimes CST evaluations are conducted long before hearings, allowing ample time for a defendant's psychotic symptoms to re-emerge and render them incompetent (assuming that it is the psychotic symptoms that affected their competence), especially if they do not receive treatment after they return to jail. Since cognitive symptoms in schizophrenia are generally stable, this is not likely relevant unless there is an interval event or condition onset. While acute psychotic states may add some amount of increased burden, perhaps mostly due to reduced cognitive control processes, at that point it's more likely that one's delusions especially will interfere with trial processes. This scenario will likely result in the need for an updated CST evaluation. Extended time between evaluation and a court hearing can be particularly problematic for persons with schizophrenia for whom medication non-adherence can have rapid and negative consequences.

A dilemma that a forensic neuropsychologist may face is that of assessing whether a defendant is unrestorably incompetent (Mossman, 2007). In *Jackson v. Indiana* (406 U.S. 715; 1972), the United States Supreme Court ruled that states may not indefinitely confine criminal defendants solely on the basis of incompetence to stand trial. This ruling left unresolved whether states could indefinitely maintain criminal charges against incompetent defendants. However, in 2008, the Indiana Supreme Court (*Indiana v. Davis*; 898 N.E.2d. 281, 2008) unanimously ruled that holding criminal charges over the head of a permanently incompetent defendant, when pretrial confinement extended beyond the maximum period of any sentence the trial court could impose, violated the basic notions of fundamental fairness embodied in the Due Process Clause of the Fourteenth Amendment.

It has been estimated that approximately 20% of CST evaluations result in a finding of incompetence (Warren, Fitch, Dietz, & Rosenfeld, 1991). According to Zapf and Roesch (2011), most (approximately 75%) incompetent defendants are restored to competence within 6 months. There is a small portion that remains incompetent for some time and may not be restorable, but clinicians are notoriously unreliable in their ability to predict which patients are unrestorable. In general, the base rate of unrestorable incompetence among persons with schizophrenia is higher than other mental illnesses. There are numerous potential explanations for this, not the least of which is the many overlapping risk factors and comorbid conditions in schizophrenia. Given this multitude of risk factors, it is not surprising that a forensic evaluator might opine that a person with schizophrenia may be unrestorable to trial competence. A patient with "deficit" schizophrenia may indeed be unrestorable because of profound negative symptoms and cognitive deficits as well as treatment-resistant symptoms. Mossman (2007) reviewed records of 351 pre-trial defendants at a state psychiatric hospital and found that the defendants least likely to be restored had lengthy histories of active psychosis and poor response to treatment. He also found that those unrestorable defendants were more likely to have a static cognitive disorder such as mental retardation. Neuropsychological assessment can help differentiate and quantify the cognitive deficits in schizophrenia and suggest whether they can be remediated or compensated for to achieve trial competence. For instance, Schwalbe and Medalia (2007) proposed that cognitive remediation of the cognitive deficits in schizophrenia might positively impact trial competence restoration efforts.

MSO The impact of schizophrenia in insanity determinations has been highlighted in several studies. For instance, research conducted nearly two decades ago by Warren and colleagues (1991) examined 894 pretrial referrals in Virginia, 617 of which were referred for MSO and/or CST. Evaluators reached an opinion supporting an insanity claim in only 47 (8%) of the cases, and psychiatric diagnoses were significantly related to the legal opinion. Schizophrenia (13 defendants, 28%) was the most frequently cited diagnostic category among the 47 defendants opined to be insane. These findings replicate conclusions from Melton, Petrila, Poythress, and Slobogin (1997) who reviewed six small studies conducted across four states at different points between 1967 and 1987. The authors concluded that "data suggest that the presence of a major psychosis is required for the insanity defense to succeed ..." (p. 216). Callahan, Steadman, McGreevy, and Robins (1991) reported that 55% of those who pled not guilty by reason of insanity and 84% of those acquitted as such were diagnosed with "schizophrenia or another major mental illness (other psychotic or affective disorder)" (p. 336).

In 2001, Cochrane, Grisso, and Frederick examined trial competence and sanity opinions among 1710 federal pretrial defendants. Results were similar to the aforementioned and reflected a strong relationship between diagnoses and psycholegal opinion. Specifically, 40% of defendants with psychotic disorders were opined to be insane as compared to only 6% of those with personality disorders. Regarding criminal charges, insanity rates varied greatly based on the type of offense. For example, those charged with threatening a government official or assault were most likely to be found insane by forensic examiners (36% and 31%, respectively), as compared with none of the defendants charged with sex crimes or kidnapping. In this same study, a unique finding emerged in the relationship between diagnoses and charges. The authors proposed that the high rates of insanity for certain crime categories were best explained by the high rates of psychotic diagnoses for defendants within these crime categories. Consistent with their hypotheses, logistic regression revealed that there were no significant relationships between charges and psycholegal opinion once diagnoses were also considered. Rather, diagnoses were related to the types of offense the defendant committed and diagnostic presentation was the main variable to affect psycholegal opinion.

Warren, Murrie, Chauhan, Dietz, and Morris (2004) investigated the content and process of 5,175 sanity evaluations conducted in Virginia by a cohort of psychiatrists and clinical psychologists over a 10-year period. The study examined factors related to a psycholegal opinion involving insanity, the process used by psychologists and psychiatrists in reaching their conclusions, disciplinary differences in opinion formation, and the consistency and change in these opinions. In this study, 13% and 20% of the evaluations resulted in an opinion of insanity by psychologists and psychiatrists, respectively. Opinions about MSO were derived using the three prongs of the insanity standard as defined in Virginia: (a) ability to understand the nature, character, and consequences of the act; (b) ability to distinguish right from wrong; and (c) ability to resist the impulse of the act. Overall, the study found that the finding of insanity was consistent with national trends.

Consistent with previous findings, Warren et al. (2004) found that a history of serious mental illness was the most prominent clinical factor. Specifically, individuals with a psychotic diagnosis were over five times more likely to be found insane than those without such a diagnosis. The study found that evaluators relied more on the cognitive prongs, versus the volitional prong, to form an opinion. Indeed, in 91% of the opinions supporting insanity, examiners identified at least one of the two cognitive prongs of the insanity standard as relevant to their opinion. The authors highlighted how this pattern reflects the difficulty that examiners have in differentiating between an irresistible impulse and an impulse not resisted. Psychotic delusions are typically essential to a determination that the defendant was not able to differentiate right from wrong at the time of an offense.

Research data clearly illustrate that psychotic symptoms heavily influence evaluator opinions about sanity. But what specific cognitive deficits of schizophrenia should be considered in MSO evaluations? Impaired memory for the alleged offense(s) is one of the most frequently cited dilemmas. As we know, severe mental illness, such as schizophrenia, can result in memory and learning impairment. The type of memory most relevant to an MSO evaluation would be autobiographical memory, which is the ability to reconstruct past personal events. Persons with schizophrenia have been found to generate fewer autobiographical memories than normal controls, presumably due to problems with memory acquisition (Elvevåg, Kerbs, Malley, Seeley, & Goldberg, 2003). Combined with the state dependent amnesia that many patients experience during acute psychotic episodes, it can be very difficult to obtain accurate reports regarding the events surrounding the alleged offense.

Although memory deficits can be a valid consideration in defendants with schizophrenia who claim amnesia, forensic evaluators are cautioned not to assume that just because a patient has a diagnosis of schizophrenia, that he/she has diminished culpability. The degree of reported amnesia must be carefully examined. Despite the fact that severe retrograde amnesia is rare in the absence of severe brain injury, claims of remote memory loss related to criminal activity are quite common (Schacter, 1986). Thirty percent of criminals claim they cannot remember their crimes (e.g., Taylor & Kopelman, 1984; Cima, Nijman, Merckelbach, Kremer, & Hollnack, 2004). Denney and Sullivan (2008) reviewed the literature and found that reported amnesia for behavior associated with homicide charges is estimated to range from 23%–65%. Many researchers suggest that a significant portion of these claims are feigned. As such, it is essential to consider all of the characteristics of a defendant's behavior prior to, during, and after the alleged offense(s) and when severe amnesia is reported, symptom validity testing should be employed to help assess the veracity of assessment results. Furthermore, because MSO evaluations are often conducted days, weeks, months, and at times years, after an alleged offense(s), it can be particularly difficult to obtain sufficient details, even from individuals who do not have a mental illness and are putting forth good effort. This highlights the necessity of collateral information, which may be the only way to collect relevant information about an alleged incident, especially when evaluating individuals with severe mental illness and/or severe brain injury.

It is also challenging, to evaluate teenagers or young adults who may have committed a crime during his/her first psychotic episode. Assessment of prodromal symptoms and related risk factors is a first step to disentangling behavior attributable to an initial psychotic episode versus behavior attributable to other sources (e.g., substance-induced psychotic behavior). First-episode psychosis is inherently challenging in MSO evaluations given that a prominent component of most successful insanity defense strategies is the individual's longstanding, and often documented, history of severe mental illness. Of course, in an individual with new onset schizophrenia, such a history will not exist. In fact, few, if any, symptoms may be documented potentially due to inaccurate diagnoses, the belief that the individual was just "different" or "going through a teenage phase."

Risk Assessment With respect to risk assessment, whether for conditional release, sexual violent predator (SVP) proceedings, etc. an evaluator should take into consideration several factors when evaluating an individual with schizophrenia (Fujii, 2002). First, it may be difficult to evaluate risk for future dangerousness because one's behavior may be unpredictable if unmedicated. Therefore, it will be important for an evaluator to consider the importance of medication and structured mental health follow-up. An individual with schizophrenia may misperceive his/her environment, which could lead to a potential for violence. Learning impairments may impede a person with schizophrenia's ability to learn from mistakes, or to learn to identify triggers for violent behavior. When evaluating persons with schizophrenia, it will be necessary to consider how treatment responsibilities will affect, or be related to, conditional release. Acute, untreated symptoms of psychosis, or the memory deficits typically observed in schizophrenia, may make adherence to conditional release particularly difficult.

Remorse is a subject worthy of mention as it may be related to future dangerousness. Persons with schizophrenia often have difficulty with perspective-taking, attributable in large part to their executive dysfunction and thus may appear to experience minimal, or any, remorse. This is particularly true if psychotic symptoms clouded their memory of the alleged event. *Theory of Mind* (ToM) may explain why persons with schizophrenia have difficulty with remorse or other emotions. ToM refers to the capacity to infer one's own and other persons' mental states. Substantial empirical evidence exists that posits that ToM is specifically impaired in schizophrenia and that many psychotic symptoms, such as delusions of persecution, thought and language disorganization, and other behavioral symptoms, may best be understood in the context of a disturbed capacity in persons with schizophrenia to relate their own intentions to behavior and to monitor others' intentions (Brüne, 2005). A lack of remorse can be perceived in several ways in the courtroom and is typically considered callous by laymen who are unaware of the ways in which severe mental illness can negate this emotion. It is important to assess the etiology of an absence of remorse, particularly given that it is often considered in conjunction with insight into one's illness and circumstances. The latter is one of the most salient factors addressed in dangerousness evaluations. Persons with schizophrenia frequently have poor insight into their deficits, which is a risk factor for poor adherence to treatment (Mohamed et al., 2009; Smith et al., 1999).

Also salient is the effect that positive symptoms of schizophrenia, such as suspiciousness and persecutory delusions, have been associated with higher rates of violence (Odds Ratio = 1.46 Swanson et al., 2006). Torrey (1994) noted that a history of previous violence, substance abuse, and medication non-adherence are significant predictors of future violence in persons with schizophrenia. As such, it is necessary to consider the individual's history of, and current, symptom presentation, as this may have implications for future risk.

When asking about a patient's history, regardless of the type of forensic evaluation, it is important to consider the impact of head injuries on behavior and future risk. Violent and explosive behavior has been associated with brain injury particularly to the Frontal lobes (Tateno, Jorge, & Robinson, 2003). This aggressive behavior is typically reactive and impulsive. Damage to the frontal areas of the brain can result in disinhibition and may exacerbate difficulties with executive dysfunction already present in persons with schizophrenia. For instance, Dinn, Gansler, Moczynski, and Fulwiler (2009) found that 36.8% of violent patients with a primary diagnosis of schizophrenia had a history of closed-head injury whereas none of the nonviolent patients with schizophrenia had such a history.

Indeed, traumatic brain injury is very common in adult prisoners. The Centers for Disease Control and Prevention (CDC) found that between 25% and

87% of men and women imprisoned for violent crimes have suffered a TBI prior to incarceration. Although this range is large, in general it is about three times higher than the rate of TBI in the general population (8.5%) In addition to the behavioral sequelae of a TBI, cognitive deficits can emerge. Individuals who have suffered a TBI may have difficulty remembering regimented rules, coping with emotions, planning, and communicating. The combination of a head injury and schizophrenia (and any other comorbid illnesses) may intensify one's impairments and further impact daily functioning. This constellation of difficulties can contribute to recidivism rates. Thus, head injuries must be thoughtfully considered when assessing most psycholegal questions, especially those of risk.

Finally, given that social functioning is a robust predictor of long-term outcome including relapse and re-hospitalizations (Harrison, Croudace, Mason, Glazenbrook, & Medley, 1996), dangerousness evaluations often include assessment of an individual's ability to integrate into functional daily living, including employment. Persons with schizophrenia may have difficulty obtaining a job without significant social support. The cognitive deficits associated with schizophrenia may make it difficult for an individual to learn new job skills and to engage in effective decision making. Attentional deficits may make it difficult for the persons with schizophrenia to attend to important information. Due to cognitive inflexibility and inefficiency, persons with schizophrenia have difficulty altering their behaviors and implementing coping strategies. In fact, response processing speed has been found to predict level of care needed by persons with schizophrenia post-discharge (Wykes et al., 1990; see Kurtz this volume).

FORENSIC ASSESSMENT STRATEGIES FOR PERSONS WITH SCHIZOPHRENIA

Neuropsychological assessment of persons with schizophrenia can provide relevant information for both clinical and functional outcome, each or both of which can have forensic implications. Research has found that factors associated with functional outcome, such as psychosocial skill acquisition, social problem solving, and successful community living, are predicted by neurocognitive measures (see Kurtz, this volume). Furthermore, impairments in cognitive, social perception, and behavior skills can explain the difficulties of persons with schizophrenia to relate effectively to others (Bellack, Sayers, Mueser, & Bennett, 1994), and identifying these deficits may be critical to future intervention. Acknowledging the idiosyncrasies involved in evaluating persons with schizophrenia, the following sections will focus on unique interviewing and evaluation considerations for this population.

Interviewing Considerations

Obtaining self-report data from a person with schizophrenia can be particularly challenging, especially in forensic contexts where paranoia is prominent, even among non-psychotic defendants, and insight into one's psychological and legal circumstances is often poor. Persons with schizophrenia who are hospitalized are particularly cautious about neuropsychological evaluation, often fearing that it will prolong their hospitalization (Marcopulos et al., 2008). It is important to recognize that forensic evaluation does not require patient consent, as typical clinical evaluation does. However, it is imperative for defendants to understand the limits (or lack) of confidentiality, the purpose of the exam, who will receive the information, etc. Defendants being treated at a psychiatric hospital often have difficulty grasping the difference between a forensic and clinical exam. Also, although defendants have a right to refuse testing, doing so may have de facto repercussions which a person with schizophrenia may not understand. As such, defendants are even more likely to be angry or frustrated by the evaluation, which may affect their effort and the validity of the results.

Rudnick and Roe (2008) offer several guidelines for interviewing persons with schizophrenia. First, they suggest that some challenges may emerge before the interview, related to the patient's feelings, expectations, and concerns, some of which may stem from previous experiences. The authors note that persons with schizophrenia may feel threatened and as a result, be very guarded, or aggressive. Also, an interviewee may be concerned with the consequences of the interview and therefore may respond in the way he/she sees best, which may invalidate the data. These risks are almost certainly amplified in a forensic context. Another challenge is the lack of insight typical in schizophrenia. Confrontation or repeating questions is not useful. Rather, any information collected from a person with schizophrenia, regardless of how minimal, may provide priceless insight into one's functioning. In a forensic context, neuropsychologists will have to balance the need for relevant information with the needs of the persons with schizophrenia, and learn to collect all necessary information from additional sources, as previously discussed. Often, if a defendant is too impaired to engage in a brief clinical interview, this may be foreshadowing for his/her ability to stand trial.

Persons with schizophrenia may be guarded and suggestible, and it is important to avoid leading questions, or implicit pressure to provide the "right" answer, especially in a forensic setting. Although cognitive impairment and psychosis may impede self-report of symptoms, interacting with a person with schizophrenia can provide very useful insight into the individual's current level of functioning. Of course, symptoms can be so acute that they preclude an interview. This can be addressed in several ways, such as providing many breaks during the interview, or extending the interview over several days. The evaluator is encouraged to determine at the onset, if possible, whether or not a patient can understand the purpose of the evaluation, and participate meaningfully, before continuing with an interview. If this is not possible, it is necessary that the evaluator return when the symptoms have sufficiently remitted.

Testing Considerations

Given the relevance of brain-behavior relationships to many psycholegal questions, neuropsychological test data can provide useful insight. Despite this, the frequency at which psychological and neuropsychological testing is utilized in forensic evaluations is variable. For example, Heilbrun and Collins (1995) investigated CST, MSO, or both, community and inpatient-hospital-based forensic evaluation reports, to explore differences between settings. For cases in which sanity was the key issue (either independently or in addition to competence), the authors presented information only on procedures used by the community sample. A clinical interview was used in 98-100% of cases, a mental status exam was performed in 67%–69% of cases, but psychological testing was only utilized in 16% of the reports, with the Minnesota Multiphasic Personality Inventory and the Wechsler Adult Intelligence Scales-Revised cited most frequently. Testing was used more often in hospital-based reports, but this appeared to be primarily a function of the evaluators' discipline; hospital-based evaluators were psychologists, whereas most community-based evaluators were psychiatrists. Warren et al. (2003) found that out of 5,175 sanity evaluations, 22% of psychologists and 6% of psychiatrists utilized psychological assessment, while only 10% of psychologists used neuropsychological testing and 2% of psychiatrists used such testing.

Two hypotheses about why psychological testing is relatively infrequently employed include: (a) such testing is simply not necessary to answer the psycholegal question, and/or (b) the determination of a necessary and sufficient forensic neuropsychological test battery has been highly debated (Heilbronner, 2004). Although a specific battery of tests has not been determined the "gold standard" for forensic neuropsychological evaluation, often a comprehensive battery sufficient to address the specific question(s) is preferred, and tests should be chosen in accord with *Daubert*. Under *Daubert*, the four criteria used to distinguish "pseudoscience" from science in the courtroom are: (a) the theory or technique is falsifiable (it can be and has been tested), (b) the theory or technique has been subjected to peer review and published in professional journals, (c) the theory or technique has a "known or potential rate of error" and there are "standards controlling the technique's operation," and (d) the theory or technique enjoys "general acceptance" within a "relevant scientific community." These criteria are not exhaustive, and the court did not rule that testimony had to include all four elements. Currently, the *Daubert* standard is the rule of evidence in United States federal legal proceedings and in many states; however, there are some jurisdictions which continue to adhere to other less stringent standards (e.g., *Frye* standard, Rule 702 of the Federal Rules of Evidence (FRE), or a variation of these standards).

Several factors must be considered before the initiation of testing. First, consider which tests are culturally appropriate to administer. Does a particular test have appropriate norms? How far did the individual being tested go in school? Does he or she speak another language besides English? Is an interpreter available? After considering these factors, given the importance of cooperation in order to produce the best effort on neuropsychological tests, to the extent possible, testing should only occur when his/her symptoms are under control (see Fujii, this volume). Otherwise, it is ideal to postpone assessment until acute symptoms have diminished. A battery must be chosen with the individual's ability to sustain attention and motivation in mind. Longer test batteries may require more frequent breaks. Incentives and positive verbal reinforcement are also likely to ensure completion of tests (Schmand, Kuipers, van der Gaag, Bosveld, Bulthuis, & Jellena, 1994). Briefer testing may be necessary if the individual is unable to complete a more thorough battery. While evaluating a defendant with schizophrenia, it is also important to remember that this diagnosis does not render immunity for other neurological conditions. As such, neuropsychological testing can be useful to rule out other conditions. For instance, if an evaluator notices rapid forgetting in a person with schizophrenia, this may be indicative of a secondary condition (Savla, Moore, & Palmer, 2008). Lezak, Howiesen, and Loring (2004) note that cultural relevancy and biases are also important factors to consider when choosing a test battery (see Marcopulos & Fujii this volume). One category of tests that must be included in forensic neuropsychological evaluations is that of symptom validity and effort.

Malingering, Poor Effort, and Symptom Exaggeration

Assessment of effort and malingering are integral components of forensic neuropsychological evaluation, so much so that the National Academy of Neuropsychology has published a position paper (Bush et al., 2005) that delineates the purposes and methods of symptom validity testing (SVT). According to this paper, "The potential for symptom fabrication or exaggeration is higher in forensic contexts than in many clinical contexts. As a result of the increased incentive to mislead the examiner, neuropsychologists have a responsibility to conduct more extensive assessment of symptom validity" (p. 423). Malingering can be perceived as consisting of two elements: response bias and conscious intention (Denney, 2008). Response bias has been defined as a systematic pattern of performance in which the obtained results do not reflect what the tests were purported to measure. Forensic neuropsychologists are concerned with negative response bias. Once this has been detected, malingering is suspected when there is potential for secondary gain. It is difficult to determine the prevalence of negative response bias in a criminal forensic population, particularly due to the difficulty with malingering detection and misclassification (Rosenfeld, Sands, &Van Gorp, 2000). Nevertheless, some prevalence data exist. Lewis, Simcox, and Berry (2002) found that 31.4% of pretrial criminal defendants feigned psychiatric illness. Cornell and Hawk (1989) found that 8% of pretrial criminal defendants feigned psychosis. Denney (2007) found that the base rate of a population of male criminal defendants referred for neuropsychological assessment of malingering was over 50%. Mittenberg et al. (2002) examined neurocognitive exaggeration in criminals and found that 19%–23% tended to exaggerate symptoms, though rates of malingering conclusions were lower when cases were referred by the defense. A more recent study of 100 males undergoing CST evaluation in a forensic hospital found 21% of the sample was deemed probable malingerers based on the SIRS (Vitacco, Rogers, Gabel, & Munizza, 2007). Ardolf, Denney, and Houston (2007) found negative response bias rates higher than 50% and possibly as high as 70% for a consecutive series of 105 pre-sentence male defendants in federal prison referred due to neurocognitive concerns. The variability in incidence reported could be due to the forensic context in which these evaluations were performed (federal prison versus hospital).

It is recommended that effort testing is given at the beginning of an assessment to help maximize rapport (as these tests are typically easy) and patient confidence. Also, if a person with schizophrenia fails an effort test at the beginning of the assessment, it is pertinent to consider discontinuing further testing until full effort can be provided. This may be possible after symptoms of psychosis are treated, sustained attention is improved, or external incentives for malingering are no longer present. The evaluator is cautioned not to assume that failure on an effort test equates to malingering. Rather, as the name of such tests implies, they measure a lack of effort or biased responding (Franzen & Iverson, 1997). Furthermore, research by Gorissen, Sanz de la Torre, and Schmand (2005) and Weinborn, Orr, Woods, Conover, and Feix (2003) found that compared to both neurologically intact and neurologically disordered individuals, persons with schizophrenia perform more poorly on effort tests. This poor effort may not always be entirely volitional. This is not surprising given that avolition is a common negative symptom observed in schizophrenia-spectrum disorders. Goldberg, Back-Madruga, and Boone (2007) noted the risk of false positives on cognitive symptom validity tests due to negative symptoms, impaired attention and concentration, and low education in psychiatric patients. Such factors must be taken into consideration when evaluating this population. For a comprehensive review of malingering, see Rogers (2008) and Boone (2007).

Writing the Report

Forensic referrals are unique for a variety of reasons, not the least of which is the ways in which assessment results are conveyed. Within this context, it is ultimately up to the referring attorney to determine how information will be relayed. Some attorneys may not want a report, whereas others may want a brief, summary report, and yet others may prefer an extensive forensic report. It is important to clarify the attorney's expectations at the onset of the evaluation. Melton, Petrila, Poythress, and Slobogin (2007) suggest presenting an oral summary of findings to the attorney and then allowing him/her to decide the next step. We are not suggesting that evaluators tailor or omit information to satisfy the wishes of the referring source. Rather, we are recommending that efforts are made to clarify with the referring attorney immediately what he/she would like/need to have in the beginning. The goal of a forensic report is to elucidate and synthesize any relevant mental health information for the trier of fact, which necessitates collection of self-report as well as collateral data. Skeem, Golding, Cohen, and Berge (1998, p. 542) stated, "Examiners who fail to review and incorporate 'outside' evidence leave themselves vulnerable to adversarial attack. Attorneys can easily assail uninformed examiners on the witness stand with evidence that contradicts their reports or conclusions." A good report often bears resemblance to a scholarly article (e.g., introduction, methods, results, and discussion). It is important that the logic one uses to derive a forensic opinion is clearly articulated (Wettstein, 2010; Melton et al., 2007). When writing, an extremely conscientious approach is recommended. For example, it is useful to think very carefully about each and every statement, and ask yourself "How would I respond if I were cross-examined about this statement/question?" It is useful to write every report as if you will be testifying about it, even though this will not be the reality.

An excellent forensic report should be written at a level that is commensurate with the audience, thus void of unnecessary psychological jargon. Indeed, overuse of psychological jargon was the most frequent complaint found in past and present research on consumer satisfaction (Brenner, 2003). A forensic report should be objective, clearly list the referral source, purpose for the evaluation, details of the informed consent waiver, and the sources of information. The assessment process should be clearly articulated. Evaluators are encouraged to avoid prejudicial information in reports. This is of great importance in a CST report, which is typically provided to all counsel, and the judge. Thus, incriminating information about the alleged offense(s), regardless of disclosure of such, should not be included in the report. A coherent story should be conveyed, and direct quotes from the defendant can help create such a story. Speculation should be avoided, and excessive qualification may be an indicator that one is speculating. Also, the evaluator is reminded that any information written in interview notes, etc. but excluded from the forensic report can be fodder for cross-examination. If found, an expert may be accused of selectively including only information which supports his/her overall opinion ("cherry picking"). Thus, a forensic neuropsychologist should carefully consider what he/she documents during the process. Behavioral observations, including any particular comorbid variables which may have affected test performance, and the defendant's overall effort and thus validity of the results, should be included. One should be ready to defend test methodology per *Daubert*.

The report should conclude with a conceptualization that integrates all aforementioned data to address the legal question. It is important that this conceptualization is presented in a facts-based, objective manner that is scientifically sound. All inferences should be defensible. Forensic evaluators are encouraged to avoid conclusive testimony regarding the ultimate issue, or the legal issue at stake that is currently being prosecuted. For instance, an evaluator is cautioned to avoid statements such as, "The defendant's history and current evaluation data suggest that he was insane at the time of the alleged offense." Such an opinion should be left to the trier(s) of fact.

Quality assurance in forensic report writing is gaining increasing attention in the field. To add to the previous suggestions, Melton and colleagues (2007) offer four specific recommendations for forensic reports: (a) separate facts from inferences; (b) stay within the scope of the referral question; (c) avoid information over and under-kill; and (d) minimize clinical jargon. Conroy (2006) noted that good forensic report writing includes: (a) identification of the forensic reason for the referral; (b) documented confidentiality warning; (c) listing of all sources of collateral data; (d) listing of procedures followed; (e) rationale for forensic conclusions; (f) exploration of alternative hypotheses; (g) avoidance of jargon; (h) avoidance of irrelevant details; and (i) avoidance of inclusion of prejudicial or pejorative information. Common errors in forensic report writing were recently detailed by Grisso (2010). Examination of a national sample of criminal and civil forensic reports submitted to the American Board of Forensic Psychology by candidates for forensic board examination revealed the following pitfalls: opinions without sufficient explanation; forensic purpose was unclear; organization problems; irrelevant data or opinions; failure to consider alternative hypotheses; inadequate data; data and interpretation mixed; over-reliance on a single source of data; language problems; improper test uses (Grisso, 2010).

CONSIDERATIONS FOR TESTIMONY

Forensic neuropsychologists evaluating persons with schizophrenia have a unique opportunity to contribute to a defendant's legal proceedings thanks to *Jenkins v. United States* (1962). This landmark decision set the precedent for psychologists serving as expert witnesses on the question of mental disease as it relates to legal issues. According to Lees-Haley and Cohen (1999), there are three cardinal guidelines for neuropsychological testimony: (a) practice scientific and ethical neuropsychology, (b) utilize your specialized knowledge during testimony to help the trier of fact understand the evidence or determine the facts in issue, and (c) avoid technical jargon. Denney and Sullivan (2008) offer three additional guidelines: (d) always tell the truth, (e) organize file materials well and have them ready for courtroom testimony, and (f) be knowledgeable about neuropsychological method skeptics.

As has been previously mentioned, avoiding partisanship is essential. This will be particularly useful during testimony when an expert, during voir dire (review of qualifications for acceptance as an expert), may be asked to disclose how many times he/she has testified for defense versus prosecution. As such, to the extent possible, a forensic expert should attempt to conduct evaluations for both sides. Experts are strongly encouraged to meet with the retaining attorney prior to testimony to discuss potential lines of questioning and content of examination.

Once in the courtroom, voir dire may or may not commence (e.g., counsel may stipulate to an expert without voir dire). Once accepted as an expert, direct testimony will ensue. Experts should strive to be articulate, concise, and void of arrogance. Brodsky (1991, 2004), Brodsky and Galloway (2003), and Blau (1984) offer excellent strategies for mental health testimony. During the direct testimony, an expert should be prepared to discuss the entire assessment process, including, but not limited to, obtainment of collateral data, rationale for utilization of tests, test construction and validity, and his/her conclusions. Cross-examination will follow, which is often perceived by the mental health expert as the most adversarial component of the testimony experience. Cross-examination is when opposing counsel has an opportunity to neutralize or refute an expert's direct testimony. Denney and Sullivan (2008) offer two strategies for coping with cross-examination: performing excellent work that you can defend, and remaining calm, regardless of how challenging cross-examination may be. During this time, it is important to remember that it is acceptable to state that you do not know an answer, and it is essential not to give in to pressure to create an answer. It is also necessary to remember that you know much more about the mental health issues to which you are testifying than most of the individuals in the courtroom, and likely more than the attorney questioning you. Also, you are not on trial.

CONCLUSIONS

Criminal forensic neuropsychological assessment of persons with schizophrenia is unique, and equally complex. Many variables must be considered when working within this context, such as one's competence to perform such evaluations, the best tests to utilize with persons with schizophrenia in order to address a forensic question, and the most effective way to disseminate assessment results. The field is evolving so that the demand for such evaluations is likely going to increase, and necessarily, the standards for competent practice in this niche will continue to be refined. Neuropsychologists have an excellent opportunity to contribute to the realm of criminal forensic evaluation, particularly given their unique understanding of the science of brain-behavior relationships and the impact of cognitive impairment on functional abilities as well as expertise in the detection of non-credible self-presentations.

FORENSIC CASE EXAMPLES & DISCUSSIONS

Case 1

Mr. C, a 34-year-old Caucasian male, was hospitalized for a pretrial evaluation. He was charged with assault and battery against a law enforcement officer. His mother reported that he was very paranoid and had barricaded himself in her basement, thus prompting her to call the police to take him to the hospital. He believed that aliens had taken over the earth. He was non-adherent to outpatient treatment and he had not been taking his medications for at least eight months.

Mr. C had a long history of mental illness with onset of psychosis at age 17. Prior to that, he had a difficult school history with a significant learning disability in reading and Attention Deficit/Hyperactivity Disorder. He dropped out of school during grade 10 and had always lived at home. He had no significant job history, but occasionally worked for an uncle's landscaping business.

In jail, Mr. C. refused to speak, eat, or drink and was obviously acutely paranoid and psychotic. He was transferred to the local state psychiatric hospital for pre-trial treatment and evaluation of competency to stand trial as well as mental status at time of the offense. With treatment, his acute paranoia and mutism attenuated somewhat, but he had profound negative symptoms marked by asociality, flat affect, very poor hygiene, long response latencies, anhedonia, and paucity of speech. Mr. C was referred for neuropsychological assessment to evaluate cognitive functions vis-à-vis restoration efforts that occurred for several months. A brief battery was administered considering his negative symptoms and difficulty with social engagement. He completed the Test of Memory Malingering (TOMM), a formal test of effort, the Wechsler Abbreviated Scale of Intelligence (WASI), and Repeated Battery for the Assessment of Neuropsychological Status (RBANS), a brief screening measure that has normative data for people with schizophrenia (see Marcopulos & Fujii, this volume) with difficulty over a 2-day period. On Trial 1 of the TOMM he scored a 39/50 and on Trial 2 a 45/50. The testing revealed an estimated IQ in the low Borderline range (FSIQ = 70) and significant cognitive deficits on the RBANS (Total Standard Score = 68) which were maximized in attention and memory. His profile fit a person with premorbid cognitive limitations and schizophrenia with the deficit syndrome. The neuropsychologist noted in his report that restoration attempts might be difficult given Mr. C's significant longstanding cognitive impairment and continued symptomatology. The treatment team opined to the courts that Mr. C was currently incompetent to stand trial.

After 6 months of restoration efforts and aggressive pharmacological and psychosocial treatment, Mr. C.'s clinical status changed little. A repeat RBANS using the alternate form revealed no significant change in cognitive functioning. His forensic psychologist wrote a letter to the court opining that he might be unrestorable due to continued severe negative symptomatology and cognitive impairment. Despite ongoing education, he had been unable to demonstrate a working knowledge of courtroom personnel and procedures and was unable to work effectively with his attorney due to his profound negative symptoms such as paucity of speech and extremely long response latencies.

Discussion

Sometimes, neuropsychological evaluations can provide information to help decide whether a forensic patient may be so impaired as to be considered possibly unrestorably incompetent to stand trial. Factors which are associated with unrestorable trial competence include schizophrenia-spectrum illness, history of cognitive impairment and intellectual deficits(Leong, 2007; Mossman, 2007). A person with schizophrenia with the so-called "deficit syndrome" which is characterized by negative symptoms such as poverty of speech that persist after adequate treatment (Buchanan et al., 1994; Carpenter, Heinrichs, & Wagman, 1988; Cascella et al., 2008) might be more likely to be deemed unrestorable. Case 1 illustrates a patient who had the deficit form of schizophrenia and posed significant challenges for restoring to trial competence.

Case 2

Mr. D is an 18-year-old male hospitalized at State Psychiatric Hospital for emergency treatment as well as for evaluation of trial competence and sanity at the time of the alleged offense. Mr. D has been charged with Armed Robbery.

Mr. D was referred for emergency treatment and for CST/MSO evaluation after receiving a psychological evaluation while he was at the Adult Detention Center (ADC). At that time he reported auditory hallucinations, specifically command hallucinations from "Mr. Gaga" telling him to injure himself. Mr. D's behavioral status at the ADC worsened in spite of treatment with mood stabilizing and antipsychotic medications. He was transferred to the state psychiatric hospital after engaging in self-injurious behavior (biting his finger) allegedly in response to command hallucinations.

Mr. D has a long history of behavioral and mood difficulties resulting in expulsion from school, legal charges, and psychiatric hospitalizations for suicidal and aggressive behaviors. He was diagnosed with ADHD in first grade and was prescribed Ritalin. He also had trials of Adderall, Tofranil, Seroquel, and Abilify, but records reported poor adherence and limited efficacy. He started using marijuana and alcohol at age 15. He was frequently expelled/suspended from school for behavioral issues (fighting). He was in special education in residential programs to address his behavioral problems. According to his teachers, he was capable of performing well academically, but he frequently acted out in the classroom. During his teen years, he had criminal charges and was placed in detention where he completed his high school requirements.

Several years previous to the current offense, Mr. D was hospitalized after threatening to jump in front of a train after a breakup with his girlfriend. During this hospitalization, he reported to staff that he was "only kidding" about his suicidal threats. Hospital staff described him as emotionally reactive and impulsive. He did not appear anxious or depressed, and there were no psychotic symptoms. He was diagnosed with Conduct Disorder; Mood Disorder; and Bipolar Disorder.

Two months prior to the offense, Mr. D was hit by a car on his bicycle while eluding police. He was not wearing a helmet. His Glasgow Coma Scale at the scene was 14. He was described as alert and oriented, but with some confusion at the scene. He was treated at the local hospital for multiple orthopedic and internal injuries, as well as a right frontal skull fracture and subarachnoid hemorrhage. Mr. D was subsequently transferred to Rehabilitation Hospital and stayed for 10 days.

He was described as cooperative with care, but a psychology note stated that he was "manipulative" and did not like to follow rules. Mr. D was well oriented to self, place, and date. He demonstrated poor frustration tolerance and poor problem solving abilities, which was aggravated by fatigue and decreased motivation. His thinking was described as concrete with reduced executive functioning and superficial insight into his deficits. He was described as having poor attention span and irritability. He refused to complete formal psychological testing, but was described as having significant memory deficits for recent events. The discharge note one month prior to the index offense indicated physical and cognitive improvements, but continued difficulties with task planning and execution, unrealistic planning for the future, poor ability to think about consequences, and limited motivation to continue to engage in recovery. Although he was treated with Lithium and Seroquel during his hospitalization and rehab stay, none of the records reviewed noted that Mr. D exhibited symptoms of psychosis (e.g., hearing voices) during his hospitalization.

Mr. D's behavior on the Forensic Unit of the State Psychiatric Hospital ward was described as "child-like" and "attention-seeking." He was often seen smiling and laughing. He was very talkative, frequently interacting with staff and other patients. He claimed he started hearing "Mr. Gaga" ("Lady Gaga's husband") when he was in jail and continued to report these hallucinations while hospitalized. However, staff did not observe Mr. D responding to internal stimuli. He reported hearing the voice of "Mr. Gaga" telling him to harm himself, but Mr. D did not engage in any self-injurious behaviors since coming to State Psychiatric Hospital. Staff described him as energetic and irritable, cursing and threatening with aggressive behavior. He claimed that he "sees things—good people and bad people." He said the hallucinations are much worse when he is alone or in jail. Mr. D's current diagnoses were Alcohol Abuse; Cannabis Abuse; and Personality Disorder, Not Otherwise Specified. He was taking psychotropic medications (Gabapentin, Lithium, and Perphenazine). He said these medications had no effect on his auditory hallucinations of "Mr. Gaga." He said that the only thing that helps is being distracted by watching the cartoon network or being with staff.

Collateral information was obtained from Mr. D's mother. She described her son as very immature and impulsive long before his accident, but believes this may have been exacerbated by his right frontal lobe injury. Regarding "Mr. Gaga," Mr. D's mother said this is a character that her son devised as a gaming persona several years ago and does not believe he is hallucinating.

Mr. D was referred for psychological and neuropsychological testing to clarify whether his psychotic symptoms are a product of neurologic insult subsequent to the bike accident or intentional deception or exaggeration. Mr. D completed the Personality Assessment Inventory (PAI) which indicated that he was grossly over-reporting and possibly feigning his current symptoms. He reported an extreme degree of psychotic experiences (T = 98), even more than is typical for a person with an established psychotic disorder diagnosis. Mr. D did not cooperate fully to complete the neuropsychological evaluation. He discontinued testing prior to completion, stating he was too sleepy to participate. He resisted efforts to reschedule, eventually refusing altogether. Limited testing available, combined with behavioral observations on the unit and during several interviews, suggested no significant cognitive impairment in attention, memory, language, or reasoning that would have a significant bearing on his capacity for competence to stand trial. He completed an RBANS which was in the average range except for visuospatial functions. While it is probable that he had residual cognitive impairment resulting from the traumatic brain injury and premorbid LD and AD/HD, which might been revealed with comprehensive neurocognitive testing, his daily functioning was not impaired because of cognitive deficits. He demonstrated good memory for events, staff names and their roles, and learned the ward routine, schedule of events, and group treatments for his ward. He did not demonstrate any confusion or deficits in his understanding during verbal communication nor has he had difficulty expressing himself clearly to staff and patients.

Mr. D was intermittently cooperative with the forensic interviews for CST/ MSO. He was particularly interested to know whether the interview would be the test for insanity and competency to stand trial. Mr. D vacillated between being very forthcoming with information and being evasive or claiming he could not remember. He provided numerous details about his auditory and visual hallucinations. Although Mr. D was able to provide many details about his recent history, he initially stated he could not remember anything about the offense. Mr. D attributed his poor memory to the brain injury he reportedly received after he was hit by a car while riding his bicycle and eluding police.

During the evaluation, Mr. D described his mood as "happy and hyper, and occasionally depressed." He frequently complained of sedation from the psychotropic medications and needed much prompting and encouragement to complete the interview and questionnaires. He interacted with the examiner in a child-like manner, sometimes giving facetious and "silly" answers. For instance, when asked, "What does a judge do?" he responded, "I love Jimmy Neutron." At other times he claimed that he could not recall the information being requested. His mood/affect varied from dysphoric to euphoric. Mr. D's thought processes were mostly logical and linear. His eye contact was good, except when he was dozing off. His hygiene and grooming were good.

Mr. D completed a semi-structured clinical interview (Evaluation of Competency to Stand Trial-Revised; ECST-R) to evaluate his competence to stand trial. This is an empirically validated instrument which uses the Dusky Standard as a measure of trial competence, and it also screens for potential feigned incompetency (Atypical Presentation Scales - ATP Scales). Mr. D was readily able to state his charge (armed robbery). Initially, he claimed he could not remember anything about the alleged offense, but later was able to give a coherent account of the events that was consistent with other sources (e.g., the arresting officer, his mother, his attorney). At times during the CST evaluation, Mr. D appeared disinterested or, as previously noted, provided facetious, "silly" responses to questions. However, during other conversations about the legal situation, he was able to discuss the roles of various courtroom personnel accurately. For instance, regarding courtroom behavior, initially he claimed that he would burst into song and ask the judge to sing along with him. However, at another time during the interview, he indicated he understood the importance of appropriate courtroom behavior. For example, he asked if he would know he was going to court in advance because he wanted to do his laundry. He asserted that it was important that he look presentable in front of the judge and "not like a bum" because the judge was "the boss."

Overall, Mr. D's performance on the ECST-R suggested that he had adequate abilities for factual understanding of courtroom proceedings, rational understanding of courtroom proceedings, and ability to consult with counsel. However, his responses on the ECST-R ATP scales suggested the possibility of feigning psychotic symptoms.

In summary, there were psychological and cognitive factors that had the potential to impact Mr. D's behavior in the courtroom and make him appear less capable of participation than he was able to demonstrate during this evaluation. These factors included developmental immaturity, poor judgment, instability of mood, and impulsivity possibly exacerbated by a recent brain injury. It was unclear whether Mr. D's self-report of auditory command hallucinations ("Mr. Gaga") was due to a genuine psychotic disorder. Mr. D did not demonstrate a consistent constellation of symptoms and behaviors indicating a psychotic illness while hospitalized at State Psychiatric Hospital, and standardized testing suggested feigning. Regardless of his self-report of psychotic symptoms, it was opined that Mr. D possessed sufficient capacity to demonstrate factual and rational competence to stand trial. He also demonstrated the capacity and willingness to work effectively with his attorney with the joint goal of obtaining a favorable outcome in his case.

As for his Mental Status at Time of Offense, Mr. D claimed he was experiencing auditory command hallucinations at the time of the alleged offense. These command hallucinations told him to listen to the gang members. However, it was the gang members who told him to commit the crime. Thus, the proximate cause was Mr. D's desire to be part of the gang and to follow their orders out of fear of being harmed. Mr. D was susceptible to such peer pressure due to longstanding emotional and behavioral issues that may have been exacerbated by a recent brain injury, as well as a fear of physical harm by gang members if he did not comply.

Regarding the state insanity standard, Mr. D did have a mental defect at the time of the offense. Most likely he was suffering from depression and experiencing cognitive sequelae from a traumatic brain injury incurred several months prior to his offense, of note, shortly after he committed the offense (20 days), he admitted himself to a psychiatric hospital where he was treated for depression and suicidal ideation. At no time during that hospitalization did he report symptoms of auditory hallucinations nor did the psychiatric staff observe any psychotic symptoms. Detectives who arrested Mr. D and took his statement noted he seemed "sad and emotionally needy," but did not report any behaviors consistent with a psychotic illness. Mr. D did not report to the detective that he heard voices telling him to listen to the gang members. Observations by clinical staff, clinical interview, and standardized psychological and forensic assessments suggest possible feigning of symptoms and cast doubt that Mr. D is suffering from a psychotic illness. There was no evidence from Mr. D's statements that he did not understand the nature, character, or consequences of his act. He understood that what he did was wrong and that he was facing serious legal consequences. The details of the crime did not reveal a situation where the defendant acted with irresistible impulse, possibly aggravated by a recent brain injury.

Discussion

There are a number of lessons learned from this case. It can be extraordinarily difficult to discriminate feigned from genuine symptoms. Taking a careful history and getting collateral information from a number of sources is critical. It is also difficult to determine which symptoms are germane for CST/MSO—cognitive, psychiatric, both. In this case, this defendant had the possibility of both psychiatric and cognitive impairment. He also had the possibility of feigning both psychiatric and cognitive impairment. Cognitive impairment as sequelae of a brain injury was likely, and perhaps contributed to his poor judgment and impulse control leading up to the crime. However, it did not rise to the level that it significantly impaired his CST or appreciation of the wrongfulness of his actions (MSO). The defendant emphasized psychotic symptoms in his presentation, which were not supported by in-patient observation or psychiatric history.

The input from a neuropsychologist was very helpful in this case to help the courts understand the expected sequelae from brain injury (i.e., auditory hallucinations are not common) and ascertain the presence/absence of psychiatric and cognitive impairment. It was important to utilize both cognitive and psychiatric measures of malingering. This defendant had a genuine head injury but beyond vague complaints of memory loss, did not "use" these symptoms extensively to argue IST or insanity. His TOMM indicated adequate effort and on the very few cognitive tests he completed he demonstrated good effort. However, Mr. D was clearly feigning psychiatric symptoms on the PAI, and in his interactions with staff on the ward. Believing naively that auditory and visual hallucinations can result from TBI (although symptoms of psychosis can emerge after a TBI (see Flashman and McAllister, this volume), Mr. D seemed to "use" auditory hallucinations as an excuse for the alleged crime and as the basis for a claim of IST.

REFERENCES

American Psychological Association. (2010). Ethical principles of psychologists and code of conduct. Retrieved January 1, 2011, from http://www.apa.org/ethics/code/index.aspx

American Psychology-Law Society. (n.d.). *Specialty guidelines for forensic psychologists* - fifth draft. Retrieved October 1, 2010. from http://www.apls.org

Arango, C., Calcedo-Barba, A., González-Salvador, T., & Calcedo-Ordóñez, A. (1999). Violence in inpatients with schizophrenia: A prospective. *Schizophrenia Bulletin, 25*, 493–503.

Ardolf, B. R., Denney, R. L., & Houston, C. M. (2007). Base rates of negative response bias and malingered neurocognitive dysfunction among criminal defendants referred for neuropsychological evaluation. *The Clinical Neuropsychologist, 21,* 899–916.

Arsenault, L., Moffitt, T. E. Caspi, A, Taylor, P. J., & Silva, P. A. (2000). Mental disorders and violence in a total birth cohort: results from the Dunedin study *Archives of General Psychiatry, 57,* 968–979.

Barr, W. (2008). Neuropsychological approaches to criminality and violence. In R. Denney & J. Sullivan (Eds.), *Clinical neuropsychology in the criminal forensic setting* (238–272). New York: Guilford Press.

Bellack, A. S., Sayers, M., Mueser, K.T., & Bennett, M. (1994). Evaluation of social problem solving in schizophrenia. *Journal of Abnormal Psychology, 103,* 371–378.

Blau, T. H. (1984). Psychological tests in the courtroom. *Professional Psychology: Research and Practice, 15,* 176–186.

Boone, K. B. (2007). A reconsideration of the Slick et al. (1999) criteria for malingered neurocognitive dysfunction. In K. B. Boone (Ed.). *Assessment of feigned cognitive impairment* (pp. 29–49). New York: Guilford Press.

Borum, R., & Grisso, T. (1995). Psychological test use in criminal forensic evaluations. *Professional Psychology: Research and Practice, 26,* 465–473.

Brennan, P., Mednick, S. A., & Hodgins, S. (2000). Major mental disorders and criminal violence in a Danish birth cohort. *Archives of General Psychiatry, 57,* 494–500.

Brenner, E. (2003). Consumer-focused psychological assessment. *Professional Psychology: Research and Practice, 34,* 240–247.

Brodsky, S. L. (1991). *Testifying in court: Guidelines and maxims for the expert witness.* Washington, DC: American Psychological Association.

Brodsky, S. L., & Galloway, V. A. (2003). Ethical and professional demands for forensic mental health professionals in the post-Atkins era. *Ethics & Behavior, 13,* 3–9.

Brodsky, S. L. (2004). *Coping with cross-examination and other pathways to effective testimony.* Washington, DC: American Psychological Association.

Brüne, M. (2005). "Theory of Mind" in schizophrenia: A review of the literature. *Schizophrenia Bulletin, 31,* 21–42.

Buchanan, R. W., Strauss, M. E., Kirkpatrick, B., Holstein, C., Breier, A., & Carpenter, W. T. (1994). Neuropsychological impairment in deficit and nondeficit forms of schizophrenia. *Archives of General Psychiatry, 51,* 804–811.

Bureau of Justice Statistics. (2006). *Special report, Mental health problems of prison and jail inmates.* Washington, DC: U.S. Department of Justice, Office of Justice Programs, Bureau of Justice Statistics.

Bush S., Ruff, R. M., Tröster, A. I., Barth, J. T., Koffler, S. P., Pliskin, N. H., et al. (2005). Symptom validity assessment: Practice issues and medical necessity. *Archives of Clinical Neuropsychology, 20,* 419–426.

Cascella, N. G., Testa, S. M., Meyer, S. M., Rao, V. A., Diaz-Asper, C. M., Pearlson, G. D., et al. (2008). Neuropsychological impairment in deficit vs. non-deficit schizophrenia. *Journal of Psychiatric Research, 42,* 930–937.

Callahan, L. A., Steadman, H. J., McGreevy, M. A., & Robins, P. C. (1991). The volume and characteristics of insanity defense pleas: An eight-state study. *Bulletin of the American Academy of Psychiatry & the Law, 19,* 331–338.

Carpenter, W. T., Heinrichs, D. W., & Wagman, A. M.(1988). Deficit and nondeficit forms of schizophrenia: The concept. *The American Journal of Psychiatry, 145,* 578–583.

Centers for Disease Control and Prevention (CDC). *Traumatic brain injury in prisons and jails.* http://www.cdc.gov/traumaticbraininjury/pdf/Prisoner_TBI_Prof-a.pdf

Choe, J. Y., Teplin, L. A., & Abram, K. M. (2008). Perpetration of violence, violent victimization, and severe mental illness: Balancing public health concerns. *Psychiatric Services, 59*, 153–164.

Cima, M., Nijman, H., Merckelbach, H, Kremer, K., & Hollnack, S. (2004). Claims of crime-related amnesia in forensic patients. *International Journal of Law and Psychiatry, 27*, 215–221.

Cochrane, R., Grisso, T., & Frederick, R. I. (2001). The relationship between criminal charges, diagnoses, and psycholegal opinions among federal defendants. *Behavioral Sciences and the Law, 19*, 565–582.

Committee on the Revision of the Specialty Guidelines for Forensic Psychology. (2011). *Specialty guidelines for forensic psychologists.* Manuscript in press.

Conroy, M. A. (2006). Report writing and testimony. *Applied Psychology in Criminal Justice, 2*, 237–260.

Cornell, D., & Hawk, G. (1989). Clinical presentation of malingerers diagnosed by experienced forensic examiners. *Law and Human Behavior, 13*, 375–383.

Cuffel, B. J., Shumway, M., Choujian, T. L., & MacDonald, T. (1994). A longitudinal study of substance use and community violence in schizophrenia. *Journal of Nervous and Mental Disease, 182*, 704–708.

Daubert v. Merrell Dow Pharmaceuticals, Inc., 509 U.S. 579, 113 S. Ct. 2786 (1993).

Denney, R. L. (2005). Criminal forensic neuropsychology and assessment of competency. In G. J. Larrabee (Ed.), *Forensic neuropsychology: A scientific approach* (pp. 378–424). New York: Oxford University Press.

Denney, R. L. (2007) Assessment of malingering in criminal forensic neuropsychological settings. In K. B. Boone (Ed.), *Assessment of feigned cognitive impairment* (pp. 428–452). New York: Guilford Press.

Denney, R., & Sullivan, J. (2008). *Clinical neuropsychology in the criminal forensic setting.* New York: Guilford Press.

Denney, R. L., & Wynkoop, T. F. (2000). Clinical neuropsychology in the criminal forensic setting. *Journal of Head Trauma Rehabilitation, 15*, 804–828.

Diamond, P. M., Wang, E. W., Holzer, C. E., Thomas, C. E., & Cruser, D. A. (2001). The prevalence of mental illness in prison. *Administration and Policy in Mental Health, 29*, 21–40.

Dinn, W. M., Gansler, D. A., Moczynski, N., & Fulwiler, C. (2009). Brain dysfunction and community violence in patients with major mental illness. *Criminal Justice and Behavior* 36, 117–136.

Douglas, K. S., Guy, L. S., & Hart, S. D. (2009). Psychosis as a risk factor for violence to others: A meta-analysis. *Psychological Bulletin, 135*, 679–706.

Dusky v. United States, 362 U.S. 402 (1960).

Evaluation of Competency to Stand Trial-Revised (ECST-R) and professional manual. (2004). R. Rogers, C. E. Tillbrook, & K. W. Sewell (Eds.). Lutz, FL: Psychological Assessment Resources

Elvevåg, B., Kerbs, K. M., Malley, J. D., Seeley, E., & Goldberg, T. E. (2003). Autobiographical memory in schizophrenia: An examination of the distribution of memories. *Neuropsychology, 17*, 402–409.

Fisher, W. H., Geller, J. L., & Pandiani, J. A. (2009). The changing role of the state psychiatric hospital. *Health Affairs, 28*, 676–684.

Franzen, M. D., & Iverson, G. R. (1997). The detection of biased responding in neuropsychological assessment. In A. MacNeill-Horton, D. Wedding, & J. Webster

(Eds.), *The neuropsychology handbook.(vol. 1), Foundations and assessment* (pp. 393–422). New York: Springer.

Frye v. United States 292 F. 1013 (D.C. Cir. 1923).

Fujii, D. (2002). *Hawaii State Hospital neuropsychology training manual.* Unpublished manuscript.

Goldberg, H. E., Back-Madruga, C., & Boone, K. B. (2007). The impact of psychiatric disorders on cognitive symptom validity test scores. In K. B. Boone (Eds.), *Assessment of feigned cognitive impairment* (pp. 281–309). New York: Guilford Press.

Gorissen, M., Sanz de la Torre, J. C., & Schmand, B. (2005). Effort and cognition in schizophrenia patients. *Schizophrenia Research, 78,* 199–208.

Greiffenstein, M. F. (2008). Basics of forensic neuropsychology. In J. E. Morgan & J. H. Ricker (Eds.), *Textbook of clinical neuropsychology* (pp. 905–941). New York: Psychology Press.

Greiffenstein, M. F., & Cohen, L. (2005). Neuropsychology and the law: Principles of productive attorney-neuropsychologist relations. In G. J. Larrabee (Ed.), *Forensic neuropsychology: A scientific approach* (pp. 29–91). New York: Oxford University Press.

Grisso, T. (2003). *Evaluating competencies: Forensic assessments and instruments* (2nd ed.). New York: Springer.

Grisso, T. (2010). Guidance for improving forensic reports: A review of common errors. *Open Access Journal of Forensic Psychology, 2.* Retrieved October 1, 2010, from http://works.bepress.com/thomas_grisso/4

Harrison, G., Croudace, T., Mason, P., Glazenbrook, C., & Medley, I. (1996). Predicting the long-term outcome of schizophrenia. *Psychological Medicine, 26,* 697–705.

Wettstein, R. M. (2010). The forensic psychiatric examination and report. In R. I. Simon & L .H. Gold (Eds.), *Textbook of forensic psychiatry: Second edition* (pp. 175–206). Washington, DC: American Psychiatric Publishing.

Heck, A. L., & Herrick, S. M. (2007). Geriatric considerations in restoration of competence to stand trial: Two cases of impaired cognition. *Journal of Forensic Psychology Practice, 7,* 73–82.

Heilbronner, R. L. (2004). A status report on the practice of forensic neuropsychology. *The Clinical Neuropsychologist, 18,* 312–326.

Heilbrun, K., & Collins, S. (1995). Evaluations of trial competency and mental state at time of offense: Report characteristics. *Professional Psychology: Research and Practice, 26,* 61–67.

Hodgins, S., Calem, M., Shimel, R., Williams, A., Harleston, D., Morgan, C., et al. (2011). Criminal offending and distinguishing features of offenders among persons experiencing a first episode of psychosis. *Early Intervention in Psychiatry, 5,* 15–23.

Hodgins, S., Mednick, S. A., Brennan, P., Schulsinger, F., & Engberg, M. (1996). Mental disorder and crime: evidence from a Danish birth cohort. *Archives of General Psychiatry, 53,* 489–496.

Hubbard, K. L., Zapf, P. A., & Ronan, K. A. (2003). Competency restoration: An examination of the differences between defendants predicted restorable and not restorable to competency. *Law and Human Behavior, 27,* 127–139.

Indiana v. Davis, 898 N.E.2d.281 (2008).

Jackson v. Indiana , 406 U.S. 715 (1972).

Jenkins v. United States, 307 F.2D 637 (DC Cir. 1962).

Lamb, H. R., Weinberger, L. E., & Gross, B. H. (2004). Mentally ill persons in the criminal justice system: Some perspectives. *Psychiatric Quarterly, 75,* 107–126.

Lamb, R. H., & Weinberger, L. E. (2005). The shift of psychiatric inpatient care from hospitals to jails and prisons. *Journal of the American Academy of Psychiatry and Law, 33,* 529–534.

Lees-Haley, P., & Cohen (1999), The neuropsychologist as expert witness: Toward credible science in the courtroom. In J. J. Sweet (Ed.), *Forensic neuropsychology: Fundamentals and practice,* (pp. 443–468). Lisse, Netherlands: Swets & Zeitlinger.

Leong, G. B. (2007). Commentary: Restorability of incompetence to stand trial—implications beyond predictive equations. *Journal of the American Academy of Psychiatry and the Law, 35,* 44–46.

Lewis, J. L., Simcox, A. M., & Berry, D. T. R. (2002). Screening for feigned psychiatric symptoms in a forensic sample by using the MMPI–2 and the Structured Inventory of Malingered Symptomatology. *Psychological Assessment, 14,* 170–176.

Lezak, M. D., Howiesen, D. B., Loring, & D. W. (2004). *Neuropsychological Assessment (4'h ed.).* New York: Oxford University Press.

Link, B. G., Cullen, F. T., Frank, J., & Wozniak, J. F. (1987). The social rejection of former mental patients: Understanding why labels matter. *American Journal of Sociology, 96,* 1461–1500.

Marcopulos, B. A., Fujii, D., O'Grady, J., Shaver, G., Manley, J., & Aucone, E. (2008). Providing neuropsychological services for persons with schizophrenia: A review of the literature and prescription for practice. In J. Morgan & J. Ricker (Eds.), *Textbook of clinical neuropsychology* (pp. 743–761). New York: Taylor & Francis.

Marcopulos, B. A., Morgan, J. E., & Denney, R. L. (2008). Neuropsychological evaluation of competency to proceed. In R. L. Denney & J. P. Sullivan (Eds.), *Clinical Neuropsychology in the criminal forensic setting* (pp. 176–203). New York: Guilford.

Press, Melton, G. B., Petrila, J., Poythress, N. G., & Slobogin, C. (1997). *Psychological evaluations for the courts: A handbook for mental health professionals and lawyers* (2nd ed.). New York: Guilford Press.

Melton, G. B., Petrila, J., Poythress, N. G., & Slobogin, C. (2007). *Psychological evaluations for the courts: A handbook for mental health professionals and lawyers (3rd ed.).* New York: Guilford Press.

Miranda v. Arizona, 384 U.S. 436, 86 S. Ct. 1602, 16 L. Ed. 2d 694 (1966)

Mittenberg, W., Patton, C. Canyock, E. M., & Condit, D. C. (2002). Base rates of malingering and symptom exaggeration. *Journal of Clinical and Experimental Neuropsychology, 24,* 1094–1102.

Mohamed, S., Rosenheck, R., McEvoy, J., Swartz, M., Stroup, S., & Lieberman, J. A. (2009). Cross-sectional and longitudinal relationships between insight and attitudes toward medication and clinical outcomes in chronic schizophrenia. *Schizophrenia Bulletin, 35,* 336–346.

Morrissey, J. P., & Cuddeback, G. S. (2008). Treatment in jails and prisons. In K. T. Mueser & D. V. Jeste (Eds.), *Clinical handbook of schizophrenia* (pp. 524–532). New York: Guilford Press.

Mossman, D. (2007). Predicting restorability of incompetent criminal defendants. *Journal of the American Academy of Psychiatry and Law, 35,* 34–43.

Munkner, R., Haastrup, S., Joergensen, T., & Kramp, P. (2003). The temporal relationship between schizophrenia and crime. *Social Psychiatry and Psychiatric Epidemiology, 38,* 347–353.

Munkner, R., Haastrup, S., Joergensen, T., & Kramp, P. (2009). The association between psychopathology of first episode psychosis patients within the schizophrneia spectrum and previous offending. *Nordic Journal of Psychiatry, 63*, 124–131.

Nestor, P. G., Daggett, D., Haycock, J., & Price, M. (1999). Competence to stand trial: A neuropsychological inquiry. *Law and Human Behavior, 23*, 397–412.

Nicholson, R. A., & Kugler, K. E. (1991). Competent and incompetent criminal defendants: A quantitative review of comparative research. *Psychological Bulletin, 109*, 355–370.

Peters, R. H., Sherman, P. B., & Osher, F. C. (2008). Treatment in jails and prisons. In K. T. Mueser & D. V. Jeste (Eds.), *Clinical handbook of schizophrenia* (pp. 354–364). New York: Guilford Press.

Rogers, R. (2008). *Clinical assessment of malingering and deception (3rd ed.).* New York: Guilford Press.

Rosenfeld, B., Sands, S. A., & van Gorp, W. G. (2000). Have we forgotten the base rate problem? methodological issues in the detection of distortion. *Archives of Clinical Neuropsychology, 15*, 349–359.

Rudnick, A., & Roe, D. (2008). Diagnostic interviewing. In K. T. Mueser & D. V. Jeste, *Clinical handbook of schizophrenia* (pp. 117–124). New York: Guilford Press.

Schacter, D. L. (1986). Amnesia and crime: How much do we really know? *American Psychologist, 41*, 286–295.

Schmand, B., Kuipers, T., Van der Gaag, M., Bosveld, J., Bulthuis, F., & Jellema, M. (1994). Cognitive disorders and negative symptoms as correlates of motivational deficit in psychotic patients. *Psychological Medicine, 24*, 869–884.

Schwalbe, E., & Medalia, A. (2007). Cognitive dysfunction and competency restoration: Using cognitive remediation to help restore the unrestorable. *Journal of the American Academy of Psychiatry and Law, 35*, 518–525.

Skeem, J. L., Golding, S. L. , Cohn, N. B., & Berge, G. (1998). Logic and reliability of evaluations of competence to stand trial. *Law and Human Behavior, 22*, 519–547.

Slobogin, C. (2003). Pragmatic forensic psychology: A means of "scientizing" expert testimony from mental health professionals? *Psychology, Public Policy, and Law, 9*, 275–300.

Smith, T. E., Hull, J. W., Goodman, M., Hedayat-Harris, A., Willson, D., Lyssa, M., et al. (1999). The relative influences of symptoms, insight, and neurocognition on adjustment in schizophrenia and schizoaffective disorder. *Journal of Nervous and Mental Disease, 187*, 102–108.

Steadman,H. J., Mulvey, E. P., Monahan, J., & Robbins, P. C. (1998). Violence by people discharged from acute psychiatric inpatient facilities and by others in the same neighborhoods. *Archives of General Psychiatry, 155*, 393–401.

Steadman, H. J., Osher, F. C., Robbins, P. C., Case, B., & Samuels, S. (2009). Prevalence of serious mental illness among jail inmates. *Psychiatric Services, 60*, 761–765.

Swanson, J., Borum, R., & Swartz, M. S. (1996). Psychotic symptoms and disorders and the risk of violent behaviour in the community. *Criminal Behavior and Mental Health, 6*, 309–329.

Swanson, J. W., Holzer, C. E., Ganju, V. K., & Jono, R. T. (1990). Violence and psychiatric disorder in the community: evidence from the epidemiologic catchment areas surveys. *Hospital and Community Psychiatry, 41*, 761–770.

Swanson, J. W., Swartz, M. S., Van Dorn, R. A., Elbogen, E. B., Wagner, H. R., Rosenheck, R. A., et al. (2006). A national study of violent behavior in persons with schizophrenia. *Archives of General Psychiatry, 63*, 490–499.

Tardiff, K., Marzuk, P., Leon, A., & Portera, L. (1997). A prospective study of violence by psychiatric patients after hospital discharge. *Psychiatric Services, 48,* 678.

Tateno, A., Jorge, R., & Robinson, R. (2003). Clinical correlates of aggressive behavior after traumatic brain injury. *Journal of Neuropsychiatry and Clinical Neurosciences, 15,* 155–160.

Taylor, P. J., & Kopelman, M. D. (1984). Amnesia for criminal offences. *Psychological Medicine, 14,* 581–588.

Teplin, A.,Abram, K. M., & McClelland, G. M. (1996). Prevalence of psychiatric disorders among incarcerated women: Pretrial jail detainees. *Archives of General Psychiatry, 53,* 505–512.

Tiihonen, J., Isohanni, M., Rasenen, P., Koiranen, P., & Moring, J. (1997). Specific major mental disorders and criminality: A 26-year prospective study of the 1966 northern Finland birth cohort. *American Journal of Psychiatry, 154,* 840–845.

Torrey, E. F. (1994). Violent behavior by individuals with severe mental illness. *Hospital and Community Psychiatry, 45,* 653–662.

Vitacco, M. J., Rogers, R., Gabel, J., & Munizza, J. (2007). An evaluation of malingering screens with competency to stand trial patients: A known-groups comparison. *Law and Human Behavior, 31,* 249–260.

Wallace, C., Mullen, P. E., & Burgess, P. (2004). Criminal offending in schizophrenia over a 25-year period marked by deinstitutionalization and increasing prevalence of comorbid substance use disorders. *American Journal of Psychiatry, 161,* 716–727.

Walsh, E., Gilvarry, C., Samele, C., Harvey, K., Manley, C., Tattan, T., et al (2004). Predicting violence in schizophrenia: A prospective study. *Schizophrenia Research, 67,* 247–252.

Warren, J., Fitch, L., Dietz, P., & Rosenfeld, B. (1991). Criminal offense, psychiatric diagnosis, and psychological opinion: An analysis of 894 pretrial referrals. *Bulletin of the American Academy of Psychiatry and the Law, 19,* 63–69.

Warren, J., Murrie, D., Chauhan, P., Dietz, P., & Morris, J. (2004). Opinion formation in evaluating sanity at the time of the offense: An examination of 5175 pretrial evaluations. *Behavioral Sciences and the Law, 22,* 171–186.

Weinborn, M., Orr, T., Woods, S. P., Conover, E., & Feix, J. (2003). A validation of the test of memory malingering in a forensic psychiatric setting. *Journal of Clinical & Experimental Neuropsychology, 25*(7), 979–990.

Wettstein, R. M. (2010). The forensic psychiatric examination and report. In R. I. Simon & L. H. Gold (Eds.), *Textbook of forensic psychiatry: Second Edition* (pp. 175–206). Washington, DC: American Psychiatric Publishing.

Wohlheiter, K., & Dixon, L. (2008). Assessment of co-occurring disorders. In K. T. Mueser & D. V. Jeste, *Clinical handbook of schizophrenia* (pp. 125–134). New York: Guilford Press.

Wykes, T., Sturt, E., & Katz, R. (1990). The prediction of rehabilitative success after three years: The use of social, symptom, and cognitive variables. *British Journal of Psychiatry, 157,* 865–870.

Wynkoop, T. F., & Denney, R. L. (1999). Exaggeration of neuropsychological deficit in competency to stand trial. *Journal of Forensic Neuropsychology, 1,* 29–53.

Yates, K. F., & Denney, R. L. (2008). Neuropsychology in the assessment of mental state at the time of the offense. In R. L. Denney & J. P. Sullivan (Eds.), *Clinical Neuropsychology in the criminal forensic setting* (pp. 204–237). New York: Guilford Press.

Zapf, P. A., & Roesch, R. (2011). Future directions in the restoration of competence to stand trial. *Current Directions in Psychological Science, 20,* 43–47.

BOX 13.1 SCHIZOPHRENIA AND CRIME

1. There dramatic increase of mentally ill individuals in jails and prisons is due to deinstitutionalization, changes in civil commitment criteria, inadequate community resources, and the role of law enforcement in managing psychiatric crises.
2. There is a higher prevalence of criminal offenses among persons with schizophrenia and schizoaffective disorder compared with the general population, as well as with other persons with severe mental illness.
3. Comorbid substance abuse, psychotropic medication non-adherence, and active psychotic symptoms have been the most common factors implicated in increased risk of violence in people with schizophrenia.
4. Violence victimization for those with serious mental illness is also higher than the general population. Negative symptoms, including cognitive impairment, can make persons with schizophrenia more vulnerable to victimization.

BOX 13.2 TYPES OF FORENSIC ASSESSMENTS

1. Competency to Stand Trial (CST), Mental Status at Time of Offense (MSO) and Risk assessments are the most common evaluations in forensic psychiatric settings.
2. Dusky v. United States established that for a defendant to be competent to stand trial they must understand the court proceedings and be able to work effectively with their attorney.
3. Psychosis is the most common reason for trial incompetence, but cognitive impairment also increases the likelihood that a defendant will be deemed incompetent.
4. The legal term "insanity" consists of two prongs: the cognitive prong (inability to appreciate the nature, character, and consequences of his/her act because of an underlying mental illness) and the "volitional" prong (the defendant would have committed the act even if a policeman was present).
5. Schizophrenia is the most common diagnosis for defendants found insane.
6. Dynamic risk factors (those subject to change or intervention) and static risk factors (usually historical such as gender, past violence or history of brain injury) are considered in risk assessments.

BOX 13.3 ETHICAL CONSIDERATIONS FOR FORENSIC NEUROPSYCHOLOGICAL ASSESSMENT

1. Neuropsychologists conducting forensic evaluations must always consider the possibility of feigning or exaggerating either psychopathology, cognitive impairment, or both.
2. The task of a forensic neuropsychologist is typically to provide information and/or education to the court rather than the traditional helping role for the patient.
3. A patient's self-report should always be corroborated by external data, and collateral sources of information obtained.
4. The Fifth, Sixth, Eighth, and Fourteenth Amendments are considered the most relevant for criminal forensic practice.

BOX 13.4 COGNITIVE DEFICITS IN SCHIZOPHRENIA AND FORENSIC ASSESSMENT.

1. Although most defendants are found incompetent to stand trial due to psychotic symptoms, cognitive deficits in attention, memory, processing speed, and abstract reasoning impact the defendant's ability to follow legal proceedings and work with their attorneys.
2. Claims of amnesia are very common in criminals. Neuropsychological evaluation can help discern genuine from feigned memory deficits.
3. Most defendants (75%) are restored to competency within 6 months due to successful treatment of psychotic symptoms.
4. Defendants who are found unrestorable often have histories of active psychosis, poor response to treatment and "static" cognitive deficits such intellectual disability.
5. Schizophrenia is the most frequent diagnosis for those defendants found legally insane.
6. *Theory of Mind* (ToM) which refers to the capacity to infer one's own and other persons' mental states, is impaired in schizophrenia and may explain difficulty expressing remorse or other emotions.
7. Poor insight is a risk factor for poor adherence to treatment.
8. Brain injury has been associated with increased aggression. Persons with schizophrenia with a history of violence were more likely to have a history of brain injury.

BOX 13.5 FORENSIC ASSESSMENT STRATEGIES

1. A significant number of defendants feign psychiatric or cognitive illness therefore formal assessment of symptom validity is necessary.
2. Persons with schizophrenia perform more poorly on effort tests and it may be due to negative symptoms rather than deliberate feigning.
3. There is an increased risk of false positives on cognitive symptom validity tests due to negative symptoms, impaired attention & concentration, and low education in psychiatric patients.
4. A forensic report should be objective, clearly list the referral source, purpose for the evaluation, details of the informed consent waiver, and the sources of collateral information.
5. Incriminating information about the alleged offense(s), regardless of disclosure of such, should not be included in a CST report.

CONTINUING EDUCATION QUESTIONS

1. What are some reasons why there are so many psychiatrically disabled persons in jails and prisons compared to the general population?
   a. Changes in commitment laws
   b. Deinstitutionalization
   c. Inadequate community resources
   d. Social stigma
   e. All of the above
2. What is the most important risk factor for violence in severe mental illness?
   a. Substance abuse
   b. Previous history of violence
   c. Treatment nonadherence
   d. Social stigma
   e. Active psychotic symptoms
3. Dusky v. United States established
   a. A defendant's right to a competency evaluation prior to trial
   b. Criteria for insanity
   c. Protection against self-incrimination
   d. Right to a speedy trial
4. Negative symptoms of schizophrenia
   a. Increase the risk of violence
   b. Increase the risk of victimization
   c. Are more likely to improve with medication than positive symptoms
   d. Are more common in the prison population

5. The cognitive prong for legal insanity involves
   a. Assessing whether the defendant meets criteria for intellectual disability
   b. Determining whether the defendant appreciates the nature, character, and consequences of his/her act
   c. Evaluating whether the defendant understand his or her legal charges
   d. B & C

Index

T

For Product Safety Concerns and Information please contact our EU representative GPSR@taylorandfrancis.com Taylor & Francis Verlag GmbH, Kaufingerstraße 24, 80331 München, Germany